SUPERSTARS, STARS, AND JUST PLAIN HEROES

Also by Nathan Salant

This Date in New York Yankees History

SUPERSTARS, STARS, AND JUST PLAIN HEROES

NATHAN SALANT

STEIN AND DAY/*Publishers*/New York

All photographs not otherwise attributed are reprinted courtesy of the New York Yankees or are from the author's personal collection.

First published in 1982
Copyright © 1982 by Nathan Salant
All rights reserved
Designed by Louis A. Ditizio
Printed in the United States of America
STEIN AND DAY/*Publishers*
Scarborough House
Briarcliff Manor, N.Y. 10510

Library of Congress Cataloging in Publication Data

Salant, Nathan.
   Superstars, stars, and just plain heroes.

   1. Baseball players—United States—Biography.
I. Title.
GV865.A1S24   796.357′092′2 [B]   79-3877
ISBN 0-8128-2716-3   AACR2

To the 1979 Spring Valley Pirates, Rockland Big League Champions. A team of superstars, stars . . .

Lenny Adametz
Steve Adler
Ken Bachert
Gene Badolato
Alan Bellando
Andre Chiavelli
Bob Conklin
Wayne Fabbri
Pat Fucci
Jim Harrison
Ed Moss
Les Saland
Carl Wolfson

. . . and a just plain hero named **Howie Suckle.**

This book is also dedicated to **Bob Nadal** and **Emil Willis** out of loyalty and respect, and with eternal thanks for their time, interest, and cooperation.

CONTENTS

Introduction	xi
The Media	xix
Superstars and Stars: Batters	1
The Homerun	3
"Cap" Anson	5
Ty Cobb	13
Honus Wagner	21
Rogers Hornsby	29
George Sisler	35
Pie Traynor	41
Tris Speaker	47
Al Simmons	57
Mickey Cochrane	65
Ben Chapman	75
Hank Greenberg	83
Jimmie Foxx	97
Ralph Kiner	105
Mil Ott	111
Duke Snider	119

Superstars and Stars: Pitchers 129

    Christy Mathewson 131
    Rube Marquard 139
    Grover Cleveland Alexander 147
    Walter Johnson 153
    Eddie Plank 161
    Carl Mays 167
    Carl Hubbell 173
    Dizzy Dean 181
    Lefty Grove 195
    Sandy Koufax 201
    Don Drysdale 215
    Mel Stottlemyre 223

Just Plain Heroes 231

    George Rohe 233
    John "Home Run" Baker 237
    George Whiteman 245
    Howard Ehmke 249
    Al Gionfriddo 253
    Dusty Rhodes 259
    Sandy Amoros 265
    Don Larsen 273
    Bill Mazeroski 279
    Al Weis 285
    Chris Chambliss 291
    Bucky Dent 297

Conclusion 305

General Index 307

Index of Teams 317

Illustrations between pages 230 and 231

Acknowledgments

Without the cooperation of dozens of people, this book would never have been possible. Among the many who provided essential information and support were—

Jack Redding, Cliff Kachline, and the library staff at the National Baseball Hall of Fame, Cooperstown, N.Y. . . .

Cedric Tallis, Larry Wahl, David Szen, Betsy Leesman, Joe D'Ambrosio, Bob Pellegrino, Mike Rendine, Betty Rosenblum, Marty Rothe, Luis Morales, Dale Weeks, Annie Mileo, Bob Sheppard, and Pete Sheehy of the New York Yankees . . .

Bob Broeg, sportswriter emeritus of the *Sporting News* and *St. Louis Post-Dispatch* . . .

the late Fred Leib, perhaps the greatest sportswriter who ever lived . . .

Hal Lebovitz of the *Cleveland Plain-Dealer*, and his library staff . . .

Mel Allen, Phil Rizzuto, Frank Messer, Bill White, Fran Healy, and the other broadcasters with whom the author has had contact . . .

Dick Gutwillig of the *Rockland Journal-News* . . .

Mickey Morabito (A's), Joe Wetton (Dodgers), Bob Korch (Braves), Chuck Shriver (White Sox), Arthur Richmond (Mets), Marty Appel (Baseball Commissioner's Office) for their aid in tracking down former players and providing other information . . .

Stan Fischler, my mentor in the literary world . . .

Bob Nadal, for taking the time to read several sample chapters and give his opinion of the direction this endeavor should take . . .

Stefanie Letvak for the reference books she supplied . . .

Carl Wolfson, for proofreading several chapters, and a continuing friendship that began on the baseball field, and has extended through two published works . . .

Rich Levinson, for research help with some of the chapters included herein . . .

Art Ballant, my editor at Stein and Day . . .
Sol Stein, for aiding in the development of the idea behind this book . . .
My parents and Uncle Sam, who provided constructive criticism.

I would also like to thank the former and current major leaguers who answered my questions, particularly Yogi Berra, Andy Carey, Ben Chapman, Paul Dean, Bill Dickey, Joe DiMaggio, Joe Dugan, Bob Feller, Whitey Ford, Joe Garagiola, Al Gionfriddo, Hank Greenberg, Elston Howard, Carl Hubbell, Monte Irvin, Al Kaline, Ralph Kiner, Don Larsen, Whitey Lockman, Sal Maglie, Mickey Mantle, Roger Maris, Billy Martin, Rube Marquard, Willie Mays, Bill Mazeroski, Dusty Rhodes, Phil Rizzuto, Bob Shawkey, Duke Snider, Mel Stottlemyre, Ralph Terry, Bobby Thomson, and Al Weis.

I would also like to make special mention of Joe Sewell, who has been incredibly cooperative in all of my efforts. He has spent countless hours on the phone, and responded to many, many letters, about his former teammates and opponents.

Last, but not least, go my thanks to the 1979 Spring Valley Pirates, for providing me with a wonderful summer, and the first of three consecutive championships in my coaching career.

Introduction

Who are the true superstars of baseball history, and how do they differ from the mere stars—and from the just plain heroes? Is there a clear-cut standard by which the dozens of outstanding players can be measured for true-superstar status, or must we settle for vague, subjective notions of the individual fan?

Is a .400 season that qualifies for the batting title sufficient? What about 50 or more homeruns? One hundred twenty runs batted in? A gold glove? Leading the league in assists? All of them? Three out of four?

Suppose a player bats .300 for 15 or more seasons? Is he automatically a superstar? Must he also hit 500 career homeruns and drive in 1,500 runs? Can he be slow on the basepaths, but otherwise a great offensive threat? How much of a role should clutch-hitting play? Must he play for a championship team? Make a minimum salary? Drive an expensive sports car? Have a candy bar named after him? Endorse a pair of jeans? Have an honorary "Day" at the end of his career?

What are the standards for pitchers? Is a no-hitter enough? A perfect game? Twenty wins in a season? Leading the league in wins and earned run average? Winning the Cy Young Award? Striking out 15 men in a game? Two hundred in a season? All of the above? Some?

Will 300 career victories do it? Two thousand strikeouts? A lifetime earned run average under 3.00? Five Cy Young Awards? Seven World Series triumphs? A 100-miles-per-hour fastball? Killing a batter with a pitch? Throwing temper tantrums on the field? Election to the National Baseball Hall of Fame?

Have these questions clouded the already vague notion of what a superstar really is?

This book stands for the proposition that there is a very measurable standard for determining whether the superstar label accurately applies to any ballplayer. There are many criteria that lead up to superstardom, but in the end, the true measure of that status is immortality. Has the player in question become more than a mortal man?

Has his name remained a household word after his retirement? His death? Is his bat a prized possession sought by every fan? Would his autograph be stored in a safety deposit box? Will the next-door neighbor's 12-year-old son recognize that former player's name? Will the current player be remembered that way 30 years from now? Fifty? For all eternity?

If his name has survived, is it only vaguely familiar? Is the player only remembered for one great moment in his career, a moment in which he rose to the occasion and performed a seemingly impossible feat, or led his team to a crucial victory? Does the neighbor's 12-year-old son know anything about him? Are his statistics and accomplishments on the tips of the average fans' tongues, coast to coast? Will every bleacherite at the ballpark be certain of the teams he played for? The positions he played? Whether he threw left-handed? Did he become a national entity eternally linked with the word "baseball"? Has his popularity or notoriety decreased over the years? Did he become a legend in his day, and has that legend survived the ultimate measure of life: death?

This book concerns itself with three categories of ballplayers: superstars, stars, and just plain heroes. The true superstar is a great athlete who ranks among the leaders in every category during his career. The public perceives him as the "straw that stirs the drink," the player who must hit or pitch if his team is to win the key game. He must come through in the clutch—not once, not twice, but dozens of times. As the years go by, and he reaches the height of his career, the team becomes merged into the superstar (mention the Yankees, and the names Babe Ruth, Lou Gehrig, Joe DiMaggio, Mickey Mantle, and today, Reggie Jackson, pop into mind). As he piles success on top of success, his notoriety extends beyond the region in which he plays. Fans across the nation take note of his consistent performance at a level well above the average ballplayer's. He begins to dominate the sports pages and sports reports. His bat becomes the best bat, his glove the mark of excellence, his signature an autograph. Advertisers seek him out for endorsements. The fans talk about his clothes, the restaurants he frequents, the cars he drives, the company he keeps. A night in his bed is transformed from an act of promiscuity to an achievement worth bragging about.

At that point, the ballplayer is still a mere star. He has not crossed the essential threshold into the ranks of the immortals. He will be forgotten after he retires. He may even suffer the ignominy of hearing the crowd boo his performance when he fails to get the crucial hit. The ultimate insult of demands that he be replaced by a younger player will echo through the ballpark as age slows his every step and dulls his reflexes.

But a chosen few will never hear those boos. Their failures will be forgiven. Their every at-bat is a cherished moment greeted with cheers, even if they strike out with the bases loaded in the last inning.

Each of these men is a true superstar. He was once a mere star, but, at some specific

Introduction

moment in his career, performed an outstanding feat that enabled him to vault from the ranks of the mere stars up to the Olympus of immortals. The mention of his name immediately evokes a response which includes that great moment, as well as other events, sidelights, personality traits, and even weaknesses that that ballplayer had. More than his name survives. His immortality is insured.

Consider the case of Babe Ruth. The mention of his name calls to mind 60 homeruns in one season, 714 in a career, a "called" homerun in the World Series, promising to hit a homerun for a seriously ill child (and delivering), an insatiable appetite for food and women, a salary higher than the President's... a living legend to this day, despite his death in 1948.

Although the Babe enjoyed tremendous success as a pitcher with the Red Sox (89-46) from 1914-19, he emerged as baseball's greatest star after the sensational trade that sent him to the Yankees. In 1920, he belted an unheard-of 54 homeruns in one season, and lifted the perennially mediocre New Yorkers into pennant contention. A year later, he slammed 59 four-baggers, and led the Yankees to the World Series. After an injury-plagued off-season in 1922, he led the league with 41 homers and 131 runs batted in, batted .393, and carried the ballclub to the world championship.

Along the way, he revolutionized the game, transforming the homerun from a freak incident into the deadliest, and most popular, offensive weapon. He not only hit them with unparalleled frequency, but drove the baseball incredible distances, while fielding like a gold glover, and also maintaining a .342 career average. His wild personal life, unique relationship with the media, and tremendous knack for getting along with the fans easily enabled him to dominate the sports pages, and merge the Yankee team identity into himself. Across the nation, thousands flocked to local ballparks to watch him play in exhibition games. Hundreds jammed even the tiniest of railroad stations, hoping for a glimpse of the homerun king when the Yankees train pulled through. Even the Yankee-haters, a new, but rapidly growing breed of aficionado in those days of Prohibition, doffed their hats to the Babe's feats.

Yet, as high as Ruth's star had risen by the time the 1927 season came around, he had not yet attained true superstar status. The proof of his mere star status came in 1925, when he was suspended for insubordination, publicly embarrassed, and roundly booed upon his return to action. After a stinging diatribe against his behavior at the Annual Baseball Writers' Association banquet after the season, Ruth made a public apology to the youth of America, and vowed to return a new man in 1926. He came through with a great year, and led the team back to the World Series.

As the 1927 season dawned, Ruth was only 32 years old. But his well-publicized excesses had led the media, and many fans, to conclude that he was still on his way down. Preseason predictions had Ruth dropping to the low .300s at the plate, and the low 20s in homeruns.... All he did was bat .356 with 60 homers, thereby conquering

Father Time, and vaulting into the domain of the immortals. From that point on, the Babe was never booed again. He had become a true superstar, whose name would last forever.

Consider the case of Hank Aaron, perhaps the best example of the importance of that one great event in a player's career that transforms him from a mere star into a true superstar. If Aaron had not caught, and surpassed, Ruth's career homerun mark, his name would gradually fade away, just as those of Mel Ott, Eddie Mathews, and Jimmy Foxx have slipped into obscurity. When Al Downing served up Aaron's 715th homerun, Hammerin' Hank accomplished the "impossible"—he had hit more career round-trippers than the immortal Ruth himself.

What else does anyone else remember about Aaron, who retired as an active player after the 1976 season? Did he bat left-handed? What positions did he play in the field? Which teams did he play for? How many times did he hit 50 homeruns in one season? Besides career homeruns, what three other significant offensive categories does Aaron rank first in? Is he married? Does he have any children? What is he doing today?

Odds are, the average fan does not even know the exact number of homeruns that Aaron hit (755), let alone the fact that he is the all-time leader in games played (3,298), at-bats (12,364), and runs batted in (2,297). He was also a lifetime .305 hitter, and is one of the handful of major leaguers who hit 30 homers and stole 30 bases in one season (1963: 44 homers, 31 stolen bases). He never hit more than 47 homers in his 23 seasons, but saw action at every infield position, as well as in the outfield and as designated hitter, while playing for the Milwaukee/Atlanta Braves and Milwaukee Brewers. Today, he is the Braves Vice-President of Player Development.

The point is simple: Had Aaron not broken Ruth's mark, had he finished just one homerun short of the magic 714, he would fade into obscurity and eventually be forgotten by the average fan 30 years from now. In other words, in the long run, he might just as well have never even played the game of baseball!

Fortunately, Aaron broke the record, and although fans may never be as familiar with his exact total as they were with Ruth's 714, more than just the name of Hank Aaron will survive.

In contrast, consider the cases of Jimmy Foxx, George Sisler, and Tris Speaker. Foxx was a lifetime .325 hitter who slugged 534 homeruns from the right side of the plate during his 20-year career. In 1932, he hit 58 homeruns and drove in 169 runs, the greatest offensive production since Ruth's 60 and 164 in 1927. He ranked second on the all-time homerun list from his retirement in 1945 through September 1968, when Mickey Mantle hit his 535th. He led the Philadelphia Athletics to three consecutive pennants and two world championships. He played every position on the diamond, except second base. But who ever hears his name anymore?

Consider the case of George Sisler, the outstanding first baseman for the St. Louis

Introduction

Browns in the late 'teens and twenties. He was a lifetime .340 hitter who twice broke the .400 mark (.407 in 1920, .420 in 1922). He is recognized universally as the finest fielding first baseman in major league history. He was the only shining light in the Browns' otherwise dismal history. He led the American League in stolen bases four times, including 51 thefts in 1922. His 257 hits in 1920 remains the record for a single season. Yet, who ever hears a word about him anymore, either?

Perhaps the saddest case of all is that of Tris Speaker. For years, "Spoke" was the centerfielder on every all-time major league team. Then along came Willie Mays, and Speaker was quickly forgotten. It seems unfair. Speaker out-averaged Mays (.344-.302), out-doubled him (793-523), out-tripled him (224-140), out-hit him (3,515-3,283), stole more bases (433-338), struck out incredibly fewer times (220 in 10,208 at-bats, to May's 1,526 in 10,881), and nearly matched Mays in every other offensive category except homeruns.

"No offense to Willie Mays, but if 'Spoke' had played the bulk of his career in the lively ball era, he would have hit an awful lot of homeruns," fellow Hall-of-Famer Joe Sewell said. "And you also have to remember that Speaker was also managing our ballclub for many of those years."

In the field, well, no one was better than Speaker, but the one thing he never did was make the great catch that turned a World Series around the ways Mays did in 1954. He also never benefited from radio and television the way Mays did, and his Cleveland teams made it to the World Series just once in his 22-year career. Speaker was simply a great all-around player, who did the spectacular every day, but never did the impossible . . . and never became a superstar.

Foxx, Sisler, and Speaker are good examples of why mere statistics are not enough to create a superstar. There are other very solid examples. Twenty-three former major leaguers batted .333 or more for careers that included at least 4,000 at-bats: Ty Cobb (.367), Rogers Hornsby (.358), Joe Jackson (.356), Ed Delahanty (.346), Wee Willie Keeler (.345), Ted Williams (.344), Speaker (.344), Billy Hamilton (.343), Pete Browning (.343), Ruth (.342), Harry Heilman (.342), Bill Terry (.341), Jesse Burkett (.340), Sisler (.340), Lou Gehrig (.340), Nap Lajoie (.339), Riggs Stephenson (.336), Al Simmons (.334), Paul Waner (.333), Eddie Collins (.333), and Cap Anson (.333). Are Delahanty, Hamilton, and Browning household names? What positions did Stephenson, Collins, Burkett, and Heilman play? For whom did Hornsby, Jackson, Simmons, and Lajoie perform?

A similar example exists among pitchers. Thirteen men recorded 300 or more major league victories: Cy Young (511-313), Walter Johnson (416-279), Grover Cleveland Alexander (373-208), Christy Mathewson (373-188), Warren Spahn (363-245), Pud Galvin (361-309), Kid Nichols (360-202), Tim Keefe (344-225), John Clarkson (327-177), Eddie Plank (327-192), Mickey Welch (311-207), Old Hoss Radbourn (310-192),

Lefty Grove (300-207), and Early Wynn (300-244). Who were the southpaws? For whom did Galvin, Nichols, Keefe, and Clarkson pitch? What was Plank's nickname? Did any of them strike out more than 2,500 batters?

This is not to say that the above-named men were not great performers. Obviously, they rank among the greatest players of all time. It simply means that they never captured the hearts of the nation, never had that one great moment that vaulted them into immortality, and never became true superstars.

It is important to understand exactly what classification as a star means. It in no way demeans the ballplayer's ability—many stars actually outperformed the superstars (as in the Speaker-Mays example). In some cases, the only difference may seem to be that the star never had the opportunity to win the crucial game, or if he did, he failed to take advantage of it. (In the latter case, consider Carl Yastrzemski, who suffered the agony of making the final out in the 1978 American League Eastern Division playoff game, with the Red Sox trailing by a run, and two men on base.) There is also something to be said for the argument that the true superstar propels his team into contention, and then gets the key hits that win the pennant.

Refer back to Ruth again. Until his arrival in New York, the Yankees were second-class citizens behind the better established, more successful Giants. They had not been serious contenders for 15 years. Then, along came Ruth, and the Yankees were converted into contenders in one year, pennant-winners a year later, and world champions two years after that. Admittedly, the supporting cast had largely been assembled prior to Ruth's arrival, but it took the "Big Man," with his awesome homeruns and consistent clutch hits, to push the Yankees over the top. Like any true superstar, he was at his best under pressure. His gamewinning homers and World Series feats are well known. His legendary "called" homerun off Charlie Root in the 1932 World Series has been the subject of great debate for years—did the Babe really call his shot? Recent testimony tends to prove he did not mean to point to the centerfield bleachers before the famous blow, and even if it is ever conclusively proven that he did not call the shot, fans will still talk about it, and tell the story of the "called" homerun, for as long as there is baseball.

Ironically, while great ballplayers like Foxx, Speaker, and Sisler never achieved superstar status and never attained the essential immortality, another, inferior class of performers shares the eternal spotlight with the true superstars: the just plain heroes. A hero, in the athletic sense of the word, is the individual who rises to the occasion and comes through with the clutch hit or outstanding performance when it is least expected. He is an athlete whose record simply does not give rise to expectations of success, let alone a shocking blow that wins a pennant or a World Series, or is so overwhelming in and of itself that it cannot be forgotten.

The rest of the hero's career is irrelevant; frequently, it was so average, or fringe, that it is not worth mentioning. The rest of his on-the-field career—let alone his off-the-field life—is irrelevant. All that matters is that one moment in which he accomplished the incredible.

The quintessential hero was Bobby Thomson, whose two-out, three-run homerun in the bottom of the ninth inning lifted the New York Giants to a shocking 5-4 victory in the decisive game of the 1951 National League playoff against the Brooklyn Dodgers. To fully understand the nature of the feat, consider the overall situation. The Giants trailed the Dodgers by 13½ games in mid-August. They rallied to tie the Dodgers with two games remaining in the regular season, and finished in a tie. New York won the first game of the playoff (on a homerun by Thomson, off Ralph Branca, no less—and how many fans remember that!), but dropped the second, 10-0.

Both teams had their aces ready for the decisive game: Don Newcombe versus Sal Maglie. Newk handcuffed the Giants on four hits and one run for the first eight frames, and carried a 4-1 lead into the bottom of the ninth. Thousands of fans headed for the exits, positive that the Dodgers had pulled the pennant out after all. New York club owner Horace Stoneham had already made his way down to the Giants clubhouse, prepared to console his team by reminding them of the tremendous battle they had waged in the final seven weeks of the season. Most of the newspapermen present had completed their stories, recounting the Dodgers win, and needing only a summary of the ninth inning, and a few quotes, to be complete. No reasonable man expected that the Giants would rally to win the game, and no one could have foreseen the role Thomson was about to play.

The Giants were not dead. Alvin Dark and Don Mueller singled to open the ninth. Monte Irvin popped up, but Whitey Lockman doubled, scoring Dark, and chasing Newcombe to the showers. Dodgers manager Charlie Dressen summoned Branca to face the next batter: Thomson.

Bobby had enjoyed his finest regular season that year: .293, 27 doubles, 8 triples, 32 homers and 101 RBIs. He would remain in the major leagues for 15 years, and finish at .270 with 264 homeruns. Fine statistics, but no one would argue that he was as good a third baseman as Eddie Mathews. Thomson was not even a bona fide star. A three-run homerun simply was unexpected. In fact, it was more than that—it was unthinkable.

Of course, that is exactly what happened. Branca's first pitch was taken for strike one. The next offering was a high, inside fastball. Thomson swung, and drove a line drive deep to left field, straight at the 315-foot marker. Leftfielder Andy Pafko went back to the wall. For a split second, the entire stadium froze, waiting to see where the ball would land. When time resumed, Pafko's look of horror was matched only by the wild exuberance of the crowd, as the ball sailed into the seats in left field, for an incredible, shocking, three-run homerun. The Giants had won the pennant.

In comparison, none of Aaron's homeruns had that type of effect. Nor did those of Foxx, Ernie Banks, and Frank Robinson, or Killibrew's or Hank Greenberg's.

But Bill Mazeroski's, Chris Chambliss's, and Bucky Dent's did, and that's why each of them, unlikely homerun threats as they were, are remembered forever, while Greenberg, who hit 331 in his career (including 58 in one season), and the others are forgotten. By comparison none of their homeruns really seem to have mattered.

In the field, Willie Mays made a great catch in the 1954 World Series, a catch which is acclaimed as the key to the Giants upset sweep of the Indians. He went on to hit 660 homeruns, but it was that catch which vaulted him into superstar status. Tris Speaker made a career out of impossible catches, and batted .344—.042 more than Mays—but none of his hits or catches came in that type of situation, so Spoke never became a superstar, and is forgotten. Sandy Amoros, a lifetime .255 hitter who spent parts of seven years in the major leagues, made one great catch to save the 1955 World Series, and is remembered forever. Could Amoros carry Speaker's glove or bat? No. Was Mays as good a ballplayer as Speaker? Maybe, but probably not. Yet, who survives, and will survive for all eternity? Amoros and Mays—the hero and the superstar. The star is forgotten.

In the pages that follow, the lives and careers of 39 ballplayers are examined in depth. Each biographical chapter is designed to bring the accomplishments and highlights of each player's career to the forefront. Each chapter also includes a summary in which a judgment is offered regarding the correct classification of the player as a superstar, star, or just plain hero.

Some of the players covered will be very familiar. Others will be vague names out of the past. Others will be total unknowns.

Consider the standards. Understand that the mere star is a great athlete who simply never achieved immortality. Then, ask where your favorites fit in: Superstars? Stars? Or just plain heroes?

THE MEDIA

Can the media really create a superstar? Must a great ballplayer cater to reporters and broadcasters in order to attain superstar status? What effect has the advent of radio and television had upon the projection of a ballplayer's image? Can a ballplayer be hated by "the knights of the keyboard," and still achieve immortality?

The importance of a good relationship with the media cannot be overemphasized. Although allegations that the media can turn a good ballplayer into a superstar are ridiculous (you cannot turn chicken feathers into chicken salad), the media are decisive in determining whether a player ever reaches the threshold level from which the vault into superstardom may be made. Obviously, an athlete can never capture the hearts of the fans, let alone dominate the sports pages, if reporters choose to ignore him, or portray him in a consistently negative light. Similarly, those players who curry favor with the press are at a distinct advantage (provided they produce on the field).

The ultimate example of media detraction involved the manager of the Brooklyn Dodgers, Wilbert Robinson, who so infuriated a Brooklyn newspaper that the daily ceased using the manager's name. Managerial decisions were either ignored, or simply reported as "the Brooklyn manager did (such and such)."

A similar situation involved Rogers Hornsby who simply was not liked by anyone. His feats were duly reported, and dully reported. He was traded so many times that people came to believe he was a troublemaker. No one wrote any articles about his off-the-field life because he had none worthwhile writing about, and preferred to be left alone.

Ted Williams almost got caught up in the same trap, but the Boston media were always split on the Splendid Splinter. While some hated him with a passion, others were equally quick to rise up in his defense. Furthermore, Williams's relationship with the out-of-town media, and particularly the New York reporters, was always cordial and cooperative. Thus, the fans always read and heard two sides, and were left to decide for themselves.

Perhaps the best way to examine the essential role of a "good press" is to consider the formation of fan impressions. The simple fact is that very few fans ever meet a major league ballplayer, and many fans never even go to a major league game. This has not changed much over the years. In 1903, 2,390,362 fans paid their way into National League ballparks, and 2,344,888 watched the American League. The population of the United States was roughly 78,000,000, so if each fan went to only one game, 6.1 percent of the populace attended a major league baseball game that year. (Obviously, that was not the case. Many fans attended more than one game, so the real percentage was probably closer to 4 percent.)

Fifty years later, the Nationals played before 7,419,721 and the Americans attracted 6,964,076. Approximately 153,000,000 people lived in the United States, so the unadjusted percentage that attended baseball games was 9.4, but the real figure (adjusted for repeat attendance) was probably about 5 percent.

In 1978, the totals were 20,106,924 and 20,529,965. The estimated population was 212,000,000, so the unadjusted percentage was 18.7, and the adjusted figure was probably about 9 percent.

Why all of the statistical examination? To point out that most fans do not even see a major league game during any given year. They rely solely on the media, plus an occasional exhibition game that might be played in their town, and word of mouth from someone lucky enough to see a game, to develop their notions of who the great ballplayers are.

Prior to the late 1920s, the only medium for dispensing information was printed. Fans pored over newspapers, magazines, and the like to learn about their favorite players, newcomers, enemies, and leaders. The writers had the players at their mercy—a negative wire service story could destroy a player's reputation. An article that referred to a player as "lazy" might label him permanently. Certainly, nicknames evolved in that manner, and certain players were the victims of some rather brutal, and unfair, criticism. There was no rush to sue for defamation of character—the average ballplayer knew nothing about torts, let alone agents and the like.

Radio broadcasting added a new dimension. Fans heard blow-by-blow descriptions of the action—subject to the prejudices of the announcers, who were sometimes paid by the teams, and always selected with the approval of the team. How objective can an announcer afford to be if his job security rests with the ballclub he is talking about! Thus, a 450-foot homerun over the bleachers and on to the street could be "a tremendous line drive, hit deep to left centerfield, way back there, that ball is going, going, it is gone! A homerun for Mickey Mantle, and one of the longest I've ever seen, clear over the rear wall of the bleachers..."; or merely "there's a long drive to deep left centerfield, and it's out of here."

In effect, an audible version of the prejudiced newspaper article that would appear

The Media

the next day, only slanted towards the broadcaster's audience. Very few announcers were considered impartial; in fact, the job was to act as a combination cheerleader/publicity/public relations man, to put bodies in seats. The fan received a second-hand report.

The advent of television, and particularly the network Game of the Week, altered the spectrum slightly. Finally, fans were exposed to games without actually sitting in the ballpark. Opinions about ballplayers could now be influenced by visual observation, as well as by the spoken and written word; but the bottom line had changed very little. The broadcast is punctuated with the wisdom of one or more commentators, who favor certain teams and players. Although major league attendance exceeded 43,000,000 in 1980, the majority of fans attending saw only three or four teams play —not much of an opportunity to formulate first-hand opinions about ballplayers. In other words, the fan is still overwhelmingly dependent upon the media for his impressions, and the number one source remains the newspaper.

It follows that the more media coverage, the better the opportunity for achieving star, and superstar, status. The larger the city, the larger the media. The more successful the franchise, the more coverage it gets from that media, and the more likely that it will be featured on national broadcasts. And, which teams are on the airwaves most often? The winning teams. And who do the fans want to see? The winning teams. And who makes a team win? A superstar, star, or just plain hero.

SUPERSTARS, STARS, AND JUST PLAIN HEROES

NATHAN SALANT

STEIN AND DAY/*Publishers*/New York

THE HOMERUN

Baseball has come a long way since Roscoe Barnes (Chicago White Stockings) and Charlie Jones (Cincinnati Red Legs) hit the first homeruns in major league history (May 21, 1876). Contemporary accounts glorified the events as "prodigious and tremendous clouts which traveled clear beyond the confines of the playing field," and predicted a "glorious future for the player who might consistently smite the ball in such a manner." (For the record, the first American League homerun was hit by Cleveland's Erwin T. Beck on April 25, 1901.)

The writer was years ahead of his time. Not only did the names of Barnes and Jones fade into oblivion, but the homerun came close to joining them when several teams opted for ground-rule doubles on hits into the stands. In fact, for the next 43 years, the homerun was the scourge of baseball, frowned upon by fans and players alike, who joined in condemning it in favor of John McGraw's "scientific baseball." (A single, a stolen base, a bunt, and a hit through the infield to score the run.)

By the turn of the century, the record for homeruns in a season was 27, hit by Edward (Ned) Williamson of the Chicago White Stockings (not the White Sox of the future American League, but the nineteenth century predecessors of the National League's Chicago Cubs) in 1884. Twenty-five of his homeruns were hit in Chicago's home field, which is listed in some accounts as Lakefront Park, and in others, Congress Avenue Grounds. In either case, the right field foul pole was a mere 215 feet from home plate. Williamson became the first player to hit three homeruns in one game (May 30, 1884)... and he also saw his season total drop to three homeruns when the Stockings moved to the more spacious West Side Park in 1885! In fact, Williamson never hit more than 9 homeruns in one season after that, but his name remained in the record books until Rogers Hornsby broke his National League mark with 42 in 1922.

Similarly, the record for career homeruns was 136, hit by Roger Connor during 17

National League and one Players League seasons. His best year was 1887, when he hit 17 homeruns in 127 games. Connor's name is listed in the Baseball Hall of Fame—probably because of his lifetime .318 average, .487 slugging percentage, and 233 career triples (5th in major league history).

The baseball fan of today is more than familiar with the homerun, and will undoubtedly agree that it has been responsible for creating more superstars, stars, and just plain heroes than any other offensive weapon. The first player to benefit from using the "weapon" was John Franklin "Homerun" Baker, whose two game-winning homeruns in the 1911 World Series brought national recognition to his name, and focused brief attention on the potential for stardom and heroism that the homerun offered.

Of course, the real homerun explosion began with that fellow named George Herman "Babe" Ruth. . . .

"CAP" ANSON

Get that nigger off the field.

—Adrian "Cap" Anson

Baseball was a man's game in my day. The pitchers were allowed 7 to 9 balls before you walked. They delivered the ball from 45, and then 50, feet, and they pitched from a box that was six or seven feet long, not a slab. They were even allowed to take a running start before they threw.

I'd like to see what today's boys would do against the likes of [Old Hoss] Radbourn, [Pud] Galvin, [Tim] Keefe, and [John] Clarkson. I'd like to see Cobb and [Joe] Jackson and Ruth against them . . . why, they probably wouldn't bat .350 between them.

—Remarks ascribed to Cap Anson in an old column in the Hall of Fame archives.

For more than a quarter of a century, Adrian (Cap) Anson was the best-known and most respected baseball player in the world. During his record 27-year career, Anson dominated the sports pages from Boston to San Francisco as the athlete idol of America, and with good reason: In the eyes of his contemporaries, he represented all that was good about America.

"He is a family man who knows the meaning of hard work and fair play," wrote one reporter, "and a religious Christian who never fails to attend a church service on Sunday. His honesty is unquestioned, and at the bat, he is unapproached."

Clergymen across the nation frequently used Anson as a model for boys, who responded (undoubtedly more because of Cap's ability than the sermons) by purchasing anything endorsed by Anson. An Anson model bat was a treasured possession. To break one was worse than the most crushing defeat on the field. An Anson baseball card or photograph, regardless of condition, was cherished second only to the family Bible. To damage or lose one was an act of blasphemy.

By 1895, Anson's 25th year in the major leagues, the idol of American youth was so well-known that playwright Charles Hoyt wrote and produced "A Runaway Colt," a play detailing Cap's life. Naturally, the superstar played the lead role, and Cap proved to be a "good actor, [who] would never make Henry Irving or Richard Mansfield safeguard their laurels," according to one critic. (After a three-week run in Syracuse, the performance shifted to New York, where it had a short run.)

Most significantly, like a turn-of-the-century E. F. Hutton, when Cap Anson spoke, the whole world (or at least the baseball world) listened. For example, in 1890, when the fledgling Players League threatened to destroy the National League with its offer of a league run for the players, by the players, and of the players, Anson dealt the new league a fatal blow by not only refusing to sign with it, but publicly deriding it.

"They won't draw," he told a Chicago reporter. "They're just a bunch of old stiffs, and I have no faith in their movement. They may draw a few fans at the beginning, but it will simply be the novelty, and not the merit of the attraction. The league will collapse, and the ingrates who betrayed the National League will be begging to return."

Of course, Anson conveniently forgot to add that he owned stock in the National League's Chicago White Stockings, but his assessment of the Players League proved correct—it folded after one season.

Generally, Anson used his influence in positive ways. He was the first manager to take his team south for spring training (Hot Springs, Arkansas, 1885), although he later rejected the idea because he feared the change in weather would have an adverse effect on the players when they returned to the north. His White Stockings were also the first team to be housed in first-class hotels on road trips, and Cap even provided carriages to transport the players to and from the ballpark.

On the field, Cap revolutionized the game by introducing the concepts of team defense, the hit-and-run, hand signals for pitchers and coaches, and the platoon system, all of which were copied with great success by John McGraw's Baltimore Orioles. Contemporaries were particularly impressed with his institution of relay systems for hits to the outfield, and his requirement that every ballplayer be moving to back up someone if he was not actually fielding the ball.

Unfortunately, not all of Anson's influence was good, and today he is best remembered for his role in excluding blacks from the major leagues. In 1884, Cap's White

Stockings were scheduled to play an exhibition game against Toledo. Before the game, Anson noticed catcher Moses Fleetwood Walker, one of two black brothers who played for the Mudhens (William Welday Walker was an outfielder).

"If you want me to play, you'll have to get that nigger off the field," Anson announced.

"If you want to get paid for this game, you'd better be out there when the first pitch is thrown," was the Toledo reply.

Anson balked at taking the field, and delayed the game for more than an hour, before finally "condescending" to play. It was the first and last time he competed against blacks, and was the first in a series of outbursts that culminated with Anson's successful battle with John Montgomery Ward over Ward's desire to sign a black ballplayer named George Stovey.

"He was so vehement about it that I couldn't sign George Stovey," Ward told reporters. "You simply cannot cross swords with Cap. He is too popular."

Anson carried his anti-black crusade one step further when he published his autobiography, *A Ballplayer's Career* (Era Publishing Company, 1900), the first nonfiction book ever written about a major league ballplayer. At every opportunity, he took a shot at minorities:

> Clarence Duval was a little darkey ... a singer and a dancer of no mean ability, and a little coon ... I engaged him as a mascot. He was an ungrateful little rascal, however, and deserted me for Mlle. Jarbeau, the actress. ... He was a no-account nigger.

His description of "John Chinaman" and his addiction to gambling, opium, and living in squalor in San Francisco was another low point, but the book was a tremendous success. It still makes interesting reading, largely because of the vivid descriptions of nineteenth century baseball, and the diarylike account of the team's trip around the world.

No one has ever explained Anson's intolerance. Born in April 1851, in Marshalltown, Iowa, the 6'3" 220-pound Cap grew up among the Potawatomi Indians, and spoke very favorably about them (although he does refer to their penchant for firewater in his biography). He had no contact with any other minorities in his youth, and while he probably picked up a touch of intolerance from his background, the extent to which it dominated his social views remains a mystery.

Anson's mother died when he was seven years old, leaving his dad to raise the family and maintain the farm. Cap stayed in school and graduated from high school in 1867, despite majoring in sports and rarely going to his classes. His athletic ability attracted offers from Iowa State and Notre Dame, and he attended each of them for short periods of time.

The turning point came during the summer of 1870, when Anson's hometown independent baseball club challenged the Rockford Forrest Cities of the National Association to an exhibition series. Cap, Dad, and a brother all played for the locals, who were trounced 17–3 in the opener, and 7–1 in game two. As was the custom of the day, an enormous amount of betting went on, and Anson's dad lost the family's prize cow. "When the series ended, Marshalltown was bankrupt," Anson recalled, twenty years later. "And imagine umpiring a game in which people had their entire life's savings on the line. No easy job."

Cap had a fine series, and impressed Rockford owner Al Spaulding enough to send for the 18-year-old the following spring. The highly touted rookie went 1-for-4 (a double) in his first professional appearance (versus Cleveland), and finished the year at .352, while seeing action at second, third, catcher, and the outfield.

The Philadelphia Athletics (National Association—not to be confused with the Athletics who joined the American League in 1900) lured Anson east for the 1872 season, and he proved to be a worthwhile investment. Cap batted .381, and quickly established himself as the greatest hitter of the day. In 20 of his remaining 22 seasons, Anson batted .302 or better, including marks of .407 (1879) and .421 (1887). Strangely enough, neither mark led the league. In 1879, Anson came to bat only 227 times, and did not qualify for the title, which was captured by Providence centerfielder Pinky Hines (.357 in 409 at-bats). In 1887, St. Louis outfielder Tip O'Neill came home at .492, but that was the year in which walks were counted as hits. When the averages were adjusted to reflect modern methods of computation, O'Neill dropped to .435, and Anson plummeted to .347 (he had 60 walks).

Cap did lead the league in batting average twice: .399, with a league-leading 137 hits and 82 RBIs, in 1881; and, .344, with 177 hits, 20 doubles, 12 triples, 12 homeruns, 101 runs scored, and 84 RBIs, in 1888. His best overall year was 1886, when he recorded a career-high 187 hits, 35 doubles, and 147 RBIs, along with 11 triples, 10 homeruns, 117 runs scored, and 29 stolen bases.

Anson stood deep in the batter's box, fully erect, facing the pitcher, and used a 52-ounce bat. He always took at least one strike, and often two, and he invariably argued every one of them. When he finally set his bat in motion, he stepped into the pitch and "pushed" at the ball, rather than take a real swing at it. The result was usually a line drive.

How tough was it to get Anson out? Despite his policy of taking one or more strikes, Cap never struck out more than 30 times in one season, finishing with 294 strikeouts in 9,120 National League at-bats. (No strikeout statistics are available for the 1,222 at-bats in his four years in the National Association.) He made 3,041 hits in the National League (the first man to break the 3,000-hit plateau), and finished with a .333 mark in the senior circuit. Add in his 430 hits in 1,222 at-bats in the N.A., and the average climbs to .338 (18th on the all-time list). He was also the first man to hit homeruns in five consecutive at-bats (August 1884).

Yet, perhaps the greatest record Anson holds is the .302 average he recorded in 114 games as the player-manager of the White Stockings in 1897. Cap was 46 years old at the time, but still broke the 100-hit plateau and stole 11 bases.

As tough as he was at the plate, Anson was equally *bad* in the field. He was slow as molasses, and as mobile as an elephant in quicksand. His most dubious distinction is his record for most seasons leading the league in errors (five). For his first eight seasons, Cap played virtually every position on the diamond, as manager after manager tried to hide him where he could do the least amount of damage. In 1879, when Cap was named co-manager of the White Stockings, he decided that first base was the best place for him to "hide" while his club was in the field. The result: a record 58 errors in 1884!

Cap also had one other weakness: He loved to bet on his team. Frequently, Cap wagered $1,000 or more, and he rarely lost his hard-earned money, even when the teams he managed were finishing 10th in a 12-team league. Perhaps his most famous wager came in 1894, when he wagered $1,000 that his team would defeat the opposition. As a rider, he promised not to use his ace reliever, Clark Griffith, before the eighth inning. Of course, the unnamed starter was pounded in the seventh, leaving Cap with a choice of losing the game or the grand . . . and in the spirit of winning and honesty, he sacrificed his money in favor of the game. The move received tremendous publicity, and won over even the most doubtful of fans.

Wherever he went, Anson was the center of attention, no more so than in 1876, when he jumped from Philadelphia to the White Stockings. The uproar in Philly was tremendous. More than two dozen local businessmen met with Cap and induced him to repudiate the Chicago contract, but White Stockings owner William A. Hulbert refused to accept the repudiation. Anson came to Chicago's training camp and offered Hulbert $1,000 for his release. No dice, came the reply.

Newspapers across the country carried a daily "play-by-play" of the contract squabble, and when Anson finally agreed to play for Chicago, the decision made banner headlines. (Hulbert knew his ballplayers—with Anson, the Stockings won pennants in 1876, 1878, 1880-82, and 1885-86.)

After a year as co-manager in 1879, Anson took full control of the team's reins. From 1880-87, he won five N.L. flags, and the reputation as an autocrat whose temper knew no bounds. Any injury short of a fracture was insufficient reason for a player to miss a game. Since he had sworn off alcohol after spending a night in jail for drunkenness, Anson required that his players remain "dry" or face a $100 fine. He tried to control every aspect of the game, and used hand signals to instruct his pitchers on what to throw on every pitch.

Cap's players hated him, largely because he took all of the fun out of the game, and they often went out of their way to get even. Perhaps the most embarrassing hoax concerned the 1884 season-opening series at Louisville. After game one was played with what appeared to be defective baseballs ("soft and kept on splitting," Anson told reporters), Cap blamed Louisville's manager Bill Barnie. The next morning, several members of the White Stockings approached sportswriter Hugh Fullerton and asked him for a telegraph message form. He supplied them with one, and one of the pranksters typed in a "message" from Chicago President James A. Hart: "A. C. Anson, Chicago Baseball Club, Louisville Hotel, Louisville, Ky.: Don't play with Barnie's balls. (*signed*) JAMES A. HART."

Anson arrived at the park the next day, and brought along his own box of balls in response to the "telegram." When umpire John Gaffney refused to use the visiting team's balls, Cap told his team, "Get in the carriages, boys. Hart upholds me." The team returned to the hotel, where Anson wired Hart, informing him that the team had followed Hart's directions and forfeited the game. One can only imagine Hart's reaction, especially when the League Board of Directors fined the franchise $1,000!

In the end, Fullerton confessed to Hart and the Board (without revealing the names of the perpetrators), and the fine was rescinded.

By 1897, the White Stockings were in open revolt against their player-manager. The club had not won a pennant in 10 years, so Anson's irascibility was no longer cloaked by success. The club did not offer him a contract for 1898, and he spent the winter and spring brooding about his future. In June, New York Giants owner Andrew Freeman offered him the managerial reins of his Polo Grounders, and Anson accepted. Less than a month later, Anson resigned, citing irreconcilable differences with the owner, and particularly Freeman's decision to release outfielder Tom McCreery over Anson's objections.

After his resignation, Cap began a serious career in vaudeville. At first, fans flocked to see him in action, but the novelty soon wore off, and Anson began the descent into poverty. When word of his meager existence filtered back to baseball moguls, the National League's owners organized a $50,000 banquet in his honor, but Cap refused to attend.

"Since when has Anson fallen so low that they seek charity for him in his name," thundered the former idol of American youth. "Tell the world that Anson can still take care of himself and those dependent upon him!"

Anson continued to dabble in vaudeville, taking time out in 1911 to organize a group that bid unsuccessfully for the St. Louis Cardinals. That proved to be his final attempt at getting back into the game he loved. Much as baseball would exclude its next great name, George Herman Ruth, from its managerial ranks, so too was Anson summarily dismissed. When Anson died on April 14, 1922, just three days short of his

72nd birthday, he again garnered banner headlines—for the final time. His funeral was attended by tens of thousands of people, and even in death, Anson set a record—it was the largest funeral ever held in memory of an American athlete.

More than 83 years have passed since Adrian "Cap" Anson played the final game of his professional baseball career. He has been dead for more than 58 years. In life, he was the equivalent of Babe Ruth (minus the homeruns, of course) and Lou Gehrig wrapped up in one.

Yet today, with the passage of time, Anson is a forgotten man. The "team" concepts he introduced have erroneously been credited to John McGraw, largely because "Mugsy" refined them and developed them into a science. His lifetime .333 batting average is suspect, at best, because of the haphazard nature of the statistics that were "kept" in the nineteenth century. (His 1879 mark of .407 has been challenged because the league's official scorer allegedly added extra hits to the totals of his favorite players, and historians have reduced that season to a .396 mark.) The many positive innovations he made are overshadowed by his virulent racism. Despite early success in his managerial career, he finished with a 1,297-957 record, and did not come close to a pennant in his final seven seasons.

What then, if anything, survives this alleged nineteenth century Babe Ruth beyond a plaque in the Baseball Hall of Fame? One sentence, for which he will be eternally linked to an evil of society: "Get that nigger off the field." For that reason—and because he is probably the only player who completed his career before the turn of the century whose name is even familiar to today's fans—Anson has to be ranked among the game's superstars.

TY COBB

I was playing at the Augusta Country Club under all the handicaps a President of the United States puts up with when playing golf [the late Dwight D. Eisenhower recalled]. I'd take a shot, then wait patiently while the familiar army of Secret Servicemen swept down the fairway clearing the way for me. It was slow golf, and it was accepted by everybody. That is, everybody but one.

On the fifth green, I bent over to address my ball, when suddenly the air was shattered by a shrieking voice from back down the course:

"Get the hell out of my way! I'm coming through!"

Well, I paused momentarily and looked around, then resumed my putting stance. Again the sharp command from back down the fairway: "Do you hear me? Get out of my way!"

So I stepped aside—to let Ty Cobb come through. I guess nobody but the great Cobb would have dared drive through the President of the United States.

—from: *Ty Cobb,* by John McCallum, Praeger Publishers, Inc., 1975.*

To this day, baseball fans remain in awe of the name Tyrus Raymond Cobb.

Born on December 18, 1886, in a rural Georgia village known as Narrows, Cobb's

---

*The perspective offered by John McCallum in *Ty Cobb* (Praeger, 1975), is probably the most illuminating biography of a baseball player that I have ever read.

24-year career with the Tigers and Athletics is a veritable record book in itself, and his life is undoubtedly an ideal plot for a Greek tragedy.

His all-time records include: the highest lifetime batting average, .367; most career hits, 4,191; most runs scored, 2,244; 12 batting titles in 13 years, including nine consecutive between 1907–15; the only man to hit over .400 three times; a .420 average in 1911, tying him for the highest single season mark in A.L. history...

The list goes on and on.

But there is so much more to the legend that was, and is, Cobb, a legend of agony and ecstasy seldom duplicated in sports history. As fine a ballplayer as he was, he was hated by most of his contemporaries and teammates, and once told a close friend that he'd have traded it all in for the warmth and friendships he never really had. His first wife divorced him, his two sons died in the prime of life, and when he died, Cobb was living proof that money (he was a millionaire several times over) could not buy happiness.

Indeed, death played a part in Cobb's life at too early an age, and in a horrible way. His mother shot and killed Ty's father when she allegedly mistook him for a burglar. The shooting was the subject of great controversy, and all sorts of scandalous behavior was rumored, but Cobb always said that his mother was innocent of any wrongdoing. He also never understood why his father attempted to enter the house via the bedroom window that night, rather than through a door, which resulted in the shooting. Ty's mother was indicted for voluntary manslaughter, but was never tried. The trial wouldn't have mattered much—Ty had lost his closest friend and staunchest supporter, and the scars never healed.

Yet, it was for the life he led, and the feats he performed, that Cobb is best remembered. As the late Earl Combs once said, "He was a hard-nosed, physical, battling ballplayer when he played against us, and that was towards the end of his career. He probably was never as rough as history has made him out to be, but one thing is certain: he had no qualms about baiting, indeed fighting, anyone. And I mean anyone."

Billy Martin is the recognized pugilist of the 1950s, and he has maintained that reputation as a manager to this date; yet, Cobb's reputation for such activities makes Martin's pale, indeed shrivel up into dust, by comparison.

Who else but Cobb would not only challenge an umpire to a fight over a disputed call, but meet the umpire under the stands after the game, get his brains beat in, demand a return match the following year, and nearly kill the man in blue the second time around?

Who else but Cobb could torment the mild-mannered Lou Gehrig to the point where Gehrig charged the Philadelphia Athletics dugout, seeking Cobb's blood, only to draw his own when he slammed his head into the dugout roof on the way down the steps? (But, according to contemporaries, Cobb ran like hell to get away from Gehrig, who was one man Cobb had no intention of fighting.)

And who else but Cobb would dare to break the unwritten rule guaranteeing the sanctity of the fans in the stands? It was on May 15, 1912, that an infuriated Cobb vaulted the left field wall in Hilltop Park, in New York, to go after a creature named Claude Leuker. Leuker, known as a "derelict par non," needed a lesson in manners, and Cobb pummelled him, according to contemporary accounts, after listening to his vile epithets for four-and-one-half innings.

Needless to say, that assault "endeared" the "Georgia Peach" to the fans around the league; and as miserable as they had made him up to that time, well, the treatment was magnified tenfold. That act also solidified his reputation for violence, and led to the first players' strike in modern major league history when A.L. President Ban Johnson suspended him indefinitely.

One has to realize that Cobb's teammates were often reluctant to risk their necks on his behalf, and occasionally admitted that they enjoyed those rare days when Cobb met his match. Most of them pursued a policy of armed coexistence, knowing that, at any moment, Cobb could turn on them as if they were the enemy. They certainly avoided him as much as possible.

But on this one occasion, they rallied around their superstar outfielder and sent a telegram to Johnson, demanding that Cobb be reinstated, and refusing to play without him. When Johnson refused to reinstate Cobb, the Tigers took off their uniforms and left the ballpark, forcing Detroit to field a team of semipro, college, and sandlot players. The Athletics won handily, 24–2, and Johnson was livid with rage, in the mistaken belief that Cobb had instigated the sit-out. Ty was to prove him wrong.

In a unique twist, Cobb played the role of peacemaker, urging his teammates to return to the diamond rather than incur the wrath, and life suspensions, that Johnson threatened.

Who else but Cobb would dare to become modern baseball's first contract "holdout"? In 1908, at the tender age of 21, Cobb demanded a $5,000 salary and a no-cut contract—more than double the $2,400 he earned in 1907. The Tigers offered him $3,000, a virtually unheard of $600 raise in those days, but Ty angrily declined, and threatened to retire and go to college. Detroit owner Frank Navin countered with threats of his own, and told the press that the Tigers would do fine without the ungrateful lad.

After a great deal of publicity and horn blowing, Navin reluctantly agreed to meet with Cobb for the final time, in hopes of convincing him of the foolhardiness of his demands and ways. And, as would always be the case thereafter, Navin "pursuaded"

Cobb to "give in and be realistic," and sign for $4,000, plus an $800 bonus if he batted over .300 and fielded over .900 (Cobb hit .324 that year, and easily broke the .900 mark afield.)

What did Cobb do with his hard-earned dollars? Invest. He bought thousands of shares of stock, and had an incredible knack for playing the securities and stock markets successfully. He eventually owned 20,000 shares of Coca Cola (he bought that one when the price was $1/share), and 7,500 shares of Chevrolet, according to McCallum. Cobb also told reporters that he was worth somewhere between $4 million and $12 million, depending upon who he was "admitting" to.

Despite his money, Cobb always had the reputation for being a cheapskate. McCallum confirmed that Cobb not only refused to answer fan mail, but actually clipped the stamps off the return envelopes for his personal use. Similarly, while en route to Cooperstown, Cobb ordered McCallum to turn off the highway and drive two miles out of his way to get gasoline at a particular station because that one offered the savings stamps Ty collected!

Clearly, controversy followed Cobb wherever he went, as often by coincidence as by design. In 1910, Cobb went neck and neck down the stretch for the batting championship with Cleveland's Nap Lajoie. Lajoie was a fan favorite around the league, and was known for his manners and clean living. Cobb's reputation needs no further elaboration.

Ty led Lajoie by several points as the teams entered the final doubleheader of the season. The Indians faced the Browns, and Lajoie made eight hits in eight at-bats, including seven bunt singles. One of those singles was originally scored an error, but St. Louis scout Harry Howell allegedly bribed the official scorer into changing the ruling. Contemporary newspaper accounts also questioned the "wisdom" of playing the infield back on the edge of the outfield grass every time Lajoie batted, but Browns manager Jack O'Connor claimed that Lajoie had outfoxed his defense.

Fortunately, another sportswriter in the press box, Hugh Fullerton, smelled a rat. He went to Cobb and explained the situation, and although Cobb told him to forget it, Fullerton did not. Instead, he went back through the scorebook, found a game he scored in which Cobb was safe on an "error," and changed that to a hit. That was enough to save the title for Ty, .3849 to Lajoie's .3841. O'Connor and Howell were banished for life after an investigation by Johnson.

Cobb always played the game to the hilt, and would resort to psychological mind games when all else failed. In 1911, Cobb trailed Chicago White Sox star "Shoeless" Joe Jackson by more than 30 points in the race for the batting title. As the season neared its end, the Tigers and Sox squared off for a six-game series in Chicago. Cobb had been hot at the plate of late, and had closed the gap, but he knew that unless Jackson slumped badly, the title was out of reach. Furthermore, Jackson and Cobb were very good friends, and how many of those did Ty have, especially on other teams?

So, what did Cobb do? He began by totally ignoring Jackson, and then started to curse him out and tell him to "get lost," according to McCallum. Then, after the totally bewildered Jackson had given up trying to figure out why Cobb was angry at him, Ty turned around in game six and greeted Jackson as if nothing had ever happened! Jackson realized he had been duped, but it was too late. He had slumped, possibly because his concentration was broken by his amazement at Cobb's behavior, and Cobb won the title.

Then, there was Cobb's sense of humor. He once managed to appear in the same photo, twice! No trick photography, just a panorama camera (a moving camera that exposes only a small portion of film at a time while the lens travels on an arc across the field to be pictured). The Tigers were lined up for their team picture, the line was too long for a regular camera, and Cobb knew the mechanics behind the panorama camera. He lined up fourth from the left at the start. As soon as the lens passed him, he raced behind the line and arrived at the side of Manager Hughie Jennings, who was fourth from the right!

He also enjoyed taking advantage of his teammates. On a sunny Sunday in New York City, Cobb once bet Herman "Germany" Schaeffer that he could cross the East River without getting wet. Schaeffer was foolish enough to bet on it. The pair went downtown, to the Brooklyn Bridge, whereupon Cobb walked across and back in a matter of minutes. Schaeffer paid up!

That trick was all the more appropriate because it victimized Schaeffer, a man who specialized in running the bases backward, and playing similar pranks on teammates. Perhaps Schaeffer's best move was the time he bet Davey Jones that the world does not rotate on its axis. The pair returned to their hotel room, whereupon Schaeffer filled the bathtub to the top with water, told Jones to look at it, and went to sleep. The following morning, Schaeffer dragged Jones into the bathroom and triumphantly showed him the bathtub, which was still full of water. While spinning a glass full of water, and pointing at the drops that spilled over the sides of the glass, Schaeffer pointed out that if the earth rotated, the water would also have spilled out of the tub. Jones conceded defeat, and paid! (If you don't see the wisdom, try it on a friend.)

Above all else, Cobb was always in the news. Anything he did was covered, either on page one, or the sports pages:

> (May 23, 1911, Associated Press) ... After a sensational sprint across Cadilac Square last night [Ty Cobb] succeeded in recovering his automobile and capturing 19-year-old John Miles, who borrowed it without permission.
>
> Cobb's automobile, which was presented to him last fall for his batting prowess, was

standing empty in front of a hotel, but the owner (Cobb) was . . . nearby, when Miles cranked it up.

A few minutes later, the chase was on, and after a sprint of over 100 yards, Cobb, disregarding consequences, leaped into the front seat and hurled the youth into the street.

The story continued, and revealed an often-overlooked aspect of the Cobbian personality:

Miles was apprehended and arraigned, but Cobb declined to press charges because Miles was a newlywed and "they have been married only a little while and things have not been breaking well with them."

Yes, Cobb could not only be compassionate, but even charitable. His Cobb Educational Foundation paid the way for hundreds of needy youths to go to college. He built a modern hospital in Royston, Georgia (the place he called home for most of his life), and he named the structure after his parents. Many an indigent former ballplayer, and many a widow, found a check in the mail once a month, courtesy of Cobb.

So, there you have it: an incredible enigma; a man who could be the devil incarnate on one hand, and a charitable saint on the other. Yet, if one strips away the man from the statistics, the statistics themselves are simply awesome.

How great was Ty Cobb, the hitter? His closest competitor in total hits, Hank Aaron, finished with 3,771—some 420 less than Cobb; and Aaron had 935 more career at-bats. Aaron and Babe Ruth each scored 2,174 runs—70 less than Cobb, who never hit the 700 or so homeruns they did (he hit 118, and led the league once, with 9, in 1909). Rogers Hornsby is the all-time runner-up in batting average, with a .358 career mark—nine points less than Cobb. Ty's 12 batting crowns in 13 years, and nine straight 1907–15, are both unapproached, and no one else had ever hit more than .400 three times.

Furthermore, with the exception of homeruns and slugging percentage, Cobb is among the top five in every other offensive category. He finished second in games played (3,033 to Aaron's 3,298), triples (297 to teammate Sam Crawford's 312), at-bats (11,429 to Aaron's 12,364), and stolen bases (892 to Lou Brock's 917). Cobb ranks third in doubles, with 724, and fourth in total bases (5,863 to Aaron's 6,856) and runs batted in 1,959 to Aaron's 2,297).

Is it any wonder that an oldtimer, when asked what Cobb would hit today, answered .320, and when challenged on that prediction replied, "You have to remember that he'd be more than 90 years old."

Tyrus Raymond Cobb has been dead for 19 years. He played his final game on

Ty Cobb

September 11, 1928, when, at the age of 41, he pinch-hit for Jimmy Dykes and grounded out. He finished that season at .323, with 353 at-bats. He was offered a fortune to play another year, but refused because he wasn't satisfied with his performance anymore.

Dead for 19 years . . . yet the legend of Ty Cobb lives on, indeed grows, with the passage of time; and the incredible fact of the matter is that almost anything you have ever heard about him is probably true. With his statistics, and incredible life story, is it any wonder that Cobb was one of baseball's superstars?

HONUS WAGNER

When Ty Cobb reached first base for the first time in the 1909 World Series at Forbes Field, the American League's greatest hitter cupped his hands together and shouted down to shortstop Honus Wagner, "Hey, Knothead. I'm coming down on the next pitch."

Wagner, the greatest hitter in the National League, and a man whose reputation for gentlemanly conduct remains a legend to this day, smiled, and replied, "I'll be waiting."

As Pirates hurler Babe Adams delivered the next pitch, Cobb took off for second base.

In the only confrontation between the era's greatest players, Cobb came out a painful second best. As the Tigers superstar slid into second base, the gentlemanly Wagner tagged him in the face, getting the putout, and giving Cobb a lacerated lip.

Years later, Cobb recalled the play, shook his head, and said, "That goddamned Dutchman was the only man in baseball that I couldn't scare."

John Peter (Honus) Wagner looked more like a human caricature than a baseball player. The 5'11" Hall of Fame shortstop sported a 200-pound frame which was highlighted by a huge barrel chest, broad shoulders, hunched back, and the most incredibly bowed legs in baseball history. ("He could tie his shoes standing up," Lefty Gomez once quipped.) Wagner's arms stretched down to his knees, and he could hold six baseballs in each of his oversize hands. No wonder a contemporary said Wagner looked more like an actor in the movie "Freaks" than a member of the Pirates.

In the field, Wagner's style was unique. He used his huge hands like a shovel, holding his palms next to each other and scooping up the ball. When he threw over to first base, pebbles, dirt, and other debris seemed to fly over with the ball.

No other infielder was less graceful; yet no batter seemed able to hit the ball past him. Contemporary accounts describe his range as superhuman, particularly on balls hit in the hole behind third base. Former New York Giants manager John McGraw credited Wagner with more than just superhuman range—"He had an uncanny ability to accurately judge where a batter would hit the ball, making him all the more successful."

At the plate, Wagner stood deep in the batter's box, wiggling his bat like the nervous twitching of a rattlesnake, ready to lash out at every pitch. He was the classic line drive hitter, spraying the ball to all fields, depending upon where it was pitched. The strike zone was irrelevant to him—he swung at just about anything, and usually made contact. (Wagner struck out only 327 times in 10,449 career at-bats!)

Wagner batted .328 in a 21-year career that began with Louisville, in 1897, and ended with Pittsburgh, in 1917. From 1897 to 1913, Wagner recorded a record 17 consecutive seasons at or above the .300 mark, including a career-high .381 in 1900. He also led the league in doubles 7 times, triples 3 times, and hits twice. As a clutch hitter, his nine 100-RBI seasons were unmatched in the dead ball era, and he finished with a .468 slugging percentage.

He could also run the bases, earning his sobriquet "The Flying Dutchman" by stealing more than 30 bases for 11 straight years. Wagner went on to lead the league 5 times, including 61 in 1907 at the age of 33, and retired with 722, placing him fifth on the all-time major league list.

Perhaps the best measure of Wagner's ability at the plate is his record against the top six National League pitchers of his era: Amos Rusie (.524), George Wiltse (.368), Nap Rucker (.356), Kid Nichols (.352), Cy Young (.343), and Christy Mathewson (.324).

"I remember the first time I faced Honus," Mathewson recalled. "I asked our catcher what Wagner's groove [weakness] was, and he replied, 'a base on balls.'"

In fact, only one major league pitcher ever had much success against The Flying Dutchman: Jack Taylor (lifetime 150-139, 2.66 ERA), a 10-year man with the Cubs and Cardinals.

"For five years I couldn't get a hit off him," Wagner said. "Finally, I got so disgusted that I turned around and batted left-handed. I hit a triple, and he never got me out again."

Wagner was born on February 24, 1874, in Carnegie, Pennsylvania. He was one of

Honus Wagner

nine children born to a pair of German immigrants, and at the age of 12 began working in a coal mine for 70 cents a day. Baseball was his favorite pastime, and he had little difficulty competing with the friends of his older brother, Al "Butts" Wagner. ("Butts" spent a year in the major leagues, batting .226, before realizing it was not his call in life.)

When Al signed with Steubenville in the old Interstate League, Honus got serious about a baseball career. His big break came when Steubenville Manager George Moreland found himself shorthanded as opening day approached, and accepted Al's suggestion that Honus be called in to help. Honus arrived in time for the game, but had to play barefooted because no one had a size 14 shoe for him!

After a couple of years in the minors, Honus was sold to Louisville, then a National League franchise. He batted .344 in 61 games—the beginning of a 21-year career that established him as the premier shortstop and right-hand hitter of his day.

But it did not come easy. When he joined Louisville that year, the veterans resented his presence, and followed the time-honored procedure of walking all over him. In fact, Honus's career almost ended before it began, because of his reluctance to be aggressive.

"The manager was Fred Clarke, and he ordered me to go up there to take batting practice," Wagner recalled. "The veterans wouldn't let me hit. Finally, Fred said I was gone if I didn't get in there.

"So, I head back up the plate, and this one big old geezer turns around and asks me just what I think I'm doing. I told him the manager wanted me to hit, and he said that if I got near the plate he'd spit in my eye. Well, the manager had ordered me to hit, so I marched on up there, and that old geezer wheels around and lets spray a load of tobacco juice in my face and asks where I think I'm going.

"So, I hoist up my bat and take a good aim at his head, and I tell him I'm gonna hit at something, and I don't much give a damn what it is. Then, I swung at his head. Needless to say, none of my teammates ever bothered me again."

Wagner opened the season in the outfield, and would see action at every position on the diamond during his career. In later years, he claimed to have pitched and won a game in 1913 (coming on with the Pirates down 8-0 to Brooklyn, only to watch his team rally, and drive in the game-winning run himself!), but the record shows two appearances and no decisions.

"My welcome to the National League really came against the Baltimore Orioles," Wagner said. "I hit what should have been a triple, but Dirty Jack Doyle gave me the hip at first base, Hughie Jennings tripped me at second, and Mugsy McGraw blocked me off third and tagged me in the stomach so hard that he knocked the wind out of me.

"Boy, oh boy, was manager Clark angry at me about that," Wagner continued. "He threatened to send me down to the bushes if I didn't fight back. I got the message, and proved it. In my next at-bat, I belted a shot up the alley in left center. As I rounded first base, I dumped Doyle on his ass. At second, I stiff-armed Hughie and left him face down, eating dirt. But the best fun was at third base, where I stomped on McGraw's feet, kicked him in the shins, and laughed in his face. None of them ever forgot it. Not that I blame them for what they did. In those days, it was survival of the fittest, and if you fought back, the old-time players accepted you."

Wagner's first World Series appearance came in 1903, when the heavily favored Pirates were upset by the Boston Pilgrims in the first World Series ever played. Wagner batted a dismal .222, and many fans wondered if he would have been better off accepting the $20,000 the New York Highlanders had offered him to jump to the American League.

The fans would react very differently in 1909, when Wagner leaped into immortality by not only outplaying Ty Cobb (Wagner batted .333, with 6 stolen bases, to Cobb's .231, and 2 steals), but by beating Cobb at the Tiger outfielder's favorite games: physical abuse and intimidation.

"I didn't cut his lip on purpose," Wagner later explained, "but I knew he'd be coming in hard, and I wasn't about to let him nail me. Besides, if he made it once, he'd run a thousand times, and we wanted to win that World Series badly because of the way we played in 1903."

Wagner continued his outstanding play for five more seasons, before slumping to .252 in 1914. He hung on until the end of the 1917 season, in which he batted .265 at the age of 43. Ironically, Wagner's career almost ended in 1909 because of a contractual dispute with club owner Barney Dreyfuss.

"I wanted $10,000 a year, and I told him I'd retire if I didn't get it," Wagner said. "After all, I hit .354 the year before (with 201 hits, 39 doubles, 19 triples, 100 runs scored and 109 RBIs), and he didn't even offer me a raise. I was 35 years old, my legs were acting up on me, and I felt I'd earned that kind of salary."

Wagner not only got the raise, but from that year on, every contract Dreyfuss ever sent him was blank.

"He used to send me a blank contract and tell me to fill in the amount," Wagner said. "And I always sent it back with the same number filled in: $10,000. That was a lot of money in those days, and I was comfortable and single [Wagner married in 1916], so it was enough."

Perhaps a surprising remark when measured against today's salaries, but it was completely in character for Wagner.

"He was modest, conservative and particularly aware of his role as the idol of American youth," Cobb later recalled, perhaps a bit jealous of the fact that the public loved Wagner but merely respected Cobb. "I know he once turned down $1,000 a week in a vaudeville tour I was offering. He said he wasn't an actor."

Honus Wagner

Wagner never smoked and rarely drank. Perhaps the most famous story in baseball card collecting history revolves around the Honus Wagner Sweet Caporal Tobacco card. In those days, baseball cards were issued by most of the tobacco companies. Wagner had always refused to allow his name to be used because he had strong feelings against the use of tobacco, and was concerned that his picture on one of those cards would encourage youngsters to smoke. One day, Sweet Caporal approached Wagner's close friend, sportswriter John Gruber, and offered Gruber $10 if he could persuade Wagner to let Sweet Caporal use him on their cards. Gruber knew of Wagner's feelings, but told the company he was positive that it could be done, so Sweet Caporal printed up some Wagner cards. (Exactly how many is not known; but very few are known to exist today.)

When Gruber told Wagner about the deal, Wagner absolutely refused to allow his name and picture to be used. He also didn't want his friend to be out the $10, so Wagner sent the sportswriter $10 of his own!

In an era of hard-nosed, uncouth ballplayers, Wagner was a gentleman, and the fans loved him for it. He, in turn, realized that the fans paid his keep, and quickly developed that special knack for dealing with them. To this day, people remember the unique rapport he had with the fans around the country, a rapport which could be compared to that of Babe Ruth. Everywhere he went, he was in demand, and everywhere he went, he tried to be accommodating.

One day in St. Louis, Wagner was walking down the street when he passed a couple of street urchins who greeted him as if they'd known him for years. Wagner stopped, smiled, and said, "Oh, hello fellows. Sorry I didn't recognize you at first," and stopped for a 15-minute chat.

The Flying Dutchman's sense of humor also kept him in the public eye. On July 4, 1909, Wagner came to the plate with a torpedo shaped like a bat. He swung at the first pitch, and "exploded" a base hit, scaring the daylights out of just about everyone in the ballpark—but, then again, what could you expect from a man who spent his spare time collecting chickens! (Undoubtedly the strangest hobby in baseball history.)

Another side of Wagner's character that is always overlooked is his understanding of the psychological side of baseball. Despite his portrayal as a "dumb Dutchman," Wagner was the equal of anyone, including Cobb and McGraw, when it came to distracting opponents or breaking the other team's concentration.

His favorite story was the time he so rattled a St. Louis pitcher that the rookie hurler blew a 4-0 lead.

"We were losing, and the kid was untouchable," Wagner said. "I came to the plate in the seventh inning, and took two strikes. The next pitch was his best fastball, right over the middle, and I reached out and caught it barehanded, threw it back to him, and yelled out 'Changeup, huh.' You should have seen the look on his face, and even though I was called out, the poor sucker walked the next five straight batters and we came back to win."

In July 1917, the Pirates were mired in last place with a 20-40 record. Owner Barney Dreyfuss decided that a new manager was needed, and he asked Wagner to take over. Honus assumed the managerial reins on July 1, and resigned on July 4. The Pirates went 1-4 under his brief regime.

"I wasn't ready for it," he said. "I just couldn't get mad at anybody."

After the season ended, Wagner retired. He coached baseball and basketball at Carnegie Tech for a while, and later served as sergeant at arms for the Pennsylvania legislature (a job he quit because "it was too boring"). In 1927, he and Pie Traynor opened a sporting goods store, but that collapsed during the Depression.

By 1932, Wagner was unemployed. He desperately wanted to get back into baseball, and was seriously considered for the Cincinnati Reds manager's spot before Heinie Groh was hired. As his personal depression over his unemployment increased, his wife decided to take matters into her own hands. She telephoned the new Pirates team owner, Bill Benswanger, and told him how much Honus missed the game. Benswanger was well aware of Wagner's public appeal, and immediately signed the 59-year-old as a coach.

Wagner remained on the field, in uniform, until 1949, when his age (78) and arthritis made it impossible for him to continue. During those 18 seasons, he kept the fans and media well entertained with his stories about crazy plays he'd seen—or conjured up. Wagner's favorite involved a hapless outfielder who leaped up against the outfield fence to attempt a spectacular catch, only to get caught on the wire and hang there, red-faced, while the ball hit the wall, remained in play, and the batter circled the bases.

In 1946, the Pirates threatened to strike. During a radio interview, Benswanger vowed that there would be nine men on the field, "even if Honus Wagner has to play shortstop." The story was carried all over the country, and the next morning, the owner arrived at Forbes Field at 9 A.M. to discover a 75-year-old man and his grandson, waiting to buy tickets for the 2 P.M. game. When Benswanger asked why the pair were there so early, the elderly fellow replied that they'd "flown all the way from South Carolina just to see the great Wagner play one more time."

On April 30, 1955, the city of Pittsburgh and the Pirates baseball club erected a statue of Wagner in Schenley Park. The 81-year-old Hall-of-Famer somehow managed to attend the unveiling ceremonies, despite failing health. It was his final appearance before a public that still adored him. He died on December 6, less than three months short of his 82nd birthday.

How great was Wagner? When he retired, Honus led all National League hitters in career at-bats (10,449), hits (3,430), singles (2,527), doubles (651), triples (252), and games played (2,789). He still leads the League in singles and triples, and ranks third on the all-time major league list in triples, and fifth in hits, doubles, and stolen bases.

There is one final postscript. In 1969, as part of the Baseball Centennial, 100 of the nation's leading sportswriters were asked to vote on the All-Time Major League Team, by position. Only one name appeared on every ballot: shortstop, Honus Wagner, superstar.

ROGERS HORNSBY

I told Landis that playing the horses is like playing the stock market, except that I get my answers in a couple of hours. I don't care what he says or threatens. I will never stop going to the track, and the Judge had better set his own house in order before he interferes with mine.

—Rogers Hornsby

One day the St. Louis Cardinals were playing the Brooklyn Dodgers. A rookie was on the mound for Brooklyn, and first baseman Jack Fournier was coaching the kid on how to pitch to each batter.

Things worked out well until a menacing-looking right-hand hitter stepped in.

"Keep the ball inside for this fellow," Fournier said. "Don't give him anything outside to hit."

The rookie obeyed the order, and the batter lashed a low line drive down the third base line. It went for a triple, whereupon the kid walked over to Fournier and said, "I thought this guy couldn't hit inside pitches."

"Oh, no, I didn't say that," Fournier replied. "I said not to give him one outside—what the hell do you think I want to get a leg taken off for? That batter was Hornsby!"

Rogers Hornsby never won any popularity contests, and he could not have cared less.

The controversial, tactless, insensitive man who set the modern single season record by batting .424 in 1924 never gave a damn what his teammates thought of him, and had even less respect for the managers and owners he played under. He even dared to tackle the iron-willed Commissioner of Baseball, Judge Landis, and actually won, when he successfully resisted the Judge's order to stop playing the horses.

"I told Landis that playing the horses is like playing the stock market," Hornsby recalled, hinting at Landis's penchant for stocks and lack of success in reading the market, "except that I get my answers in a couple of hours. I will never stop going to the track, and I told him that he'd better set his own house in order before he interferes with mine."

The Rajah's track record (six teams in 23 seasons) gives some idea of how impossible he was to get along with. He batted more than .400 three times in his first 10 major league seasons, and was named player-manager of the Cardinals midway through the 1925 season. After piloting the club to its first pennant and world championship in 1926, he was traded to the New York Giants for Hall-of-Famer Frankie Frisch and pitcher Jimmy Ring.

The trade stemmed from an incident with team owner Sam Breadon over an exhibition game that Hornsby wanted cancelled.

"We were in the thick of the pennant race and had what should have been a badly needed day off," Hornsby said, "but Breadon wouldn't cancel that goddamned game. He came into the clubhouse after a tough loss, and told me that we had to play. Naturally, I told him where to go, and what he could do with that game, but he was the owner, so we had to play."

He batted .361 in 155 games for the Giants in 1927, but couldn't get along with owner Horace Stoneham. Again, an incident in the clubhouse was the catalyst.

"John McGraw was sick all July, so I took over as manager for the month," Hornsby said. "The team played at a .597 clip—better than it had been going under McGraw. Then, one day, Stoneham comes in after a loss and tries to tell me how to run the club. I told him to look after the stock market and I'll run the ballclub."

The Rajah was sent packing to Boston, where he led the Braves and the National League with a .387 average. Hornsby was happy in Boston, but owner Emil Fuchs could not afford to keep the high-salaried second baseman. At his own suggestion, Hornsby was dealt to the Cubs for five no-names and $200,000.

"I told him to trade me so he could get the money he needed," Hornsby explained. "Besides, I don't think he ever forgave me for the time I told a sportswriter that that team of humpty-dumpties had about as much chance of winning the pennant as an icicle's chance in hell."

He lasted four years in Chicago, and was fired midway through the '32 season. When he left, the Cubbies were in second place, and they went on to win the pennant under Joe McCarthy. When the losers' shares of the World Series money were divided up, the team "thanked" their former manager by voting him a zero share!

In 1933, Hornsby returned to the Cardinals, but they forwarded him to their cross-town rivals, the Browns, so he could be their player-manager. By this time, age had reduced the Rajah to a pinch hitter, and even his self-esteemed genius couldn't lift "those humpty dumpties" out of the second division.

The Browns fired him in 1937 (after he had bad-mouthed team president Don Barnes), but brought him back for the 1952 season. He lasted 50 games before being relieved by Bill Veeck, and the players were so glad to see him go that they are said to have presented Veeck with a silver plaque "in recognition of the greatest play since the Emancipation Proclamation."

His final managerial post was with the Reds, where he finished sixth for two years and was dismissed. In 1962, the New York Mets hired him as their batting instructor, and the irascible Hornsby used the appointment to get into yet another baseball battle, this time with Roger Maris.

Prior to the season, Hornsby had written an autobiography in which he knocked Maris as a .260 hitter. As the Mets and Yankees prepared for a spring training game, a UPI photographer tried to set up a Maris-Hornsby photo. The Rajah agreed, and headed over to the Yankee dugout, but Maris ignored the Hall-of-Famer and continued signing autographs for the fans.

"What do you think of that bush leaguer!" Hornsby exploded. "He refused to pose with me. I've posed with some real major leaguers, but no bush leaguers like he is. He couldn't carry my bat. He didn't hit in two seasons what I hit in one."

Why was Hornsby so impossible to get along with?

"He was very set in his ways, and believed that everyone should do things the way he did," a former player recalled. "He never smoke or drank, and refused to go to movies during his career because he was afraid they would hurt his eyes. He was the last person you'd invite to a party. The problem was, he expected grown men to emulate him, and you can't limit the lives of ballplayers the way the Rajah wanted to."

Hornsby was born on April 26, 1896, in Winters, Texas. He came from Scotch-Irish stock, and sported a round, unsmiling face which was highlighted by deep piercing eyes and a personality to match. No one ever got very close to him, including the two women he married, and divorced. Virtually nothing is known about his childhood, and he might as well have been born wearing the uniform of Denison in the Class D Western Association, because that's where Cardinals scout Bob Connery first spotted him.

"The Cardinals were a tight-fisted organization in those days," Connery said. "Manager Miller Huggins knew it all too well, so he told me not to bother scouting the top minor leagues because the owners wouldn't spend the money to sign the good talent. Miller said to stick to the locals, and I found Hornsby there, in Denison's spring training camp. He impressed me enough to remember him, and in 1915, we bought him for $50.

"To be honest, I was not too impressed with his hitting," Connery continued. "He was a loose, gangling kid with a good pair of hands, a strong arm, and a world of life and pep on the ballfield. I also noted that his eyes were clear."

When the 5'11", 140-pound rookie reported to St. Louis, Huggins inserted him into the lineup, and Hornsby batted .246 in 18 games. At the end of the season, the kid asked the veteran manager, "What do you think of me?"

"Well, young man, I like your hustle, but you're young and need to put on some weight, so I'll have to put you out on the farm next year."

"Oh, you needn't do that," the naive Hornsby replied. "I can go to my father's farm this winter."

In spring training the following year, Huggins saw something he liked, and Hornsby remained with the club. He responded with a .313 average while seeing action at every infield position. A year later, Hornsby was the regular shortstop and batted .327. Injuries and alleged fears of the draft slumped the star to .281 in 1918, but in 1919 he rebounded to .318.

The year 1920 began with Hornsby inserted at second base, a position he handled superbly. Although opponents were quick to note his weakness in fielding pop flies ("He never hit any, so how would he know how to catch them," quipped Lefty Gomez), he was so good that he'd have been a regular if he'd only hit .280.

When 1920 ended, Hornsby had finished with five league-leading marks: .370 average, .559 slugging percentage, 94 RBIs, 44 doubles, and 218 hits. As things turned out, he was only warming up.

From 1921 to 1925, Hornsby won five consecutive batting titles with marks of .397, .401, .384, .424, and .403. His five year average was .402. He also led the National League in slugging percentage every year (.639, .722, .627, .696, .756); RBIs, hits, and runs scored, three times; and doubles and homeruns twice.

His best season was his triple crown year, 1922, when he led the league with a .401 average, belted 42 homeruns, and drove in 152 runs. He also led the league in hits (250, a mark surpassed just twice in National League history, by Bill Terry and Lefty O'Doul, each with 254), doubles (46), runs scored (141), and slugging percentage (.722). His 14 triples also placed him among the leaders.

When Hornsby hit .424, only two pitching staffs held him below the .400 mark: Pittsburgh (.393) and Chicago (.387). Add on his 89 walks, and he was on base 316 times in 625 trips to the plate—better than a 50-50 shot every time!

The streak ended in 1926, and Hornsby blamed the player-manager role for his drop to .317. He rebounded to .361 in '27, led the league for the seventh and final time with a .387 mark in '28, and had his final outstanding year in '29, when he hit .380 for the N.L. champion Chicago Cubs.

As an all-around hitter, Hornsby was clearly the greatest from the right side of the plate. He combined a high lifetime batting average (.358, second on the all-time list) with power (541 doubles, 302 homeruns), lashing line drives from deep in the batter's box to every corner of the ballpark. The Rajah also had good speed, as evidenced by his 168 career triples, and superior success on the basepaths.

"When I came to the plate, I felt sorry for the pitchers," he said. "They had to try to get me out. They had to put the ball over the plate, and I could hit it."

Opponents tried every trick in the book to stop him. One day, Braves catcher Al Spohrer tried to distract Hornsby by bringing up the Rajah's favorite topic: food.

"My wife has discovered a butcher who sells the finest steaks," the catcher said.

"That so?" Hornsby replied.

Strike one, called.

"Not only that, but she can prepare them better than anyone I know," Spohrer continued.

Strike two, called.

"What Grace and I thought, Rog, was that the next time you're in Boston, Rog, you might come to the house and have a steak with us."

Crraack!

As Hornsby crossed home plate with a homerun, he said, "What night shall we make it, Al?"

Strangely enough, one group of people Hornsby did get along with was the umpires. He was ejected from only one game in his entire career, and on that occasion, veteran umpire Bill Klem convinced the ejecting umpire to reinstate Hornsby!

"Hell, umpires are human beings with a job to do, and they don't beat you," he explained. "The only thing I hated to see 'em do was miss a third strike on me so I didn't get a chance to swing."

Off the field, Hornsby remained a recluse. His only hobby was sitting in hotel lobbies, watching people go by, and occasionally talking to youngsters and fans. He refused to engage in other sports because he feared they might sap his strength, or cause injury. The Rajah particularly despised golf.

"When I hit a ball, I want someone to chase it," he sneered, after turning down an invitation to a tournament. "Women play golf."

In 1944, Hornsby took his act south of the border to manage the Veracruz Blues in Jorge Pasquel's Mexican League. Rumor had it that the games were fixed, and Hornsby discovered it to be true in a unique way. (The first two games of each three game series were to be split, thereby guaranteeing a large crowd for game three.)

The Blues won on Friday, and trailed by three runs with two outs in the bottom of the ninth the next day. Pasquel got Hornsby's attention, and convinced the 48-year-old manager to pinch-hit. Naturally, the Rajah hit a grand slam to win the game—and kill the attendance for game three. When Pasquel complained, Hornsby told him off, and Pasquel sent him back to Texas.

After his final stint with the Reds, Hornsby was often called upon as a source for articles about baseball, and he always managed to live up to his reputation as the most outspoken of players. In 1960, he took the soap box to preach against Al Worthington, a White Sox pitcher who quit baseball for two years to protest the use of a sign-stealing spy secreted in the Chicago scoreboard.

"His ethics are wonderful for a game between the Humane Society and the Salvation Army," Hornsby wrote, "but not for a game in the majors. The PTA would go along with him, but enforce rules against stealing signs and you wouldn't have enough guys left to play."

In 1961, *True Magazine* published a Hornsby piece entitled "You've Got to Cheat to Win in Baseball," in which Hornsby listed his Nine Commandments:

a. Bend that elbow *on* the field, too.
b. You don't need spit to throw a spitball.
c. All signals don't come from third base.
d. Some of the best kickers never saw a football.
e. That glove isn't there just to keep your hands warm.
f. A trip in the majors beats a trip to the bushes.
g. Tell the ump they were out of your shirt size.
h. A smart beanballer never misses.
i. Belts can hold up baserunners as well as pants.

After that year with the Mets, Hornsby's eyesight began failing him, and he eventually entered the hospital for cataract surgery. Ironically enough, the man who never went to the movies because they might damage his eyes died of a heart attack and stroke following the cataract surgery on January 5, 1963.

The ghost of Babe Ruth remains very much alive today, but that of Rogers Hornsby remains well buried. As great as he was on the field, he never captured the hearts of the fans. In fact, the fans joined his teammates in hating him. He never became the idol that Ruth, Gehrig, and Cobb were, thereby proving, once again, that mere statistics do not make a superstar.

Today, Hornsby is remembered as the answer to a trivia question: Who holds the record for the highest single season batting record? Next time it comes up, remember the answer: Rogers Hornsby, .424, 1924, a mere star.

GEORGE SISLER

The St. Louis Browns had the day off, and their Hall of Fame first baseman, George Sisler, decided to pay a visit to his good buddy, W. C. Fields.

Sisler caught Fields in the dressing room, and after the usual greetings, W.C. offered the star a drink.

"No thanks, I don't," was Sisler's reply.

"Oh, well," replied Fields, "even the perfect ballplayer can't have everything."

In 1920, George Harold Sisler set the all-time major league record by stroking 257 hits in one season, while leading the American League with a .407 batting average.

Two years later, Sisler set the American League record by hitting .420, while again leading the league in hits (246), and adding the league titles for triples (18), runs scored (134), and stolen bases (51). He also batted safely in 41 consecutive games, a mark which stood until Joe DiMaggio surpassed it with 56 in 1941.

By the time Sisler's 15-year career ended in 1930, he sported a .340 lifetime batting average, and a reputation as the finest fielding first baseman in the history of the game. His place in the soon-to-be-formed Hall of Fame seemed assured, as did his immortality.

Yet today, although he has been enshrined in the Hall of Fame for 41 years, George Sisler is a forgotten man. The first baseman the fans remember from that era is Lou Gehrig, even though Gehrig couldn't carry Sisler's glove.

How could a ballplayer with those credentials fade into obscurity?

Historians will argue that it was no fault of Sisler's. He spent the first 12 years of his career with the St. Louis Browns, a team renowned for its ineptness, and even Sisler could catapult them into only one pennant race (1922, when the Browns finished one game behind the Yankees). By the time the Senators acquired him in '28, Walter Johnson no longer took his turn on the mound, and they, too, had faded into mediocrity. The final two and a half years with the Braves were no improvement— their only miracle was in 1914, and they would not win again until 1948.

But the historians, God bless 'em, fail to account for the real reasons. A true superstar leads his team to victory. He is "the straw that stirs the drink," as Reggie Jackson said, and Sisler simply didn't stir it well enough on the field, and never stirred it off the field.

"He lacked the fiery flamboyance of Ty Cobb and the boisterous brilliance of Babe Ruth," was the way fellow Hall-of-Famer Eddie Collins put it. "George was a great first baseman, and a great hitter, but he was too quiet and clean-living to win headlines."

Indeed. While Cobb was punching his way through the American League, taking on fans, players, and umpires alike, Sisler behaved like a saint. Only once in his career did Sisler raise his fists in anger, and the result was a one-punch knockout of teammate Bob Groom. It came after Sisler had been slow to retrieve a bad throw, enabling a run to score from second on what should have been an inning-ending force-out. Groom had mercilessly derided him after the inning, and Sisler finally lost his temper.

While Ruth was leading the wild, scandalous life for which he is so well remembered, Sisler was home with his family, shunning publicity. The vaudeville stage and barnstorming tours were not for him—he preferred the sedentary life of a printer.

Even in his native St. Louis, Sisler was swamped by the reputation of another star, the late Rogers Hornsby, much as Bill Terry would be dwarfed in New York by Lou Gehrig. While the Rajah was telling managers, umpires, owners, and even Commissioner Landis where to go and how to get there, Sisler never argued with anyone. He was thrown out of only one game in 15 years, in an incident in which he slapped umpire George Hildebrand with his glove after a bad call at first base. Sisler apologized immediately, and where other players might have been banned for months, received a $50 fine and six-day vacation.

Born on March 24, 1893, in Manchester, Ohio, the 5'10" left-handed hitter came from a middle-class family that emphasized education. He was an outstanding high school athlete, and enrolled at the University of Michigan in 1910, where he majored in engineering. Branch Rickey guided the Wolverines baseball team, and he never forgot the incredible talents of his .400-hitting pitcher.

"In May 1911, Sisler pitched one of the most incredible games in baseball history," Rickey recalled. "He struck out 20 men in a seven-inning ballgame.

"Actually, he played everywhere, and he made it look easy," Rickey continued. "He had the greatest reflexes I've ever seen, and that was the cornerstone of his ability to play every position and make it look easy. Add to that the fact that he always wanted to win, and that he used his superior intellect to find ways to do exactly that, and you had the best ballplayer I ever saw. That's right, in 1922, he was the best, ever."

Rickey was not the only man to note the freshman's talents. A long-since-forgotten scout for Akron of the old Ohio-Penn League also saw something he liked, and inked the minor to a professional contract. When George's Dad learned that the signing would prevent his son from playing college ball, and thereby encourage George to leave school, he went to court and repudiated the contract.

While the case lingered in the courts, Akron sold Sisler to Columbus, which, in turn, forwarded his rights to the Pittsburgh Pirates.

When Sisler graduated from Michigan in 1914, Rickey inked his former star to a St. Louis Browns contract . . . and then all hell broke loose. The Pirates were furious, claiming the phenom belonged to them, and the dispute moved from the courtroom to the National Commission of Baseball, a three-man board which supervised the overall relations between the major leagues until the election of Judge Landis in 1920. After a lengthy debate, Sisler was awarded to the Browns.

George made his major league debut against the Cleveland Indians a year later, pitching three scoreless relief innings, and picking up a victory. His next appearance was against the best pitcher of the day, Walter Johnson, and Sisler defeated the "Big Train," 2-1.

"I'll never forget that one," Sisler recalled, some 20 years later. "We knew Johnson would be on the mound, but Rickey hadn't told us who would do our hurling. That night, Branch came into my room and told me I would pitch. I didn't want to sleep. The next day, I was going to pitch against Walter Johnson—and I beat him!"

Sisler would face Johnson again, in August, and decisioned the Hall-of-Famer again, this time 1-0. When 1915 ended, Sisler had gone 4-4 with a 2.83 ERA in 15 games. He also batted .285, seeing action at first base and the outfield in 66 other games.

Rickey knew his baseball, and he knew that Sisler had to play every day. The 1916 season opened with the soph at first base, and George hit .305. For the next six years, Sisler would hit .341 or better, including .407 and .420 marks.

"I always considered the 1920 season my best," Sisler said. "I led the league in at-bats with 631, set the hits record, and also had 49 doubles, 18 triples, 19 homeruns, 136 runs scored, 122 RBIs, 42 stolen bases, and a .632 slugging percentage."

But Rickey remained convinced that 1922 was George's year.

"He singlehandedly led us down to the wire in the pennant race that year," the Mahatma recalled. "Why, he only struck out 14 times in 586 at-bats. We should have won the pennant, but the Yankees edged us out."

The '22 race was a nightmare for the Browns, and Sisler in particular.

"We were beating them by one run with two outs in the ninth inning," Sisler recalled. "They loaded the bases, and Whitey Witt stepped up. It was a two-strike pitch, and he stroked it into centerfield . . . when I saw that ball sail out there and land safely, why, my heart ached. That blow not only cost us the pennant, but put the whole franchise into a state of shock from which it never recovered."

Soon after the World Series ended, rumors surfaced in the St. Louis papers, saying that Sisler would not be wearing a Browns uniform in 1923, and that a deal to the Yankees, for $200,000 and a player, was imminent. It was a near-truth. The Yankees did offer $200,000 for Sisler, who would have been a perfect replacement for the less-talented Wally Pipp (Gehrig was still a Columbia University man at that time), but the Browns turned it down, to the delight of their fans.

Unfortunately, the other part of the rumor proved to be true. Sisler would not wear a Browns uniform in 1923, but for a different reason. He wore a bathrobe in a hospital, and at home, because his severe sinusitis forced him to sit out the season.

"It was so bad that I was seeing double," Sisler said. "One day I was driving home, and I saw two cars in the left lane. I said to myself, 'George, you're going to get hurt, or even killed,' so I took the doctor's advice and hung up my spikes."

As the 1923 season progressed, and the Browns languished in fourth place, the newspapers revealed that Sisler had been advised to retire forever. The fans were horrified.

"All season long, I suffered," Sisler recalled. "I felt sorry for the fans, for my teammates, for everyone, except for myself. I planned to get back into uniform for 1924. I just had to meet a ball with a good swing again, and then run. The doctors all said I'd never play again, but when you're desperate, when you're fighting for something that actually keeps you alive—well, the human will is all you need."

The road back seemed impossible. In spring training, 1924, Sisler looked terrible, suffering from severe headaches and double vision, until, one day against the Cardinals . . .

"I was still seeing double, but I had to play. I picked out what I thought was a good pitch, swung at one of the two balls that were coming to the plate, and hit it with all my might. Luckily, there was contact, and the drive went between the outfielders. As I raced around the bases, something seemed to ease in my head, and I knew that I had the sinusitis licked."

Well, partially licked, anyway. The record shows that Sisler was never the same ballplayer he had been. In 1924, his comeback was hindered by the pressures of serving as a player-manager, and he batted only .305. A year later, he leaped to .345, and carried the Browns back up to fourth place with an 82-71 record, but a sixth-place finish in 1926, and his .290 batting average, ended George's managerial career.

"I never should have accepted the role in the first place," Sisler said. "I simply wasn't ready to manage. I was only 31, and it was too early in my career."

There would be three more .300-plus seasons in Washington and Boston, followed by a sinusitis-forced retirement at age 37. The next 12 years included a sporting goods dealership that was axed by the Depression, and a return to the printing business he always enjoyed. He also scouted for the Dodgers and Pirates, and taught his sons a bit about the game along the way.

Dick, the oldest, became a power-hitting first baseman-outfielder who lasted 8 years in the big leagues. He became a hero in 1950, when his 10th-inning homerun in the final game of the season enabled the Phillies to edge out Brooklyn for the pennant—the same team George Sr. scouted for.

George Jr. never made it to the big leagues, but enjoyed considerable success as a minor league executive, and is the President of the Columbus Clippers. When Al Rosen left the Yankees after the 1979 season, George Jr. was mentioned as a probable successor, but the nod eventually went to Gene Michael.

Dave, the youngest of the boys, spent six years on the mound with the Red Sox, Tigers, Senators, and Reds, pitching in 247 games, and finishing with a career 38-44 mark and a .157 batting average.

He also provided the final proof of George Sr.'s obscurity as a ballplayer. One day, when Dave was still a youngster, he and George Sr. were out having a catch. Dad failed to glove an "easy one," and the future pitcher blurted out: "Gosh, how did you ever play baseball!"

George Sr. put his glove down, walked into the house, and as far as any of his sons know, never put it on again.

When George Sisler Sr. passed away on March 26, 1973, he had lived a full life filled with much happiness. His name will remain enshrined in Cooperstown, where, year after year, the youth of America will learn that "Gorgeous George" was not a professional wrestler, but one of the greatest stars of the 1920s.

Perhaps if Sisler had hit homeruns instead of triples, he would be remembered as the Babe Ruth of St. Louis. Perhaps an occasional slide into third base with his spikes up would have elevated him to Cobbian status. Maybe a fight or two, and some choice language for Judge Landis, would have put him above Rogers Hornsby. And, if the sinusitis that ruined his career had caused his premature death, he might have outshone Gehrig.

But that was never Sisler's way . . . nor was it the way of a superstar.

PIE TRAYNOR

> They can substitute for him, but they can never replace him.
> —Branch Rickey's assessment of Hall
> of Fame third baseman Pie Traynor

At the height of his 17-year career with the Pittsburgh Pirates, Harold "Pie" Traynor was not only the best third baseman in the major leagues, but was also the most popular man in the Steel City.

On the field, Traynor simply had to be seen to be believed. Most defenses featured a hole between short and third through which opponents tried to hit the ball, but with Pie out there, the Pirates had little more than a crack. The Hall-of-Famer combined a magnet-like glove with lightning quickness, enabling him to do the impossible again and again. Hot shots over the bag were turned into easy putouts. Bunts down third were a waste of time. What could not be stopped with the glove was usually barehanded, and followed by a perfect throw to first.

At the plate, the 6'1" right-hander paused to kiss his 42-ounce bat before stepping in, and would send line drives screaming all over the ballpark. Traynor was a master of the hit-and-run, and perfection when it came to hitting to the opposite field. If he had a fault at the plate, it was his inability to hit the long ball (his best single-season homerun total was 12, in 1923), but he still managed to drive in 101 or more runs in seven different seasons, and was always among the league leaders in doubles and triples. Strangely enough, the lifetime .320 hitter would lead the league in only one offensive category, and that for only one season: triples, with 19 in 1923.

Off the field, Traynor had that special knack for relating to the fans. He never turned down a request for an autograph or a handshake, and gave endless hours to charity. Part of his secret was his refusal to ride to the ballpark. He often walked seven or eight miles, and for every mile he walked there were at least 100 fans waiting for him. During the 1927 World Series, Traynor walked from his hotel on 34th Street in Manhattan up to Yankee Stadium (161st Street) in the Bronx, refusing ride after ride, and ultimately arriving at the ballpark some four hours later. No wonder the Pirates were swept!

Born on November 11, 1899, in Framingham, Massachusetts, Pie was one of eight children. His schooling ended when he was 12 years old, and he began walking into Boston (a three-mile trek each way) to work as a messenger boy. When he wasn't working or walking, he was out on the sandlots, playing baseball.

"I'll never forget my first sandlot game," he recalled. "I got there late, and the only open position was catcher. In those days, masks were hard to come by, and I took a foul ball in my face. It cost me two teeth, a good paddling when I got home, and ended any thoughts of making a career out of that position. Toothless yes, but my enthusiasm was undiminished."

It was also during those childhood games that Traynor received the nickname "Pie," according to one friend. The story goes that a local priest who used to supervise the lot always treated the boys to dessert after the games. Everyone asked for ice cream—except for Harold, who always demanded a piece of pie.

Then again, another friend said the name came from the same cause (the affinity for pie), but a different source: a reward for chasing foul balls when the local men's team played. Mrs. Traynor always claimed she coined the name because he always insisted on adding pie to her shopping list.

Traynor's father had another "real" reason.

"I was a printer, and Harold used to come home from those sandlot games all dirty," the elder Traynor recalled. "The word for messed-up or dirty type is *pi*, and that's where the name really came from."

Whatever the source, the nickname stuck, to the point where Pie tried to enlist under that name, and was rejected. Eventually, he was assigned to a war-related industry: inspecting freight trains at a munitions factory. The job consisted of riding a horse 12 hours a day and making sure all was well on the railroad cars. The closest Pie came to action was when a couple of would-be graffiti vandals tried to paint a few choice words on a car, and were summarily asked to leave the yard.

The one advantage of the war-related industry was its industrial league baseball team. Pie's continued success on the field led to a tryout with the Boston Braves, but Manager George Stallings chased the youth off the field because he believed Traynor was too young. The Red Sox also took a look at the local infielder, but decided not to sign him. Undaunted by the pair of rejections on the home front, Pie continued to attend tryouts and was eventually signed by Portsmouth, Virginia, for the 1920 season.

The 21-year-old New Englander batted .270 in 1920, and the embarrassed Sox sought to rectify their error that August. By that time, Traynor had attracted the attention of the Pirates, and the bidding war was on. Boston's final offer was $9,000—one grand less than Pittsburgh's—so a mere $1,000 cost the Sox the greatest third baseman in major league history. (Actually, it also cost the Yankees a shot at Traynor, because with the way Boston started dealing away its players to the New York team, Pie probably would have wound up in the pinstripes.)

With all the fanfare surrounding his acquisition, Traynor was an immediate disappointment to the eager Pirate fans. He batted .212 in 17 games, and was very shaky in the field. At the end of the season, he was farmed out to Birmingham, where he batted .336 and stole 47 bases in 1921.

The Pirates found themselves in a rather pleasant situation in 1921. The team was battling for the pennant, and the fans were coming out in record numbers. Then, in a matter of days, Clyde Barnhart and Possum Whitted suffered season-ending injuries, and the Pirates needed infield help, pronto. Pie was summoned from Birmingham, once again arrived amidst great fanfare, and again had his troubles.

Manager George Gibson inserted Pie into the lineup against the Cubs on his first day with the team, and the future All-Star proceeded to make the game-losing error. The miscue not only lost the game, but nearly cost the youth his career. Gibson made no secret of the fact that "Traynor had lost the game," and also announced that he had no confidence in the kid, and would look elsewhere for help.

As things turned out, it was Gibson who would be looking elsewhere during the 1922 season. When the Pirates got off to a 32-33 start, he was sent packing, and Bill McKechnie came on as the new skipper. It was the best thing that ever happened to Traynor. McKechnie moved Traynor from shortstop to third, and shifted Rabbit Maranville from second to short. The pair became fixtures at their respective positions, and both are in the Hall of Fame today.

By 1925, Traynor was an established star, and in that year, he hit .320 with 39 doubles, 14 triples, 106 RBIs and 114 runs scored to lead the Bucs to a pennant. The seven-game World Series with the Senators was a classic, and provided Pie with the biggest thrills of his career.

"I hit a homerun in my first World Series at bat," he said, "and the victim was the great Walter Johnson. He was some pitcher, and I was thrilled to death that I had taken him to the seats. Of course, I'd have been a lot happier if we had won the game."

The Pirates lost game one, 4–1. A 3–2 win in game two was followed by a 4–3 loss in game three, and a whitewashing by Johnson in game four (4–0).

"We really weren't ready for the Series when it began," Pie recalled. "The National League season had ended a week before the American League, so we had gone stale. We had our backs to the wall, but we rallied to take the fifth and sixth games, largely thanks to Roger Peckinpaugh, the Washington shortstop who made eight errors in that series.

"When Johnson took the mound for game seven, we were worried," he continued, "and when they scored four runs in the first inning, we were downright scared. But, he just wasn't the same man he'd been earlier in the Series, worn out I guess, and we got to him. Peckinpaugh hit a homerun in that game, but he also made some more bad plays in the field."

The 1927 Series against the Yankees would not be as pleasant. New York swept Pittsburgh, shutting down Traynor and the Waner brothers. Legend has it that the key to the Series was a homerun barrage by Ruth, Gehrig, and Meusel during batting practice before game one, which so intimidated the Pirates that they went down quietly.

"That wasn't true," Traynor maintained. "After we took batting practice, and before they started theirs, we returned to the clubhouse. We did not watch them hit. We were indoors, and at Yankee Stadium there are no windows.

"The real reason we lost that Series was pitching," he continued. "They had a great staff, and ours was only a good one. Pennock and Hoyt are in the Hall of Fame, and Shocker and Pipgras were tremendous. They also had Wilcy Moore, one of the best relievers in the business. Heck, Pennock had a perfect game going in game three until my single with one out in the eighth."

Pittsburgh faded to fourth place in '28, despite Traynor's .337 average, and would not win another pennant until years after his retirement. There would be several near-misses, the most noteworthy coming in 1938, the year Gabby Hartnett hit his "homerun in the dark." By then, Traynor, who had become the player-manager in 1934, had relinquished his playing role.

"That was a devastating blow if there ever was one," he recalled. "Truth of the matter was that we were lucky to get that close. Our pitching never was all that good, with ace Mace Brown leading the staff at 15–9. They wound up winning 89 games to our 86."

When the Pirates collapsed to seventh place in 1939, the owners placed the blame on Pie's shoulders, and decided that a managerial change was in order. The popular Traynor could not be fired without creating a major outcry, so he was moved up into the front office as the new assistant director of the farm system. Pie tolerated the job for two boring years, before leaving in favor of the broadcasting booth. He caught on with radio station KQV, and continued to work there until the late 1950s. By then, he was ready to retire, and he led a comfortable, pleasant life until his death on March 16, 1972, in his beloved adopted home of Pittsburgh.

How good was Pie Traynor? Those who saw him play say that Clete Boyer, Graig Nettles, and Billy Cox approached his excellence in the field, and that Brooks Robinson would have given him a run for his money in overall ability... but Traynor outhit all of them by 45-90 points every year!

The late Frank Grahame, a sportswriter of great repute, always wondered why Pie was more or less a forgotten man. "It is curious that his fame down through the years has not matched his skills because there wasn't anything he couldn't do extraordinarily well," was the way Grahame put it.

Why, then, is Pie Traynor's name not as well known as that of Brooks Robinson? Is it merely the passage of time, or are there other factors?

Obviously, the answer is that Traynor, for all his grace afield, .320 batting average, and selection in 1969 as the greatest third baseman in baseball history, was never a superstar. Part of the reason is that he was a line drive hitter in an era when the public was preoccupied with homeruns, and the public has remained "homerun-hungry" to this very day. Hand in hand with this is the fact that Traynor was a league leader in only one category, triples, and for only one year. How many runners-up in the homerun race can even the best trivia expert name, let alone in less important categories?

Off the field, great as was the rapport he had with the fans, his life was not flamboyant, and his name was not in the news. No one knew where he ate, or what he wore, and no one really cared. He was just your "average" .320 hitter, who came to the ballpark, did his job, and went home to his family.

Perhaps if Traynor had managed more than 58 homeruns in his 17-year career, he would be remembered. Perhaps if he had led the league in hitting a few times, or come through with the gamewinning hit in the World Series, he would be remembered. Maybe a fight or two, or at least an occasional spikes-up slide into third base, would have helped. But the fact remains that the Greatest Third Baseman in Baseball History was a mere star whose name, and fame, fizzled out.

TRIS SPEAKER

You can talk about Willie Mays and Joe DiMaggio and all the other great centerfielders you want, but none of them, and I mean *none* of them, could carry Tris Speaker's glove.
—Joe Sewell, Hall-of-Famer,
Cleveland Indians (1920–30),
New York Yankees (1931–33)

Only a herculean effort by the greatest centerfielder in major league history saved the 1920 American League pennant for the Cleveland Indians.

The Tribe was locked in a season-long three-way race with the White Sox and Yankees, when disaster struck in mid-August. Their talented, popular shortstop, Ray Chapman, was beaned by a Carl Mays fastball that fractured his skull, and died the next day. A day later, the Indians went into a serious slump. After splitting a pair in New York, they dropped three out of four games in Boston, and fell out of first place. In Philadelphia, they dropped the first two games of a four-game series to the last-place A's, and suddenly found themselves 3½ games behind the Yankees.

Player-manager Tris Speaker ("Spoke") summoned his troops to a closed-door pregame meeting the next day, knowing that he had to exorcise the depression out of the ballclub.

"What's happened to Chappie cannot be changed," the centerfielder told his troops, according to Joe Sewell, "but I know one thing: if Chappie were here now, if he could speak, he'd be telling us to go out and finish the job he started—to win the pennant."

"And that's all he said," Sewell recalled, "but then he went out and got four hits (two doubles, two singles), stole home, and led us to a 10-4 win. That's the kind of man

Spoke was. He was the greatest centerfielder I ever saw, and a truly great leader of men."

The Indians snapped out of their slump, winning 18 of their next 23 games, to regain the league lead. Leading the Indians' charge was Speaker. In a key doubleheader versus the Browns, Spoke drove in the tying run with two outs in the ninth inning of the opener, and scored the game-winner, and made two spectacular catches in the nightcap. On September 9th, he doubled, walked twice, and sacrificed in Cleveland's essential victory over the second-place Yankees. By the time the Indians squared off with the White Sox for a late-September three-game series, Spoke was batting nearly .400, and the Indians were in first place by 1½ games.

Chicago pounded the Tribe in the opener, 10–3, to trim the lead to a half-game. The next day, the Indians carried a 2–0 lead into the sixth inning, when Duster Mails weakened and walked three in a row to load the bases with one out. Spoke called time, marched in from centerfield, and asked his favorite reclamation project (Mails had bombed with Brooklyn four years earlier) if he could get the next two batters: Buck Weaver (a .333 hitter that year) and Hall-of-Famer Eddie Collins (.369).

"No problem," Mails replied. "It's as good as done."

So, Speaker left the southpaw in there, and he proceeded to strike Weaver and Collins out!

Over the passage of time, stories arose claiming that Speaker himself made a great catch to save that game. The batter was Joe Jackson, the bases were loaded with two outs in the ninth—or so the story goes—when Spoke raced back to the wall, leaped, snared a sure extra-base hit, smashed into the concrete, collapsed, but held on to the ball.

Careful investigation reveals that no such play occurred in that series, which was the only meeting of the pennant contenders during the final seven weeks of the season. As the reader will discover, Tris made so many phenomenal catches in his 22-year career that such a legend was bound to spring up. Although there is nothing in the play-by-play accounts of the game* to explain how the legend arose, it is most likely a combination of events. There is no doubt that Speaker made dozens of great catches in September 1920, and any one of them could have saved the pennant—Cleveland edged out Chicago by two games.

One great catch which has been recorded occurred in game one of the 1920 World Series at Ebbet's Field, and although even teammate Joe Sewell originally thought it was a regular-season sensation, a check of his scrapbook got the setting straight. The dangerous Hy Myers (.304 that year, with 36 doubles, a league-leading 22 triples, and

---

*Joe Scminick, librarian for the *Cleveland Plain Dealer*, checked the September 24th issue, which was the customary play-by-play account that prevailed in those days. He reported finding no mention of the "catch."

80 RBIs) was the batter. Speaker shaded him toward left center, but the right-handed slugger crossed up the defense by clouting a tremendous drive up the alley in right center....

"I thought for sure that it would hit that big old concrete wall, or maybe even go over it," Sewell recalled. "But when I looked up, there was Spoke, racing the ball to the wall. Well, he gets there ahead of it and puts his left foot up on the wall like he was climbin' up stairs, and then makes the catch with his back to the infield and crashes into the wall. That was poured concrete out there, and Spoke was out like a light, but he held on to the ball and saved us the game. You know, we had to pry that ball out of his hands, unconscious as he was and all.

"I'll tell you something else," Sewell continued. "That wasn't but one of many great catches Spoke made. He was so great at making the impossible easy that pretty soon I wasn't as impressed by it anymore. Hell, I was just a rookie back then, and I'd never seen a man do that, but Spoke had been doing it for years, so everyone else was used to it.

"And I'll tell you another thing about him. He had a great arm, stronger than any I've seen in 60 years, except for Bob Meusel (New York Yankees, 1920–29; Cincinnati Reds, 1930), and Meusel was never as accurate. Why, when Spoke threw the ball in, all you did was straddle the base. The throw would be there on one hop, every time.

"You know, you don't hear too much about Spoke any more. He's pretty much forgotten. Why, not too long after he finished playing, people had already forgotten how great a hitter he was, and a fine baserunner, too. He finished at .344 for 22 years (seventh on the all-time list), and hit more doubles (793) than any man who ever played baseball. He could steal a base for you, too. Stole fifty-some-odd (52) one year (1912). Why, the only one better at the game was Ty Cobb, and Cobb was never the fielder that Spoke was. But they've all heard of Cobb today, and they've both been dead for about 20 years. It's hard to understand . . ."

As far as any oldtimer is concerned, Tristam (Tris) E. Speaker was head and shoulders better than any other centerfielder, especially as a ball hawk. For all but the most powerful hitters, the 5'11½" Hall-of-Famer stationed himself no more than 50 feet behind second base, enabling him to grab dozens of line drives that were "hits" in any other outfield.... And when an opposing batter drove one over the Gray Eagle's head (premature graying of the hair made that nickname ideal), he simply turned his back, raced out to the spot where the ball would come down, turned around if there was time, and, invariably, make the catch.

"It was uncanny, just uncanny, the way he could do that," Sewell said. "Sometimes he'd be off and running before I could turn my head to follow the flight of the ball. It had to be the most incredible case of instinct in baseball history. And he never misjudged them, either. Why, it got to the point where the official scorers expected him to catch everything, so he'd pick up an error where no other man would have even gotten near the ball."

Speaker credited fellow Hall-of-Famer Cy Young with developing that ball hawk "instinct."

"When I was a rookie with Boston in 1909, Cy was still there," Speaker said in 1937, when he became the seventh man inducted into Baseball's Hall of Fame. "He used to hit fungoes to me for 30 minutes a day. Cy could place the ball just one step out of my reach, so I started watching where he'd hit the ball on the bat, and thus sharpen my sense of anticipation. I guess it became an instinct after a while."

Tris' unique positioning enabled the Red Sox (1909–15) and Indians (1916–26) to employ revolutionary defense in bunt situations. For example, with runners on first and second, "Spoke," would come charging in to cover second as the pitch was released, thereby freeing the shortstop to outleg the lead runner to third. At other times, and particularly when only first base was occupied, Speaker would wait until the batter laid the ball down, and then break for second. The idea was to make the out at first, and then fire the ball to Speaker covering second, hoping to catch the runner making too big a turn.

"You'd be surprised how often it worked on young fellows," Sewell said. "We used to practice those plays a lot, and we won a lot of games that way."

The shallow defense also enabled Speaker to turn many unassisted double plays. In 1919, he turned two in an 11-day span. A year later, according to Sewell, Spoke turned two in one game!

"Of course, when he couldn't do it himself, he was the best at throwing men out," second baseman Bill Wambsganss recalled. "Why, he set the league record for assists by a centerfielder before he came to Cleveland (35 in 1909) and then did it again (1912)."*

Although Speaker led American League centerfielders in assists and double plays six times in his career, he threw out 20 or more runners in 13 of his 22 seasons. He is far and away the all-time career leader among outfielders with 448—Cobb is second with 392.

Completely forgotten is the Gray Eagle's offensive output. Tris batted .344, including five seasons at .380 or better, and finished with more doubles (793) than any man in major league history. He batted more than .300 eighteen times, but won only one

---

*The modern record for the most assists by an outfielder in one season is 44, by Chuck Klein (right fielder, Philadelphia Phillies) in 1930. Klein had the advantage of playing his home games in tiny Baker Bowl, where the 270-foot foul line made stretching singles into doubles a rather dangerous business.

The all-time record is 51, by Tom Dolan (St. Louis, American Association) in 1883.

batting crown (1916: .386, a league-leading 41 doubles and 211 hits, plus 8 triples and 35 stolen bases). Cobb topped his .383 in 1912 by batting .410. George Sisler bettered Spoke's .388 by 19 points in 1920. Harry Heilman turned in marks of .403 (1923) and .393 (1925) while Tris was finishing at .380 and .389.

"Funny how he never seemed to win those batting crowns," Sewell said. "You'd see Spoke get up there, holding the bat an inch above the knob, resting it down low by his hip, then waving it menacingly, and you knew he could hit. Why, he'd stare out at the pitcher without batting an eyelash, and then suddenly cock the bat as the pitcher threw. He was intense."

If Speaker's batting prowess is forgotten, then his baserunning ability is dead and buried. In 1912, he stole 52 bases. Tris swiped 30 or more in six other seasons, and finished with 433 career thefts. He was rarely thrown out going from first to third, and always a threat to take the extra base on a hit.

"It's hard for me to accept today that nobody really remembers Spoke," Sewell said. "That man was probably the greatest outfielder ever, the seventh best hitter in terms of career average, a superb baserunner, and a great leader of men, but today, well, except for the people whose lives he touched, he might almost as well have never played the game."

Ironically enough, if Tris Speaker's mother had had her way, Tris never would have played professional baseball. She had heard all about the way that teams sold and traded their players like cattle. There was no way her Tris was going to be "sold into slavery." So, when Doak Roberts, owner of the Cleburne (North Texas League) team needed her permission for 17-year-old Tris to sign with his team, she refused.

Trouble was, the boy had ideas of his own. Ever since his dad had passed away in 1898 (when the boy was 10 years old), Tris had been an independent youngster who did as he pleased. He starred in football and baseball during his high school days, and spent his spare time bronco-busting wild horses. The latter hobby nearly ended his athletic career before he ever donned a Red Sox uniform. One day, Tris was tossed from a mount and broke his right arm so badly that he had to convert to a left-handed thrower (no mean feat at that point of his life, because he was a pitcher). A few years later, a compound fracture of the left arm was so serious that the doctors wanted to amputate, but Speaker preferred to risk gangrene, and the limb healed completely.

In 1905, Tris graduated from high school and enrolled at Fort Worth Polytechnic Institute, where he starred as a moundsman. Roberts happened to drop by for a game during Speaker's sophomore year, and all the kid did was hit two homeruns and pitch a shutout. Roberts offered him $50 a month, and over Mother Speaker's objections, Tris joined the Cleburne club.

Speaker's first start came a few days later, and he pitched well in a one-run loss.

Unfortunately, that was the extent of his success on the mound. The next day, he was pounded for 22 hits, all of them for extra bases, before manager Benny Shelton ambled over to the mound.

"Stay in there, kid," Shelton quipped. "There hasn't been a *single* hit all day."

On the same day that his pitching career ended, his outfield career more or less began. After the game, Speaker learned that rightfielder Dude Ransom had broken his cheekbone and would be lost for the season. Speaker overheard Shelton bemoaning the loss, and told the manager that he would be a great rightfielder. For some reason, Shelton listened, and inserted Spoke in the outfield. He proved to be a natural, batting .314, and drawing a great deal of attention from other clubs.

Among the most interested was St. Louis Browns Manager Jim McAleer, who obtained an option on Speaker, but never exercised it. Part of the problem was the asking price—Roberts wanted $1,500 for his star outfielder, and the Browns were pennypinchers. McAleer said he would consider taking Speaker when "Roberts said the kid was ready," but failed to exercise the option, despite two mid-season letters to that effect. Finally, Roberts got disgusted, and sold Speaker to the Boston Red Sox for $800.

Boston summoned him in September, and Tris was something less than a success—he batted .158, and the Sox did not even offer the future Hall-of-Famer a contract for 1908! Speaker took advantage of his free agency by going to the New York Giants training camp the following year, where he twice approached Manager John McGraw about a job in his outfield, but Mugsy was not interested.

"Young man, I have too many ballplayers in camp now," the Little Napoleon said. "I wish I had time to give you a tryout, but I can't."

Reluctantly, Spoke left the Giants, and paid his way to the Red Sox camp, where the Sox eventually signed him. Speaker came through with a tremendous exhibition season, but did not go north with the big league team. Instead, he was left in Little Rock in lieu of payments for rental of the facility for spring training! Owner Mickey Finn agreed to sell Speaker to Boston for $500 if they ever wanted him, and when Spoke batted .350 for Finn, half a dozen other teams began offering substantial money for him. Fortunately for Boston, Finn was a man of his word, and sold Speaker to Boston in the latter half of the 1908 season.

Tris batted .220 in 31 games, but drew rave reviews for his defense. The Sox kept him as a utility player in 1909, and it paid off handsomely. The 21-year-old, 193-pounder won the starting job in centerfield, and batted .309 (26 doubles, 13 triples, 77 RBIs, and 35 stolen bases). A year later, Harry Hooper replaced Dan Gessler in right field, and Duffy Lewis took over for Harry Niles in left, completing the great outfield that led the Sox to the world championship in 1912 and 1915.

The 1912 series was the more memorable for Speaker, largely because of his role in the seventh game. (Actually, it was the eighth game. Game 2 was called by darkness as a 6-6 tie.) The Giants carried a 2-1 lead into the bottom of the tenth inning behind the seven-hit pitching of Christy Mathewson. Pinch-hitter Clyde Engel led off the inning with a sinking line drive that Fred Snodgrass dropped in left field. After Hooper flied out, Steve Yerkes walked, and up to the plate stepped Speaker.

Spoke popped a Mathewson fastball into foul territory between first and home for what should have been an easy out . . . but it fell to earth untouched!

"I figured I'd blown it," Speaker told reporters after the game, "and then I hear Matty calling for their catcher, Chief Meyers, to take it. I couldn't believe my ears. There was no way Meyers could get it. The wind was carrying the ball away from him, and he never did catch up to it. First baseman Fred Merkle, the man who could have caught it easily, stabbed at it too late. Matty had made a mistake, and I knew it would cost him.

"I could have jumped for joy when he called Meyers," Speaker continued. "I was so excited that I yelled out to Matty, 'You just blew the championship!'"

Sure enough, Speaker followed with a base hit to right, scoring Engel with the tying run. Duffy Lewis walked, and Larry Gardner followed with a sacrifice fly that won the game and the championship.

Speaker batted an even .300 for the Series, including a double and two triples, to cap a great regular season (.383, a league-leading 53 doubles, 13 triples, 9 homeruns, 136 runs scored, 98 RBIs, and 52 stolen bases).

Boston went to the Series again in 1915, despite Speaker's off-year (.322, 25 doubles, 12 triples, no homeruns, 108 runs, 69 RBIs, and 29 stolen bases), and took the Phillies in five games. Spoke batted .294 with one triple, but made two errors. The first came on a fly ball he lost in the sun, but he made up for it by tripling off Grover Cleveland Alexander in his next at-bat. The other muff cost Ernie Shore a shutout in game four, but the Sox won, 2-1.

Two shocks were in store for Tris in the off-season. First, the Federal League settled its anti-trust suit against major league baseball, ending the salary war that had raised major league pay by more than 30 percent. Boston owner Joe Lannin was determined to recoup some of the extra dollars that war had cost him, so he sent Spoke a 1916 contract for $9,000—a fifty-percent cut. Speaker was furious. He had expected a raise, originally thought about settling for no less than the $18,000 he earned in 1915, but then announced he would play for $15,000—and not one penny less. He even refused to go to spring training, until manager Bill Carrigan arranged for him to be paid on a game-by-game basis during the exhibition season.

"I had a great spring, and topped it off with a game-winning homerun off Rube Marquard right before the season started," Speaker recalled in 1950. "As a result, Lannin came to see me and told me he would sign me for the $18,000 as soon as we got to Boston. I was happy as a lark... and then I get a phone call from Bob McRoy, the Cleveland Indians general manager. He tells me he's downstairs and he wants to see me.

"So, I invite him up to my hotel room, and after the usual talk, he springs a surprise on me," Speaker continued, "by asking me how I'd like to play in Cleveland. I was honest. I told him he not only had a bad team, but that Cleveland was a bad baseball town. Then, the bomb dropped—he tells me that he wishes I didn't feel that way because they'd just made a deal for me."

"At first, I told him to cancel the trade. There was no way I was going to Cleveland. But, I knew I really had no choice, so I asked him about the trade. He said the Indians had given up a couple of players (pitcher Sam Jones and infielder Fred Thomas) plus $50,000. So, I told him I'd play in Cleveland if he gave me $10,000 as my share of the deal. He knew I was serious about going home, so he gave me the money; or, as I recall, Lannin had to give me the money or blow the deal, so he did."

Spoke had a great year with the Indians in 1916, leading the league in batting (.386), slugging percentage (.502), doubles (41), and hits (211). While Speaker led the way, Cleveland improved steadily over the next three years, and by the time Speaker replaced manager Lee Fohl midway through the 1919 season, the Indians were ready to challenge for the pennant. The rookie manager brought them home second in 1919 (39-21 under his leadership), although the strain of managing contributed to his first sub-.300 year in 10 seasons (.296).

A year later, Tris rebounded to .388 (including a league-leading 50 doubles, 11 triples, 8 homeruns, 137 runs scored, 107 RBIs, and 214 hits) and the Indians won their first pennant and world championship. The road to the pennant was not easy. A wild three-club race and the loss of shortstop Chapman made it a trying experience, but in the end, Spoke pulled his team through.

Speaker also led the way past the Dodgers in a wild seven-game set. Cleveland trailed the Series, three games to two, when the teams began game six at League Park. For five innings, Sherry Smith and Duster Mails traded goose eggs, until Speaker singled with two outs in the sixth. George Burns followed with a double down the right field line, and Tris scored all the way from first on the hit. It was the only run of the game.

In game seven, Speaker came through with a clutch triple off Burleigh Grimes to pace the Indians 3-0 win.

"It was the greatest achievement of my career," Spoke recalled at his Hall of Fame induction in 1937. "It's one thing to play for a champion. It's even more rewarding to play and manage it."

Although the Indians remained very competitive, largely due to Speaker's revolu-

Tris Speaker

tionary platooning system (righty-lefty), they were unable to catch the Yankees and Senators over the next five years. Tris' last great season was 1925 (.389, 35 doubles, 5 triples, 12 homeruns in 117 games). A year later, the 38-year-old player-manager plummeted to .304, and was ready to retire....

And then came the second great shock of Speaker's career: He was named as a co-conspirator in a game-fixing scandal that nearly retired him into disgrace.

To this day, the exact events surrounding this episode remain unclear. Apparently, American League President Ban Johnson obtained a pair of letters, one written by Ty Cobb, the other by Speaker's close friend, Joe Wood, which strongly implied that the pair had conspired with pitcher Hub Leonard to throw a game in 1919. The subject was a very suspicious 9-5 Tigers victory over the Indians in late September, at a time when the Tigers were battling the Yankees for third place (and a share of the World Series pool). Cleveland had already clinched second place; the White Sox were World-Series-bound.

Johnson believed the implications, and publicly accused Cobb, Leonard, Wood, and Speaker of "fixing" the game. Exactly how Speaker's name became involved remains a mystery. He was never mentioned in the letters, and had four hits in the game in question. The best guess is that Johnson knew that Wood and Speaker were the best of friends, and that Cobb and Speaker were also pals. He also knew the obvious: as manager of the Indians, Spoke was in an ideal position to at least know about any fix, so he may have assumed that Speaker had given his tacit approval.

When Johnson revealed the allegations, he announced that Speaker and Cobb would never play in the American League again. The owners of their respective teams suspended the pair without pay, and then the excrement hit the fan.

"No one in Cleveland believed those charges for one minute," Sewell recalled. "It was ridiculous. Even the newspapers knew that Spoke had two triples and two singles in that game. Petitions were signed, people wired Johnson and Commissioner Landis, and there were all sorts of protests."

Speaker was content to leave the game without a fight (which always left skeptics wondering about whether he really did know that something was up), but Cobb was furious. He appealed to Landis, and the Judge ordered all four named players to report for a hearing in New York. Leonard refused to show (ostensibly because he was afraid Cobb would kill him). As a former federal court judge, Landis knew that the Constitution guaranteed a man the right to confront his accusers, and maintained the accused's innocence until proven guilty, so he had no choice but to reinstate them.

The exonerated Speaker signed as a free agent (Cleveland had released him) with Washington, where he had a solid year (.327 in 141 games), but became expendable because of his $50,000 salary. Owner Clark Griffith gave Speaker permission to make his own deal, and the 40-year-old outfielder arranged a cash swap that landed him in an A's uniform for his final big league season. Tris appeared in 64 games, batted .267, and retired after the season.

Speaker spent the next two years as the player-manager of Newark, but quit to become a broadcaster in Chicago. When friends asked him to become co-owner of the Kansas City Blues, he joined their investment group, but the venture failed during the Depression. His next stop was Cleveland, where he rejoined the Indians, this time as a broadcaster. He channeled some of his savings into a liquor dealership, and also accepted an executive position as a representative for a steel firm.

In 1947, Indians owner Bill Veeck lured Speaker back on to the playing field in a special coaching role. His main project was the conversion of infielder Larry Doby into outfielder Larry Doby. Evidently, Spoke could teach what he could do so well—Doby led the Indians to the world championship in 1948—but Speaker did not enjoy the coaching chores and left baseball again.

On December 8, 1958, Speaker and a friend were returning from a fishing trip when the 70-year-old Hall-of-Famer collapsed. He opened his eyes once, told his pal "My name is Tris Speaker," and died.

Tristam E. Speaker may have been the greatest star the game ever knew, but he never made the leap into the immortality reserved for true superstars. The reasons are easily ascertained. At the plate, he was always overshadowed by Cobb as a pure hitter, and by Ruth for power. In the field, he did not have the arm that Meusel did; but great fielders rarely attain notoriety, let alone immortality, anyway. As a manager, he won only one pennant, and was overshadowed by Miller Huggins, John McGraw, and even Connie Mack. As a person, he could be smooth and friendly, but he never truly captured the hearts of the fans across the nation, and his reluctance to fight the "scandal" case left many wondering about a real "fix." In the end, as good as he was, as fine a statistic as his .344 average is (seventh on the all-time list), and as great an accomplishment as his all-time record of 793 doubles is, Speaker simply did not become the center of attraction for the baseball fans of the world. After all, who cares who led the league in doubles in any given year, anyway, let alone in a career—or, to put it another way, how many league leaders in doubles can you name? It's like naming runners-up in the batting and homerun races.

There is one final irony to the career and life of Tris Speaker. Al Gionfriddo, a man who could not even carry Speaker's cap, made one great catch and became a hero. Willie Mays made a catch in the 1954 World Series that vaulted him into superstardom. But Tris Speaker, the man who made more great catches than anyone else, is a forgotten man, buried somewhere in the graveyard of baseball stars.

AL SIMMONS

If I didn't get a hit, I thought the pitcher was a lucky stiff. There wasn't a pitcher in the world who could fool me, and even if he did, I had a good enough pair of wrists that I could alter my swing and slap that ball around at the last split second.

Yeah, I was superstitious. In 1927 I ordered my bats one inch too long. The trainer filed them down for me. I hit .392 that year, and every year after that, I'd order the bats too big, and he'd whittle them down for me.

—Al Simmons

If Rogers Hornsby was the greatest right-hand hitter in baseball history, Al Simmons was a close second.

For most of his 20-year career, the 5-11, 190-pound Hall of Fame outfielder terrorized the American League, batting over .300 fifteen times, and finishing with a lifetime .334 mark. Beginning with a .308 mark as a rookie in 1924, Simmons strung together eleven consecutive .300-plus seasons, including a career-high .392 in 1927. From 1925 to 1931 his record reads .384, .343, .392, .351, .365, .381, and .390—a composite .371 over seven seasons.

Simmons did more than hit for average. He was a tremendous clutch hitter who drove in 102 or more runs 12 times. His 1,827 runs batted in place him tenth on the all-time list. Al slugged 31 or more doubles ten times, ten or more triples seven times, and made 200 or more hits six times.

He also saved some of his greatest performances for the four World Series he played in, recording the fourth best career slugging percentage (.658) in Series history. He also batted .462 in the first three All-Star Games.

With all that offensive production, it's no wonder that Al's defensive abilities were always overlooked.

"There never was a better left fielder when it came to going into the corner to cut off a sure double," Hall-of-Famer Bill Dickey said. "He never threw to the wrong base and often dared the runners to challenge him."

"Even when he coached third base in the '40s, he never made a mistake," added Joe Cronin. "He had remarkable baseball sense and was really a perfect player."

Born to a pair of poor Polish immigrants on May 22, 1902, Aloysius Harry Szymanski grew up in the South Side of Milwaukee. He was a tremendous high school athlete, and received a football scholarship to Stevens Point Teachers College, but from Day One he only thought in terms of baseball as a career.

"I guess it was in my blood or something," Simmons said. "I always put baseball above all else, even though I had the football scholarship. I wanted baseball so badly that I wrote to every team I ever heard of asking for a tryout."

A letter to Toledo manager Roger Bresnahan, himself a Hall-of-Famer, went unanswered. Had Roger bothered to reply, odds are Simmons would have wound up in a New York Giants uniform, swinging at those invitingly close fences in the old Polo Grounds, because Bresnahan always sent his best talent to his former field boss, John McGraw.

"There's no doubt that a career in New York would have meant more homeruns than [the 307] I hit with the A's," Simmons said. "The Polo Grounds were only 280 feet to left field, compared to 334 at Shibe Park. But had I been in New York, I would never have played for those great teams of 1929–31."

The big break came while Al was playing semipro ball for Juneau, Wisconsin. He pinch-hit an inside-the-park homerun for a 1–0 win over the Milwaukee Red Sox, and word of his ability began filtering back to the American Association Milwaukee Brewers. Eventually, owner Otto Borchert summoned him for an interview.

"I had a hell of a time convincing him that I was a baseball player," Simmons recalled. "He was very involved in promoting boxing matches, and he thought I was in his office to set up a ring appearance. Finally, their business manager, Lou Nahin, showed up, and confirmed that I was a ballplayer."

Al signed with Milwaukee for 1922, had a tremendous spring training, but was farmed out to Aberdeen, where he batted .365. Milwaukee sent him to Shreveport for 1923, where Simmons was batting well over .300 when the Brewers received a startling telegram from the Texas team manager: "Simmons won't do. Will give him his unconditional release."

Nahin knew Simmons was having a fine year, and suspected the manager was trying to pull a fast one. He wired Shreveport not to release the youth, and demanded that Simmons be returned to Milwaukee on the next available train.

Shortly thereafter, the Texas League Club reported that Simmons had improved, and offered to purchase his contract for $1,500!

Nahin and Borchert were furious at the attempted swindle, and threatened a lawsuit if Simmons were not returned immediately. According to Bob Broeg, the Brewers' owner later told sportswriter Sam Levy, "Can you imagine that guy in Shreveport trying to outsmart me? He'd pay me $1,500 for a player he wanted to release a week before!"

After returning to Milwaukee, Simmons batted .398 in 24 games. By that time, Connie Mack's talent search had focused in on him, and The Grand Old Man exchanged $68,000 and a handful of minor leaguers for Simmons.

Surprisingly enough, Simmons arrival in the A's spring training camp went largely ignored. Mack had also invested $100,000 in an outfielder named Paul Strand, a phenom from the Pacific Coast League who had batted .394 with 325 hits for Salt Lake City the year before. As things turned out, Strand was the first $100,000 flop in baseball history—he hit .228 in 47 games, and was returned to the Coast. While the media focused its attention on Strand, Simmons had a solid exhibition season and went on to hit .308 in 152 games.

Simmons first drew attention because of his unique batting stance, which included a pronounced stride toward third every time he swung ("stepping in the bucket"). Mack tried to change the step, but Simmons refused to alter his stance, and became known as "Bucketfoot Al."

"I utterly despised that nickname because as far as I was concerned, it questioned my courage," he said. "It sounded like I was afraid of the ball. After a while, they stopped calling me by that name, because they knew it made me angry, and the angrier I got, the better I hit."

For the next 19 seasons, baseball purists continued to find fault with his stance, but Al had such strong forearms and wrists, and used such a long bat (38 inches), that the stride had no effect on his power. He would take his stance deep in the batter's box, and would swivel his hips and body so as to negate the bucket step. "He hit everything everywhere," was the way one opposing pitcher put it, "and he was a notorious bad ball hitter."

Simmons' sophomore year was little short of incredible: .384, a league-leading 253 hits, and 658 at-bats, including 43 doubles, 12 triples, and 24 homeruns... but he did not lead the league in percentage—Harry Heilman hit .393. A drop to .343 in 1926 was followed by an explosion to .392—and again Simmons finished behind Heilman (.398).

By the time 1929 rolled around, and the A's won the first of three consecutive pennants, Simmons was sandwiched between Mickey Cochrane and Jimmy Foxx in one of the most awesome lineups in baseball history. He batted .365, with a league-leading 157 runs batted in, despite missing 11 games. In the World Series against the Cubs, Al batted .300 with 2 homeruns, the most memorable of which led off the famous ten-run seventh inning that enabled the A's to overcome an 8–0 deficit in game four. (The A's batted around, and Simmons' second hit of the inning was a single that moved the tying run to second base. Foxx singled to tie the score, and then Jimmy Dykes doubled both men home to put the A's on top.)

Simmons was also instrumental in the A's Series-clinching come-from-behind win the next day. Chicago entered the ninth leading 2–0, only to watch Mule Haas slug a game-tying homerun. Simmons followed with a double, and after Foxx was intentionally walked, Miller doubled Al home to win it.

Simmons finally led the league in hitting with a .381 mark in 1930 (including 41 doubles, 16 triples, 36 homeruns, and 165 RBIs.). He also played the greatest doubleheader of his career on Memorial Day against the Senators. In the opener, Simmons went 0-for-4 before coming to bat with two outs and two on in the ninth, and the A's down by three. For the first time in his career, he was roundly booed by the home fans.

"I was furious, absolutely seething, when I heard those boos," said the man who modeled himself after Ty Cobb (they were teammates and roommates in 1927–28). "I'll never forget that at-bat. I really got a hold of one of Ad Liska's submarine pitches, and drove it out for a three-run homerun."

In the eleventh, Simmons doubled; in the thirteenth, he singled; but both times, he was left stranded. He added another double in the fifteenth, and when Foxx was safe on an infield hit, Al wrenched his knee sliding into third. He refused to leave the game, and by the time Eric McNair singled him home with the winning run, the knee had blown up like a balloon. The injury was diagnosed as a broken blood vessel, and the team physician ordered him to sit out the second game.

Al sat until the fourth inning, when the A's loaded the bases. Washington led by 3. Mack asked Simmons if he could hit, and "Bucketfoot" limped up to the plate. His appearance was greeted by a long ovation . . . an ovation which was dwarfed by the one he received after drilling the first pitch for a grand slam. (The A's went on to a 14–7 win.)

The World Series was another success for Al and the A's. Simmons batted .364 with 2 homeruns, and Philadelphia beat the Gashouse Gang in six games.

"I still haven't forgotten the first one he hit in that Series," said opposing pitcher Burleigh Grimes. "It was an 0–2 spitter a foot-and-a-half outside. Afterwards, I told the newspaper men, 'Where the hell's this guy's weakness—right over the plate?'"

By 1931, Simmons was established as the game's most dangerous hitter, and he

Al Simmons

decided it was time to be paid like one. He held out for a substantial raise all winter, and refused to join the A's for spring training. Minutes before the home opener, Al signed a three-year deal for $100,000 . . . and was in the starting lineup . . . and belted the first pitch he had seen that year for a homerun! He went on to lead the league again, this time at .390, and reached the 200-hit plateau for the fourth straight year. His World Series was another success (.333, two homeruns, 8 RBIs), but the A's dropped the seven-game series to St. Louis.

After another solid year (.322, a league-leading 216 hits), Simmons was dealt to the White Sox (along with Dykes and Haas) for $150,000 Depression dollars. The Windy City treated him well for two years (.331, .344), but when Al plummeted to .267 in 1935, the Sox decided to sell him. Detroit and New York expressed interest, and Al picked the Tigers.

"It was the worst decision I ever made," he later lamented. "If I'd gone with the Yankees, I'd have played on four consecutive pennant winners.

"Besides, the Tigers were winners in 1934 and '35." he continued, "so the attitude was 'we were winners without you, so we don't need your help.'"

Simmons batted .327 in 143 games, but the Tigers fell 19½ games behind the Yankees, and dealt him to Washington after the season.

Simmons batted .279 in 1937. The following year, owner Cal Griffith renewed his contract, but added a bonus clause: If the 36-year-old star hit over .300, he was to receive $200. As the season wound down, Al was batting .302, when he and Griffith got into a tremendous fight.

Griffith claimed that Simmons had cursed at a fan, and fined him $200. Simmons swore he was innocent, claimed the owner had fabricated the incident to save himself $200, and appealed to the commissioner. Judge Landis held a hearing, and ruled in Griffith's favor, based on testimony of alleged spectators, the clubhouse boy, and others.

After the hearing, Cal unloaded the veteran to the Braves (.282 in 93 games), who shipped him to Cincinnati toward the end of the season (.143 in 9 games). In 1940, he returned to the A's and batted .309 in 37 games. Simmons dropped to .125 for 9 games in 1941, and retired.

When World War II claimed most of the major leaguers, the Red Sox asked Al to come out of retirement, and he hit .203 in 133 at-bats in 1943. Mack brought him back to Philadelphia as a player-coach for 1944, and the future Hall-of-Famer went 3-for-6 to close out his career with 2,927 hits.

Simmons remained with the A's as a coach for five years, spent a year with the Indians in a similar capacity, and then retired. By that time, he had saved $100,000 in a bank account, held $200,000 in annuities, and owned several choice parcels of land in Milwaukee. Somehow, he managed to dissipate all of it in a few short years, and when he died on May 26, 1956, he was wracked by the ballplayer's common enemy: alcoholism.

There was another side of Aloysius Harry Szymanski, an aspect of his character that was never publicized: He loved children. Years ago, teammate Bing Miller shed some light on the extent to which Simmons would go out of his way to brighten the life of a child.

"It was an off day, and we were supposed to go fishing with a group of people," Miller said. "It was time to leave, and all of a sudden he turns around and says he can't go because he's 'got to go down to Gettysburg to see a very sick boy' who had begged him for a visit. 'I don't want you to think I don't want to join you,' Al told me, 'but this kid probably leads a drab life, and if I can put some pleasure into it, I'm going to.' He was a great man. A lot of what he did off the field never got into the papers, but that's the way he wanted it."

How could a man who did everything so well be forgotten so soon after his death? Simmons was not just a great ballplayer—he was the second greatest right-handed hitter in the history of the game, and as fine a fielder as the major leagues have ever seen. He led his team to three consecutive pennants, and those 1929–31 A's are ranked among the top five teams in history. "Bucketfoot" batted over .300 fifteen times, and compiled a wealth of other statistics that are overwhelmingly impressive.

Yet today, Al Simmons is a forgotten man. Why?

It is true that Simmons shunned publicity, particularly off-the-field. He also played in a small city whose fans were fiercely divided between the Phillies and A's. Another key was his failure to capture the hearts of the fans around the country, a fact he admitted.

"Ty Cobb was my idol," Simmons said. "A lot of him rubbed off on me. I tried to model myself after him, and maybe I was too successful in some ways."

In fact, Simmons often adopted Cobb's belligerent attitude toward the fans around the league, and was known to antagonize them intentionally. At times, he even had trouble dealing with the hometown folks, as in the infamous "cursing incident" with the Senators.

By the same token, he was not "bad enough" to attain immortality like Cobb. Nor did he have the benefit of the New York media, à la Reggie Jackson, a man who is despised by fans across the country, but is also grudgingly respected for his on-the-field performance.

One other factor to be considered is that, while Simmons could hit homeruns, he never compared to teammate Jimmie Foxx for power and frequency. Babe Ruth had revolutionized the game a few years before Simmons reached the majors, and the public wanted the long ball. On a team like the A's, which had so many outstanding players and unique personalities, Simmons simply did not shine a cut above the rest . . . and even the Groves and Foxxes are not well remembered, either. Once again, the fate of a mere star, no matter his statistics, is obscurity. Aloysius Harry Szymanski, or Al Simmons, has suffered that fate.

MICKEY COCHRANE

Mickey Cochrane was batting. There was a man on first, two men out, and the count was 3-and-1. The next pitch was a fastball that sailed high and inside, and it struck him on the left side of the head. It made a sickening thud, and dropped straight off his head on to the plate. He dropped to the ground like he'd been shot. I thought he was dead. God, it was awful. I saw his eyes rolling, and I thought he was dead.

—Bill Dickey, catcher, New York Yankees

On May 26, 1937, the baseball world sat solemnly, waiting to learn the fate of the popular Detroit Tigers player-manager, Mickey Cochrane.

The future Hall-of-Famer had been struck by a Bump Hadley fastball during the preceding day's game at Yankee Stadium. He had collapsed immediately, rolled over, and then appeared to be dead. The vast throng on hand for this early-season battle between the anticipated pennant contenders fell strangely silent, and watched in horror as Cochrane was carried off the field. Normally, only those in the outer reaches of the upper deck could hear the sounds of life outside the mammoth stadium, but on that day, all present heard the unmistakable wail of the ambulance's siren.

Cochrane was rushed to St. Elizabeth's Hospital, where doctors began a week-long battle to save the catcher's life. X rays revealed that his skull had been fractured in three places. His sinus cavity had also been cracked. Cochrane lapsed in and out of consciousness for 10 days, before he was finally well enough to be sent back home to Detroit. He spent the next six months recuperating at his home.

The following spring, the 34-year-old manager demanded that he be allowed to resume his on-the-field duties, but Tigers owner Walter Briggs refused to allow Mickey to don the so-called "tools of ignorance." Cochrane's playing days were over, and on August 7, 1938, his managerial career was over, too. He simply could not lead from the sidelines. The man who led the Tigers to consecutive pennants, and a world championship, was finished. He would never be the same "Black Mike," the greatest catcher in Tigers history.

Born to Scotch-Irish parents on April 6, 1903, in Bridgewater, Massachusetts, Gordon Stanley (Mickey) Cochrane always wanted to play major league baseball, and he always wanted to become a big league manager, too.

"Lots of kids wanted to be big league players," Cochrane told reporter Frank Graham, "but I wanted even then to become a manager. What makes a kid think like that? Maybe I just had to be the boss."

As a boy, Mickey spent his time avoiding his chores, and developing a reputation as the most competitive, hard-nosed kid in town. He always loved to run, and at one point began training for the 440-yard run in the Olympics. His track ran right past the local cemetery, and since the bulk of his running was done at twilight or later, no one ever ran a quarter of a mile faster than he.

Although he proved to be a fine shortstop (and a good student) in high school, and set records in the 440, those endeavors took a back seat to the other sport in his life: football. Cochrane used his tremendous speed and agility to develop into one of the finest high school running backs in New England. When none of the Ivy League schools came through with a scholarship, the 5'10½", 160-pound speedster opted for Boston University.

The Terriers were not among the better football schools of the day, but with Cochrane, they suddenly became respectable. Their practices were held on a vacant lot between the Charles River and the railroad tracks below Braves Field. The sessions invariably consisted of 11 players kicking off to Cochrane, and the star runner racing up the field in an attempt to score. Practices often ran for hours, largely because Cochrane was never satisfied until he had bettered the previous practice's score.

Football played an important role in Mickey's life. It not only provided an avenue for venting steam, but exposed his intense competitive nature, and never-say-die attitude, to the media. Once, against Brown University, Cochrane was called upon to punt from the Boston 48-yard line. He took one look at the distant goalposts, said "to hell with punting," and drop-kicked a 52-yard field goal! In the same game, he was later knocked unconscious and carried off the field, only to return two plays later and make a game-saving tackle.

Cochrane never earned All-America honors, a recognition that would have been automatic at a larger, or more successful, school, but his gridiron exploits earned him a spot on a Providence, Rhode Island, semipro team that brought in some badly needed dollars on Sundays. He also washed dishes at a local tavern, ushered at the ancient Boston Arena, and played the saxophone in a band.

After the football season, Cochrane donned the gloves and trunks of the Terriers' boxing squad, where he earned quite a reputation in the ring. He stunned his teammates, early on, when he scored a one-punch knockout of a Rhode Island heavyweight who tipped the scales at 280 pounds—more than 120 pounds above Cochrane's weight!

Of course, the spring and summer were reserved for his favorite sport: baseball. The B.U. season was not much—in more ways than one. In his freshman year, Cochrane failed to make the squad as a shortstop. In 1921, he did not make the junior varsity. For the '22 season, he switched to third base, and made the grade. As things turned out, despite the bad weather that is spring in Boston, Cochrane saw action in the outfield, on the mound, at the hot corner, and when the regular catcher broke a finger, Mickey volunteered to catch the final ten games of the season.

Summer ball was a different story. Cochrane earned a sizable salary in the "hotel league" in the Adirondack Mountains, where he doubled as a waiter at a Saranac Lake resort, and a star infielder for their team. He played under the pseudonym "Frank King" to protect his amateur status.

When the Saranac team folded in 1922, Mickey followed a teammate to Dover, Delaware (Eastern Shore League), hoping to land a spot as an extra infielder. Manager Jiggs Donahue made it clear that infielders were "a dime a dozen," but that what he really needed was a catcher. "I've done some catching," the B.U. kid told Donahue, and the manager agreed to give him a shot *if* he could catch.

"At first, it was touch and go," Cochrane recalled. "I had a helluva time. Must have missed a dozen foul pops in my first game. It got to the point where every guy who came up wanted to hit a foul so they could watch me stumble around under it. Fortunately, I hit pretty good (.327 in 65 games), so they kept me around and worked with me."

The turning point came on a day when Portland (Pacific Coast League) team owner Tom Turner happened to be in the ballpark. Cochrane went 4-for-5 at the plate, and made four errors behind it, but Turner was so impressed with the youth's bat and aggressiveness, that he offered Mickey $1,000 if he would join the Portland club.

"That looked like a pile of money," Cochrane told reporters. "I was hungry, and I could not eat a college degree, so I quit college in February and went West."

Mickey batted .333 in 199 games for Portland, and major league scouts began keeping tabs on the phenom. Some were scared off when Turner's price tag was $35,000 for Cochrane, but Tigers scout Carl Zamloch wired Detroit owner Frank Navin early in the PCL season, and urged him to grab the kid immediately. Navin did not have the money, and was not satisfied with the youth's behind-the-plate skills, so they passed him up. A few months later, when Navin realized his mistake, the price tag had jumped to $75,000, and the Tigers owner told Zamloch that "nobody could be that good." (Actually, Navin simply could not afford the $75,000.)

Connie Mack was next in line. By that time, the price was $150,000, and the Shibe family balked at paying that kind of money for another West Coast phenom. (Mack had spent a similar sum to acquire a fellow named Paul Strand a few years earlier, and Strand proved to be a flash in the pan.) Mack returned to the Shibes and told them that if they did not want to buy the kid, they should buy the Portland team, and they did! The new owners' first act was to "sell" Cochrane to the A's for $50,000 and five players. (Mack later admitted that the real price was closer to $250,000—"$50,000 for Mickey, and $200,000 the Shibes lost in running that minor league club.")

Mickey joined the A's in spring training (1925) with less than a season-and-a-half's worth of catching experience, and it showed.

"He was positively awful behind the plate, and especially on pop fouls," teammate Cy Perkins, the light-hitting, 17-year veteran, incumbent backstop, recalled. "He was so bad that Mr. Mack tried him at third base, but that was no good either. Finally, Mr. Mack decided that the future of the A's depended on the kid, so he asked me to work with him. I started teaching him everything I knew, from how to keep your bare hand out of the way to what pitches to throw to which hitters. I guess he was a good student—he never broke a finger, and he made the Hall of Fame—or maybe I was a good teacher?"

When the season began, Perkins was still *numero uno* until "the eighth inning of our opening game, when Mr. Mack sent the kid up to bat for me. He doubled off the wall in right center, and I knew I'd lost my job. I guess I can't complain too loudly. His record speaks for itself, and when he went to Detroit as player-manager in '34, he took me along as his assistant."

Cochrane batted .331 (21 doubles, 5 triples, 6 homers, and 55 RBIs) in 134 games. More importantly, his quickness behind the plate saved many a wild pitch, and his lightning bolt arm gunned down runner after runner. He also assumed the role of team leader, and had no trouble harnessing even the most time-honored of veterans. One day, 41-year-old hurler Jack Quinn was pitching a shutout, when he suddenly called time and summoned his kid catcher to the mound. "When the hell will you call for the spitter?" the grizzled veteran, whose bread and butter offering was the wet one, demanded. "I'm tired of throwing fastballs."

Cochrane pointed out to the scoreboard in right center, glared at the pitcher, and icily replied, "When those numbers [a string of zeroes] change, I'll call for a change. Until then, you throw what I tell ya."

Another time, fellow youngster Rube Walberg walked four consecutive batters.

Cochrane called time, walked out to the mound, and kicked the hurler in the rear end!

"Settle down, Rube," Cochrane warned, "or else."

Cochrane had no qualms about taking on the whole ballclub when he had to. One hot summer afternoon, the A's fell behind the Yankees by four early runs, and seemed ready to just play out the nine as quickly as possible, so as to escape the heat. Cochrane stewed for five innings, and then hurled his equipment into the dugout.

"Why you dirty yellow bums!" he raged. "Are you quittin'? You . . ." A few more choice words followed, and then Cochrane stormed out to lead off the inning. He lined a single to center field. Al Simmons followed with a base hit to left, and Cochrane surprised Bob Meusel by racing all the way to third. Jimmy Foxx followed with a double . . . and the A's came from behind to win.

Strangely enough, as hard as Cochrane played on the field, during his early years, he could relax equally well when he left the ballpark. He sang and played the saxophone, frequently searching for good jazz bands when on the road. He also loved to play practical jokes, his favorite targets being George Earnshaw and the grizzly old Quinn.

Mack rarely interfered in Cochrane's life, but when he learned that the 22-year-old catcher had taken up glider piloting, it was too much. The Grand Old Man ordered Mickey to cease and desist—he was too valuable to the ballclub that would win three pennants (1929-31) and two world championships to be allowed such hobbies.

In 1929, the 26-year-old, black-haired, blue-eyed catcher batted .331 (37 doubles, 8 triples, 7 homeruns, and 95 RBIs) in the regular season, and topped that off with a .400 mark against the Cubs. That World Series featured the most remarkable comeback inning in Series history. Chicago led game four, 8-0, in the seventh inning, when the A's exploded for 10 runs. Cochrane's contribution at the plate was minimal: a walk (he scored the tying run) and a ground out. However, his constant razzing of the Chicagoans (with the help of his teammates, of course), and the Cubs' equally abrasive replies, led to personal intervention by Commissioner Landis, who ordered a truce. Mickey got the last word in, though. In the fifth and final game, "Black Mike" waited while a Chicago batter took his time getting into the batter's box.

"Hurry up, sweetheart!" he screamed, using a high-pitched, feminine-sounding voice. "We're serving tea at four o'clock!"

The 1930 Series against the Cardinals was anticlimactic by comparison. Mickey had batted .357 (42 doubles, 5 triples, 10 homers, and 85 RBIs) in the regular season, but was held to a .222 mark in October. However, two of his four hits off Cardinals pitching were game-winning homeruns, and another was a key ninth inning double in game five (he scored on Foxx's game-winning homerun).

Unfortunately, the '31 Series was a disaster. Plagued by the loss of his investments (due to the Depression) off the field, and by Pepper Martin, sinusitis, and nagging leg injuries on the field, Cochrane batted a dismal .160, and was blamed for Martin's five stolen bases and .500 average. (Fact of the matter was that Martin did his dirty work on the pitchers, taking incredible advantage of Earnshaw and Lefty Grove, neither of whom were adept at holding a runner close to first base.) The Cardinals took the crown in seven games, and the A's would not win another pennant for nearly 40 years.

The Yankees rebounded to dethrone the A's in '32. Cochrane slumped to .293 at the plate, but hit a career-high 23 homeruns, and broke the 100-RBI-plateau (112) for the only time in his career. The failure to reach the World Series, coupled with the depths of the Depression, sent the A's into a financial shock from which the franchise never recovered. Mack was forced to sell his players, and a year later, Cochrane was dealt to the Tigers for $100,000 and a catcher named John Pasek (2 years, 28 games, .257 average).

Actually, the deal was not all that simple. Detroit owner Frank Navin had decided it was time for a managerial change. Bucky Harris had finished no better than fifth in his five-year tenure, and Navin wanted new blood. At first, the owner planned to hire Babe Ruth, particularly because the aging slugger would hype the gate in a player-manager role. But Ruth foolishly broke an appointment with Navin in favor of a barnstorming tour, and the owner reconsidered.

"I'm not sure what to do for a manager," Navin confided in H. G. Salsinger, a well-respected Detroit sportswriter. "I can get Babe Ruth from the Yankees for little or nothing, or I can buy Mickey Cochrane from the A's for $100,000. Which would you take?"

"What do you want him for?" Salsinger asked.

"Manager," the owner replied.

"Then get Cochrane," the reporter concluded. "You need a manager, and you also need a catcher."

The owner heeded the advice, and it paid tremendous dividends. In spring training, the newcomer told the world that his young Tigers ballclub would win the pennant... and led by Charlie Gehringer, Hank Greenberg, Goose Goslin, Tommy Bridges, and Schoolboy Rowe, they did exactly that. Cochrane seemed to work magic in coaxing, conniving, begging, and threatening the most out of his players. Several had the finest years of their careers under Cochrane. (Witness third baseman Marv Owen, a lifetime .275 hitter who batted .317 with 34 doubles, 9 triples, 8 homeruns, and 96 RBIs that year; also, Bridges, who entered the '34 season with a four-year 39-32 record, and proceeded to win 22 games against 11 defeats.)

Cochrane batted .320 himself, but by the time the World Series against the Cardinals began, he was so exhausted that he had to spend his nights in a hospital bed. The strain of the pennant race may have also affected his attitude, because he refused to match Rowe against Cardinals ace Dizzy Dean in the Series. Many people said it was the equivalent of conceding defeat before the Series even began—a most un-Cochrane-like maneuver.

As things turned out, the Tigers did lose in seven games, and Cochrane had another rough Series (.214).

Things were different a year later. Cochrane turned in his last great season (.319, 33 doubles, 3 triples, 5 homers, but a slump to 47 RBIs), and capped it off with a solid performance (.292) in Detroit's six-game conquest of the Cubs.

"Winning that sixth game was the greatest thrill of my career," he said more than 25 years later. "We were tied, 3–3, in the ninth inning, when [Chicago third baseman] Stan Hack led off with a triple. I went out to the mound to talk to Tommy Bridges, and told him to throw nothing but breaking balls to their next hitter, Billy Jurges. Bridges did exactly what I told him, but the second pitch got away from him and bounced in the dirt in front of the plate. I thought we were goners, but I blocked the ball and held the runner at third. Then, Bridges struck out Jurges, gets Larry French to bounce right back to the mound, and Augie Galan flies out. They didn't score, and we knew we had them.

"Then, in the bottom of the inning, I led off with a single," he continued. "Gehringer was next, and he smashed a grounder over first base which, I'm told, their first baseman, Phil Cavaretta, dove for, blocked, picked up and stepped on first base to get Charlie, and then wheeled around and threw to second. Well, the throw hit me as I was sliding—course I didn't actually see it—and I was safe. I always figured I'd have been safe anyway because they'd a' had to tag me. Anyway, Goslin was next for us, and he lined one into the outfield for a base hit. When I reached home plate with the Series-winning run, I kept jumping up and down on it. It was the greatest moment of my career."

Sadly enough, it also proved to be his last day in the limelight. The Tigers got off to a horrendous start in 1936. Slugger Hank Greenberg broke his wrist and was out for virtually the whole season. Injuries and disappointments abounded, and Cochrane simply could not handle it. Midway through the season, he suffered a severe nervous breakdown, and was ordered to leave Detroit for at least a month. By the time he returned, Cochrane had resigned himself to a second-place finish, and began planning for 1937.

That '37 season opened on a bright note. The Tigers were healthy, Cochrane was batting over .300, and it looked like the fight for the pennant would go down to the wire. Detroit moved into Yankee Stadium on May 25th with Cochrane confident that his Tigers could dethrone the defending league champions.

Irving "Bump" Hadley was on the mound for New York. Cochrane touched him for a game-tying homerun in the third inning, and faced the hurler with a man on first and two out in the fateful fifth. The count reached three balls, one strike. Hadley's next pitch was a fastball that Cochrane recalled tensing for, ready to swing, and then relaxing when he realized that the pitch was ball four. A split second later, the ball struck him—he later said he had simply lost sight of it.

"... I thought he was dead," Bill Dickey said. "I'd heard all about the Ray Chapman thing [when the Cleveland shortstop was hit by a Carl Mays pitch and died], and, well, as scared as I was, it was something of a relief to see him roll over and hear him say something like 'Good God Almighty.'"

Cochrane was carried to the clubhouse, where he briefly regained consciousness and asked that the game be delayed until he was ready to return. He lapsed back into unconsciousness, and remained in serious condition for the next several days.

On June 7th, he was stable enough to be moved. An ambulance carried him to Grand Central Station, where he was placed on a special "hospital car" for the train ride back to Detroit. Mickey spent the rest of the summer recuperating, and signed a two-year managerial contract in September.

When Cochrane rejoined the club for spring training, he begged Briggs to allow him to return to the playing field, but the owner absolutely refused the manager's requests. Resigned to a nonplaying role, Cochrane soon found that he could not handle sitting on the bench and giving orders. Several players began openly grumbling about the manager. As the season began, there was serious doubt that he would be around at the end. In July, the Tigers returned from a bad road trip, and word had it that Cochrane was about to be axed. More than 10,000 people turned out to welcome the team home, and show their support of the manager.

The large turnout merely delayed the inevitable. Players began griping directly to Briggs, claiming that Cochrane was a slave-driver and impossible to play for. Finally, on August 6th, Briggs summoned the manager and informed him that Del Baker was taking over. Cochrane was heartbroken.

There would be one more display of affection for the fallen leader. When word got out that he was leaving town for good, thousands of people again made the trek to support him. This time, the demonstration was at the airport, where the fans said their final goodbyes.

After a brief vacation, Cochrane joined the Dryden Rubber Company in an executive capacity. When World War II broke out, he enlisted in the Navy, where he spent three years coaching the Great Lakes Naval Center baseball team. His squad won 166 games against 26 losses. In 1945, he was sent to the Pacific, where he received word that his only son, Gordon Jr., had been killed in action. Psychologically, that blow finished Mickey off, too.

In 1949, he rejoined the Athletics as a coach, and a year later, was named the general manager when Connie Mack stepped aside. A bright future as an executive seemed realistic, but a squabble developed between the new owner of the team, Connie Mack

Jr., and Cochrane, and he resigned. Mickey resurfaced in baseball again in 1955, when he was hired as a scout by the Yankees. In 1960, he returned to the Tigers in a similar capacity. By that time, the cancer that would claim his life two years later had begun to finish what a Bump Hadley fastball, and the death of Gordon Jr., had already begun. The man who was arguably the greatest catcher in baseball history remained unhappy, and died on June 28, 1962, in Lake Forrest, Illinois.

How great a catcher was Mickey Cochrane? The statistics are impressive: 13 years, 1,482 games, 5,169 career at-bats, a .320 lifetime batting average, 333 doubles, 64 triples.... Admittedly, he was never a consistent homerun hitter, but most of the four-baggers he smacked were game-tying or -winning blows.

But the real story of Mickey Cochrane's greatness goes beyond the statistics. He was a tremendous baserunner, and probably the finest defensive catcher in baseball history. He was also as hard-nosed as they came. Most importantly, he was a leader, and when he led from the field, he was a winner.

"More than any other player, Mickey Cochrane was the one responsible for the three pennants and two world championships we won from 1929–31," Connie Mack recalled.

"He took a second division ballclub and not only taught them how to win, but won two pennants in a row, and brought Detroit its first world championship," Briggs said.

But perhaps the man who saw so many of the great ones, Branch Rickey, put it best: "I don't know any catcher who could outrun him, and no catcher could outthrow him. For both batting average and power, he was superb. He also had great baseball sense, was a take-charge guy, and could teach every aspect of the game—something most of the great players could not do. How many others ever won 5 pennants in 13 years?"

What then, is the legacy of Gordon Stanley Cochrane? Does the man for whom another legend, Mickey Mantle, was named, dwell in the house of the superstars?

The answer is "yes." The proof is simple. When the fans around the country were asked to name the greatest catcher of all time, he won hands down over Dickey and Hartnett, his chief rivals. Cochrane's name is still familiar to the average fan. When the Cincinnati Reds began touting Johnny Bench as the next great catcher in baseball history, his defensive skills were not compared to those of Dickey, Hartnett, or Berra; they were compared to Cochrane's. His leadership ability was also compared to Cochrane's, and his clutch hitting was compared to "Black Mike" as well as the other three.

Cochrane has attained immortality, and remains the standard against which the great catchers are measured. Such is the stuff that superstars are made of.

BEN CHAPMAN

One day three black sportswriters from a Pittsburgh newspaper came to see me in my office. I think they were from the *Courier*. I was managing the Phillies at the time.

They said they wanted to ask me a few questions, and they asked me if my ballclub was riding Jackie Robinson, and if we were, why.

I told them it was true, we were riding him.

And I also said, "Before you go any further, I'd like to ask all of you a question: Do you want that man to make it like every white man has made it, or do you want us to pave the way for him?"

They said all they wanted was for him to be treated like a white man.

I said, "That's exactly what my ballclub is doing."

Now was I right or wrong?

—Ben Chapman

More than 33 years have passed since William Benjamin (Ben) Chapman uttered those, and many other, fateful words.

And the lifetime .302 hitter is still haunted by history's version of his treatment of Jackie Robinson, and alleged bigotry.

"After all," as one elderly fan put it, "from the day Chapman joined the Yankees in 1930, he always had the reputation for being anti-Catholic, anti-Jewish, anti-black and anti-Northerners."

Yet, the writer who talks to Chapman today comes away wondering if those allegations are true.

And today, at age 71, with the doors of Baseball's Hall of Fame still closed to him, Chapman has given up trying to clear his name.

"I was a Southerner playing baseball in the North in 1930," Chapman said. "It was the Depression, and in those days people were still fighting the Civil War. To them, I was a Rebel. The first words I heard from the fans at the Yankee Stadium were: 'You Southern son-of-a-bitch, why don't you go back to Alabama where you belong.'"

"People automatically assumed that I was anti-everybody," he continued, "but it's not true. If I was that way, why did I hire three Catholic coaches while I was managing the Phillies? I always used to tell them to light a candle for me, because I'd need it. If I was anti-Jewish, then why is my house graced with a beautiful oil portrait painted by one of my best friends, Johnny Maxwell? And, you know, Johnny called me every name in the book when we played against each other, and I returned the favor. But that was baseball back then.

"As for being anti-black, well, then why did I keep five black players on my Tampa minor league team 20 years ago, in an era when racial tensions were terrible? And, why did I race Bojangles Robinson at Yankee Stadium in 1936? All my friends wanted to know what the hell I was doing racing a black man, and I told them that it was because he was my friend. He used to travel with us some of the time, and we were close.

"People can be indoctrinated by the press. If you try to explain the situation, they say you're just alibiing, so I just don't bother any more."

The arrival of Jackie Robinson brought it all to a rather nasty head, with Chapman repeatedly portrayed as an arch villain. Robinson himself told many people that Chapman's team treated him the worst, always throwing at him and using the crudest possible language.

"Yes, we jumped all over Jackie Robinson," Chapman admitted. "But, in those days, you jumped all over every rookie. You have to understand that baseball was a lot different in those days. It was dog eat dog. When I joined the Big Leagues, when the Ruths, Foxxes, Gehrigs, and Greenbergs joined the Big Leagues, there was a certain price you had to pay. They'd get two strikes on you, and they'd knock you down. They can't do that anymore because the rules forbid it. And, they also called you everything in the book. Nothing was sacred, and if you belonged, you took it.

"Hell, when I was first starting, and for years thereafter, Ruth or Gehrig would hit a homerun, and I'd get knocked down."

History shows that at least one team, the St. Louis Cardinals, voted to boycott any games Robinson played in, but that never even came up on the Phillies.

"Another team voted not to play against him, and didn't until they were ordered to,"

Ben Chapman

Chapman recalled. "We never thought or even talked like that. We played against him, and we treated him like any other rookie.

"Jackie Robinson never wanted any favors," he continued. "The real problem was that some of the people behind Jackie wanted the road made easy for him. But, how could anyone expect the same ballplayers who'd been thrown at, and rode on, when they were rookies, to turn around and say, 'Leave this guy alone, he gets an easy in'?"

Chapman, an only child, was born in Nashville, Tennessee, in 1908. His family moved to Birmingham, Alabama, five years later, and he has called that city home ever since.

In high school, he played four sports: baseball, football, basketball, and track. The All-State Selections Committees honored him in the three team sports; strangely enough, despite a 10.0-second record in the 100-yard dash, he was ignored when it came to track honors.

A football and basketball scholarship to Purdue came through, and Chapman accepted it . . . for a few days, anyway.

"I went up to Purdue, looked it over, and stayed about ten days," he recalled. "Then, I told the football coach that I was going to play professional baseball. The Yankees were after me, and I signed with them.

"Baseball was the direction I always pointed in," he continued. "I always felt I could play. My dad was an ex-ballplayer. It was the only sport that paid any money in those days. Those were Depression years, you know, and ballplaying meant money. When I was a kid, you were lucky to have a pair of roller skates.

"But, getting back to the Yankees, I knew it would be them, because in 1926 I was their batboy during an exhibition series in Birmingham."

Chapman was originally an infielder, but literally threw himself into the outfield.

"Whenever the ball was hit my way, the fans behind first base would yell 'duck, he's got it again,' and they'd scatter. Once I made the switch to the outfield, I started leading the league in assists!"

Ironically, the lifetime .302 hitter was cut by six City League teams because he couldn't hit a lick!

"I was batting around .110 or .120 with each team," he recalled. "So, each time I'd get cut, I'd go out and hit 200 or 300 balls a day, and it worked in the end."

Of course, there was the thing he always did well: running.

He led the League in stolen bases, and is third among all-time New York Yankees base-stealers with 184 in just over five seasons.

"I had a high school coach named Ernest Tucker who taught me how to run the bases," Chapman said. "We won the state championship that year, and seven other players on that team played professional baseball. Tucker used to have us running and sliding until we had strawberries on one side, and then he'd turn us around and have us slide until we got them on the other. After that, we slid on our stomachs. I don't have to tell you what we looked like when we finished."

After two years in the minor leagues, Chapman stuck with the big club in 1930. He saw action at second and third in 138 games, and batted .316, despite a horrendous slump in the first month of the season.

"Branch Rickey once told me that if you let a young ballplayer beat his brains out in a slump, he'll come to you to ask for advice, and he'll be ready to accept it," Chapman recalled. "But, if you go and offer advice to someone who's in a slump, he'll resent it. Rickey told me that when I was on his ballclub, but as a player, I was the same way. Things got so bad when I started in 1930 that I was asking everyone for help, but I still finished at .316."

Chapman's first game was against Lefty Grove. Before stepping into the batter's box, Ben had a quick talk with Lou Gehrig.

"He told me to forget about trying to pull Grove because Grove was too fast," Chapman recalled. "But, I wouldn't listen. I was pretty cocky. I'd hit 31 homeruns the year before in the minor leagues, and I said to myself: 'I can pull anybody.' Well, I hit one foul ball, and Lefty struck me out four times!"

The relationship between Chapman and Babe Ruth was a saga in itself. In the beginning, Chapman was in awe of the big fellow, but that was gone by the middle of the 1931 season.

"We had a big game in '31, and I made a bad play trying to steal third base," Chapman remembered. "When I played, I was over-aggressive. Hell, I was out, and I was angry. I came back to the bench, and there was Ruth, sitting right next to Joe McCarthy (the manager). The Babe was angry, too, and with Joe sitting right there, Ruth said, 'Chapman, when I'm the manager next year, you won't be stealing.'

"Well, I came right back at him and said that when he got to be the manager, he should trade me to St. Louis, which was the Siberia of baseball in those days. I told Ruth that I was tired of playing centerfield while covering all of left field for him, and that he ought to pay to get in to the ballpark.

"Of course, I should never have said that, and I apologized the next day. We didn't get along for the next three years."

In 1932, there was the famous "sun field incident." Ruth always refused to play the outfield position that faced into the sun (left field at Yankee Stadium, right field at most other stadia). That left fellows like Ben Chapman staring into the brilliance, and one day the "Rebel" challenged Ruth about it.

The Babe explained that the sun hurt his eyes. Chapman told Ruth that the sun hurt his eyes, too, so Ruth switched to a more convincing argument.

"Babe told me that the sun hurt his hitting," Chapman recalled. "And I told him that

Ben Chapman

the sun also hurt my hitting. Whereupon, Ruth replied, 'Chapman, I want to tell you something. Nobody comes out to see you hit.'

"Well, I agreed with him," Chapman continued, "but they did come out to see me steal bases. I always had the green light, except when we were down two runs, or ahead by three. If we were down by a pair or more, it wasn't worth the risk because we had so many power hitters. And, if we were up by three or more, it wasn't worth the risk because I could get hurt."

There was a final episode to the Chapman-Ruth saga, and it led to rumors of a fight between the two.

In 1934, a pair of New York sportswriters, Dick Vidmer and Rud Rennie, went around to all of the Yankees and asked if Ruth should retire. Every player said "yes," and many choice comments were printed, including "he's got to the point where he can't even go 15 feet for a fly ball."

"Well, Ruth was furious, and McCarthy warned me," Chapman recalled. "Babe called a team meeting, and proceeded to curse and curse and curse everybody on the ballclub. After about a half hour, I got disgusted, so I walked over to Ruth and told him that I was one of the guys who'd talked to the newspaper men. He said, 'I knew you had to be one of them.' And then I told him exactly what I'd said:'If I had your career and your record, I would not stand out there every day and let the fans boo me the way they're booing you. I'd retire.'

"Of course I didn't know what his reaction would be, but he put his arm around me and said he was glad that at least one of us had the guts to say it to his face, and that from that day on, I was okay in his book," Chapman continued. "And, from that day on, we were good friends. He even visited me during spring training in his last year, while he was dying from cancer. I was managing the Philadelphia club in Clearwater, and he sat with me and my two boys for several hours."

The 1932 world championship was the highlight of Chapman's career. In game four, the Cubs walked Bill Dickey to load the bases. There were two outs, and Chapman was the next hitter. He lined a base hit to centerfield, scoring the game-winning runs. Chapman also recalled a running, one-hand catch he made off Gabby Hartnett in game 2, a catch that saved the game for Lefty Gomez. And, the statistics show that he tied Ruth with six runs batted in for the series, second only to Gehrig's eight.

Unfortunately, Chapman never really liked New York, and the fans made the feeling mutual. One day, a fan called him a "Southern son-of-a-bitch," among other things, and Ben vaulted the railing into the stands.

"It was unreal the way people thought that anyone from the South hated everybody," he said. "And sometimes I think that a lot of people still believe that nonsense."

In 1936, he was relieved to be traded to the Senators.

"They had to trade me because Joe DiMaggio was brought up," Ben recalled. "They knew he would be a superstar, and a superstar belongs in centerfield. He played his first 20 or so games in left, alongside me, until I was traded."

The trade hurt Chapman's pocketbook, because the Yankees were pennant-winners in 1936–39 and '41–'43. "Those World Series checks would have offset the fact that the Yankees paid me my lowest salaries in my career," he said. "I never made more than $12,000 a year in New York. They paid me $16,000 everywhere else."

"I was bitter about the trade—so bitter that I went down to Washington and hit .330-something, and J. Edgar Hoover had to give me a most valuable player trophy," he laughed. "Then, I got traded up to Boston, where that short left field raised my average to .340."

Chapman still recalls the Yankees of the era with his fondest memories, despite being overshadowed by Ruth, Gehrig, and company.

"They were better than I was," he explained. "I should have been overshadowed. All I ever was was a guy who hit .315, .320. I once hit .340. I could also steal bases. But Ruth was the greatest ballplayer who ever lived. He put thousands of people into the seats. Sometimes, we'd follow the Senators into St. Louis, and we'd read in the paper that they drew 3,500 people to their game. Then, with Ruth in town, playing, they'd draw 35,000."

"Gehrig was a great line-drive hitter," he continued, "and DiMaggio was voted the Greatest Living Player. They were supergreats. The Hall of Fame was created for them, not for guys who just hit .300. Today, they even put .260 hitters in the Hall of Fame, so now I believe that I belong in there."

The other side of Chapman's playing career came in the 1940s, when he pitched 25 games and recorded an 8–6 mark. It began in the minor leagues, while he was managing Richmond, a team that had only five pitchers, but had five doubleheaders in a row! He liked it, was successful, and was bought by Branch Rickey. Those were the war years, and when the "real hitters" came back from Europe and the Pacific, Chapman retired.

He managed the Phillies in 1945–48. Their best finish was fifth—if you don't have the horses, you can't go to the races.

After leaving Philadelphia, he managed Tampa in the Florida State League, and was voted the Top Athlete in the State of Florida in 1951. The notoriety created an offer to join an insurance company as a life insurance agent, and his wife persuaded him to give it a shot. Not a bad move, considering that he has sold more than one million dollars' worth of policies in seven different years!

For at least 10 of his 15 seasons, Ben Chapman was a force to be reckoned with in the American League. He batted .300 or better six times, and finished at .297 and .299

in two other years. On four occasions, he led the league in stolen bases, including 61 thefts in 1931.

Yet, when the great hitters of the era are mentioned, Chapman's name is omitted; and when the art of base stealing is elaborated upon, he is ignored.

Case in point: In 1976, the Cincinnati Reds' Joe Morgan stole 60 bases, scored 113 runs, and drove in 111. An article appeared in the Cincinnati *Red Alert,* lauding Morgan's accomplishment of becoming the "third player in the history of baseball to steal 60 bases, score 110 runs, and drive in 110 in one season." The writer said that that "guaranteed him a niche in the Hall of Fame, next to the other two who did it: Ty Cobb and Honus Wagner . . .", according to Chapman, who has the article.

"But in 1931, I hit .315, stole 61 bases, drove in 122 runs, and scored 120," Ben continued. "So, I wrote the reporter a letter, and got no response. He never corrected the error, and never even answered me. I guess he preferred to forget about it."

To this day, the doors of the Baseball Hall of Fame remain closed to William Benjamin Chapman. His name is omitted from the list of invitees to Old Timers' Days at Yankee Stadium, even though he is their third-ranking all-time base-stealer, and one of seven Yankees to bat .300 for a career of 800 or more at-bats. He could ably represent the 1932 world champions. He could be given an opportunity to explain his side of the Jackie Robinson incident. Even his letter to an errant sportswriter need not go ignored.

Then again, perhaps it is Robinson who is (was) right and Chapman who is (was) wrong. Robinson never forgave Chapman for the treatment he received, and Dick Young still carries a grudge against Chapman. Teammates and opponents line up on both sides of the fence. Perhaps the real truth is demonstrated by the fact that, today, Ben Chapman is ignored, forgotten, and maligned.

For Ben Chapman, a star of the 1930s, the truth, whatever it is, still hurts.

HANK GREENBERG

> We shall miss him in the infield,
> and we shall miss him at the bat,
> But he's true to his religion,
> and I honor him for that.
> —Edgar Guest (honoring Hank Greenberg's
> decision not to play on Yom Kippur)

On September 27, 1938, Henry Benjamin Greenberg had the baseball world on edge. He had just slammed his 57th and 58th homeruns of the season, and with five games left to play, the future Hall-of-Famer had a clear shot at Babe Ruth's record of 60 in one season.

The schedule called for two games in Detroit versus the Browns, followed by three in Cleveland. The Yankees had already clinched the American League pennant, and despite a down-to-the-wire battle between the Pirates and Cubs in the National League, Greenberg was the center of attention.

In the opener against St. Louis, "Hammerin' Hank" came to the plate five times and drew four walks against an erratic lefty named Howard Mills. The next day, Greenberg's personal nemesis, Bobo Newsom was on the mound, and the crafty right-hander held Hank to one single in four at-bats.

The setting switched to Cleveland, where Denny Galehouse held the slugger hitless in the opening game at ancient League Park. The second and third games were also scheduled for the old ballpark, but then the almighty dollar intervened.

Cleveland had the hottest ticket in sports, and the team's management knew it.

League Park held 21,414 fans, but just a few miles away sat cavernous Cleveland Municipal Stadium. That monstrous ballpark sat 77,797, and crowds occasionally exceeded the 80,000 mark. Bearing that in mind, the Indians decided to cancel the Saturday afternoon contest at League Park, and play a Sunday doubleheader at Municipal Stadium.

The older park was tough enough on right-handed hitters (376 feet down the left field line, 415 to left center, and 460 straightaway), but Municipal Stadium was virtually impossible (435, 463, and 490). No one consulted Greenberg about the switch, and he never complained about it either.

The Indians spent three days promoting the doubleheader, which featured the added attraction of 19-year-old sensation Bob Feller as the guaranteed starter in the first game.

More than 40,000 fans filled the stands by the time Feller threw his first pitch, and the superstar flamethrower responded with an 18-strikeout performance. Greenberg went down on strikes twice, and did not come close to a homerun.

So, it all came down to the final game of the season, and once again other powers intervened. There were no lights in major league ballparks in 1938. As the afternoon wore on, Greenberg found himself battling more than southpaw Johnny Humphries as the sun began settling in the west. Three times Hammerin' Hank pounded the ball, once off the 450 marker in left, twice he had to settle for a double and a single on drives that might have been homeruns in League Park.

In the sixth inning, umpire George Moriarty turned to the slugger and said, "I'm sorry, Hank, but this is as far as I can let the game go."

"That's all right," the weary giant replied. "This is as far as I can go, too."

If ever there was a self-made ballplayer, then Hank Greenberg was the one. No one ever worked harder at becoming a success, and few have been more successful than "Hammerin' Hank."

Born to a pair of Romanian immigrants on January 1, 1911, Greenberg was as hungry and determined to succeed in athletics as any man who ever lived... and he had more than his share of obstacles to overcome. For one thing, there was his size: 6'3¾", and 210 pounds, by the time he was 18 years old, and always awkwardly larger than his peers. For another, a set of successful middle-class parents who had their son ticketed for a college education and the robes of a doctor or lawyer afterward, and who had very little faith in a career in baseball.

"They always had a certain amount of difficulty dealing with my interest in sports," Greenberg said. "In fact, when the neighbors would ask why I was growing up to become 'a bum,' my parents had a tough time answering. But when I became famous, their attitude, and the questions, changed quite a bit."

And last, but certainly not least: Hank was a Jew who dared to tread where few of his "lantzleit" had gone before. This was held against him on numerous occasions, as the Gashouse Gang made poignantly clear in the 1934 World Series.

But back to Greenberg's childhood for a while. When Hank was seven years old, his parents purchased a comfortable home near Crotona Park in the Bronx, New York. His dad was in the textile business. Summers were spent on the New Jersey shore. Beautiful Crotona Park was down the block from the family's 16-room house. Hank played his first organized baseball while attending P.S. 44, and quickly developed the reputation of being able to hit the ball harder and farther than any of his friends. Hand in hand with his size and power was his awkwardness. The result was a deep-seated fear of looking foolish, and it drove him to practice more often, and try substantially harder, than anyone else.

Perhaps the most famous Greenberg boyhood tale involved the day his father came home and discovered a pile of sawdust spread all over the front lawn. David Greenberg was furious—vandals in such a nice neighborhood, he assumed—and was even angrier when he discovered that the culprit was his own son. The explanation that the sawdust was there to provide Hank with a sliding pit for practice did little to placate the elder Greenberg, and Hank was ordered to get the sawdust out of there, and keep it out. The youth could not bear to lose his practice area, nor was he one to openly defy his father, so he compromised: the sawdust went on the lawn after David went to work in the morning, and was gone before he came home at night.

Hank played basketball and baseball at James Monroe High School, where he attracted the attention of Yankees superscout Paul Krichell. General manager Ed Barrow subsequently contacted David, and offered him $1,000 if Henry would sign with the Bronx Bombers. David Greenberg shrugged it off. His son was going to college, and $1,000 would not get the boy very far. Barrow gradually upped the ante to $7,500 and threw in a warning against the dangers of signing with an out-of-town team, but David Greenberg would not hear of it.

The Washington Senators were next in line. Scout Joe Engel offered $12,000, but David Greenberg still was not interested. Detroit's Jean Dubuc came around with a $9,000 offer, and the constant attention began to raise some doubts in the senior Greenberg's mind. Perhaps he was passing up a great opportunity for his son.

Fortunately, the textile worker had a banking friend. The banker had another good friend named John McGraw. The Giants czar had always wanted a Jewish baseball player, and David Greenberg figured there was no better authority to go to. What did McGraw do when he had the opportunity to sign the greatest Jewish hitter ever? The Giants manager told Greenberg's friend that Hank was too slow and awkward. As far as he was concerned, the gigantic first baseman would never make it.

The opinion shocked David Greenberg, and hurt his pride. When Dubuc came back with a new offer that allowed Hank to go to college, David Greenberg gave in, and left the final decision up to his son.

"The Yankees had Lou Gehrig," Hank reasoned, "and I figured it would be impossible to displace him. I also knew how badly my parents wanted me to go to college, so I accepted the Tigers offer."

Greenberg enrolled at New York University that fall, but found that college life just was not for him. He contacted the Tigers in the spring, signed his contract, and reported to Hartford. After 19 games, the Tigers sent him down to Raleigh, North Carolina (Piedmont League), where he batted .314 with 19 homeruns and 93 RBIs. His offensive display so intrigued the Detroit front office that they summoned him at the end of the season to see what he could do at Briggs Stadium. The 19-year-old slugger saw action in one game, in a pinch-hitting role, and flew out deep to left field.

After two more solid seasons in the minors, Detroit added him to their varsity roster for 1933. Unfortunately, Manager Bucky Harris had spent at least $50,000 the year before in a deal that brought slick-fielding first baseman Harry Davis (a lifetime .277 hitter over 22 major league seasons) to his ballclub. The manager was reluctant to insert the awkward-looking rookie in place of the proven quantity, but after Hank spent the exhibition season destroying the opposing moundsmen, Bucky had no choice. Greenberg went on to bat .301 (33 doubles, 12 homers, and 87 RBIs).

His performance was merely a sample of what was yet to come. Mickey Cochrane joined the Tigers as player-manager in 1934, and one of his first acts was to insert the hard-hitting first baseman into the clean-up spot in the batting order. For the next several years, he teamed with fellow future Hall-of-Famers Charlie Gehringer and Goose Goslin to form Detroit's own version of the infamous "G-Men." Hank batted .339 (26 homers, a league-leading 63 doubles—four short of the record set by Boston's Earl Webb—and 139 RBIs), and led the Tigers into a three-way, down-to-the-wire pennant race against the Yankees and Indians.

By the time September rolled around, the giant first baseman had established himself as an essential cog in Detroit's pennant-contending machine. When he announced that he would not play in a mid-September contest against the Red Sox because it fell on Rosh Hashanah (the Jewish New Year, and an important High Holiday), thousands of Tigers fans were outraged. Piles of letters filled the Detroit front office, demanding that the slugger be forced into the lineup, but Cochrane left the decision entirely up to the young man.

It was the first, but far from the last, time that Hammerin' Hank's religion was the subject of some unwanted publicity. Ironically, Greenberg was never a very religious man. However, he did not want to upset his parents by playing on the High Holiday, and also admitted a certain amount of wonderment about violating the sanctity of the day.

On the other hand, he did not want to offend his teammates and fans by sitting out a crucial game. Caught in a terrible bind, Hank did what many a young Jew did in the past: Consult local rabbis. The first ruling left the decision up to Greenberg—

Judaism leaves each person free to make his or her own decision, and accountable to God for his or her acts. Still not satisfied, he pressed a second rabbi for more information. To their mutual astonishment, a reference to ballplaying was discovered in the Talmud (a book of Jewish Law and interpretations), and based on the language in the 900-year-old guide, Greenberg elected to play. As things turned out, he hit two homeruns in the Tigers 2–1 victory.

Eight days later, Greenberg faced a similar dilemma. This time the holiday was Yom Kippur (the Day of Atonement, a solemn day reserved for fasting and prayer), and Greenberg absolutely refused to play. The Tigers lost without him, but he earned national acclaim for placing religion above baseball, and folk poet Edgar Guest saluted him with the four-line ditty that opened this chapter:

> We shall miss him in the infield,
> and we shall miss him at the bat,
> But he's true to his religion,
> and I honor him for that.

Evidently, he made the right decision, because the Tigers went on to win the pennant (their first in 25 years).

The St. Louis Cardinals were the National League champions. Known eternally as the "Gashouse Gang," they featured Dizzy and Daffy Dean on the mound, and Hall-of-Famers Frank Frisch and Joe Medwick in the field. They also featured a brand of anti-Semitism that Greenberg found hard to swallow.

From the first round of batting practice, straight through the seven-game classic, the Cardinals directed barb after barb at the Jewish first baseman. It began with taunts of "Moe," and degenerated into the most grotesque and disgusting riding.

The verbal assault seemed to take its toll on the 23-year-old slugger. In the third inning of game one, with runners on second and third and two outs, Greenberg struck out on four pitches. He singled leading off the sixth, and hit a solo homerun in the eighth, but by then the Cardinals were ahead by six runs. The game ended 8–3. After the game, Dizzy Dean told the world that the Tigers were not as good as four other National League teams, and predicted an easy victory.

Game two was even worse. Greenberg was held hitless, although his walk in the bottom of the 12th inning pushed the game-winning run into scoring position. Previously, he had twice struck out with men on base, and also drawn a walk.

The worst of it came in game three, when Greenberg again struck out with runners on second and third in the third inning, and the Tigers lost, 4–1. Greenberg accounted for the Tigers lone tally with a two-out run-scoring triple in the ninth, but he was left stranded.

Sometimes the sleeping giant is best left alone, or so the old saying goes, and

Greenberg bore blunt testimony to its veracity by exploding for two singles and two doubles in game four. His infield hit in the third inning drove in a run. His seventh inning double broke a 4-4 tie, and his eighth inning two-bagger scored another pair, as the Tigers went on to a 10-4 victory.

Greenberg also turned in the fielding gem of the day. With the score tied at 4, the Cardinals placed runners on first and second with one out in the fifth. Ernie Orsatti drove a line drive down the line. Greenberg speared it, dove toward first base in an attempt to double up Bill DeLancey, but arrived a split second too late. Without hesitating, Hank whipped the ball to second, and caught Joe Medwick off the bag for an inning ending double play.

Detroit faced Dizzy again in game five, and Manager Cochrane decided to take some of the pressure off his young slugger by dropping him to sixth in the batting order. The Cardinals let him know all about it his first time up, but Greenberg walked, and scored on a double by Pete Fox. In the fourth, Dizzy made him look foolish, and struck Hank out with two runners on base. Greenberg turned the tables on Dean in the sixth, when his sacrifice fly scored an insurance run in the Tigers 3-1 win.

Cochrane moved Greenberg back into the clean-up spot for game six. He struck out leading off the second, and fouled out with two outs in the fourth. The sixth inning was another story. Hammerin' Hank came to bat with Gehringer on second and two men out. The Tigers trailed by a run. Hank slashed a wicked line drive into centerfield to tie the ballgame. In the eighth, he had the opportunity to go home a hero, but Paul Dean got him to foul out with runners on first and third and two outs.

Game seven was a disaster. Hank came up with a man on first and one out in the second inning, and Dizzy struck him out again. In the fifth, he singled leading off, but was left stranded. Dean struck him out in the seventh, and by the time Greenberg batted in the ninth, St. Louis led, 11-0. Dean added insult to injury by striking Hank out again, this time with two on and one out, and the Series was over.

There were some who thought Greenberg "choked" in the Series, but his statistics tell a different story: .321, one homer, two doubles, one triple and 7 RBIs. The only man who really stopped him was Diz, and in '35, Diz stopped just about everyone, anyway.

The same folks who thought Hank blew the Series also thought he would never be the same ballplayer who hit .339, but the fans stuck with him. (Even at the height of frustration, game six of the Series, he received a standing ovation from the Detroit crowd that had read plenty of the remarks the "Gang" was making.)

This time, the fans knew more than the writers. Hank led the league with 36 homeruns and 170 RBIs in 1935, while batting .328 and slamming 46 doubles. He easily captured the American League's Most Valuable Player Award, and entered the

World Series against the Cubs confident that he would silence the lingering critics of 1934.

Lon Warneke gave those critics added fuel for their fires by holding Greenberg hitless in game one, as Detroit lost, 3-0. Hank put a stop to the criticism early in game two. He came to bat with a man on in the first inning, and drove a Charlie Root offering into the upper deck in left field, to start Detroit on its way to an 8-3 win. Unfortunately, the homerun proved to be his only hit of the Series—in the seventh inning, reliever Fabian Kowalik nailed Hank with a fastball on the left wrist. Greenberg took his base, in obvious pain, and further aggravated the injury in a collision with catcher Gabby Hartnett. Overnight, the wrist ballooned up to the size of his biceps, and X rays revealed a clean fracture that sidelined him for the rest of the Series (won by the Tigers in six games).

Once again, the critics predicted that Hank would no longer do much "Hammerin'," but Greenberg opened the '36 campaign with a hot streak that placed him just under .350 for the first 12 games. Again, fate intervened and ordained more suffering for the gentle giant. In game number 13, Washington's Jake Powell collided with Greenberg on a play at first base, caught his left arm under Greenberg's left arm, spun him to the ground, and the wrist was fractured again. Greenberg was lost for the season, and the critics believed the slugger was finished.

When spring training opened in 1937, the "word" was that Hank's power was gone. The "cripple" went on to hit 40 homeruns, 14 triples, and 49 doubles, and drove in 183 RBIs—one short of Lou Gehrig's American League record. Greenberg batted .337, but the Tigers were slow getting out of the starting gate, and finished 13 games behind the Yankees.

The best was yet to come, although his slow start in 1938 got the critics going again.

"I started so badly I was afraid that I was in for a really lousy season," he recalled. "When I did get any hits, they were homeruns, but I paid no attention to them. I was worried about my batting average."

He was mired in the .250s in the early part of June, but a hot streak carried him to .292 just before the All-Star break. Hank was selected to the All-Star squad, but refused to play.

"I was angry at the manager [of the All-Star Team, Joe McCarthy]," he explained. "In 1937, I'd been elected to the team, but I sat and signed autographs because McCarthy never put me into the game. I was not about to sit again."

When the season resumed, Greenberg's bat remained hot. He hit two homeruns in one game on eight separate occasions after the All-Star break, giving him a record 11 two-homer games in the season. His average gradually climbed to .315, and the chase for homerun number 60 was on.

"Not until I hit my 57th and 58th homeruns in the same afternoon did I really think I had a genuine chance of breaking Babe Ruth's record," he said, after the season was over. "I had five games left, and it was not unreasonable to assume that I might get 3 more. As it turned out, I didn't even get one." More unfortunately, the Tigers dropped to fourth, 15 games behind the Yankees, and Greenberg had to watch the World Series again.

The year 1939 proved to be another solid year (.312, 33 homers, 42 doubles, and 112 RBIs), but when his 1940 contract arrived in the off season, it called for a $10,000 pay cut.

"I was shocked, and leery," he recalled. "They said the only way to avoid it was to move to left field because they wanted to get Rudy York's bat into the lineup, and the only position he could play was first base. Naturally, I was suspicious, so I told general manager Jack Zeller that I'd make the switch, but that since I was the one who would be taking a chance, I wanted a $10,000 raise if I started out there in left field on opening day."

Zeller agreed, and Hank spent the spring working dozens of extra hours chasing fungoes and practicing relays until he became an adequate outfielder. The work paid off in more ways than one. He not only made the grade on opening day (thereby earning the raise), but had his best full-season batting average (.340), and led the league in homeruns (41), doubles (50), and RBIs (150). Even better, the Yankees finally had an off year, and Detroit won the pennant, enabling Greenberg to take home an additional $3,519 as his World Series share.

Again, the postseason games proved to be a mixed bag. Greenberg batted .357 (10-for-28) with 2 doubles, one triple, one homer, and six RBIs, but the Tigers lost the series, four games to three. Again, Greenberg came under criticism for not coming through in the "clutch," particularly in the sixth and seventh games. However, a close examination of the Series as a whole, and those games in particular, disproves the allegation.

Detroit won the first game, 7-2, with Greenberg going 1-for-3 with a run scored. In game two, a 5-3 loss, he hit into a double play with runners on first and third and no outs in the first inning (the runner on third scored); walked in the fourth; doubled home a run in the sixth, and drove left fielder Jimmy Ripple to the wall with a ninth-inning drive that came within inches of being a homerun. In game three, he struck out in the second, hit into another run-scoring double play in the fourth, and singled and scored on Rudy York's homerun in the seventh. (Detroit won, 7-4.) Cincinnati took the fourth game, 5-2. Greenberg led off the second inning with a fly to center, doubled with two outs to drive in a run in the third, bounced out with no one on base in the sixth, and drove Ripple to the wall again with a two-out shot in the ninth with a man on first.

No one could fault his performance in game five. He started his day with a two-out single in the first inning, drove a three-run homerun into the upper deck in left field in the third, hit a bases-loaded sacrifice fly an inning later, flew out in the sixth, and led off the eighth with a base hit. Detroit won the game, 8–0.

Bucky Walters spun a five-hitter to pull the Reds even (4–0) in game six. Greenberg struck out, fouled out, and bounced out in his first three at-bats (with no men on base), and then walked with a man on first and one out in the ninth.

Game seven was an agonizing experience. Hank led off the second with a single, but was left stranded. He came up with two men on and two outs in the third, but Paul Derringer fanned him. His sixth-inning single was wasted again, and in the eighth, when he came to the plate with the tying run on first and no outs, he ripped a line drive right to the shortstop.

Disappointing, yes. "Choke," no way. What's a man to do—hit a homerun every time he's up?

As Detroit headed into the 1941 season, Greenberg's future once again looked bright . . . but again, fate had ordained suffering and disappointment. The clouds of war were on the horizon, and the nation had re-instituted the selective service draft. Hank's number was among the first to be pulled, and after 19 games, he was inducted into the Army . . . but not before a rousing farewell appearance at Brigg's Stadium, in which he hit two homeruns off the Yankees' "Tiny" Bonham, to lead Detroit to a 7–4 win.

In December, it looked like the Tigers slugger would be back in baseball two years earlier than expected. The Selective Service Act was modified to release all men over 28 years of age (Hank was 30), and he was "released" on December 5th. Two days later, the Japanese bombed Pearl Harbor, and Hank re-enlisted immediately.

All told, he would miss a total of 4½ years, thereby earning the dubious honor of losing more career seasons to the service than any other slugger besides Ted Williams.

Captain Greenberg served with distinction in the Army Air Force, and was released on June 14, 1945. The Tigers announced that he would return to the lineup for their July 1st doubleheader with the A's, and some 47,729 fans jammed Brigg's Stadium to welcome their hero home.

In his first three at-bats, Greenberg grounded out. The fourth time up, he walked and scored on York's three-run homer that keyed the game-winning rally. Then, batting with no one on and the crowd screaming for a homer in the eighth, Hank sent a Milt Gassaway fastball into the upper deck, his first homerun in more than four years.

There would be one more great moment reserved for the slugging first baseman. Detroit and Washington battled neck and neck down to the last day of the season in the quest for the A.L. pennant. Entering action on September 30th, the teams were separated by one game in the loss column. Detroit had a twin bill scheduled in St.

Louis—a win in either game meant the pennant. For eight innings, the lead seesawed back and forth, until the Tigers found themselves trailing by a run as they batted in the ninth. Hub Walker led off the inning and singled. Skeeter Webb laid down a perfect bunt, and both men were safe when Walker beat first baseman George McQuinn's throw to second. Jack Mayo followed with a successful sacrifice bunt, bringing "Doc" Cramer (a lifetime .296 hitter) to the plate. Manager Luke Sewell ordered his pitcher (Nelson Potter) to walk Cramer and go after Greenberg, who had been held to one single in three at-bats. The slugger ripped a screwball deep into the bleachers in left field, just inside the foul line, and the Tigers went back to Detroit with another pennant. (The second game was rained out.)

That time, Greenberg and the Tigers brought home all the "beef fry" (a kosher substitute for bacon). Hank batted .304 (three doubles, two homers, seven RBIs) and had the game-winning hits in games two (a three-run homer) and five (three doubles).

At long last, the "choke" adjective had been shed, and Greenberg's future again looked great. The off-season made him even happier. Team owner Walter Briggs raised his slugger's salary to $75,000 for 1946. Detroit dealt York to Boston, enabling Greenberg to return to first base. And, although he had slowed up a bit, and found the sudden starts and stops at first increasingly difficult on his legs, Hammerin' Hank led the league with 44 homers and 127 RBIs. Unfortunately, 1946 was Boston's year, and the Sox blew the race open with a 16-game winning streak in June. Detroit finished second, 12 games out.

And then came the greatest shock of Greenberg's life: While driving in his car he heard a radio report that he had been waived out of the American League, and claimed by the lowly Pittsburgh Pirates. No Detroit official ever contacted him.

At first, Greenberg planned to retire. He had built up a small fortune through wise investments, and had married Carol Gimbel a year before. However, when the new owners of the Pirates (Bing Crosby, John Galbreath, and Frank McKinney) offered him $100,000 for 1947, he agreed to the terms.

"For years, everyone thought Stan Musial was the first $100,000 ballplayer in the National League," Greenberg said in 1970. "Well, now you know the truth. Ten years before Stan got his 100-grand, I had already reached that plateau."

That final major league season was agony—in a physical sense. Greenberg's legs were not up to the strain, and each day in the field was tougher. The Pirates shortened their left field line from 365 feet to 335, and reduced the power alley from a staggering 457 to a more reasonable 355 (right field was only 300 feet, similar to the old Yankee Stadium), in hopes of increasing Greenberg's homerun totals and helping their young slugger, Ralph Kiner. The newly fenced area became known as "Greenberg Gardens" because the grounds crew filled the former playing area with a large vegetable spread.

Hank struggled through 125 of the 154 games the Pirates played that year, batting

.249 (13 doubles, 2 triples, and 25 homeruns) and led the National League with 104 walks. His real contributions were as a gate attraction, and as a mentor for Kiner, who has always credited Greenberg with teaching him all the inside things about baseball that enabled Kiner to lead the league in homeruns for 7 straight years.

After the season, Cleveland owner Bill Veeck asked Greenberg to join the Indians as a coach–pinch-hitter. The real lure was an eventual front office position, and after a short-lived attempt at spring training, Hank hung up his spikes and was named farm director. Two years later, he advanced to the general manager's post, and immediately infuriated the Cleveland fans by trading the popular shortstop-manager Lou Boudreau for Al Lopez. Al eventually silenced the critics by winning the pennant in 1954, and when Greenberg moved over to the White Sox a few years later, Lopez followed him west and won another flag.

The final baseball honor was paid in 1956, when the man who hit 331 homeruns in 1,394 games was elected to the Baseball Hall of Fame.

"I thought about all the hours I'd spent on the ball field, and how all the time I spent improving myself as a player was worth it," he told reporters, after learning of his election. "I never thought I'd be rewarded this way."

In 1969, Greenberg was mentioned as a possible successor to Ford Frick as the next Commissioner of Baseball, but the Hall-of-Famer pushed for his friend, Bill Veeck, instead.

"I never really wanted it," Greenberg said. "The man they should have hired was Bill Veeck. The game was faced with tough competition from hockey, football, and basketball, and needed a shot in the arm and revolutionary ideas. He would have been the man to do it, bringing in things like interleague play."

Today, Greenberg, who divorced Ms. Gimble and married Mary Jo Tarola in 1966, is a renowned tennis star in the "senior circuit."

From 1933 to 1946, Hank Greenberg terrorized American League pitchers. Allowing for the years he missed in the service, and the time he lost due to injuries, and adding in his year with Pittsburgh, Hank hit 331 homeruns in less than 10 full seasons, while batting .313. His .605 slugging percentage ranks him fifth in major league history. The four pennants Detroit captured during his prime are more than the Tigers won with Ty Cobb and Al Kaline (Kaline never won any). His World Series record, despite the "choke" reputation, shows a .318 average, with 5 homers, 7 doubles, 2 triples, 22 RBIs, and 19 strikeouts. Most of all, the fans in Detroit loved him, and he remains the greatest Jewish slugger of all time.

Yet, for all of his towering homeruns, and for all of the love the fans had for him in his heyday, today Henry Benjamin Greenberg is fading away in memory. In another

20 years, he will be forgotten. How is it that a man of his strength and reputation could be counted among the finest of the mere stars?

Greenberg had several things working against him, two of which were not of his own making. Genetics determined his size, and resulted in a less graceful appearance in the field, and a less than fast pace on the basepaths. While he only led the league in errors twice (1940 and 1946, with 15 in each season), he was never compared to men like Bill Terry and Hal Chase as a defensive first baseman. Critics also point out that he only stole 58 bases in his career, but very few power hitters are also base stealers, and those that were (i.e., Willie Mays) are more likely to be superstars.

The other aspect of Hank Greenberg over which the man had no control was his religion. Hank played in the most anti-Semitic era of United States history. While he was belting homeruns out of Tigers Stadium, men like Henry Ford and Father Coughlin were preaching hatred against his co-religionists. (In fact, in 1934, Ford hosted the Dean Brothers and Frankie Frisch during the World Series against St. Louis, despite the fact that Ford was a native Detroiter.) When Greenberg made a run at Ruth's record, thousands of fans and dozens of major leaguers did not want to see a Jew break the mark.

Of course, the fact that he was the greatest among the handful of Jewish players in major league history also operated in his favor. Certainly, most Jews, be they fans or not, at least recognize his name, but there are only 6,000,000 Jews in the United States. There is no doubt that he will always be remembered by Jewish fans, but that is not enough to qualify him as a superstar.

(How much of a difference is there between "ethnic" immortality and "favored son" immortality? Virtually none. Just as Jews will always remember Greenberg, Bostonians will revere Carl Yastrzemski . . . but the Gentiles of St. Louis and Chicago will forget them both.)

However, there are other factors which detract from any Greenberg claims to superstar status. Regardless of the reality of the claims, the fact that he had the reputation for "choking" in the World Series is the most severe blow. The statistics may "prove" otherwise, but what the fans read and remember were the strikeouts at the hands of Dizzy Dean and company. The one great triumph in 1945 simply was not enough to wash away the bad taste of '34.

Finally, the other insurmountable obstacles: Greenberg played in a small city, and at a position that was dominated by Lou Gehrig in his early years, and the memories of Gehrig as time wore on. And, of course, the effect of World War II on his career cannot be accurately gauged. Had he hit 33 homeruns in each of those seasons (his average over 10 years), he would have approached the 500-homerun mark. Had that been the case, things might have been different.

Similarly, had he caught Ruth in 1938, things more than likely would be different . . . but the true superstar does not fail, and Greenberg failed in 1938, and was perceived to have failed in '34, and '40 . . . and must therefore be relegated to mere star status.

JIMMIE FOXX

"We were playing the Athletics back in 1933," former Yankee left-hander Lefty Gomez recalled. "I was in a jam. They had runners on first and third, and 'the Beast,' Jimmie Foxx, stepped up to hit. Now, I never could get him out. Bill Dickey was catching, and he kept giving me sign after sign, and I kept shaking him off. Finally, Bill called time out, and came out to the mound.

"'Well, you've got to throw something,' Bill said, knowing full well that Foxx would hit whatever I threw.

"'Not necessarily,' I replied. 'Maybe if I stand here long enough, he'll go away.'

"Well, he didn't, but the next pitch I threw sure did—away into the upper deck in left field in the old Yankee Stadium, the longest homerun I ever did see.

"You know, I thought it was a fastball when I threw it. After 'the Beast' hit it, I *knew* it was a fastball. Took me 20 minutes to walk up to where it landed, and all I found was a shattered seat."

James Emory "Double X" Foxx was the most powerful right-handed batter in the history of baseball. From 1925 to 1945, he slugged 534 homeruns, and virtually every one of them was "the longest homerun ever hit" in that ballpark, or at least the longest one since Foxx's last visit!

The Associated Press report of July 17, 1936, was typical: "The longest homerun ever hit at Comiskey Park (modern-day White Sox Stadium), and one of the longest ever hit in major league history, was launched into orbit this afternoon by James Foxx of the Philadelphia club. The ball sailed completely over the left field upper deck roof, landed in a playground north of the Park, and bounced against a fieldhouse at 33rd Street...."

Three years earlier, he had hit the longest homerun in the history of Shibe Park in Philadelphia.

"The pitcher was Bump Hadley," Hall-of-Famer Leon "Goose" Goslin recalled. "The pitch was a fastball, and Double X hit it over the two-deck stand. It sailed clear across Somerset Avenue, and finally came down on the roof of a house across the street. It travelled more than 550 feet."

The amazing thing about "The Beast" was that he was more than just a brute power hitter. He batted over .330 nine times, including a career-high .364 (with 213 hits) in 1932, and finished his 20-year-career at .325. In fact, he is one of the few players to play in more than 2,000 games and make more hits (2,646) than games played (2,317).

Unfortunately, as hard as Foxx could hit a baseball, he was himself hit by even harder luck. His minor league owner-manager, Frank "Home Run" Baker, offered him to the Yankees before selling him to the A's, but the Yankees said they were satisfied with Wally Schang. (A year later, they dealt Schang to Boston, but Foxx had missed out on an opportunity to play with Babe Ruth and be the catcher on the '27 Yankees!) Connie Mack bought him on Baker's recommendation, knowing full well that the 19-year-old could not possibly take the starting job away from Mickey Cochrane.

Foxx spent three years as Cochrane's understudy, before Connie Mack finally put him at first base.

In 1932, Jimmie entered the month of September with 48 homeruns, well ahead of Ruth's 1927 pace, only to fall off a ladder in his home and break his wrist. Foxx refused to sit out and let the injury heal, and he finished with 58.

"Not only the injury," he recalled, "but I had two homeruns that were rained out. I also lost three homeruns in St. Louis, and at least four or five in Cleveland, because they put fences on top of the lower walls. Those fences weren't there when Ruth hit 60."

He also missed winning the Triple Crown that year because his .364 average (213 hits in 585 at bats in 154 games) placed him second behind Dale Alexander (.367 in 392 at-bats over 124 games). (Of course, the rules were changed afterward to require at least 499 at-bats.)

Off the field, hard luck followed Jimmie wherever he went. In 1929–30, he invested all of his savings in a business, but the Depression wiped it out. Toward the end of his career, he invested all of his money in a golf course/residential club in Florida, and World War II wiped it out.

Jimmie Foxx

He retired one year before the Major League Baseball Pension Plan went into effect, and held one unsuccessful job after another. In 1958, when the Boston Chapter of the Baseball Writers Association sought to honor him as their annual guest, the world was shocked to learn that Double X had turned down the invitation because he had no money for travel. Of course, the association raised the necessary cash, and started a campaign to get Jimmie started in a new business, but the restaurant he co-owned also failed.

"I guess I was born to be broke," is the way Foxx explained his misfortunes to the hordes of reporters he saw at the dinner. "I earned more than $250,000 in my career, and now I don't have a penny. The money I lost was my own fault, but I'd like to give something to my children."

Finally, in the ultimate of tragedies, Double X died in poverty on July 7, 1967. Cause of death: choking to death on some meat while dining at his brother's home in Florida.

Jimmie Foxx was born on October 22, 1907, in Sudlersville, Maryland. His parents were "dirt farmers," and "money was hard to come by." "Christmas was nothing, nothing at all," he said. "We were doing good just to eat."

Perhaps that was the reason why Foxx ran away from home when he was 10 years old, although he always claimed it was because he "wanted to become a drummer boy in World War I."

"My grandfather used to tell me all about the Civil War," he said. "I wanted to live that kind of exciting life. Now, I doubt that I could have ever killed anything, except maybe a baseball."

Foxx was an incredible natural athlete who combined speed, power, and strength. As he grew to his adult height (6 feet) and weight (195 pounds), his first love was track, but as he grew more muscular, he lost some of his speed. Jimmy was an outstanding pitcher in high school, and attracted the attention of the local Easton minor league club, managed by Frank "Home Run" Baker. Baker signed the 16-year-old to a one-year contract, and soon discovered that the kid could hit a baseball even harder than he could throw it. Baker realized he had a true gem on his hands, and immediately began contacting major league clubs. At first, he offered Foxx to the Yankees, but they were satisfied with veteran Wally Schang. His next stop was Philadelphia, where he brought the youth to see Connie Mack. The Grand Old Man heard his former third baseman's rave report, and purchased Foxx's contract for $2,000.

"The Beast" first attracted attention as a brash, phenom rookie in 1925. "He talked big, but as things turned out, he could back it up," Hall of Famer Al Simmons recalled. "One day, he comes up to me and says, 'See that palm tree out there?' while pointing to a large tree some 400 feet away. 'Down at Easton, I hit 'em longer than that.'

"Well, I took a long look at him and said, 'Oh yeah. Well, we play with baseballs in this league, not golf balls.' Didn't rattle him a bit. Next time up, he hit one over that tree!"

When the season opened, Jimmie found himself parked on the bench behind Cochrane and veteran Cy Perkins. He played in 10 games that year, went 6-for-9, and presented Mr. Mack with a very pleasant problem: how to get his bat into the lineup. In 1926, he saw action as a catcher and outfielder in 26 games, and batted .313. He did not hit his first homerun until 1927, when he batted .323 with 6 doubles, 5 triples, 3 homeruns, and 20 RBIs in 61 games, 32 of which were played at first base.

A year later, Mack gave him a shot at third, but the hot corner was too hot for Foxx to handle. Despite his problems in the field, the 20-year-old batted .328 (29 doubles, 10 triples, 13 homeruns, 79 RBIs, and 43 strikeouts in just 400 at-bats). One day, Mack surprised the kid by asking if he had a first baseman's mitt.

"No sir," came the reply.

"Better find one," the manager explained, "because from now on, you're a first baseman."

Given the starting role prior to the 1929 season, Double X responded with the first of 12 consecutive great seasons, batting .354 with 33 homeruns and 118 RBIs. In each of those 12 years, Jimmie hit 30 or more homeruns, a feat that not even Ruth achieved.

The A's won the pennant by 18 games, and Foxx batted .350 in his first World Series. That '29 Series featured the famous 10-run sixth inning in game four that brought the A's back from an 8-0 deficit, and carried them to victory. Foxx singled twice in that frame; his second hit scored Mickey Cochrane with the tying run.

Foxx was even more outstanding in 1930 (.335, 33 doubles, 13 triples, 37 homeruns, 127 runs scored, 156 RBIs... but his only league-leading category was strikeouts, 66), and again led the A's to the world championship. This time, the opposition was more formidable. The St. Louis Cardinals (alias "The Gashouse Gang") had edged out Joe McCarthy's Cubs by two games, and matched up extraordinarily well against the A's. The result was a thrilling six-game World Series, with Foxx providing the key blow in the all-important fifth game.

The A's entered the game with the series tied at two games apiece, and facing the Cardinals ace, Burleigh Grimes, in St. Louis. In the top of the ninth, with the score 0-0, Foxx launched Grimes' second offering (a slow curve) into the seats in left field for a two-run homerun. It was the most important hit of his career, and the most memorable.

"Grimes was quite a bench jockey," Foxx explained, years later. "He even got on Mr. Mack, and that was against the rules. The first pitch to me was a big roundhouse curve, and I just watched it go by for a strike. I said, 'I'll be damned. I wonder if he'll do that again?', because he was a spitballer normally. He did, and a guy in the stands barely caught it before it went clear out of the ballpark."

The importance of the blow even attracted the attention of a future President. At that time, the gentleman was a judge in Missouri. He had pulled into a gas station, and the station attendant heard the radio blaring the World Series wrap-up.

"Who won the game?" the youth asked.

The judge snapped back, "Jimmie Foxx 2, St. Louis 0."

Harry Truman was a Cardinals fan.

The next day, Philadelphia battered Bill Halahan, and the A's were world champions again. Foxx, Mack, and Philadelphia would never win another.

The 1931 regular season was one that Double X preferred to forget. He slumped to .291, 30 homeruns, and 120 RBIs, but rebounded to star in a losing effort against the Cardinals in his final World Series. Jimmie batted .348, hit his fourth postseason homerun, and cried for 45 minutes after the Cards won game seven, 4-2.

His outstanding series earned him a raise to $16,333 for 1932, and he earned every penny by turning in the finest season of his career. He led the league in homeruns (58), runs scored (151), RBIs (169), and slugging percentage (.749), while batting a career-high .364. Only the fall off a ladder, and a quirk in the batting championship rules, denied him the homerun immortality and triple crown he otherwise deserved.

A year later, Foxx had turned in another superlative season. Among the highlights were four homeruns in four consecutive at-bats (his last at-bat on June 7th and his first three on the eighth), and an A.L. record 9 RBIs in one nine-inning game (a two-run triple, a grand slam homerun, a run-scoring single, and a strikeout) against the Indians. His .356 batting average, .703 slugging percentage, 48 homeruns, 163 RBIs, and 93 strikeouts led the league again.

What did the 26-year-old slugger receive for his efforts? A $333 salary cut! The A's had fallen on hard times, along with the rest of the Depression-held nation, and Mr. Mack had already begun to sell off his stars. Foxx was the old man's favorite, and would be the last to go (in 1935), but not before turning in three more stellar seasons.

Foxx never complained about the low salary structure of the A's (Lou Gehrig was earning twice that amount in New York, and Ruth had seen $80,000 in his best years). In fact, he never really complained about anything. His physical condition was never at issue. The trainers never saw him, other than when it was time to give out the uniforms. His only gripes were reserved for the wealthy men he passed on his way to the ballpark, men who could have helped the street urchins and orphans, but chose not to do so. His favorite pastime was to watch children playing in the city sandlots, and buying them ice cream after their games were over.

When Mr. Mack could no longer afford to keep Double X, he sent the slugger north to the cozy confines of Fenway Park, hoping that the 315-foot green monster in left field would aid Jimmie in the pursuit of future homerun titles. Mack sent pitcher John Marcum (65–63, 4.66 ERA over 7 seasons) along with Foxx in return for pitcher Gordon Rhodes (43–74, 4.85, 8 years), catcher George Savino (no major league statistics), and $150,000.

When word of the deal broke, the Red Sox fans pronounced an end to the New York Yankees and Detroit Tigers mastery of the American League. Everyone expected Foxx and company to have a field day in cozy little Fenway, but as things turned out, the Sox and Foxx were a big disappointment. Many of Jimmie's line drives struck the fence on the rise, costing him dozens of homeruns. Not that he had bad years in Boston—he had five fine seasons, including 1938 statistics as follow: a league-leading .349 average, .704 slugging percentage, 119 walks, and 175 RBIs; 50 homeruns, 33 doubles, 9 triples, 139 runs scored, and only 76 strikeouts. Strangely enough, the 50 homeruns ranked him second to Greenberg's 58, but when Jimmie hit 35 the following year, he led the league for the fourth and final time.

Foxx turned in his last big year in 1940, when he batted .297 with 30 doubles, 36 homeruns, and 119 RBIs. When catcher Gene DeSautels was injured and placed on the disabled list, Foxx volunteered to catch, and did a credible job in 42 games. When his homerun output faded to 19 a year later, Boston waived him to the Cubs. He managed only 8 homeruns and a .226 average for Chicago, and retired to become the manager of Chicago's Portsmouth franchise in the Piedmont League.

"Managing was not for me," is the way Foxx recalled his one season at the helm. "It was a lot easier to hit homeruns than to handle 17 guys who think they are homerun hitters."

When World War II claimed most of the able-bodied ballplayers, Foxx attempted a comeback in 1944. He made one double in 20 at-bats, and went back to the coaching box. A year later, his old buddy, Ben Chapman, asked him to play for the Phillies as a pitcher-utility player, and Jimmie agreed. "Double X" pitched in nine games, recorded one win against no defeats, and showed a 1.59 ERA. He also added 7 homeruns to his total, and ended his career with 534, the most ever hit by a right-hander at that time.

When the war ended, Foxx opted for permanent retirement from baseball, and returned to St. Petersburg, Florida, where he accepted a job as a truck driver. A couple of years later, he switched to a South Miami fishing equipment manufacturer, then to the restaurant business, and then to poverty and total obscurity.

For all intents and purposes, Foxx's career was over after the 1941 season. He was only 34 years old at the time, and a man of his size and strength should have lasted another four or five seasons. (Ruth played until he was 41, and hit 244 homeruns after his 34th birthday. In fact, he led the league three times during that span, and hit 40 or more homeruns four times.)

What curtailed Double X's career? Double shots. At the height of his career, Foxx used to brag that he could drink 15 nips (the small bottles served on trains and planes) of scotch in one sitting, and frequently drank more. His penchant for alcohol, combined with his refusal to obey doctors' orders for allowing injuries to heal, forced his premature retirement.

Off the field, "The Beast" was "a generous and kindly fellow who always picked up the check," according to his former manager, Ben Chapman. "He'd give you the shirt off his back, and did everything for his friends. Then, when a lot of those friends started ignoring him because he wasn't playing any more, he couldn't handle it. What a shame!"

When James Emory Foxx retired after the 1945 season, he had played in 2,317 games, batted 8,134 times, and made 2,646 hits—a .325 career average. Only Babe Ruth had hit more homeruns in a single season (59 and 60) *and* in a career (714) than Double X. Only Roger Maris has beaten the single-season mark. As time has gone by, Foxx has dropped to ninth on the all-time homerun list.

His .609 slugging percentage trailed only Ruth (.690) and Gehrig (.632)—only teammate Ted Williams has exceeded that mark (.634). Similarly, Foxx's 1,922 RBIs placed him fourth behind Ruth (2,204), Gehrig (1,991), and Cobb (1,959)—only Hank Aaron (2,297) and Stan Musial (1,951) have surpassed him. He was an overwhelming choice for the Baseball Hall of Fame in 1951.

Yet, when the ranks of baseball's true superstars are numbered, the name of James Emory Foxx does not appear. For all of his power and strength, for all of his run-producing statistics and tape-measure homeruns, for all of his good-naturedness and the ice cream cones he bought for hundreds of youngsters, Double X has been forgotten.

Considering his superb statistics, how is it possible that a ballplayer of Double X's ability could fade into oblivion? There are a few reasons, the most significant being Babe Ruth. To understand Ruth's effect on Foxx's legacy, one must realize that from 1920 to 1932, only Ruth had been able to hit for high average and with consistent power. Gehrig and Foxx were the challengers, and the only other ballplayers of the era who approached the Babe in those categories.

Foxx had a golden opportunity to write his name into the record books, and probably into the ranks of the superstars, when he made a run at Ruth's single-season homerun mark in 1932, but he failed. (By comparison, when Ruth hit 60 homeruns in 1927, he broke his own mark of 59.) The result was that Foxx was statistically almost as good as Ruth, and that was not enough. Foxx was up against the entrenched superstar, and like a heavyweight boxing match, the only way to dethrone the champion is to knock him out. Foxx did not even manage a split decision.

By the time Ruth retired, the A's were no longer a pennant-contending club, and the media's attention had shifted away from Philadelphia. The only way to regain that attention would have been another assault on the record book, but by 1935, Foxx was no longer the dominant power hitter he had been. Other names like Gehrig and Greenberg had come along, and their teams were winning pennants while the A's and Red Sox were runners-up at best.

The other side of the coin involved the A's themselves. Although the 1929-31 clubs ranked among the greatest teams in major league history, they were probably the least exciting of the greats. Nicknames often tell a story in themselves, and while the Yankees were either "Murderers Row" or the "Bronx Bombers," and the Cardinals were "The Gashouse Gang," the A's were "Mr. Mack's Boys" or "The Mackmen." Sounds rather limp-wrist by comparison, but the nickname was accurate to the extent that the team was dominated by Connie Mack. None of its members attained superstar status during their Philadelphia days because the players had to mirror Mr. Mack's business-like manner and quiet, efficient style. Even the few eccentrics he tolerated, like Lefty Grove (or Rube Waddell some 20 years earlier), had to knuckle under to Connie's way of doing things.

Last but not least, there was Foxx himself. He never craved headlines, he was always crowd-shy, he never had the flair for the dramatic (no called homeruns from the superstitious and cautious Double X), and he had very little luck. He never denied his bad luck, either.

Perhaps if Jimmie had been born 20 years later it would have been different. Certainly, had he surpassed Ruth in either of the key categories, things would have been different. Homeruns that travel tremendous distances might well be known as "Foxxian" blasts instead of "Ruthian"s, but when Jimmie had to perform the superhuman task of eclipsing Ruth, he came up short, and missed out on his once-in-a-lifetime opportunity.

Today, Jimmie Foxx is a forgotten man. The only time his name ever comes up is when another in the long line of great homerun hitters blasts number 535, and thereby drives "The Beast" one step further into the endless abyss of oblivion, the final resting place for all mere stars.

RALPH KINER

Mr. Kiner, without your 37 homeruns we'd still finish last.
—Branch Rickey

———————————

Yesterday doesn't count anymore, only today. I've reached the point where I'm surprised when I'm asked for an autograph.
—Ralph Kiner, 1961

Who is the only player in major league history to lead or tie for the league lead in homeruns in seven consecutive seasons?

Need a hint? He is also the only rookie to win a major league homerun title, and his career homerun percentage (7.1) is second only to that of Babe Ruth!

Still uncertain? He twice hit homeruns in four consecutive at-bats, twice broke the 50-homerun plateau, and even hit 12 grand slams.

Does the fact that the Pittsburgh Pirates traded him to the Chicago Cubs after taking batting practice *on a day they were playing each other* stir the memory?

Still stumped? Well, here is the giveaway for New York fans: He currently shares the play-by-play duties for the New York Mets.

Ralph Kiner.

Born on October 27, 1922, in Santa Rita, New Mexico, Ralph McPherran Kiner grew up in Alhambra, California. The future Hall-of-Famer began his baseball playing shagging flies for his neighbor's son. By the time he was nine years old, the local sandlots had become a favorite hangout, although he also enjoyed football, running, and whatever else the radio and newspapers were highlighting.

As a child of the Depression, Kiner was called upon to help makes ends meet, and served as a magazine carrier . . . until he realized that the periodicals had to be delivered during the afternoon, and would prevent him from playing baseball. The solution was unique, and simple: Kiner buried the papers daily, and mowed neighborhood lawns to pay for them! It worked for a while, until his mother found out. The punishment was military school!

"It wasn't until high school that I really got serious about baseball," Kiner said at his Hall of Fame induction in 1975. "By then, the scouts were watching me regularly, and with that great California weather, I was playing 200 games a year. Also, since I was always bigger and stronger than my peers, I could hit the ball a long way, and that attracted a great deal of attention."

Kiner grew to 6'2" and 195 pounds, and eventually joined the New York Yankees Juniors in Los Angeles. Although the amateur club was indirectly linked to the Yankees, Kiner never seriously considered a career in the Pinstripes because the New York outfield consisted of Tommy Henrich, Joe DiMaggio, and Charlie Keller.

"That outfield seemed impregnable," he said, "so I accepted an offer from the Pirates. It was $3,000 to sign, $5,000 if I ever made it to the majors, and a minor league Class A contract. In those days, Pittsburgh had a very weak team, and I figured it was a faster route to the majors."

That was in 1941, and when Kiner got his first look at the since-demolished Forbes Field, the right-hander immediately regretted his decision.

"When I saw that 365-foot marker down the left field foul line, I could have strangled the guy who signed me, Hollis Thurston," he said. "It was even worse than Yankee Stadium, and I was a pull hitter. Why, centerfield was 457 feet in Forbes—just six feet less than in the stadium. No one had ever told me about that distance, and I'd never thought to ask."

In spring training, Kiner got off to a tremendous start: two homeruns against the White Sox in his first game. He cooled off a bit, and the decision was made to send him down to Albany—possibly influenced by the Pirates' reluctance to pay him the $5,000 his contract required if he made the big club. Kiner cleaned up in Albany, recording two outstanding years. In 1943, he was promoted to Toronto (International League), but after five weeks, he was drafted into the Navy.

"As soon as I was released in December 1945, I began working out," he said. "By the time spring training began, I was in superb condition. I'd heard that they'd earmarked me for the Pacific Coast League, but I was determined to stick with the big team."

Kiner had an incredible spring, including 14 homeruns and better than 30 RBIs. He slammed his way into the starting centerfielder's role, and went 1-for-4 (a double) on opening day. Two days later, he hit the first of his 369 career homeruns. The victim was St. Louis' Howie Pollet. When the season ended, Kiner had led the National

League in homers (23) and driven in 81 runs in 502 at-bats. Less impressive were his .247 batting average and league-leading 109 strikeouts.

The Pirates rewarded their phenom by doubling his salary (to $10,000) for 1947, but the off-season acquisition of fellow Hall of Fame slugger Hank Greenberg did more for Kiner than the extra cash. (The Tigers were a disappointing second in 1946, and the aging slugger was made the scapegoat, despite a league-leading 44 homers.) "As Yogi Berra put it in reference to Bill Dickey, Hank learned me all his experience," Kiner said.

"We were a pretty wild bunch on those Pirates," he explained. "There was a lot of carousing and late-night night life. Anyway, one day Hank sat me down and told me to tone down my off-the-field life. He said that I had a chance to really make something out of myself, but I couldn't sit at a bar and whistle at girls all night, and then go out to the park the next day and produce.

"On the field, he also took me under his wings. He moved me closer to the plate to protect the outside corner, and enable me to pull the outside pitches. He spread my feet a bit, too, opening my stance to 27 or 28 inches, and cutting my stride to about six. The resulting compact stance, in which I let the ball come to me, rather than going out after it, meant a lot. It not only improved my average, but proved to be the difference between hitting a couple of dozen homeruns a year and hitting 40 or 50.

"You know, Hank did more for me than any man I ever knew," Kiner continued. "That talk about cutting down my after-hours life came at a crucial time. I had gotten off to a horrendous start, and was ticketed for the minors after the first month of the season. I was striking out two or three times a game, and sometimes even more. But Hank went to the team owner and told him to keep me with the big club, that I was just about to turn the corner." (At the end of the season, Kiner presented Greenberg with a gold watch in token of his appreciation.)

"Well, it was a close call, but he was right. At the end of May, I had hit only three homeruns, but I hit 48 more, and wound up tying Johnny Mize for the league title. Of course, a lot of that was not only based on Hank's instruction—there was something to be said for hitting ahead of Hank in the batting order. Pitchers had to throw me strikes to prevent him from getting up there with men on base. If you look at my totals over the next several years, I was walked 100 or more times in many of them. After 1947, there was no Hank Greenberg batting behind me, and they did a great job of pitching around me.

"There was also another great thing about Hank coming to the club. When we signed him, the owners put up an auxiliary fence that reduced the distance down the left field line to 335 feet. The enclosed area became known as 'Greenberg Gardens' (and subsequently, 'Kiner's Korner'), although I don't think I hit more than 8 or nine homeruns into the Garden each year."

Kiner finished the season at .313 (his best single-season mark), including 23 doubles, 4 triples, 51 homers and 127 RBIs. He led the league in slugging percentage (.639), and cut his strikeouts to 81. Unfortunately, the Pirates did not improve with their sophomore sensation. In fact, they dropped a notch in the standings, and finished last. Worse news awaited the Forbes Field faithful. Greenberg announced his retirement in the off-season, leaving Kiner as the team's only legitimate power hitter and sole gate attraction. For the next five years, Kiner alone filled the stands, enabling the Pittsburghs to break the one million mark in home attendance only because of the public's desire to see the new Babe Ruth. More often than not, the stands emptied as soon as Kiner completed his final at-bat of the game, although things improved temporarily in 1948.

"That was actually a good season for everyone," he recalled. "I led the league in homers again (40), drove in more than 120 runs (123), and cut my strikeouts to around sixty (61), and, the team finished an amazing fourth (83-71). Funny thing. A year later, we reversed our won-loss total exactly, and dropped into seventh."

In 1949, Kiner had a tremendous season, batting .310, and leading the league with 54 homers, 127 RBIs, a .658 slugging percentage, and 117 walks. Although the team finished deep in the second division, Kiner kept the eyes of the baseball world focused on Pittsburgh as the season wound down. He hit his 54th homerun in the Pirates 149th game, and needed six in the remaining five contests to tie Ruth's record. At the time, he openly admitted that he did not want to tie or break the record, and even authored an article to that effect. He also rejected manager Billy Meyer's offer to let him lead off the final half-dozen games, saying, "Whatever mark I make, I want it to be honest. I don't want anybody to say I had any help."

(Twelve years later, Kiner's feelings had changed markedly, according to a column by *New York Times* sportswriter Arthur Daley. "I've reached the point where I'm surprised when I'm asked for an autograph," Kiner said in 1961. "The only homerun hitter they know today is Mantle. Yesterday doesn't count any more.")

The slugger's production declined in 1950, but he still led the league with 47 homers, drove in 118 runs, and batted .272. Pittsburgh dropped into the cellar again, moved up to seventh in '51 and returned to the cellar in '52. Of course, Kiner led the league in homers both years (42 and 37), and also led in bases on balls (137 and 110).

The '51 campaign also featured his most memorable offensive performance. On July 18th, at Ebbet's Field, he hit a grand slam homerun off Phil Haugstad in the first inning, blasted a two-run shot off Dan Bankhead in the fourth, and with the score 12–12 in the eighth, hit what proved to be a game-winning solo homerun off reliever Erv Palica.

The '52 season was also memorable—but for the worst possible reasons.

"That Pirates team had to be the worst I ever played against," fellow Hall-of-Famer

Ralph Kiner

Stan Musial recalled, and with good reason. Pittsburgh finished 42-112—a .243 winning percentage (among the worst in major league history).*

"Musial probably had a point," Kiner conceded. "To epitomize our team, our backup catcher was a football star named Vic Janowicz; and we had the O'Brien brothers (Eddie and Johnnie), both of whom were All-Americans in basketball. We had good football players, great basketball players, but precious few baseball players."

The '52 season was Kiner's final full campaign in a Pirates uniform, and was also the last time he led the league in homeruns (37) and walks (110). His batting average plummeted from .309 to .244, and when he sought a raise from the team's new general manager, Branch Rickey, he was told, "Mr. Kiner, without your 37 homeruns we'd still finish last."

Team and slugger settled for $75,000 (a $15,000 cut), but Ralph knew he was gone. Just prior to the team's 42nd game of the year, Kiner was dealt to the Cubs along with catcher Joe Garigiola, pitcher Howie Pollet, and utility man George Metkovich in return for pitcher Bob Schulte, catcher Toby Atwell, outfielders Gene Hermanski, Preston Ward, and Bob Addis, and $100,000. Kiner was informed of the deal immediately after taking batting practice. He calmly took off his Pirates uniform, brought his belongings into the Cubs locker room, donned the Chicago colors, and went 1-for-4 (a double) for his new team.

Kiner finished the year with a combined total of 35 homers, 20 doubles, 116 RBIs, and a .279 batting average. In 1954, he batted .285 (36 doubles, 5 triples, and 22 homers), but his RBI total dropped to 73, and he struck out 90 times. The following year, he found himself wearing another new uniform, that of the Cleveland Indians. By then, the sciatica in his back had seriously reduced his effectiveness, and the slugger who averaged nearly 150 games a season for nine years was reduced to 113 games—27 of them in a pinch-hitting role. Kiner hit 18 homers and 13 doubles, drove in 54 runs, but batted only .243.

"That last season was my biggest disappointment," he recalled. "It wasn't only my performance, and the pain the back was causing. We came so close to winning the pennant—just three games behind the Yankees—and that was the closest I ever came to a World Series as a player."

After announcing his retirement, Kiner accepted a post as the general manager of

---

*The worst winning percentage in major league history was that of the Cleveland Nationals in 1899: 20-134 (.130). The lowest post-1900 marks were recorded by the 1916 Philadelphia Athletics (36-117, or .235) and the 1935 Boston Braves (35-115, or .248). The 1962 Mets hold the record for the worst percentage since the expansion to a 162-game schedule: 40-120, or .250. Other tragic clubs included: 1904 Senators (38-113) .252; 1919 Athletics (36-104) .257; 1909 Senators (42-110) .276; 1942 Phillies (42-109) .278; and the 1941 Phillies, '37 Browns, and '32 Red Sox, each of whom went 43-111 (.279).

the San Diego Pacific Coast League club, a post he retained until 1961. When he left San Diego, he accepted the color commentator's duties for the White Sox, and a year later, he hooked up with the fledgling Mets as a member of their broadcast crew. Ironically, he has already been involved in two World Series with the expansion franchise, and has no immediate plans to retire.

For ten short years, Ralph McPherran Kiner ranked among the leading power hitters in baseball. He slammed 369 homeruns in just 1,472 games (5,205 at-bats), and ranks second only to Ruth in homerun percentage. In six of those seasons, he not only led the National League in homers, but also drew 100 or more walks and drove in at least 109 runs.

But fate ordained that Kiner play eight of those ten years with second-division teams, and played a final cruel trick by placing him on the Indians the year after they won the pennant.

Today, Mets fans recognize Kiner as their colorman, but have by and large forgotten his on-the-field feats. Kiner's Korner also lives on, but not as a portion of Forbes Field (which was demolished nearly ten years ago). Today, the pseudonym refers to the postgame show the former slugger hosts, and few fans, if any, know its origin.

Perhaps if the Pirates had won even one pennant in all those years, things would be different for the forgotten star of the longball. Certainly, had he tied or broken Ruth's mark in 1949, he would be well known today. Then again, the sciatic condition that shortened his career was also a factor. It lacked the sudden tragedy of a crippling automobile accident, or the gradual deterioration of arterial lateral sclerosis. None of the above came to be, and today, Ralph Kiner is just another star whose brilliance has been reduced to a mere flicker in the broadcasting booth above the fields he once played on.

MEL OTT

"Look at that kid closely," New York Giants manager John McGraw told reporters in spring training, 1926. "He's got the finest natural swing I've ever seen. His name's Ott, and I'll miss my guess if he doesn't become the greatest hitter we've ever had at the Polo Grounds."

Leo Durocher always criticized Ott as too nice a guy. One day, Durocher was riding Ott from the Dodgers dugout, when writer Frank Graham tried to tone him down a bit.
    "Take it easy, Leo," Graham said. "Your team is leading the league. Why don't you be a nice guy?"
    "Why should I," Durocher snarled, pointing at Ott in the Giants dugout. "*Nice guys finish last.*"

Only one man wearing a Giants uniform was ever cheered in Ebbet's Field: Hall-of-Famer Melvin Thomas Ott.
    As heated and vicious as the old Brooklyn–New York rivalry was, and as nasty as the Dodgers fans could get in their home ballpark, they always greeted "Master Melvin" with polite applause, and responded to his homeruns with uncharacteristic silence—and, occasionally, wonder of wonders, a smattering of applause!
    In retrospect, their reaction is easily understood. It was hard to dislike, let alone "hate," the soft-spoken, mild-mannered, gentlemanly slugger who was the closest thing to Babe Ruth on the field, and Lou Gehrig off it, on the National League's side of the playing field.

Born on March 2, 1909, in Gretna, Louisiana, the 5'9", 170-pound left-hander possessed a fine sense of humor—and a powerful pull-hitter's swing tailor-made for the "short porch" in right field at the old Polo Grounds. In fact, Mel hit 324 of his 511 homeruns over or near the 257 marker under the ancient ballpark's right field foul pole, and retired as the senior circuit's all-time homerun, RBI, runs scored, and total bases champion. (Hank Aaron and Stan Musial have long since eclipsed those marks.)

Interestingly enough, Ott did just about everything "wrong" at the plate. His unorthodox style featured a high-stepping stride just before he brought his bat around—an act which should have robbed him of all his power, and should have made him an easy out on inside fastballs.

"He looked more like he was stepping over a fence than hitting a baseball," teammate Carl Hubbell recalled. "Why, if he were playing in high school today, no coach would let him use that kind of a stance. It'd be changed immediately."

Given the opportunity, his minor league manager Casey Stengel would have done exactly that—but Giants czar John McGraw never gave him the opportunity.

"I was just thinking, Mac," Stengel told Mugsy one day, "that a year in the minors might help develop that boy of yours—what's his name—Mel Ott."

"Neither you, nor any other minor league manager is going to ruin him by changing his style," McGraw exploded, in response. "The kid stays with me. Period."

The incident was well-publicized, and the 16-year-old Ott was immediately nicknamed "Mr. McGraw's Boy," a sobriquet he carried for most of his 22-year career.

Ott was a rarity among major leaguers because he never played any formal minor league ball, and played less than a season in semi-pro competition.

"Lester Ruprich and I were the pitcher and catcher for Gretna High and we tried out for the New Orleans Pelicans in 1926," Ott recalled. "He was three years older than I, and had finished school, but I still had a year to go. New Orleans owner, Ernie Heinemann, saw me and asked my age.

"'I'm only 15, but I'll be 16 in a couple of weeks.' I told him. His reply certainly shocked me: 'We don't need children in this league, but as long as you are the catcher for your friend, you can put on a uniform and work out for a few days. Then, if you still want to play ball, I can fix you up with a semipro team in Patterson. Just tell Harry Williams (a close friend of John McGraw) I sent you.'

"Of course, I went to Patterson, and Williams paid me $150 a month, and covered all my expenses," he continued. "And when I say expenses, I mean everything from haircuts to movies. I played for him for 6 weeks, and hit so well that I got a letter from Heinemann offering $300 a month to return to New Orleans. I was going to jump at it, but I thought it was only fair to show it to Mr. Williams. Imagine my feelings when he told me to forget it!

"Why, all I could think was that I had a chance to go to New Orleans, and Mr. Williams was trying to keep me in Patterson all my life. But, I stayed with Patterson's team, and in August, I got a postcard from Mr. Williams, saying I should report to the Polo Grounds in New York for a tryout on September first. I thought it was a joke, so I ignored it. In fact, I was actually catching a ballgame for Patterson, when Mr. Williams returned from his vacation on September first. Imagine his eyes when he saw me!

"Anyway, he put me on the first train to New York, and when I arrived there, Mr. McGraw watched me hit, and then signed me. After one day behind the plate, I was switched to the outfield."

(McGraw later told reporters that the reason for the switch was because of Ott's thick, muscular legs. "They'd knot up from all the squatting," Mugsy said. "We were taping his legs before every game to prevent charliehorses, and it got ridiculous. Finally, I told him to forget about the catcher's position.")

Ott saw very little action in 1926, appearing in 35 games (25 in a pinch-hitter's role), and batting .383 (two doubles, no triples, and no homeruns). He did manage to draw the wrath of the manager when Mugsy caught his protégé playing poker with several veterans.

"You're too young to play cards," the stern manager told his 16-year-old favorite. "That will cost you $100."

(The fine was refunded via a $100 bonus at the end of the season, according to Ott.)

A year later, Ott saw action in 82 ballgames (50 as a pinch-hitter) and hit his first homerun (an inside-the-park shot off Chicago's Hal Carlson).

"Mr. McGraw kept telling me to be patient, that I'd be out there regular soon enough," Ott recalled at his Hall of Fame induction in 1951. "He'd sit beside me on the bench, telling me everything he knew about every aspect of the game, so that when I got out there, I'd be ready.

"Well, in spring training in 1928, I figured something was up, because all of a sudden he's got me working out in centerfield, too," Ott continued. "One day, I was headed in from the outfield, and I stopped to take a few grounders at second. Mr. McGraw saw it, and ordered me to start working out there, too!

"Anyway, the season opened with Andy Cohen at second, Jimmy Welsh in center, and George Harper in right, and me on the bench. Then, on the first road trip, Cohen came down with the flu, and Mr. McGraw put me in at second. I started hitting, and when Cohen returned, Mr. McGraw traded Harper to open up right field for me."

Ott saw action in 124 games, batted .322 (including 26 doubles, 4 triples, 18 homeruns, and 77 RBIs). By the end of the season, McGraw's two-year-old prophecy of greatness for Ott seemed a certainty.

The 1929 year was Mel's first great season, and statistically, it was his best. He led the league with 113 walks, batted .328, slugged 42 homeruns and 37 doubles, and drove in 151 runs (all career highs). He might well have won the homerun crown, but was walked five times on the final day of the season to prevent him from getting a shot at the 270-foot marker in right field at Philadelphia's Baker Bowl. (Phillies outfielder Chuck Klein entered the game with 43 round-trippers, and won the crown.)

Although Ott's power totals dropped a bit in 1930 (34 doubles, 5 triples, 25 homers, and 119 RBIs), he batted a robust .349—the best full-season average of his career. He also had a well-publicized laugh at third baseman Freddie Lindstrom's expense, when a reporter asked the pair who their boyhood heroes were.

"I had two," Lindstrom replied. "Tris Speaker and George Sisler."

"And you, Mr. Ott?" the reporter asked.

"Lindstrom," he replied.

"Why you little . . . !" Lindstrom exploded. "What are you trying to do? Put me away as an old codger?"

"No, Freddie, I mean it," he replied. "Remember the 1924 World Series? You were only 18 at the time, so you were a hero to every kid in high school, which is where I was. Course we didn't think so much of you after you let those ground balls bounce over your head . . ."

"You know, something, you ——," Lindstrom replied. "Sometimes I find it hard to remember what a child you are. Then, you say something like that, and I remember. You'd better watch out, before I put you over my knee!"

Chronic injuries limited Ott to 138 games in 1931, but he still led the league with 80 walks, and batted .292 (including 23 doubles, 8 triples, 29 homers, and 115 RBIs). Master Melvin bounced back with a fine season in '32, including the first of six homerun titles (38). He also led the league in walks (100), hit 30 doubles and 8 triples, batted .318, and drove in 123 runs. Unfortunately, the club plummeted to sixth place, and midway through the year, McGraw gave up the managerial reins to first baseman Bill Terry.

Ott slumped a bit in the 1933 regular season (.283, 36 doubles, 1 triple, 23 homers, and 103 RBIs), but the Giants won the pennant, and Ott got back in the groove in time to be the star of the World Series against the Senators. He opened the Series on a high note, making four hits (including a two-run homerun) and driving in three runs, in Carl Hubbell's 4–2 win . . . and he closed the Series with the famous "$100,000 homerun."

The Giants led Washington, 3–0, in game five, as the teams headed into the bottom of the ninth. An infield hit, a walk, and a three-run homerun by Fred Schulte sent the game into extra innings. With two outs, and two strikes on him in the top of the tenth inning, Ott drove a Jack Russell offering out of the ballpark for what proved to be the Series-clinching blow. The dramatic clout cost both teams at least $100,000 because game six would have been held at the Polo Grounds, where a crowd of more than 50,000 fans was expected.

New York finished two games behind the Gashouse Gang in 1934, despite Ott's league-leading 35 homeruns and 135 RBIs (the only time he led in the latter category). They dropped another notch in '35, although Master Melvin was outstanding again (.322, 33 doubles, 6 triples, 31 homeruns, and 114 RBIs).

Team and player returned to the top in 1936. The Giants won the pennant, and Ott led the league with 33 homeruns. He matched the 135 RBIs and six triples of the '34 season, and hit .304 against the Yankees in the subway series. His only postseason round-tripper that year was a meaningless blow in the sixth and final game, won by the Yankees, 13–5.

The pair combined effectively again in 1937, with Ott seeing action at third base in 60 games at the request of Manager Terry. Veteran Travis Jackson retired after the '36 series, and replacement Lou Chiozza was batting only .232 when Terry asked Ott to make the switch.

"I did it for the team," Ott recalled, years later, "but I firmly believe that the wear and tear of the position shortened my career. Those three seasons, alternating in and out of the infield, were exhausting."

Ott batted .311 (including a third consecutive homerun crown with 36, and 116 RBIs), but collapsed against the Yankees in the Series. He hit another meaningless homerun, drove in three runs, and was held to 4 hits in 20 at-bats.

"When I think that that was my last World Series, well, it's a disappointment," he recalled, years later. "Then again, I can't really complain too loudly. How many players have had great careers and never even played in a World Series game?"

In 1939, Ott's homerun total dropped to 27, and he drove in only 80 runs. A year later, he was down to 19 and 79. The usual murmurs that accompany a decline in performance of a star began, but the 32-year-old slugger returned to the outfield in 1941, and jumped back up to 27 homers and 90 RBIs. A fifth-place finish (four games under .500) cost Terry the managerial job; and owner Horace Stoneham tabbed Ott as the heir.

At first, the new dual role served the team and Ott well. The Giants rebounded to a third-place finish (18 games over .500), and Ott led the league in homeruns (30) for the sixth time.

It proved to be Ott's last hurrah. The 34-year-old slugger slumped to 18 homeruns and 47 RBIs in 1943, and the ballclub nosedived into last place. Both parties improved in '44—Ott to 26 homers and 82 RBIs; the team to fifth place—but stagnated a year later, when Ott dropped to 21 homers, and the team finished fifth.

Master Melvin considered a non-playing role for 1946, but owner Horace Stoneham convinced him to continue in a part-time capacity. He hit the final homerun of his career on opening day (off Philadelphia's Oscar Judd); it was one of five hits he made in 68 at-bats for the season. The Giants finished a disastrous eighth, and were the subject of an embarrassing ditty (sung to the tune of "Swinging on a Star") at the annual baseball writers' dinner:

> "... A Giant is a midget gettin' by on his past,
>   He can't hit a hook or nuthin' fast;
> The club makes money, but it's gone to pot,
>   The fans go there to dream of Hubbell and Ott . . ."

It really was not Ott's fault. The pitching staff had suffered two lethal losses when ace reliever Ace Adams (11-9, 15 saves in 1945) jumped to the Mexican League, and promising rookie Sal Maglie did likewise.

New blood, in the forms of outfielder Bobby Thomson (29 homers and 85 RBIs) and pitcher Larry Jansen (21-5) breathed new life into the franchise in 1947. Ott appeared in only four games, all in a pinch-hitting role, and went hitless, but the Giants zoomed to fourth place and set a record by hitting 221 homeruns. Had Maglie and Adams been available, they might have won the pennant.

The strong showing put pressure on Ott to produce a serious contender for 1948. When the team got off to a slow start, and gradually dropped 11 games under .500, rumors began that Ott would be replaced. Midway through the season, with the club playing at a 27-38 clip, Ott was replaced by his old antagonist, Leo Durocher. The uproar over the change centered more on the hiring of Durocher, who had only recently led the arch-rival Brooklyn Dodgers (before being suspended for alleged gambling connections), than upon the firing of the fans' former favorite, Master Melvin.

Ott was given a job as a talent scout and minor league manager, and remained with the Giants until February 15, 1953, when he left baseball in favor of an executive position with a contracting firm in New Orleans. He returned to baseball as a play-by-play commentator, and was thoroughly immersed in his new careers, when he was involved in a two-car collision on Highway 90, near Bay St. Louis, Mississippi. He lingered for one week, and died on November 21, 1958.

When Mel Ott retired as an active player, he was the all-time National League leader in homeruns (511), RBIs (1,860), runs scored (1,859), total bases (5,041) and walks (1,708). His .304 average, .533 slugging percentage, 488 doubles, and 2,876 hits also ranked him among the leaders. Ott hit 21 or more doubles in sixteen different seasons; 30 or more homeruns in eight seasons; and struck out more than 50 times in only three seasons. But most impressive was his bases-on-balls total—today, it is his only record which remains unsurpassed. The runs scored, RBIs, and total bases marks fell victim to Stan Musial, who was subsequently surpassed by Willie Mays and Hank Aaron. Mays and Aaron also eclipsed Ott's homerun totals, while Ernie Banks and Eddie Mathews edged him out with 512 each.

What then remains as a legacy of the man who ranks eighth in runs scored and RBIs among all major leaguers, and is fourth in career bases on balls? Nothing. Ott has been completely forgotten by all save those who played in his days, and those who saw him play. Today, he is associated with one statistic—511 homeruns—and only to the extent that whenever anyone reaches that magic number, the media points out that the new slugger is moving up on the all-time list.

"How could it happen," asked teammate Carl Hubbell. "How could they forget a wonderful man like Mel? He was such an outstanding person off the field, and, well, his statistics say it all for him on the field.

"Maybe if the Giants had stayed in New York, if they had maintained that tradition," he went on, reflecting on an old friend. "And he was up against Ruth in homeruns and Gehrig and then young Joe DiMaggio and others. I guess maybe Leo Durocher was right: nice guys not only finish last; they are also forgotten."

There is one final irony to the baseball life of Melvin Thomas Ott: The man who brought him to New York, the man who refused to allow him to play for any minor league team, the man who told reporters in 1927 spring training that the 16-year-old kid with the funny-looking swing would be the greatest hitter the Polo Grounds ever knew, the man who taught him everything he knew about major league ball... was John McGraw, the arch-enemy of the hit that made Ott the star he was: the homerun!

DUKE SNIDER

Duke Snider was furious.

He had just received the bunt sign from manager Burt Shotten, and could not believe his eyes. Not that Duke was against bunting in general. In fact, he had occasionally even bunted for a base hit.

But this time, there were runners on first and second, no outs, the score was 0–0 in the first inning, and Snider was batting .320 with 80 RBIs. It just did not seem to make any sense . . . but Shotten was the manager, so Duke followed orders and tried to lay one down. The result: a pop up to the first baseman, a wasted out, and an irate Snider heading back to the dugout.

"It's a goddamned shame that a .320 hitter has to bunt with two on and no outs in the first inning," he snarled in earshot of Shotten.

"And it's a goddamned shame that he has to pop it up!" the manager shot back. "And, Mr. Snider, that'll cost you $50."

It was neither the first, nor the last, time that Edwin Donald "Duke" Snider's comments got him into trouble during his 18-year major league career.

In fact, his first such run-in came in his first professional spring training in 1944, when the 17-year-old Californian was nearly run out of camp by Dodgers coach Wid Matthews.

"They said it was for lack of hustle," Snider recalled in 1981, "but in reality, it was because I spoke my mind whenever I did not like something. I was a fresh kid who had never been away from home, and I was very stubborn. When I look back, I admit that there were many times when I should have kept my mouth shut, but what's done is done.

"As for that bunt incident, I came back to the bench and said what I said because I was upset," he continued. "Who ever heard of a .320 hitter sacrificing in that exact situation? I don't care that we were having trouble scoring off their pitching. If he [Shotten] did not think I could get a hit, then why was he batting me third? But, he was the manager, and orders are orders, so I tried my best to move the runners up. And when I popped up, well, that got me even angrier. How do you think it feels to be in the major leagues and not be able to lay down a simple sacrifice bunt when you have to?"

After the game, Shotten offered to rescind the fine if Snider apologized to the team, but Snider absolutely refused.

"So, the fine stuck, but there's more to that story than has been told before," Snider said. "If you remember, on the last day of the 1950 season, we were one game behind the first-place Phillies, and we were playing them. The score was tied in the ninth inning, when Cal Abrams and Pee Wee Reese got on base with no outs. Just before I stepped in to hit, I went over to the dugout and asked Shotten if he wanted me to bunt. No, I wasn't being a wise guy—on those Dodgers teams, you played for the team, not for yourself; and in that situation, a bunt made some sense. Shotten knew I was serious, and I'll never forget what he said and did. He shook his head 'no,' and then told me to 'go out there and get a hit so we can beat these Phillies and tie them for first place.'

"Well, I did get a hit, to centerfield, but Abrams stumbled between second and third, and never should have been waved home. But the coach sent him, and he was thrown out at the plate (by Richie Ashburn), and we never scored. Then Dick Sisler hit a homerun in the tenth inning, and we lost the game."

Five years later, Snider was in hot water again. Duke was having his best year, when, while sliding into second base at Wrigley Field, he caught his spikes on second baseman Gene Baker's uniform and wrenched his knee. The injury not only ruined what might have been an immortal season (Duke had hit his 38th homerun a few days earlier, and was 7 days ahead of Babe Ruth's pace), but sent him into a horrendous slump. As Snider went, so went the rest of the team, and the Dodgers double-digit lead shrank to 8½ games in no time. The low point was reached in a home doubleheader loss to the Reds. Duke went hitless and stranded eight runners in the opener. He also went hitless in the nightcap, and was greeted by loud boos in his final two at-bats. After the game, the Duke spoke his mind.

"*Fans!?* What a bunch of cruddy frontrunners," he told reporters. "They're the worst fans in the League. They don't deserve a pennant. I hope to hell we move to Jersey City!"

"No one had to tell me I was lousy that night," Snider recalled in 1981. "I was more upset with my performance than anyone in the stands could have been, and their reaction just threw kerosene on my fire. Don't get me wrong—they paid to watch us play, and they had every right to boo. I just didn't like it when I was the victim, especially because I had been having such a strong season, so I said so.

"Of course I regretted it all night, but the next game I got three hits, and by the time I got the third one, those fans were cheering me again. You see, the Brooklyn fans were the most knowledgable in the League. You couldn't put anything over on them. You couldn't bluff your way through. You had to produce for them because they knew their baseball. As far as Brooklyn is concerned, I was born there and I died there—as a ballplayer, that is.

"And there's one other funny thing about that whole incident," he continued. "You know, 1955 was the year that President Eisenhower had his heart attack. Well, my quote and slump pushed his progress report on to page four of the New York and Brooklyn papers!"

And when Snider wasn't "popping off" himself, he was often the subject of controversial newspaper stories.

Case in point: in mid-August, 1952, Duke asked Manager Charlie Dressen to give him the night off. Dressen knew his centerfielder was exhausted, so he told Duke to relax on the bench for the evening. The Dodgers beat southpaw Curt Simmons, and a host of relievers, 15–0, and the team packed its bags for Cincinnati immediately after the game.

Back in New York, Snider's absence from the lineup had not gone unnoticed. Sportswriter Mike Gavin of the *New York Journal-American* filed a story that bluntly stated that Dressen had "made the most important decision of his managerial career (in deciding) to bench Duke Snider.... Obviously, the ulterior motive is to light a fire under the speedy and hard-hitting 26-year-old outfielder.... At the same token, he is reminded, obviously with (owner) Walter O'Malley's consent, that he is subjecting himself to a 25-percent cut in salary unless his ballplaying improves. Dressen's drastic move also tells other clubs that Snider . . . probably will be on the market next year."

The article reached the streets the next day, while Snider was in Cincinnati. His wife saw it, and was beside herself. Calls to O'Malley and general manager Buzzy Bavasi produced denials of any knowledge of Gavin's sources, but failed to placate her. She reached Duke at the hotel in Cincinnati, and filled him in. Snider was understandably furious. He confronted Gavin, demanding to know the source of the story. The reporter refused to reveal his sources, so Duke stormed over to Dressen.

"Duke, I don't know a thing about it," the manager said. "Look, I'm not even quoted in the article, right?"

Snider remained in a rage until the next day, when Bavasi flew in to calm him down.

"Buzzy used to plant those kinds of stories just to make me angry," Snider said in 1981. "It's no secret that I always played better when I was angry, and I did go on a hitting streak afterwards. Maybe he should have done it more often."

Edwin Donald Snider was born on September 19, 1926, in Los Angeles, California. Unlike most young children who merely toyed with baseball on the sandlots, Snider was "formally" practicing baseball when he was seven years old.

"My dad taught me to play, and he made sure that I batted left-handed," Snider said. "He knew that the ballparks favored lefties at the plate, and he also knew that a lefty gets a head start toward first base. Mom was a great softball player, so she joined right in with us."

By that time, he had already earned the nickname that stuck with him for the rest of his life: Duke.

"I was strutting home from school one day—it may have been my first day of kindergarten—when my dad saw me and said, 'Here comes his majesty, the Duke!'" Snider recalled. "I always liked that nickname—hell, anything's better than Edwin."

In high school, Snider starred in football and basketball, as well as on the diamond. He first attracted attention when he tossed a no-hitter against Beverly Hills High, and after that, the scouts came around very regularly to watch the slugging pitcher-outfielder. He signed with the Dodgers because his mom was very much taken with Branch Rickey's "youth movement" rebuilding program, and pocketed a $750 bonus that helped him prepare for spring training in Bear Mountain, N.Y.

"That was in 1944, when wartime travel restrictions forced the teams to train locally," he said. "The weather was terrible, and we did most of our practicing indoors, at West Point, where we shared the gym with Army's team. It was a very lonely experience, and I had a tough time adjusting."

When the teams did get outdoors, Snider's bat and speed soon made him the talk of the training camp. In his first game, he hit a towering homerun that cleared the tennis courts located behind the right field wall.

"By Judas Priest, what power that kid has," Rickey told reporters. "And that boy can run and throw too. Why, he has steel springs in his legs."

As the training camp wound down, the Dodgers were billing him as the phenom of the year, so imagine his shock when he was farmed out to Montreal! After a few bitter weeks, Snider fell in love with the city, and had a fine season. When he turned 18 in September, he joined the service. He was discharged in July 1946, and sent to Ft. Worth, Texas, to get in shape. He tore up the Texas League, and in 1947, stuck with the big club.

"A lot of people don't know this, but my first game in the majors was also Jackie

Robinson's first one," he said. "I pinch hit for Dixie Walker and singled in my first at bat, and wound up splitting the season between St. Paul and Brooklyn. I really didn't hit too well (.241, no homeruns, in 40 games) with the big club."

Snider also split the '48 campaign between Montreal and Brooklyn, where he batted .244, but hit the first five of his 407 major league homers.

A year later, Snider suddenly came into his own. He forced Carl Furillo to slide over to right field, and turned in an outstanding rookie year: .292, 28 doubles, 7 triples, 23 homeruns, 92 RBIs . . . and a league-leading 92 strikeouts. Gil Hodges, Roy Campanella, Jackie Robinson, Carl Furillo, and Pee Wee Reese all had fine seasons, and the Dodgers won the pennant.

The World Series against the Yankees was a disaster for the 23-year-old slugger. Duke struck out eight times in five games, setting a World Series record for futility. He managed only three hits (two singles and a double), and did not drive in a single run, in 21 at-bats.

"It was an awfully tough thing for me to deal with," he recalled. "When I was a kid, I dreamed of playing in a World Series. Well, I got there, and I never dreamed that it would be such a traumatic thing. Do you have any idea of how it feels to be a failure in front of the whole world?

"I was ready to quit," he continued. "I brooded over my performance for weeks. Then, one day, it suddenly hit me: I'd done as poorly as I possibly could, but I still had my friends, the finance company hadn't taken away the house, and the Dodgers had offered me a nice raise for 1950. I realized that I'd hit bottom, and it wasn't really as bad as I was afraid it would be. In the long run, the whole experience was helpful. It toughened me a bit."

Snider improved in every category in 1950, leading the league in total hits with 199, and batting .321 (including 31 doubles, 10 triples, 31 homeruns, 107 RBIs and 16 stolen bases). Only Ashburn's throw prevented the Dodgers from winning their second consecutive pennant.

After the season, Duke joined a team of barnstorming all-stars for a trip that began in Montreal, where he visited the Dodgers' top farm club's general manager, Buzzy Bavasi. As they parted, Bavasi said, "Duke, you had a great year. You should double your salary for 1951."

Shortly thereafter, Rickey was replaced by the same Bavasi as general manager of the big club. When Snider received Bavasi's contract offer for '51, it called for substantially less than double his salary, "so I sent it back with a note reminding him of our conversation. And he sent me a new one for the right amount."

Duke and the Dodgers got off to a great start in 1951. By August 11th, they were 13½ games ahead of the second place Giants . . . and then the great collapse began.

Campanella was out with an injury. Snider, Hodges, and Furillo went into terrible slumps. The lead shrank to two games as the teams entered the final two days of the season. Both clubs won on September 29th.

The next day, the Giants beat Boston, and as they left the field, the scoreboard showed Philadelphia on top of Brooklyn, 8–5, in the seventh inning. The Dodgers rallied to tie matters in the late going, sending the game into extra innings. A great catch by Robinson quashed a Phillies' rally in the bottom of the 12th, and his homerun in the 14th won the game, setting up the infamous playoff series. The Giants won the first and third games, to advance to the World Series against the Yankees, thanks to Bobby Thomson's homeruns.

"The frustration of losing that playoff is impossible to describe," Snider recalled. "Unless you were there, in Brooklyn or New York, rooting for one team or the other, you simply cannot begin to understand the bitterness of the rivalry. And unless you played on either club, you can never fully understand it.

"Why, just a few years ago, I was broadcasting in Chicago and ran into Alvin Dark after the game," he continued. "Dark played for those Giants, and was coaching the Cubs at the time. He offered me a ride to the hotel, and I accepted. When we got there, he offered his hand in a handshake, smiled, and said, 'I never dreamed I'd ever give a Brooklyn Dodger a ride anywhere!'"

In 1952, the Dodgers overall offense slumped. Snider dropped to 25 doubles, 21 homers and 92 RBIs, and was limited to 144 games thanks to a pitch thrown by Johnny Klippstein. It nailed Duke in the knee, sidelining him for a week. In August, the exhausted and aching centerfielder asked Dressen for a rest, and the result was the Gavin article.

On September 3, the Dodgers held an eight-game lead over the Giants. Ten days later, the margin was three! (Three games closer than it had been on the same date the year before!) This time, Brooklyn rallied, and with some help from the Phillies (a three-game sweep of New York) clinched the pennant.

Snider turned in a great World Series against the Yankees. In the opener, his two-run homer in the bottom of the sixth inning broke a 1–1 tie, enabling Brooklyn to beat Allie Reynolds, 4–2. Duke played the hero's role in Game Five, slamming a two-run homer, doubling home the tying run in the seventh inning, and then doubling home the gamewinner in the eleventh. In game six, he hit two solo shots off the Yankees pitchers, but the New Yorkers won, 3–2.

A final opportunity to leap into superstar status awaited Snider in game seven. The Yankees carried a two-run lead into the seventh inning, when Brooklyn loaded the bases with one out. The next batter was Snider, so manager Casey Stengel summoned southpaw reliever Bob Kuzava from the bullpen. Kuzava threw a curve, inside, and Duke popped it up. Stengel stuck with his relief ace against the right-handed Robinson, and the lefty induced Robinson to hit a similar pop fly . . . but this one seemed to mesmerize the entire Yankee infield. At the last second, Billy Martin raced in from second and made a shoetop catch, ending the rally. The Dodgers never threatened again.

"I'd have given up a year of my career to get a hit in that situation," Snider said. "Without winning the Series, the accomplishment of being only the third man to hit four homers (after Ruth and Gehrig) seemed less meaningful. You probably also know that I set a record with 24 total bases, and my six extra-base hits equaled another mark, but it was all tinted by that pop-up. We needed a hit. It just didn't happen."

A year later, Snider was leading his club into another postseason tilt with the Bronx Bombers, after completing the first of five consecutive seasons at or above the 40-homerun mark. (He hit 42 homers, batted .336, slugged 38 doubles and 4 triples, drove in 126 runs, and led the league in runs scored—132—and slugging percentage—.627.)

Once again, the Yankees prevailed, this time in six games. Duke batted .320, with three doubles and one homer, but bunched his hits in game four (2 doubles and the homerun).

In 1954, Willie Mays returned from the Korean War, and Mickey Mantle had his first great season. Suddenly, Snider found himself sharing the spotlight with two other great centerfielders, and while Dodgers fans sprang to his defense, soon found himself overshadowed by both of them. Duke and Willie engaged in a season-long battle for the league lead in virtually every offensive category. Mays captured the batting crown (.345-.341), homerun title (41-40), triples lead (13-10) and slugging award (.667-.647). Snider topped his interborough rival in RBIs (130-110), runs scored (120-119), doubles (39-33), total bases (378-377), and total hits (199-195). Mantle tossed his hat in the ring by leading the American League in runs scored (129) and strikeouts (107), thereby serving notice of his contention for the greatest centerfielder of the era.

The Mays-Snider controversy is an excellent case-in-point superstar/star distinction. In 1981, everyone still recognizes the "Say Hey Kid," while Snider is known only in Montreal (he broadcasts for the Expos) and by a saving remnant in New York. The '54 campaign is a good example of how that came to be. Mays starred in a late-season drive that carried the Giants to the pennant, while Snider was handicapped by injuries that undoubtedly reduced his effectiveness. Adding insult to injury was the way Mays edged Snider out for the batting crown: Duke entered the last day of the season leading by a few points, but while Mays went three-for-four, Snider was held hitless. And Mays led the Giants to something that, up to that time at least, had eluded Snider's club: a world championship, including the greatest catch in World Series history. And when Sniders's club did win it all in 1955, the game-saving catch by Sandy Amoros, and the pitching of Johnny Podres, overshadowed Snider's great performance.

From that point on, for the rest of his career, no matter how well Snider did it,

Willie did it better. When Snider batted .309 with 42 homers in 1955, Mays went him one better, batting .319 with 51 homers. The fact that Duke led the league in runs batted in (136) and runs scored (126) was equaled by Mays' lead in triples (13), and close call in runs scored (123) and RBIs (127).

The Mays edge went beyond mere numbers. Snider never had a catchword phrase like Willie's "Say Hey." He was never as colorful a fielder as the Giants superstar—when Mays chased a fly ball, his cap would fly off and he always seemed to make a spectacular catch, great throw, or unorthodox basket catch. Snider, on the other hand, probably covered as much ground, but did it in a quiet way.

Duke was also handicapped by the team he played for. The Dodgers were a collection of great ballplayers: Reese, Furillo, Hodges, Robinson, and Campanella. Mays was the only great one on the Giants, and only Berra rivaled Mantle in pinstripes. Mantle also did something Snider rarely did: He hit the tape-measure homerun with incredible frequency.

Lastly, Snider's publicity all too often centered on negative remarks, or technical weaknesses. Duke tended to swing at pitches outside the strike zone, and had a significantly lower batting average against southpaws (anywhere from 38-111 points less than against righties).

Of course, Snider's team did win one World Series in Brooklyn. In 1955, the Dodgers finally conquered the Yankees, and Duke led the charge again, outhitting (.320-.200) and outslugging (1 double, 4 homers, 7 RBIs—1 homer, 1 RBI) Mantle in the process. Duke starred in a losing cause in game one, including the first homer, and was held strangely silent in games two and three.

He exploded for a three-run homer that insured Brooklyn's victory in game four, and his two solo shots in game five were decisive in the Dodgers' win. Snider's bat was silenced by Whitey Ford in game six, and he was held hitless in the Series-clinching seventh game.

A year later, the same teams took the field for yet another seven-game battle, with the Yankees emerging on top. Snider had turned in another superlative year: 43 homers and 99 walks (the only time in his career that he led the league in those categories), and his .598 slugging percentage also topped all National Leaguers. But Mantle picked that season to win the Triple Crown: 52 homers, 130 RBIs, and a .353 average. The Yankee superstar continued to shine in the Series, slamming three homers and driving in four runs, while Snider managed one round-tripper and 4 RBIs.

The '57 season proved to be the Dodgers' final campaign in Brooklyn, and also turned out to be Snider's final great season. His 40 homers and 25 doubles were slugged in just 139 games, as the knee he wrenched continued to give him fits. After the season, he underwent knee surgery which was labeled a success, but really was not.

"After 1956, I never played a game without pain," Snider said. "The '57 season was agony, but '58 was even worse. I banged the knee in a car accident, thereby aggravating it, and then found out about that 385-foot marker in right center field. The ballclub slumped to seventh place. It was terrible."

In one game, Snider drove three consecutive shots 395 feet, only to watch the right fielder glide over and put them away. Duke gradually made a change to line drive hitting, sacrificing some of the old power for contact.

In 1959, the club bounced back. Snider's line drives fell to a .308 average. He hit 23 homers and drove in 88 runs in the 126 games he played in, and contributed nine game-winning hits. Los Angeles made it to its first World Series, and the Dodgers won their second championship by beating the White Sox in six games. Fittingly enough, Duke's final postseason hit was a two-run homer that put the Dodgers ahead to stay in game six. It was his 11th—still the National League record.

The 1960 season was the beginning of the end for the last of the Ebbets Field stars. Snider's production fell off, and his knee limited him to 101 games. Rumors surfaced that he would be sold to the Yankees for $50,000, but the Dodgers kept him around for three more mediocre years, before selling him to the Mets for $40,000 in 1963.

Somehow, Snider squeezed out 129 games that year, batting .243 with 14 homers and 45 RBIs, but the end of the line was near. On September 12th, New York paid a final tribute to its former star by staging "Duke Snider Night."

"I look up into the stands and it looks like Ebbets Field," the tearful centerfielder told the crowd. "The Mets are wonderful, but you can't take the Dodgers out of Brooklyn."

(Juan Marichal struck him out twice, walked him in his third at-bat, and then induced him to bounce out to shortstop.)

On April 14, 1964, the final irony was dealt upon the former Brooklyn Dodger—he was sold to the Giants for $30,000. Snider appeared in 91 games, 48 of them in a pinch-hitting role, and hit 4 homers. After the season, he hung up his spikes for the final time.

By then, Snider co-owned a bowling alley in California, and had purchased a beautiful avocado farm on a hill in Fallbrook. The Dodgers were quick to reclaim their star as a scout, and he subsequently served as manager of Spokane (1965), Kenwick (1966), and Albuquerque (1967), before returning to scouting in 1968.

When the San Diego Padres joined the league the following year, Duke switched allegiances and served as a batting instructor/broadcaster for three seasons. In 1972, he returned to the dugout as the manager of their Alexandria farm club, but when the Montreal Expos offered him a broadcasting position for 1973, he left the field again.

Today, Snider still does the Expos games. There was talk of a shift to the New York Mets broadcast booth for 1981, but the talks failed, so Duke signed a four-year deal with Montreal.

"I love that city," he said. "The people up there are wonderful fans, always were. Today, I am a proud, happy man. I guess you can say I've come a long way since 1944, when a brash, cocky kid named Snider nearly got thrown out of his first spring training camp."

When Edwin Donald Snider retired, he had played in 2,143 games. His .295 average was accomplished via 2,116 hits, 358 of which were doubles, 85 triples, and 407 homeruns. He still shares the record with Ralph Kiner for the most consecutive years at or above the 40-homerun-plateau (five), and his 11 World Series homers is still the National League best. He is also the only man to hit four homeruns in two different World Series. He was elected to the Baseball Hall of Fame in 1979—his eleventh year of eligibility.

"Today, I can't walk down the street for more than one block in New York and Montreal without being recognized," he said. "But in the other cities, like Cincinnati and Chicago, they don't know who I am—but why should they?"

Snider has a point. Perhaps if those four-homerun World Series had featured Dodgers victories, things would be different. Certainly, if there were still an Ebbets Field, or at least a Brooklyn National League franchise, the absent element of tradition would help. But in the end, the key to Snider's mere star status is simple: Two of the greatest did it better, in the same city, at the same time. Snider was the star centerfielder in New York City; Mays and Mantle were the superstars.

SUPERSTARS AND STARS: PITCHERS

CHRISTY MATHEWSON

One day a rookie drilled three hits against Hall-of-Famer Christy Mathewson, and returned to the bench with a self-satisfied smirk.

"So that's the great Mathewson," he proclaimed. "He ain't so much."

"Do you remember what pitches you hit?" the manager asked.

"Nah," said the youngster. "Why should I?"

"Because Matty will remember, and you'll never see those pitches again."

As things turned out, those were the only hits the kid ever made off Matty.

"You could catch Matty in a rocking chair."
  —Roger Bresnahan, catcher, New York Giants

When Christopher "Big Six" Mathewson exploded on to the national scene with a 30–13 record in 1903, he was just what major league baseball needed: an educated, clean-living, superstar to hold out as an example for the youth of America.

Strangely enough, the popularity of the so-called "national pastime" had declined drastically in the six years since baseball's first superstar, Cap Anson, had retired. The image of the game, and particularly that of its players, had plummeted to an all-time low. Parents, teachers, and clergymen joined in damning the "ruffians who spent their daylight hours playing a child's game, and their night-time hours drinking themselves into stupidity, and frequenting houses of ill repute." No self-respecting father would allow his son to choose baseball as a "profession."

Enter Matty, a 6-foot 1½-inch, 195-pound lad from Factoryville, Pennsylvania. During his 17-year career with the Giants and Reds, the fair-haired, blue-eyed, All-American Boy would go on to win 373 games on the field, and the hearts of thousands off of it.

While most players spent their nights out on the town, "Big Six" was at home with his family. While most of his contemporaries were hard-pressed to sign their names, Matty was not only a graduate of Bucknell University, but went on to write the first scientific study of baseball, *Pitching in a Pinch* (available from Stein & Day Publishers). On the rare occasions when ballplayers were invited to speak before civic groups, many showed up drunk, and most had little to say; but Mathewson spoke eloquently and urged children not to smoke, drink, or take their education lightly. Most of all, his reputation for honesty was in sharp contrast to that of the average ballplayers (who often bet on their own games), and Matty's well-publicized belief that baseball should not be played on Sundays also endeared him to the ministry. (He practiced what he preached, too—he never played a Sunday game in his career.)

He was always rumored to avoid all tobacco and alcohol, but this was not the case. He smoked cigarettes and a pipe. Although he was not a heavy drinker, Matty also knew the difference between gin and scotch. At the gaming tables, he was an expert at bridge and checkers—and he knew when *not* to draw in poker!

"He was a good man, but not a goody-goody," Mrs. Mathewson said in 1966. "You don't think I would have married a prude, do you?"

At the height of his career, Matty was the most recognized athlete in America. He was so popular that dozens of letters addressed to "6, New York City" were automatically forwarded to him at the Polo Grounds.

Exactly how he earned the nickname "Big Six" remains uncertain. Sportswriter Sam Crane claimed he coined the sobriquet, likening the ace right-hander to New York City's largest fire engine (also known as Big Six). Others claim the nickname was related to the pitcher's height—he was more than six feet tall, hence a "Big Six."

On the field, Mathewson was the dominant pitcher of the decade, mixing a good fastball, hard drop, and occasional change-up to set the batters up for his out pitch, the famous "fadeaway." (It was actually a screwball, which operates as a reverse curve, breaking in on righties and out on lefties when thrown by a right-hander. The pitch also puts a tremendous strain on the arm, and Matty told biographers that he rarely threw it more than 10 or 12 times a game.) The other key to Mathewson's success was his outstanding control, statistically preserved by his 3–1 strikeouts-to-walks ratio.

Over his career, the Hall-of-Famer averaged 23 wins a year, totaling 373, against 188 losses. He is tied for third in total wins with Grover Cleveland Alexander, and his 2.13 ERA ranks him fifth in major league history. Matty also threw the "goose egg" with great frequency, recording 83 career shutouts (third behind Walter Johnson and Alexander).

In 1903, Matty started a string of 3 straight seasons in which he won 30 or more games (30–13, 33–12, 31–8), and 12 straight at or above the 22-win plateau. On five occasions, he led the league in wins, strikeouts, and ERA. The ERA marks were particularly impressive because he finished under 2.00 six times, including a 1.14 mark in 1909. The only contemporary N.L. pitcher who compared was Mordecai Brown, who won 239, lost 130, and finished with the third lowest ERA in history (2.06), but he never reached the 30-win plateau.

Matty's best year was 1908: a league-leading 37 wins (the modern N.L. record), 11 losses, and league-leading marks in ERA (1.43), games pitched (56), starts (44), complete games (34), innings pitched (390.2), strikeouts (259), shutouts (12), and hits allowed (285). He walked only 42—less than one per nine-inning game.

The statistics become more impressive when one realizes that Matty was also famous for pitching only as well as he had to. If the Giants scored nine runs, he often allowed eight; if New York scored only once, he'd win 1–0. One of the late Arthur Daley's favorite baseball yarns involved Matty's penchant for "making things interesting." The year was 1908, and the Giants were leading the Cubs, 6–0, when Matty decided to make it close. The score closed to 6–5, with two men on base and no outs, when manager John McGraw yelled out, "Bear down, you big baboon." Matty feigned anger, glared into the dugout, and replied, "Take it easy, Mac. It's more fun this way." Of course he struck out the next three batters—on nine pitches!

Actually, Matty enjoyed rattling the ever-serious McGraw with his unique habits on the mound. His favorite was a 14-hit shutout against the Pirates. In each of the first seven innings, the ace retired the first two batters, allowed the next pair to single, and then struck out the fifth man. Finally, McGraw threatened to take him out of the game, so Matty settled down and retired the side in order for the final six outs.

His approach to pitching combined his fine mind with his outstanding ability.

"I always tried to learn about the hitters," he said. "Any time someone got a hit off me, I made a mental note of the pitch. He'd never see that one again."

He also loved a good challenge, his favorite being the opportunity to pitch against his arch-rival, Brown. Matty won 10 of their 18 meetings, including a 10–8 win in the final game of both of their careers in 1916.

Perhaps the greatest tribute to Mathewson was paid by his constant World Series rival, Connie Mack.

"Mathewson was the greatest pitcher who ever lived," said the man who spent 60 years as the staunchest proponent of the American League over all things belonging to the National. "He had knowledge, judgment, perfect control, and form. It was wonderful to watch him—when he wasn't pitching against us."

Yet, for all the accolades, Mathewson lost two of the most important games of his career: the 1908 playoff against the Cubs, and the seventh game of the 1912 series against the Red Sox. Bad breaks played a part in both games.

In 1908 the bad breaks actually began in a game against the Cubs on September 23rd, when Fred Merkle earned the eternal sobriquet of "Bonehead" by failing to advance to second base on what should have been a game-winning hit by Al Bridwell. Instead, "Bonehead" stood on first base, watched the "run" score, and then fled the field to escape the delirious fans. Cubs second baseman Johnny Evers called for the ball, was tossed a ball (no one knows if it was the real game ball), and tagged second for the inning-ending forceout. (Ironically, the Cubs had missed out on a similar situation a few weeks earlier, and the same umpires were in attendance.) When the men in blue could not clear the field, the game was declared a tie.

Both teams protested. Chicago claimed victory on three grounds: the field could not be cleared, and since crowd control was the responsibility of the home team, the Cubs should have won by forfeit; because a member of the Giants, Joe McGinnty, had allegedly interfered with Evers's attempts to recover the baseball (McGinnty supposedly threw it in the stands); and because the Giants refused to play out the tie the next day as prescribed by league rules. New York argued that Merkle touched second, that Evers used a non-game ball, and that the run should have scored automatically.

The League Board of Directors called in all involved parties, including the Giants pitcher, Christy Mathewson. At the time of the "hit," Matty was coaching first base. Despite knowing that his testimony would cost him the ballgame, and possibly the pennant (which it ultimately did), the hurler told the board that Merkle never touched second. Big Six's reputation for honesty made further investigation unnecessary, and the game was ordered to be replayed, in its entirety, if necessary.

The teams finished the season with identical records, and met at the Polo Grounds, October 8th, to decide the pennant. With the Giants leading 2–1, and two Cubs on base, outfielder Cy Seymour ignored Matty's warnings to play the light-hitting Joe Tinker deeper, and Tinker drove a triple over Seymour's head to win the game.

The 1912 loss was even more heartbreaking. The Giants took a 2–1 lead in the top of the 10th inning, but the roof caved in. Clyde Engel led off the Boston half of the inning with a soft fly to centerfield that Fred Snodgrass dropped, allowing him to reach second safely. Harry Hooper followed with a drive to deep center that Snodgrass snared with a spectacular catch, Engel advancing to third. Stephen Yerkes walked on a controversial 3–2 pitch, putting runners on the corners. Tris Speaker followed, and lifted a foul pop-up by the first base coach's box. For some inexplicable reason, first baseman Merkle never moved for the ball, which fell to earth safely, in foul ground. Given a second chance, Speaker singled home Engel, with Yerkes advancing to third. A sacrifice fly scored Yerkes, and Matty was a loser.

After the game, Mathewson talked at length with the writers, telling them not to blame Snodgrass and Merkle, and then went over to console them. "They felt worse than any of us," Matty recalled in 1920.

Fortunately, postseason competition did not always treat Mathewson so cruelly. Actually, Matty enjoyed his greatest moment, in fact launched himself into superstardom, when he pitched three shutouts against the Athletics in the 1905 World Series. The Giants ace opened the Series with a four-hitter, took game three in identical style, and allowed six hits in the clincher. The feat remains unmatched in World Series play.

With any luck, Matty might have gone undefeated in the fall classic, rather than a deceptive 5–5. In 1911, he went 1–2: a six-hit, 2–1 win in game one; a 3–2, 11-inning loss in game three (including Frank Baker's two-out game-tying homerun in the ninth inning); and an 11-hit, 4–2 loss in game four. The 1912 Series was even more traumatic. Big Six pitched an 11-inning tie in game two, dropped a 2–1 decision on an error by Jack Doyle in game five, and was victimized by Merkle and Snodgrass in game seven. His final postseason appearances were in 1913, when he won game three (3–0 in 10 innings), but dropped the final game (3–1), without allowing an earned run. His career World Series ERA was 1.15 in 101⅔ innings.

Mathewson's background was atypical of the turn-of-the-century ballplayer. He was the oldest of five children born to a middle-class family that emphasized education and hard work. At age 10, Matty began pitching, and by the time he was 14, the future Hall-of-Famer was receiving $1/game to pitch semipro ball. Two years later, his hometown men's team found themselves in need of a pitcher for a challenge game against Scranton. They summoned the 16-year-old from the stands, and he struck out 15.

After graduating from the prestigious Keystone Academy, Mathewson enrolled at Bucknell, where he collected headlines in football as well as baseball. (He set the school record with a 48-yard field goal against Penn, and it has held up to this day.) Off the fields, Matty was class president, a member of Psi Gamma Delta, and a great romantic, according to his college sweetheart and future wife, Jane Stoughton.

During the summer of his freshman year, Big Six played semipro ball with Honesdale, where a forgotten pitcher named Williams first showed him the "fadeaway." In 1899, Taunton signed him to a one-year contract, and he went 5–2. Norfolk acquired him a year later, and Matty earned his $90/month by going 20–2. In June, Manager John Smith told him that the Phillies and Giants wanted to buy him, and Smith asked Matty to pick the team he preferred to play for. After studying the rosters of both clubs, Mathewson selected New York, "largely because they needed pitching." The sale price was $1,500, conditioned upon his making the big league club.

When he arrived in New York, Matty was sent out to the mound to hurl "game condition" batting practice. Manager George Davis stepped up to the plate, and the rookie fired a fastball past him.

"That's a pretty good fast one you've got there," Davis said. "Now let's have a look at your curve."

Matty threw him his best, a roundhouse curve, the pitch the newspapers said "had them standing on their heads" in the minors, and Davis drove it over the centerfielder's head.

"That old roundhouse ain't any good in this company," Davis yelled. "You can see that pitch start to break all the way from the box. A man with paralysis in both arms could get himself set for that one. Don't you throw a drop?"

Matty threw his drop, and Davis ruled it "a pretty fair pitch. Now, what else do you throw?"

"I've got sort of a freak pitch that I never use in a game," the rookie replied.

"Well, let's see it," came the fateful order.

So, Matty reached back and tossed the fadeaway, and Davis couldn't touch it. He threw it three times, and left the veteran manager shaking his head.

"You work on that pitch," he told Matty. "That's the damnedest pitch I've ever seen. No one will hit it much."

Mathewson's major league debut came on July 17, 1900, against Brooklyn. He entered the game with runners on second and third, and the score tied at 5 in the fifth inning. All told, he allowed three runs, and was tagged with the first of three losses he suffered that year (against no wins).

Davis was not impressed, and the youngster was dealt to the Reds for $300 after the season. As things turned out, he never pitched for Cincinnati.

John Brush was the president of the Reds that year, but had already planned to jump to the Giants for 1901. The man knew a pitcher when he saw one, and wanted to win at any cost. His last act before making the leap was to deal Mathewson back to New York for Amos Rusie, a nineteenth century pitcher who had been sidelined for two years with a sore arm. (Rusie came to the Reds with a 243–159 record and retired one year later with a 243–160 mark.)

Matty went 20–17 for the seventh-place Giants in 1901, a team that won only 52 games. After the season ended, he jumped to the Philadelphia Athletics of the American League, but before the start of the 1902 campaign, he jumped back to New York! (There was open warfare between the rival major leagues, and no reserve clause to contend with.)

During the 1902 season, manager Horace Fogel toyed with the idea of converting Matty into a first baseman because the youngster was a fair hitter and injuries had left the club shorthanded. Matty actually played a few games at first base. Fortunately, when John McGraw took over the managerial reins midway through the season, he stopped the experiment, although his subsequent claims that he had saved Mathewson from giving up pitching were not true.

After the season ended, Mathewson signed with the St. Louis Browns, but the Peace Commission that drew up the settlement between the rival leagues awarded him to the Giants. He responded with a 30–13 mark, and was off to superstardom.

Matty remained the idol of America, and baseball's finest moundsman, until a shoulder injury in 1914 ruined his career. The Giants dealt him to the Reds in mid-1916 so he could become their player-manager. He rallied that club to a fourth-place finish in 1917, and had them in third place the following year, before entering the Army for World War I.

Interestingly enough, had the baseball world listened to Mathewson that year, the Black Sox scandal might have been averted. The Reds numbered among their cast of players a fine fielding first baseman named Hal Chase. For years, rumor had it that Chase was serving as a go-between for gamblers and was throwing games. On August 8, 1918, Matty suspended Chase for "indifferent playing." Chase told reporters that the real reason was that he had been accused of gambling on his own games. A hearing was set for January 30, 1919. By that time, Chase's principal accuser, Christy Mathewson, was in France, and there was insufficient evidence to support a conviction. (As soon as Chase was acquitted, the Giants signed him, but in September, he disappeared from the club. The press said it was an illness or injury, but the real reason was that the league had obtained a cancelled check from a known gambler, payable to Hal Chase. Perhaps, if Chase's banishment had been well publicized, the White Sox players who threw the 1919 World Series would have thought twice about it.)

The war had a terrible effect on Mathewson, who served as a captain in the chemical warfare division. Somewhere in France, Big Six inhaled poison gas, and his lungs were permanently damaged. Some accounts say it was during a German gas attack, while others claim the gassing occurred while Matty was teaching recruits how to use a gas mask, and his mask malfunctioned. Reporters were told that the injury occurred when Matty was checking newly captured ground for lingering gas, and neglected to wear the mask.

Regardless of the circumstances, he returned home with a nagging cough, and no job. His "interim" replacement, Pat Moran, had led the Reds to the world championship. When McGraw heard that his old favorite was available, he signed Matty to a coaching job, but in 1921, the cough was diagnosed as tuberculosis.

The Mathewson family left New York City and took up residence in a sanitorium in Saranac Lake. His condition improved markedly, and in 1923, he defied his doctors and left the sanitorium to assume the presidency of the Boston Braves. It proved to be his death warrant. On the first day of the World Series that fall, he died.

Christy Mathewson left his mark on the game of baseball. He was not only the dominant pitcher of his era, but he also contributed a new pitch, the screwball, and remains among the top 10 in virtually every pitching category to this day. His performance in the 1905 World Series remains a legend. He also added qualities of honesty, sportsmanship, and eloquence that the game sorely lacked. When he sought privacy, as in 1913, when he did not join his teammates for a trip to Japan, he received headlines for it.

Everyone loved Matty. When he died, dozens of wreaths were sent to his funeral, but none was so impressive as the one signed "The Knothole Gang." It was from the poor children of Boston—those who could not pay to get into Braves Field, but were allowed to watch through holes in the fences, unmolested, on Matty's orders to the police. To the Knothole Gang, to the clergy, to the parents, and to his peers on the diamond, Matty was a champion—and a true superstar.

RUBE MARQUARD

"I was pitching for Brooklyn, and had just beaten the Braves, when the clubhouse boy came in.

"'Rube,' he said, 'there's an elderly gentleman outside who wants to see you. He says he's your father, and he's come all the way from Cleveland.'

"'He's not my father,' I replied. 'My father wouldn't go across the street to see me. But you go out and get his autograph book and bring it in, and I'll autograph it.'

"But instead of bringing the book, he brought the man in. It *was* my dad.

"'Boy, you sure are a hardhead,' he said to me. 'You know I didn't mean what I said 10 years ago.'

"'What about you, Dad?' I replied. 'You're as stubborn as I am. I thought you really meant it.

"'Did you see the game?' I asked.

"'Yes.'

"'Where did you sit?'

"'Well, you know the man who wears the funny thing on his face?'

"'You mean the mask? The catcher?'

"'I guess so. Well anyway, I was halfway between him and the number one—you know, where they run right after they hit the ball.'

"'You mean first base?'

"'I don't know. I don't know what they call it.'

"'How many times have you seen me play, Dad?'

"'This is the first.'"

When Richard "Rube" Marquard left home to join the Indianapolis club in the American Association, his father told him he never wanted to see him again.

"Baseball is for bums," the elder Marquard said. "I want my children to be real professionals—doctors, lawyers, or even teachers. People should not be paid to play games."

And for ten years, father and son never saw or spoke to each other. Whenever neighbors and friends asked Mr. Marquard if he'd heard about Rube's latest success on the field, Mr. Marquard would tell them he had no son named Rube, that he once had a son named Richard, but that that son had disappeared.

After the reunion in the Dodgers clubhouse, father and son never got along better.

"I kept him around in New York for about two weeks," Rube recalled, "and he never had a better time. I introduced him to everyone, and he loved it. When he finally went home, the reporters came and asked me where he lived in Cleveland so they could go and talk to him.

"And what do you think he told them when they asked him if he played ball when he was younger?" he continued. "Dad said he not only played, but was very good at it, and pitched, just like me. Then, they asked him if he was proud of me, and he said 'Of course. He's a great player, isn't he?' But the truth was that he hated baseball."

Born on October 9, 1889, Richard "Rube" Marquard was the son of a "professional man," the chief engineer for the city of Cleveland. There were four other children in the family (three boys, one girl), and their dad had high hopes that they would all be "professionals—teachers, doctors, or lawyers."

But spending hours in school and reading books was not Richard's idea of having a good time, and he continued to battle with his father over the youth's first love: baseball.

"Don't get the wrong idea," Rube said, shortly before his death in 1980. "I was a good student, and I could have gone to college. I just didn't want to. Baseball was what I wanted, and I was fortunate enough to be good at it."

Success indeed. Marquard was always big for his age ("My sister was the shortest. She was 6'2'''"), and his competition consisted of older boys and men. He was named a batboy for the Cleveland Naps (they later became the Indians) exhibition games, and even pitched a game for the barnstorming Tribe when he was 15 years old.

The final battle with his dad came in 1906, when Rube's friend, Howard Wakefield (catcher, 1905–7, Cleveland, Washington, Cleveland), arranged for the flame-throwing left-hander to try out with Waterloo of the Iowa State League. Rube had no money, and his father adamantly opposed anything that would further a baseball career, so the youth was forced to hitch rides and hop freight trains to get to Waterloo.

The tryout consisted of two games, a 6–2 win against Keokuk, and a 6–3 loss to the same club six days later. After the second game, he was told to go home.

"They did not pay my expenses, and I felt cheated," Marquard recalled. "The whole experience soured me on baseball, and taught me that you couldn't trust baseball owners."

When the 1907 season began, Rube was working in the Fanning (or Telling—he wasn't sure of the exact name) Ice Cream Factory, earning $25 a week, and taking home an extra $10 for pitching on Sundays. He enjoyed remarkable success in the industrial league, and it was only a matter of time before the Indians offered him a contract.

"They called me in and offered me $100 a month," he said. "They also promised me $200 a month for 1908, if I did a good job. I told them to forget it, that I was making more money in the factory."

A few weeks later, Indianapolis (American Association) wired him an offer of $200 a month, and he accepted. They optioned him to Canton (Central League), where he pitched 40 games, and went 23–13.

In 1908, the parent club retained him, and the future hall-of-famer had another outstanding year (28–19, with 250 strikeouts). The local newspapers began likening him to Rube Waddell, the flame-throwing strikeout artist with the Philadelphia Athletics, and the nickname stuck.

"Actually, that wasn't the only time the newspapers changed my name," Marquard said. "There was originally a 't' at the end of my last name, but the sports editors kept dropping it, so eventually I did, too."

Actually, the likeness to Waddell ended in the strikeout column. Marquard was never the eccentric Waddell proved to be, and was intelligent and a teetotaler, something Waddell never was.

Highlight after highlight came Marquard's way during that 1908 season. He beat the major league Indians, 2–0. Then, on September 3, several major league scouts came to watch him throw against Columbus, and Rube responded with a no-hitter. That evening, Cleveland offered $10,500 for him, and the Giants countered with $11,000—the most paid for a player in baseball history up to that time.

Marquard arrived in New York amid great fanfare, including headlines that announced the arrival of "The $11,000 Beauty." Manager John McGraw made no secret of his plans to keep the youth on the bench ("so he could learn the hitters."), but the Giants management insisted that their investment be displayed, and Marquard took the mound at the Polo Grounds on September 24, 1908. He lasted five innings, allowed five runs on six hits (including a grand slam by Hans Lobert), and left the field "waving confidently to the bleacherites."

The 1909 season was a disaster. Rube won only 5 of 18 decisions, and became known as "The $11,000 Lemon." When he turned in a mediocre (4-4) record in 1910, the Giants management began wondering if they had been duped, and considered suing Indianapolis for fraud! Fortunately, Marquard and McGraw never lost confidence in the pitcher's ability, and success was just around the corner.

During spring training 1911, coach Wilbert ("Uncle Wilbert") Robinson came to the rescue. He taught Marquard a sharp-breaking curve (instead of the roundhouse), and perfected his three-quarter-arm motion. The results were astonishing: 24-7, a league-leading 237 strikeouts, and a 2.50 ERA.

The Giants finished on top of the National League, and faced the Philadelphia Athletics and a fellow named Frank Baker in the World Series. Christy Mathewson opened the Series with a 2-1 win in New York, and Marquard took the mound to start game two. With the teams deadlocked at 1-1 in the sixth inning, Baker stepped up with a runner on first and slammed a Marquard offering into the seats in right field for what proved to be the game-winning homerun.

The next day, the papers were filled with a column, allegedly written by Mathewson, which lambasted Marquard for throwing a fastball to Baker, when McGraw had warned that only curves were to be served to him.

"Back in those days, everyone had a sportswriter who ghost-wrote articles for the World Series," Marquard recalled. "The writers knew we went over every hitter before the game, and someone must have told the guy that Baker was not to be fed any fastballs. Anyway, the pitch he hit was a curve, but that doesn't matter. What matters is that Matty never said those things, and never even knew what was in the story until it came out in the papers the next day."

Mathewson was back on the mound for game three, and entered the ninth inning leading, 2-1. He retired the first two batters, and up came Baker. The count went to no balls, two strikes, and the Hall of Fame third baseman belted Matty's next offering into the seats. The Athletics won the game in 11 innings, and went on to win the Series in six games, but not before Marquard's ghostwriter took a few ink swipes of his own.

"Will the great Mathewson tell us exactly what pitch he made to Baker?" Marquard's ghost, Frank Menke, asked. "I seem to remember that he was present at the same clubhouse meeting at which Mr. McGraw discussed Baker's weakness. Could it be that Matty, too, let go a careless pitch when it meant the ball game for our side? Or maybe Home Run Baker just doesn't have a weakness?"

"I've seen a lot of reports that said Matty and I became enemies or some such nonsense," Marquard said. "But that's not true. Why, Matty and I roomed together on the road for years afterwards. We both knew that our ghosts were just making things lively. Too bad we lost the Series."

In 1912, Marquard won his first 19 decisions, tying an ancient record set by former

New York Giant Tim Keefe in 1888, when the pitcher's mound was only 50 feet from home plate. In fact, according to today's rules, Marquard actually won 20 in a row.

"I came into a game in relief of Jeff Tesreau," Marquard said. "We were ahead, 2–1, but they had two men on base. A wild throw by our catcher, Art Wilson, allowed two runs to score, and we went into the bottom of the ninth down by a run. In the bottom of the inning we scored two runs on a homerun by Wilson, the same guy who made the error.

"But in those days," he continued, "any pitcher who started a ballgame and lasted seven or more innings won the game, no matter what, if his team won in nine innings or less. So, I lost a win. They gave it to Tesreau."

Marquard pitched 16 complete games, was relieved twice, and won a game in relief (June 19 versus Boston). He also had one "no decision"—a game the Giants eventually lost to Philadelphia, 8–6. (Mathewson took the loss.) When the streak ended in a 7–2 loss to the Cubs on July 7, Marquard had allowed just 49 runs in 20 games!

Contemporary reports told of a lunatic woman who had a hand in ending the streak. Mary Porter was hanging from a tree just outside the park, and kept shrieking "Take him out; knock him out. Knock the cover off the ball. Come on, you Cubs!" The noise so disturbed Marquard that he lost his concentration, and he complained of the "jinx" after the game.

No one could complain about Rube's pitching in the World Series that year. He won game three, 2–1, allowing six hits, and took game six, 5–2 on a seven-hitter, but the Giants lost the Series in seven games when Fred Snodgrass and company dropped one fly ball, and let another fall untouched.

After the series, Marquard made a movie with Alice Joyce and Maurice Costello called "19 Straight" and followed that with a scandalous vaudeville tour with dancer Blossom Seely. The pair were the hit of the season as they danced the "Marquard Glide," and fled the stage on more than one occasion to escape Ms. Seely's outraged husband. When Ms. Seely finally divorced Joe Kane, and married Rube, Kane sued Marquard for $25,000 for alienation of affection, and won. Three years later, Marquard and Seely divorced, too.

The 1913 season was another big one for Rube, who went 23–10, thereby running his three-year total to 73 wins, one less than the immortal Mathewson. Baker victimized him for three hits in game one of the World Series against Philadelphia, and he lost, 6–4, in his final Series appearance in a Giants uniform.

His fortunes reversed themselves in 1914. Rube lost 12 straight games and dropped to 12–22. At times he was brilliant, as in a 21-inning, 2–1 win over Babe Adams and the Pirates, but he was terribly inconsistent.

Marquard made matters worse during the off-season when he first signed with the Giants, then attempted to jump to the newly formed, and ill-fated, Federal League.

The Feds refused to take him when they discovered the previous contract with New York, and McGraw was not to forget Marquard's attempted traitorous behavior. Rube opened his season on a high note with an April 15th no-hitter against Brooklyn (the only one of his career), but was inconsistent again. He eventually fell into McGraw's doghouse, and when the manager stopped pitching him, received permission to make a deal with another team. Marquard called his old coach, Wilbert Robinson, who had since taken over the Dodgers, and for $7,500, Marquard was dealt to Brooklyn.

His first appearance was against the Giants, and he defeated his old club, 3–2, prompting McGraw to offer Brooklyn $35,000 for the return of his former ace. But Robinson would have none of the Giants' gold, and Marquard proved his value over the course of the 1916 season with a 13–6 mark that helped the Dodgers win their first pennant. The Red Sox battered him in his two World Series starts, and the fans wondered out loud if he were finished. Rube temporarily silenced the critics with a 19–12 mark in 1917, but the Doubting Thomases returned when he went 9–18 the following season, and capped the decade off by breaking his leg in 1919.

Marquard was determined to continue his career, and he rebounded to 10–7 in 1920, and lost more than the one World Series game he pitched against the Indians, when he was arrested for ticket scalping in a Cleveland hotel. Until his death in 1980, Marquard maintained that he had been framed, but Dodgers owner Charlie Ebbets would hear none of it, and traded him to the Reds in the off-season.

"I was waiting for my brother in the hotel lobby," Marquard told the late Dan Daniel. "He was late, and I had two tickets for him. Finally, I couldn't wait any longer, so I asked the hotel clerk to hold them for him. No sooner did I hand him the tickets than I was grabbed by city detectives. The plot was engineered by an employee of the Cleveland team, but the club's executives had nothing to do with it."

After a 17–14 year in Cincinnati, Marquard was sent packing to Boston, where he spent four under-.500 seasons before an appendectomy cut short his career in 1924.

Marquard remained in baseball for several years, managing and pitching for minor league teams in Providence, Baltimore, Birmingham, Jacksonville, Atlanta, and Wichita. In 1932, he finally hung up his spikes, and began working year-round as a pari-mutuel clerk at several racetracks. He was elected to the Baseball Hall of Fame in 1972, and attended every induction ceremony until his death on June 2, 1980.

Where does Richard "Rube" Marquard fit into the spectrum of superstars, stars, and just plain heroes?

On the face of it, his record seems very impressive: 204 wins, 179 losses, a 3.08 ERA, 30 career shutouts, a 19-consecutive-game winning streak, and election to the Baseball Hall of Fame. Closer examination reveals that the record is misleading. Marquard toiled for 18 years. He averaged a mere 11 wins a season. Teammate Christy Mathewson spent 17 seasons in the big leagues, and went 373-188, with a 2.13 ERA.

Marquard's claims to superstardom are further undercut by his lack of success in the World Series. He paired wins in 1912, but the Red Sox took the Giants in seven games. He was ineffective, at best, in most of his other appearances.

Yet, the most damaging blow to his statistical career is the fact that if a fan subtracts his three great years (1911-13) from his record, Marquard comes in at 131-151—hardly the stats of a superstar!

But mere statistics do not determine superstar status, and it is off the field that the heaviest blows were dealt to the Hall-of-Famer. His scandalous romance with Blossom Seely was amply covered by the newspapers, but was treated in the same manner as the paternity suits against Babe Ruth. The ticket-scalping incident, although an obvious frame-up, was looked upon as sinful behavior by a man who didn't need to raise a few extra dollars by depriving true fans of good seats. When Charlie Ebbets pronounced him a dead Dodger, there was no outcry against the decision. Surely a superstar would have been "protected" by his public.

The crowning blow to Marquard was not dealt on the field, or in the courtroom, but in the newspapers. When Menke attacked Mathewson in the classic ghostwriter's style, he made the mistake of insulting the idol of America. It did not matter that Marquard never said those words, and, in fact, had no knowledge of the content of the piece until after it was published. All that mattered was that Rube Marquard's name was on the product, and the fans never really forgave him for not only attacking their idol, but a teammate.

More than one public figure has come to learn that the pen is mightier than the sword. Unfortunately, Marquard is among their ranks, a mere star in the galaxy of fine baseball pitchers.

GROVER CLEVELAND ALEXANDER

The 1926 Chicago Cubs were in a bad slump. Manager Joe McCarthy was fed up with the off-the-field antics of his ballclub, particularly with their affinity for tipping the bottle and staying out all hours of the night.

Finally, "Marse Joe" reached the breaking point and called a team meeting designed to end the slump—and the drinking. After a lengthy sermon about the evils of alcohol, McCarthy closed the meeting with what he hoped would be an impressive demonstration of the effects of liquor.

He removed a pair of worms from a container, and dropped one into a jar of water. The worm squirmed around, seemingly savoring its fluid environment.

The second worm was less fortunate. McCarthy dropped it into a vial of gin, where it thrashed about in obvious agony, and quickly died.

Turning to Grover Cleveland Alexander, McCarthy cast a baleful look at his star hurler and asked, "Alex, have I proved my point?"

"If you're trying to tell me that I'm nothing but a worm, I've got nothing to say," Alexander replied. "The only other thing you've proved to me is that if you drink gin, you won't have worms."

The clubhouse exploded with laughter . . . and Alexander was traded the next day!

How could a man who suffered from epilepsy and alcoholism even make it to the major leagues, let alone win a National League record 373 games?

For 50 years, the baseball world has marveled at the accomplishments of the right-handed control artist who dominated the National League for 15 consecutive years, Grover Cleveland (Alex) Alexander.

And when fans learn that the sandy-haired farm boy from Gale, Nebraska, also suffered attacks of double vision, lost the hearing in his left ear when he was 31 years old, and divorced and remarried his lovely wife, Aimee, twice, they often wonder if Alex really existed!

No one will ever come up with an explanation of how the 5'11" superstar did it, but Alex was clearly among the greatest pitchers in baseball history. He exploded onto the major league scene with the Philadelphia Phillies, posting a 28-13 mark. His best pitches were a "whiplash curve" (similar to the slider), a good changeup, and a sneaky fastball that he generally kept out of the strike zone so as to tease the batter. But the real key to his success was his remarkable control.

"He was so easy to catch that one day I tossed away my mitt and used an empty can," his former batterymate and manager, Bill Killifer, recalled. "It was during practice, of course. I crouched behind the plate, and gave him the can for a target. Alex fired, and hit the can's opening, dead on. I began moving the can around the strike zone, and Alex hit it 41 times, perfect. Sounds incredible, but it's true."

From 1915 to 1917, Alexander strung together three of the finest seasons in the history of modern baseball: 31-10 (1.22 ERA), 33-12 (1.55), and 30-13 (1.86), a three-year winning percentage of .729. That 1916 season included 16 shutouts, a single-season record that remains unapproached to this day (Bob Gibson and Jack Coombs had 13, and Alex is next with 12 in 1915!). He also pitched and won a doubleheader against the Reds, beating them 1-0 in 58 minutes in the second game. His seven-year record with the Phillies (190-88, a .683 winning percentage, and ERA under 2.19) is all the more impressive because his home ballpark was tiny Baker Bowl, where straightaway right field was 275 feet. (No wonder the second baseman often collided with the right fielder when going back after pop flies.)

After the 1917 season, Alex was traded to the Cubs, but America's entry into World War I ended his season at 2-1 in May. He returned from Europe in 1919, posted a 16-11 mark, and continued his winning ways in Chicago until 1926, when Joe McCarthy took over the managerial duties.

The pair began feuding in spring training, with McCarthy the disciplinarian battling Alexander, the free-liver and free-drinker. When Alex broke his leg and was hospitalized for about three weeks, every member of the team came to visit him regularly, except McCarthy. Not only did McCarthy refuse to visit his pitcher, but

Grover Cleveland Alexander

McCarthy also forced the injured hurler to come to every spring training game, cast, crutches, and all.

Alex dug himself deeper into McCarthy's doghouse when he fell asleep during a team meeting to discuss changing the catcher's signs. (Rabbit Maranville, a former Cub, was now with the Braves, and sign-stealing was a popular art.) When Alex awakened, he told the group that there was "no need to worry about it because Rabbit will never get to second, anyway." That remark, combined with the worm tale recounted at the start of the chapter, resulted in his exile to the Cardinals. His 3–3 record with the Cubs seemed to support McCarthy's contention that Alex was "washed up" (or soaked through, as the case may have been).

But McCarthy was wrong. Alex went 9–7 for St. Louis in the second half of the season, and led the Redbirds to the pennant.

More importantly, the trade also set up Alexander's leap into superstardom, the great moment which guaranteed him the immortality his pitching deserved: game seven of the 1926 World Series.

After evening the Series at three games apiece by defeating the Yankees, 10–2, on an eight-hitter (Alex had also won game two, 6–2, allowing just four hits), Alexander was warned by manager Rogers Hornsby that he should delay his celebrating until after game seven because he might be needed as a reliever.

Legend has it that Alex ignored the warning, celebrated all night, and crawled into the ballpark with the ultimate hangover. Alexander always denied it.

"I told Rog that I'd stay with him that night," the late Hall-of-Famer recalled. "And that's what I did. We had dinner together, sat around talking for a few hours, and then went to sleep.

"The next morning, he told me that Haines was starting, and that I should be ready. Jess went great until the sixth, when a blister began bothering him, so Bill Sherdel and I began warming up. Rog called me in during the seventh.

"In [the old] Yankee Stadium, you couldn't see the game from the visitor's bullpen," he continued, "so when I got to the mound, Rog told me that there were two outs, that we were still ahead 3–2, but that the bases were loaded and Tony Lazzeri [an epileptic himself] was at-bat.

"Now you know that Rog was always a no-nonsense guy. If I were hung over, do you think he'd have let me pitch in that situation?"

The point is well made, but the cynic will point out that Alex had pitched, and won, many a game in worse condition.

"I told Rog that I was all right," Alex continued, "and that there was nothing to do except give Lazzeri hell. He asked me how I planned to do it, and I said I'd throw him two curves, and then an inside fastball, and then come back with an outside curve.

Rog didn't like the idea of letting Lazzeri see any fastballs because Lazzeri murdered them. We argued briefly, and then Rog said, 'You're the pitcher, you know what to do.'

"The count was 1-1 when I threw the fastball, and I got it too close to the plate. Lazzeri slammed it down the left field line, but it curved foul at the last second. I could feel Rog staring me down from second base, but I wasn't about to change my plan. The next pitch was a curve that I started at the center of the plate so that by the time it reached home it would be breaking sharply, outside the strike zone. I figured that even if Lazzeri took it, the count would be 2-2. But he swung and missed, and no one will ever forget it."

Alex retired the next five batters, and faced Babe Ruth with two outs in the ninth. Ruth worked out a walk on a very close three-two pitch, but was thrown out stealing while another very tough power hitter, Bob Meusel, was at-bat. It was the only baserunning mistake of Ruth's career, and the Babe always claimed he gambled on the element of surprise—a poor excuse because Meusel was a lifetime .309 hitter.

Friends urged Alex to retire as a hero after the Series. He would turn 40 in February 1927, and desperately needed to "dry out," but Alex ignored their advice and turned in a 21-10 record, his ninth and final 20-win season. Nagging injuries and bad health dropped him to 16-9 in '28, and down to 9-8 in '29. He was released at the end of the season, caught on with the Phillies, and went 0-3 before he violated his promise to stay dry and was released. A dismal end to a great career.

When Alexander's habits and ailments finally drove him from the major leagues, he led the National league in career wins (373), shutouts (90), complete games (439), innings pitched (5,189⅓), and appearances (696). The only comparable pitchers were Cy Young (who won many of his 511 games before the turn of the century) and Walter Johnson (who holds several of the major league records for shutouts), both American Leaguers; and Christy Mathewson, the ace of the New York Giants, who did all of his pitching during the dead ball era.

The first of Alex's records to be equalled was the career win mark. A scorer's error was discovered years after Mathewson's death, giving him one more win, and a 373-188 mark (to Alex's 373-208). As the years went by, the other records fell, leaving him with only the National League record for career shutouts, and the major league record for shutouts in one season.

But the passage of time, and surpassing of his records, have done little to dim the memories of those who saw "Alex the Great" mow down hitter after hitter with that easy sidearmed motion of his. And for those who never saw Alex in real life, an accurate portrayal of his life ("The Winning Team," starring Ronald Reagan and Doris Day) hits the television screens at least two or three times a year, and helps perpetuate the legend.

Unfortunately, Alex's image remains tarnished, indeed rusted through, by his well-publicized drinking, but he was so personable, enjoyed such extended success, and was articulate enough that he kept himself well within the public eye. In fact, the public was always willing to overlook his drinking—something it refused to do for many of his contemporaries, such as Hack Wilson, the Chicago Cubs star who was denied a place in the baseball Hall of Fame for years—but Alex was elected in 1939, the year the Hall opened. When he finally revealed the dual nature of his health problems, and admitted that his daily routine consisted of "two shots upon awakening, a shot after brushing his teeth, and more drinking at the clubhouse before the game," the revelations were front page news items—almost 15 years after his retirement.

Exactly when, and why, Alex first took to the bottle is one secret he never revealed. Speculation is that it coincided with the first series of epileptic attacks he suffered in 1908, following a severe beaning in the minor leagues (the same beaning which left him with double vision for more than a year). Certainly, his experiences in the trenches in World War I could not have helped, and when he returned from "the war to end all wars," he found himself fighting a battle against the bottle, a battle he never won.

Only once during his major league career did Alexander suffer an epileptic seizure on the mound. It came in 1926, against the Phillies, and it struck the pitcher as he entered his windup. Somehow, Alex completed the two-strike pitch, and the startled batter, Don Hurst, took it for a called strike three! The newspapers reported Alex's collapse on the mound as "dizziness."

"Perhaps a lot of the collapses and nights in the gutter were caused by epilepsy," Killifer said, years after Alex passed away, "but I remember one day when he staggered into the dugout about 15 minutes before game time on a day on which he was scheduled to pitch. I was the manager, and I told him he was pitching, regardless of his condition. He turned around and said, 'Who said I wasn't, Bill old boy?' Of course, he tossed a one-hit shutout."

The tragedy of Alexander came to the forefront soon after the end of his major league career. For a while, he bounced around in the minor leagues and with semipro teams, but his drinking was too much for even the bushes to handle. Less desirable forms of employment followed, until he was reduced to telling crowds about his pitching feats as a lecturer in a flea circus sideshow. Everywhere he went, his name was in the headlines, usually because he had been found lying in the street somewhere. He rapidly became an embarrassment to baseball, prompting former National League President Ford Frick to wire Cardinals owner Sam Breadon: "Is there anything we can do about Alexander?"

The equally flabbergasted Breadon later admitted that he had been sending Alex a pension of $100 a month, more than enough for a man to live on—or drink on, as the case was. Breadon, Frick, and Aimee finally got together, and agreed on one thing:

Alex had to be "dried out." They found him, brought him back to Nebraska, got him off the bottle temporarily, and began the search for gainful employment on his behalf. He began promoting recreation for youths, and was enjoying himself more than he had since his major league days until some "friends" convinced him to join them for a few brews in Burwell, Nebraska. The "few" turned into 36, and Alex was sent home. In 1939, Frick intervened again, setting Alexander up with the managerial job at the San Diego franchise in the Pacific Coast League, but Alex went out to celebrate and never showed up to cement the deal.

During World War II, Alex worked in a factory, manufacturing bombs and airplane parts. His health began to improve—he may have even gone off the bottle completely—but, ironically, another health problem struck him down: cancer. He died on November 4, 1950, ending 63 years of a life of hardship. The coroner's report is rumored to have read, in part: "Based on the condition of this man's liver, he has been dead for 10 years."

Grover Cleveland Alexander had no trouble with Ruth, Hornsby, Lazzeri, or Wagner. In fact, only one man ever got the best of the late Hall-of-Famer: Alex, himself.

This rare photo of a young Ty Cobb was taken during a game at Hilltop Park in 1908.

A posed "action shot" of Ty Cobb taken on March 16, 1921, during spring training.

In 1969, former Pittsburgh Pirate Honus Wagner was the unanimous choice of a panel of 100 sportswriters as the "Greatest Shortstop Ever," and with good reason. The incredibly popular "Flying Dutchman" batted .328 during his 21-year career, while setting the standards for speed and defense at that position.

Rogers Hornsby

Babe Ruth slides safely into second base while Rogers Hornsby clutches the late relay throw.

(below) Rogers Hornsby is on his way to first base after singling to right field during the 1926 World Series.

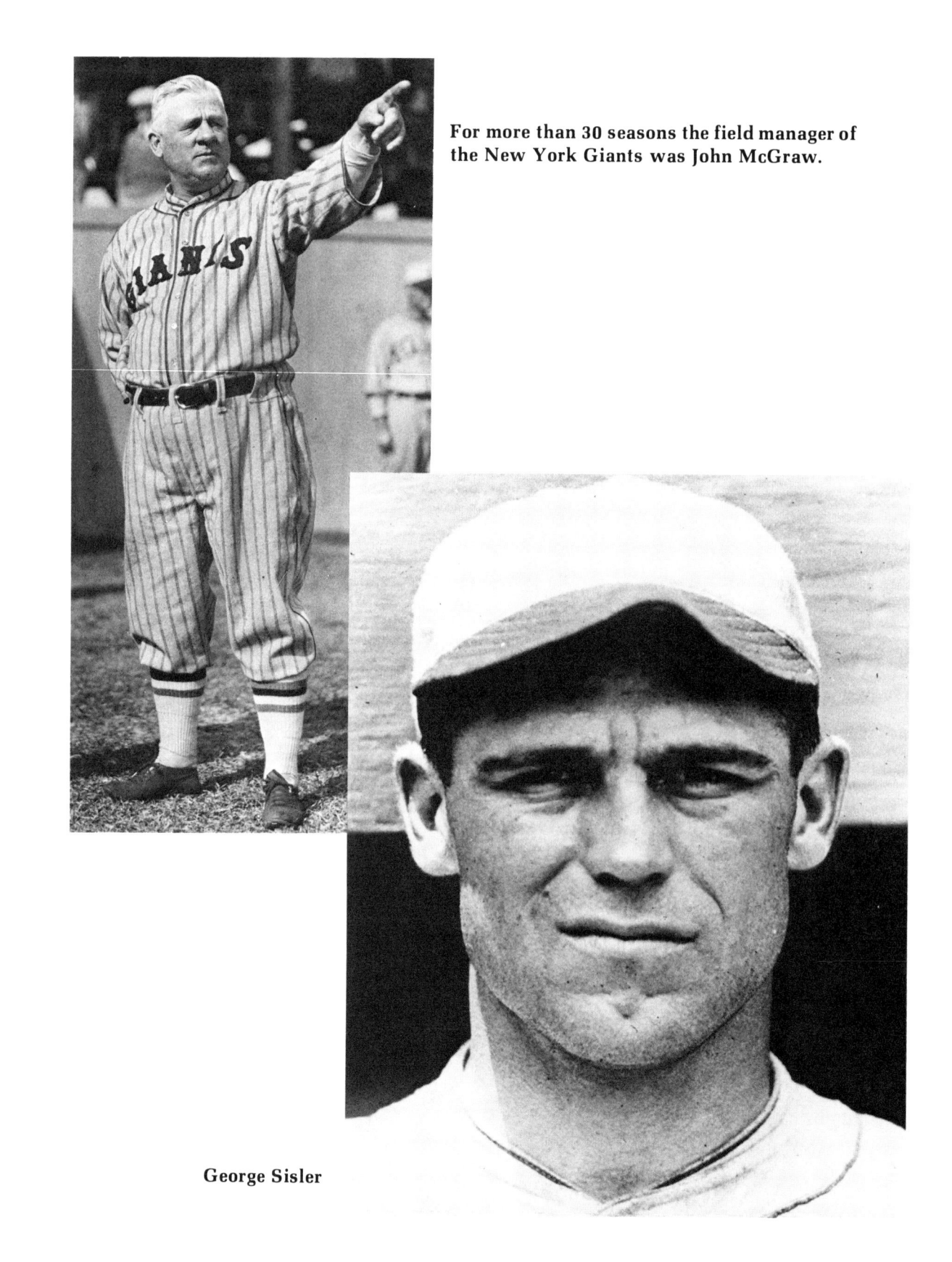

For more than 30 seasons the field manager of the New York Giants was John McGraw.

George Sisler

Hall of Famers Lou Gehrig (left), Jimmie Foxx, and Babe Ruth at Yankee Stadium in 1932.

Mickey Cochrane

ヴーログ　グツリーゲ　ズンモシ　ンーレクカ
(け投名の一界世)　(モンク・ハーホ)　(王打安)　(手捕名の一界世)
社聞新賣讀 催主手選會大球野米日秋今

(top) Hall of Famers (left to right) Lefty Grove, Lou Gehrig, Al Simmons, and Mickey Cochrane graced the cover of the Japanese Baseball Souvenir Program issued during the Connie Mack All-Star team's trip to Japan in 1933. (Courtesy of Baseball Hall of Fame)

(right) One of the stars of the Yankees of the '30s was Ben Chapman, a fine baserunner who also played for the Boston Red Sox and the Washington Senators.

This remarkable photograph was taken prior to the 1937 All-Star Game at Griffith Stadium, Washington. Pictured were seven top-ranking American League stars... and every one of them eventually was voted into the Baseball Hall of Fame at Cooperstown, N.Y. Left to right are Lou Gehrig, Joe Cronin (president of the American League in 1962), Bill Dickey, Joe DiMaggio, Charley Gehringer, Jimmie Foxx, and Hank Greenberg. The American Leaguers won the game, 8-3.

A smiling Duke Snider, the star centerfielder of the Brooklyn Dodgers.

A real rarity: an autographed picture of Grover Cleveland Alexander (the second winningest pitcher in major league history) and of the Yankees' Bob Shawkey (at the tail end of his 15-year career), taken prior to the sixth game of the 1926 World Series. Alexander outpitched Shawkey and beat the Yankees 10-2.

Walter Johnson set a major league record by striking out 3,508 batters in his 21-year career with the Washington Senators.

This series of rare photographs shows Babe Ruth batting against Hall of Famer Walter Johnson at a Yankee Stadium benefit for War Bonds during 1942. More than 60,000 fans came out to watch Ruth in what proved to be his final at-bats at Yankee Stadium. Here, the Babe gets ready to receive Johnson's 21st pitch . . .

. . . and Ruth swings, and drives the ball deep into the upper deck in right field. Although the ball hooked a few feet foul, the exhausted Ruth knew it would be his best shot, so he circled the bases for the final time in Yankee Stadium . . .

. . . while Walter Johnson looks on, smiling at Ruth's antics (for the first time in Johnson's career).

Walter Johnson

An unsmiling Dean poses for photographers after learning that his suspension for insubordination will be enforced by Cardinal management.

(left) Dizzy Dean's career continued behind the microphone after his pitching days were over. *(Photo by Todd Studios)*

(below) Hall of Fame hurler Dizzy Dean interviews fireballer, and future Hall of Famer, Bob Feller at Yankee Stadium. *(Photo by Bob Ohlen)*

Lefty Grove

"He was the meanest pitcher I ever faced," Hank Aaron said, when the name of Don Drysdale came up. "He was never afraid to pitch inside and high. He was tough."

(top) Hall of Famers Whitey Ford (left) and Sandy Koufax pose for reporters prior to the start of the 1963 World Series. *(Photo by Bob Ohlen)*

(left) Mel Stottlemyre delivers his classic sinker during a 1968 spring training game against the Orioles.

(above) Mel Stottlemyre crosses home plate after hitting his fifth career home run. *(Photo by Louis Requena)*

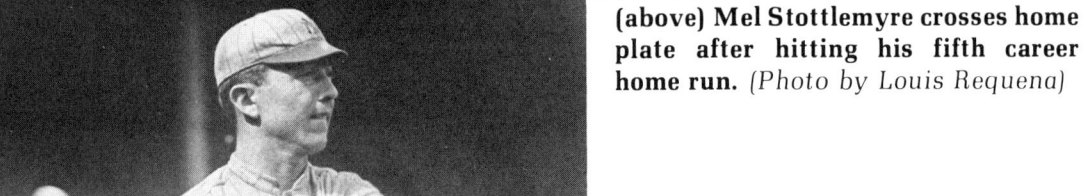

(left) "Home Run" Baker takes a batting practice swing at the Polo Grounds in 1921. Baker spent his final 6 major league seasons in a Yankee uniform. Despite the sobriquette to the contrary, Baker's home runs in a New York uniform were few and far between — he managed just 48 home runs in six Yankee years, and totalled a mere 93 for his career... but two of them came in the 1911 World Series and vaulted him into immortality.

"One ball, two strikes, two outs, bottom of the ninth inning. Larsen takes the sign and delivers to pinch hitter Dale Mitchell. Strike three! A no-hitter, a perfect game . . ." For Don Larsen, a perfect game in the World Series and instant immortality.

(left) a wildly enthusiastic Yogi Berra jumps aboard Don Larsen to celebrate the final out of the immortal perfect game that lifted Larsen into the ranks of the heroes.

(right) An autographed picture of Yankee righthander Don Larsen.

(below) A triumphant Chris Chambliss trots the final 90 feet to home plate after hitting the pennant-winning home run that vaulted him into immortality.

WALTER JOHNSON

"The big, raw rookie just took a short wind-up and let go with that ball," recalled Ed Delahanty, a member of the 1907 Senators, and the first major leaguer to face the flamethrowing Walter Johnson, albeit in batting practice. "I never had a chance to swing. The pitch was in the catcher's hands before I knew it had left Johnson's."

"When he came back with another just like it, I lay down my bat, walked over to our manager, Joe Cantillon, and said, 'I'm through.'"

"What's he got?" asked Cantillon. "Has he got a fast one?"

"Has he a fast one?" I replied. "No human being ever threw one as fast before."

"Has he got a curve?" the manager asked.

"I don't know, and I don't care," Delahanty replied. "What's more, I am not going back to bat against that guy until I learn how good his control is. From now on, he can pitch for me, but not to me."

Consider this: for the first 15 years of his career, every pitch Walter Johnson threw was a straight fastball.

Furthermore, it was common knowledge that "Barney," or "The Big Train," as Johnson was alternately known, not only refused to brush back hitters who crowded the plate, but was actually scared to death that one of his pitches would accidentally cripple or kill someone. In fact, Johnson once left a ballgame because he was too upset about an accidental beaning to continue!

What's the point? Simple: Every hitter knew exactly what was coming, knew that the pitch would come straight as an arrow, knew he could fearlessly dig in and crowd the plate . . . and still, they couldn't hit Walter Johnson!

Johnson spent 21 years (1907-27) in the major leagues, all of them with the Washington Senators. Despite the club's overall lack of success (they finished under .500 in 10 of those 21 years), Johnson won 416 games, lost 279, and compiled a 2.17 earned run average. He won 32.7 percent of the 1,359 games the Senators won during his career! "The Big Train" also managed to set two all-time marks which have withstood the test of time: career strikeouts (3,508) and shutouts (113). The runner-up in strikeouts is Gaylord Perry, who has struck out 3.336 batters, while Grover Cleveland Alexander ranks second in shutouts with 90 in 20 years. Johnson also led the league in strikeouts 12 times, including 8 straight from 1912-19.

Unfortunately, despite a string of 10 consecutive years in which Johnson won 20 or more games, the Senators did not win the pennant until 1924, when the 36-year-old righty was well past his prime, but still managed to lead the American League with a 23-7 record, 2.72 ERA, and 158 strikeouts. During the World Series against the Giants, he captured the hearts of the entire nation when, after heart-breaking losses in games one (4-3 in 12 innings) and four (6-2), he came on in relief to win game seven.

Born on November 6, 1887, in Humboldt, Kansas, the legendary flamethrower was one of six children in a Scotch-German family. He spent his winters in California, where he attracted plenty of attention as a fastball pitcher for the Fullerton High School team. In 1906, he signed with Tacoma of the Pacific Coast League, pitched a 10-inning exhibition game, and was released for "inexperience." Several other minor league clubs expressed an interest, but each feared the youngster's wildness, and declined to sign him.

Fate intervened here. Cliff Blackenship, a forgotten Senator who is not even listed in the Baseball Encyclopedia, injured his arm and was sent home early in the 1907 season. He had been instructed to look at outfielder Clyde Milan (1907-22, .285 batting average, Senators) in Wichita, Kansas, and if the opportunity presented itself, to check out a "kid named Johnson, who a local liquor salesman has been bugging us about." Blackenship was impressed with both ballplayers, and easily signed Milan, but Johnson presented a problem. The future Hall-of-Famer was only 19 years old (a minor by state law) and could not legally sign a contract, so Blackenship joined Johnson for a train ride back to Fullerton, California, and a meeting with Walter's Mom. After an hour or so of discussion, he came away with her signature, in return for a $100 signing bonus, $350/month for three months, a free return trip ticket if he failed to make the team, and Blackenship's promise to act as a chaperon.

"Best damned deal we ever did make," Manager Joe Cantillon remarked years later.

"And to think that the owners of the ballclub were furious at the $100 bonus. We got the best pitcher in history for next to nothing."

Johnson made his debut on August 2, 1907, losing to the Tigers, 3–2, in Washington. He struck out 3, walked 1, and allowed 10 hits, including a series of bunts by Ty Cobb and company which ultimately cost him the game. Afterwards, Johnson headed back to the hotel in his baseball uniform, followed by a curious crowd.

"I didn't know the team provided a bus for the players," he later laughed. "They say rookies are supposed to be green, and I guess I was the greenest one of all. Why, that same night, I was standing on the street, looking at an illuminated sign that read 'Johnson Hotel,' when a stranger came by and said, 'You're famous, kid. They've already named a hotel for you.' Do you know that I honestly believed him!"

Although a loser in his first outing, Johnson had made a permanent impression on the Washington fans with his incredible velocity. Contrary to today's notions of what a flamethrower looks like, the sandy-haired, 6'1", 200-pounder did not use an overhand delivery. Instead, he combined a big windup with a large kick, and threw across his body in a near-underhand motion that sent the ball whizzing toward the plate like a snapping whip. Everywhere he went, people began coming out to see the fastest man in baseball history, and he became a national celebrity overnight. Fortunately, the kid from Fullerton was not overwhelmed by the sudden publicity, and quickly developed a warm style for dealing with the fans.

Typical was the story told by Johnson's batterymate, Gabby Street.

"We were walking home from the ballpark when a man came up to Barney and said he knew Barney's sister," Street recalled. "They wound up talking for 20 minutes, and when it finally ended, I said to Barney, 'I never knew you had a sister.' Well, he turns around and tells me 'I don't, but I had to be nice to the man. He's one of my fans."

For all the fanfare, Johnson's 1907 record was only 5–9, but with 70 strikeouts and 17 walks in 110⅔ innings, and a sparkling 1.87 ERA.

The Big Train's first great feat occurred in September 1908, when he shut out the Highlanders on three consecutive playing dates. The string began on Friday, Sept. 4, with a six-hit, 3–0 win. On Saturday, Johnson tossed a four-hitter, winning 6–0, and after the mandatory day off on Sunday (the Blue Laws prohibited Sunday baseball), he hurled a two-hit 4–0 win in the opening game of the Labor Day doubleheader. When Manager Cantillon tabbed him to start the second game, too, Johnson put on his civies and hid under the grandstand.

"A big strong fellow like him ought to pitch two games in one day," Cantillon told reporters. "Besides, he's really got their number."

Johnson finished the year 14–14, with a 1.64 ERA and 160 strikeouts.

The 1909 season would feature another unique outing for the increasingly popular hurler. His regular batterymate, Gabby Street, suffered a wrist injury in mid-season, and the Senators acquired a semipro from New York named Heinie Beckendorf. Johnson's blazer proved too much for the rookie, and in his first game seven strikeout victims reached first base safely when Heinie couldn't hold on to the ball!

By 1910, Johnson knew the hitters and the league. He skyrocked to 25-17 (1.35 ERA and 313 strikeouts), but the Senators remained mired in seventh place, 65-85. He duplicated the win total in 1911, while losing only 13 games, but Washington dropped to 64-90.

As things turned out, that was only the beginning. For the combined years of 1912 and 1913, Johnson pitched in 98 games, winning 68, losing 19, recording a 1.12 ERA, 546 strikeouts, and 114 walks. No pitcher in major league history has approached the total dominance evidenced by those statistics. Mathewson went 64-20 in 1904-5, but his ERA was close to 1.80 and he only struck out 418 batters. Alexander's best was 64-22 with a 1.39 ERA and 408 strikeouts. Sandy Koufax was at his best in 1965-66, when he combined for 53 wins, a 1.88 ERA, and 699 strikeouts.

At one point, Johnson had recorded 16 straight wins. The streak ended on a scoring technicality that credited him with a loss in a game for which he would go to no decision today. He relieved the starter with the bases loaded, and the score tied. A wild pitch allowed one run, a single the other, and the Senators went on to lose by one run. (The Browns bombed him in his next outing, so the point may be insignificant.) Over that 16-game stretch, Johnson struck out 103, walked 20, and included a streak of 56 consecutive scoreless innings.

For his efforts over those two years, Johnson received $7,000 per annum, plus bonuses for postseason exhibition tours. It was on one such tour that he faced Christy Mathewson for the only time in his career, and Johnson emerged on top, 8-0.

Johnson "slumped" to 28-18 the following year, and nearly parted ways with the Senators when the Chicago Federal League team offered him a $16,000 salary plus a $10,000 bonus to sign with them for 1915. His loyalty to Washington wavered, and when Senators President Ben Minor heard about the offer, he told Johnson that he was not worth the 12 grand he had received in 1914 because he had won only 28 games. Walter was furious, and packed his bags, but manager Clark Griffith played on Mrs. Johnson's love for Washington, D.C., and personally guaranteed to match the Fed's offer, in order to keep him. The team's board of directors reluctantly agreed to match the $16,000 salary, but absolutely refused to pay Johnson the signing bonus. Griffith knew there was more than one way to skin a cat, so he told White Sox owner Charles Comiskey about the Chicago offer. Comiskey forked over the $10,000 rather than risk having Johnson pitching in the new league in his own backyard.

By the start of the 1920 season, Johnson had won 296 games, but had yet to toss a no-hitter or appear in a World Series. He achieved the former on July 1, stopping the

Red Sox in Boston, 1–0. Only an error by shortstop Bucky Harris prevented Johnson from attaining perfection.

The 1920 season also featured one of the tragic ironies of baseball history, as reported by Bob Broeg and confirmed first-hand by Stan Coveleski and second-hand by Joe Sewell. In an early season game, Johnson faced Cleveland shortstop Ray Chapman. His first pitch was a blue dart fastball for a called strike one. When the second pitch was a clone of the first, Chapman turned away and headed for the dugout.

"That's only two," yelled umpire Bill Evans.

"I know it," Chapman replied. "You can have the next one. What do you think I want to do, get killed?"

Less than three months later, Chapman was beaned by Carl Mays, and died of a fractured skull.

In 1923, "Barney" pitched his 100th career shutout, and it came in the same game in which the Yankees Everett Scott played his 1000th consecutive game, then a record.

And in 1924, at the age of 36, the Senators edged out the Yankees by two games and got Johnson into his first World Series.

Walter was on the mound to open the Series in Washington, and for 11 innings he matched Giants ace Art Nehf, pitch for pitch, striking out 12 and allowing 14 hits. In the 12th, New York finally broke the 3–3 tie on a hit by Ross Youngs, and the Giants won the ballgame.

Johnson was back on the mound for game five, and again came out a loser, this time by a 6–2 margin. He was tatooed for 13 hits, including a two-run homerun by pitcher Jack Bentley, and four hits by Fred Lindstrom. When he trudged off the field after the eighth inning, the Polo Grounds crowd gave him a resounding 10-minute standing ovation. No one in that crowd could have suspected that Walter would be back in a relief role in game seven.

Just as Lindstrom had had a key effect on Johnson's failure in game five, he would have an equally important effect on his success in game seven. Washington entered the bottom of the eighth inning trailing 3–1. With two outs and two men on base, Bucky Harris hit a ground ball to third that struck a pebble and bounced high over Lindstrom's head, enabling the Senators to tie the score.

When Johnson came in from the bullpen to start the ninth inning, the fans went wild. With one out in the ninth, Frankie Frisch tripled, but Johnson struck out George Kelly and got Irish Meusel to bounce out. In the tenth, Hack Wilson worked Johnson for a walk, but the veteran enticed Ross Youngs to hit into a double play. He also survived lead-off singles in the 11th and 12th, and by the time Washington came to bat in the 12th, the crowd doubted that Johnson could last much longer.

With one out, catcher Hank Gowdy dropped Muddy Ruel's pop foul, and Ruel took advantage of the reprieve to double to left field. The next batter was Walter himself, and the fans rose in mass, applauding his valiant efforts. They gasped when he slapped a ground ball to short, but cheered in unison when Travis Jackson bobbled it. The exhausted Johnson perched on first, again to the tune of a standing ovation.

Earl McNeely followed with a ground ball to third for what should have been the inning-ending double play, but the ball found that pebble again, hopped over Linstrom's head, and made Johnson a winner.

"Our clubhouse was a madhouse," Johnson recalled. "I felt like having a good cry, and I'm not ashamed to admit it. Only two days previous, the fans in New York gave me that ovation when I was knocked out. They meant it to be sympathetic, and even I thought I was through, that I'd never win a World Series game.

"But then came this last chance," he continued. "It seemed my entire baseball reputation depended on those four innings. I knew what everybody expected of me. I saw my wife, my mother, the President, the thousands of loyal fans.

"I was tired, but when Kelly fanned, I felt stronger. When I got him again in the 12th, I felt nothing could beat me. Then, before I realized it, I was sitting in the clubhouse, worn out and dazed, but oh so happy. I was more nervous after that game than I was in my first game, 18 years before."

Johnson's luck was reversed in the 1925 Series against Pittsburgh. He stopped the Pirates in games one (4–1, on five hits and 10 strikeouts) and four (4–0 on six hits), but ran out of gas in game seven (a 9–7 loss in the mud and rain in which he allowed 15 hits). That was the World Series in which shortstop Roger Peckinpaugh made eight errors and cost his club the championship.

"I felt terrible for Roger and our fans," Johnson told reporters after the Series was over. "When he hit that homerun in the seventh game, I was happier than I could have imagined, but it didn't hold up."

The 1926 season opened with Johnson on the mound, outdueling Chicago's Ed Rommel, 1–0, in a 15-inning marathon. It ended with the 38-year-old veteran showing a 15–16 mark, with a 3.61 ERA and only 125 strikeouts. He thought about retiring, but returned for spring training and looked better than he had for two years, when a line drive off the bat of Joe Judge fractured Johnson's right leg. When he recovered, he was not the same pitcher. He finished the year 5–6 with a 5.10 ERA, and rather than risk embarrassing himself, elected to call it a career.

In 1927, he managed the Newark Bears, a top-flight farm club, and made his only minor league pitching appearance. It was on Walter Johnson Day, and the management had announced that the 40-year-old superstar would be the starting pitcher. Johnson went along with the gimmick only so far—he walked lead-off hitter Maurice Archdeacon, and removed himself from the ballgame.

In 1929, the Senators summoned him to Washington, where he took over the managerial chores and led the club to a fifth-place finish. In 1930, Johnson inspired them to a second-place landing, followed by consecutive third-place finishes in '31 and '32. For reasons which remain obscure, his contract was not renewed for 1932, so he went to Cleveland, where he led the Indians to fifth-, third-, and fifth-place finishes over the next three seasons. His final managerial record added up to 530–432, and he summed it up by telling reporters, "Anybody can manage if he's got the players."

Johnson more or less faded from the major league scene, but continued to garner headlines everywhere he went. In 1942, when the nation needed money for war bonds, the American League looked to Johnson for help. The Yankees held a War Bonds Day at the Stadium, featuring a duel between Babe Ruth and Johnson. Johnson threw 21 pitches, and Ruth knocked the last one deep into the upper deck in right field, but foul by several feet. The Babe and Johnson were both exhausted by then, so Ruth trotted around the bases, and they both left the field to lengthy ovations.

It proved to be Johnson's last appearance on the field. His final visit to a ballpark came in 1946, when he watched Bob Feller fire his version of the fastball past American League batters. Naturally, comparisons had to be made, and the usually modest Johnson reluctantly told sportswriter Shirley Povich that he was faster than Feller.

"I am sure that I had more speed," Johnson stated. "But, Feller is probably more difficult to hit because of his overhand motion. I threw near-underhand, and that enabled the hitter to follow the ball all the way. His pitch comes out of his uniform, and is hard to pick up."

Which brings us to the ever-popular argument: Who was the fastest pitcher of all time? The ancients will tab Amos Rusie, a turn-of-the-century member of the New York Giants who struck out 1,957 and walked 1,716 during his 10-year career (1889–1901, 243–160, estimated 3.07 ERA), but he lacked Johnson's longevity. According to John McGraw, he also lacked Johnson's speed.

"Rusie was fast, but Johnson had a little more zip on his ball," the Giants manager told reporters during the 1924 World Series. "Also, when Rusie hurt his arm, he was finished. When Johnson got older, he made the adjustment and developed a fine curveball."

Those who remember Lefty Grove in his prime never fail to mention him as a top flamethrower. His statistics are impressive: 300 wins, 140 losses, 2,266 strikeouts, 1,187 walks, and a 3.06 ERA over a 17-year career.

The middle-aged fans always name Bob Feller: 266–162, 2,581 strikeouts, 1,764 walks, and a 3.25 ERA.

Younger folks pick Sandy Koufax: 165–87, 2,396 strikeouts, 817 walks, 2.76 ERA, 12 years.

Today's fans offer Nolan Ryan.

One man who has seen all of them (except Rusie) is Joe Sewell, himself a Hall-of-Famer, and one of the toughest men to strike out in baseball history (114 strikeouts in 7,132 at-bats).

"Nolan Ryan is the closest to Johnson," Sewell said in 1979. "Occasionally, he throws a pitch or two that compare to Johnson, but that's the difference. Johnson threw every pitch at that speed for 15 or 16 years, while Ryan can approach that speed only once in a while.

"Grove was fast, mean, and had other pitches that made him very effective," he continued. "Joe Wood had only two great years, hurt his arm, and was never the same. Koufax also had a hard curve, and he just wasn't as fast as Johnson, although he may have been tougher to hit because of his over-the-top delivery. I'll take Johnson over all of them, for his speed, and his record.

"There's one other thing you might consider," Sewell added. "For most of Johnson's career, and certainly for the first 15 years of it, most of the ballplayers were not free-swinging types looking for homeruns. They took shorter cuts, and just tried to meet the ball. It's a lot harder to strike someone out when they're just trying to lay a piece of wood on the pitch, rather than swinging from their heels. Today, Johnson would probably strike out 20 men a game, because everyone's trying to hit homeruns."

When Walter Johnson died of a brain tumor and heart attack on December 10, 1946, he was the second winningest pitcher in baseball history, the top strikeout man, the leader in shutouts, ranked second in games pitched, third in total innings, fifth in complete games and seventh in ERA. Today, he still owns the strikeout and shutout marks, remains second in wins, third in innings, fifth in complete games, and seventh in ERA. Only the advent of the relief pitcher has pushed him down in total games (sixth).

A superstar is one who not only demonstrates great ability on the field, but whose feats and records withstand the test of time. Clearly, Johnson qualifies on the statistical side. Furthermore, he remains the standard against which all fastball pitchers are compared, even though he was never electronically clocked. When he finally got into a World Series, a whole nation was rooting for him, and when he came on in relief to win the seventh game, the nation celebrated as one. He was a living legend, and remains a legend to this day, a true superstar in every sense of the word.

EDDIE PLANK

> He was not the fastest, not the trickiest, and not the possessor of the most stuff. He was just the greatest.
> —Eddie Collins, Hall-of-Famer

Trivia fans will note that, when Warren Spahn won his 328th game in 1963, he became the winningest southpaw in major league history. For substantial bonus points, whose record of 327 wins did he break?

Need a hint? Our mystery man spent 17 years in the big leagues, 14 of them with the Philadelphia Athletics. He hurled 69 shutouts (fifth on the all time list), finished with a 2.34 ERA, and won 20 or more games eight times. When he was traded to the Yankees after the 1917 season, he refused to report, preferring retirement to New York, but was so highly thought of that Miller Huggins offered him a three-year contract a year later—when the southpaw was 44 years old!

Flabbergasted? Did you guess Lefty Grove? Sorry, but Grove only won 300 games.

Let's add to the frustration a bit. Consider this: This Hall-of-Famer never played baseball until he was 16 years old, never pitched until he was nearly 18, and did not even reach the major leagues until he was almost 26 . . . but in 17 years he compiled a .630 winning percentage (327–192), and ranks ninth in career wins.

The name of the mystery man: Edward "The Gettysburg Guide" Plank.

Born on August 31, 1875, the 5′10½″ 175-pounder always insisted that his life began when he entered Gettysburg College in 1896, and based on the absence of information about his boyhood days, he may have been right. The files at the Baseball Hall of Fame reveal nothing about his early years; in fact, considering the man's achievements, the files are rather empty.

Fortunately for Plank, the baseball coach at Gettysburg was former major leaguer Frank Foreman, a moderately successful nineteenth century pitcher who was an old friend of Connie Mack. As Plank racked up win after win in the college ranks, Foreman began wiring Mack about his ace. Mack had enough confidence in his old friend to offer Plank a contract without ever seeing him pitch!

Eddie insisted on finishing his education first, and did not join the A's until 1901. He immediately impressed the manager with his control, wide assortment of pitches, and a seeming indifference to pressure situations. Plank usually threw in a three-quarter-arm motion, but frequently mixed in a sidearm whip motion that uncoiled a vicious fastball which usually found a home under the batter's chin.

Not everything the overaged rookie did pleased Mack. "I never could get used to all of his antics out there on the mound," Connie told reporters years after Plank's death. "Sure, he distracted the other team, but it also distracted me. I also had trouble getting used to his habit of talking to himself. Mr. Plank did that all the time. I once asked him what he was talking about, and all he did was glare at me, so I figured I'd better leave well enough alone.

"But from day one, I knew that fellow would do well for me," Mack continued. "He had those sharp features, a jutting jaw, well-defined lines, and a hard-nosed attitude that told me he was dead serious about his pitching, and a thinking man, too. He became the ace of my staff, and it's no wonder he won 327 games with all of his antics and talent."

Plank's delaying tactics also annoyed his teammates, who were used to finishing a game in less than two hours.

"He would fuss and fuddle with the ball, his shoes, his cap, his belt, and his shirtsleeves," teammate Eddie Collins recalled, "and then he'd try talking to the umpires. If they didn't answer him, he'd throw over to first base three or four times, and by the time he finally got around to throwing a pitch, the batter's concentration had long since been broken. It wouldn't have been so bad, except he did it on every pitch!"

(Note: Baseball rules were different in the early 1900s. There was no 20-second rule, so pitchers could take as long as they wanted between pitches, and umpires were much more reluctant to grant a batter's request for time out.)

Plank also had a special pregame routine: He absolutely refused to pitch a ballgame unless he had a bowl of tomato soup for lunch, no matter how hot the weather.

"I guess fans would get the idea that Mr. Plank was an eccentric fellow," Mack quipped, "and perhaps he was, but compared to Rube Waddell, Plank was nothing out of the ordinary.

"There's one other thing about Mr. Plank that has always been ignored," Mack continued. "He had a terrible nasal problem that made every breath he took sound like

Eddie Plank

his last. He'd be out there, wheezing and sniffing, and that had to drive the hitters crazy, too. And then there was his sore arm. Mr. Plank was always complaining about a sore arm. Funny thing about that sore arm, though—the sorer it got, the better Mr. Plank pitched."

After the 1901 season, Plank returned to Gettysburg, where he spent the off-season giving tours of the Civil War battlefield (hence the nickname, "The Gettysburg Guide"). He signed for $2,500 for 1902, and rewarded Mack by posting a 20-15 mark to lead the A's to the pennant. There was no World Series because the rival leagues had yet to settle their differences, so Plank went home without testing his mettle against the National League champion Pirates. He increased his win total to 23-16 in 1903, and then recorded back-to-back 26-win campaigns in 1904-5.

The 1905 season was also the first of several instances of bad luck that would plague Plank throughout his career. Strangely enough, none of them were of his own doing. Eddie might have won 30 games in 1905 had Rube Waddell and Andy Coakley not engaged in some horseplay that left them both sidelined with arm injuries, thereby forcing Plank to pitch every other day for the last three weeks of the season. Waddell did not pitch again until 1906.

Bad luck also plagued Eddie in his seven World Series games. He faced Mathewson three times (1-2), Joe McGinnty once (0-1), Rube Marquard (1-1), and Seattle Bill James (0-1), for an unimpressive 2-5 career mark. His 1.32 ERA is more indicative of the quality of his postseason pitching. In fact, with any luck, Plank probably would have gone 6-1 or 7-0. He opened the 1905 Series against the Giants and dropped a 3-0 game to Mathewson, who was in the process of setting the all-time record by hurling three shutouts. Plank returned for game four, allowed four hits, but lost on a pair of errors, 1-0, to McGinnty.

In 1911, after compiling a 22-8 mark, and a 2.10 ERA, Plank bested Marquard, 3-1, in a game made famous by Frank Baker's two-run homer. Mack used Eddie again that year, in relief in game five, but the southpaw was unsuccessful, coming in in the tenth inning and allowing a double by Larry Doyle, a bunt single, and a sacrifice fly. Sadly enough, Doyle never touched home, according to umpire Bill Klem, but the A's did not bother to appeal.

Plank's 26-6 (2.22 ERA) was wasted in 1912, as the A's failed to make the Series, but they returned to postseason play in 1913. Plank started game two, pitched scoreless ball for nine innings, and seemed certain to go home a winner when the A's loaded the bases with no outs in the bottom of the ninth . . . but Matty was on the mound for New York, and the wily veteran induced consecutive forceouts at the plate, followed by a one-hopper back to the mound, to get out of the jam. The disheartened Plank allowed three runs in the tenth, one of them on a hit by Matty, and went down, 3-0.

Plank finally bested Matty in game five, scattering two singles and facing only 29 men in a Series-clinching 3-1 win.

Eddie's last World Series appearance came in 1914, when the A's ran into the Miracle Boston Braves and were swept. Philadelphia might have averted the disaster had Amos Strunk not misjudged a fly ball in the bottom of the ninth in game two, but of course Plank was on the mound, and lost, 1-0, to James.

Plank pitched in one other noteworthy game, the infamous 17 inning tie that enabled the Tigers to win the 1907 pennant. Philly had opened a seven game lead in mid-September and appeared to be coasting to the flag, when Jack Coombs injured his arm and Chief Bender's arm went dead, leaving the A's with only Plank, Waddell, and a kid named Jimmy Dygert.

Detroit rapidly closed the gap and moved into Philadelphia just three percentage points behind the A's on September 27. Mack went with the overworked Plank that day, and a capacity crowd saw the Tigers edge him, 5-4, in the opener of what was supposed to be a three-game series.

The second game was rained out and re-scheduled as part of a Monday doubleheader. More than 25,000 fans jammed into ancient Columbia Park, forcing the A's to set up standing room on the outfield, and they cheered wildly as Philly opened a 7-1 lead. But Waddell couldn't hold it, and a two-run homer by Ty Cobb knotted the score at 8-8 in the ninth. Mack summoned Plank from the bullpen. He allowed a run in the tenth, but Philadelphia tied it in their half of the inning. In the fourteenth, the A's Harry Davis sent a long drive toward the standing room crowd in center field. A policeman posted to control the crowd moved in front of Detroit centerfielder Sam Crawford, and the ball bounced into the roped-off area. The Tigers claimed interference, and umpire Tom Connolly agreed. Players from both teams came off the benches, and several fights began. The police and umpires tried to break up the donnybrook, and even threatened to arrest Tiger pitcher Bill Donovan and first baseman Claude Rossman, before the battlefield cleared. The game went three more innings before the umpires called it because of darkness. Detroit went on to Washington, where they won four in a row, and captured the flag with a final record of 92-58 to Philadelphia's 88-57. (In those days, unplayed games which had not been made up during the season were not made up unless there was a dead tie on the last day of the regular season.)

In 1915, Plank jumped to the St. Louis Feds, where he posted a 21-11 mark, and he leaped back to the A.L. Browns a year later. He went 16-15 for the fifth place Brownies, but slumped to 5-6 in 1917, and was traded to the Yankees after the season. He refused to report to New York, sat out a year, turned down a three-year contract offer from the Yankees, and elected to retire. He was 44.

Plank spent the rest of his life in Gettysburg, content to give battlefield tours, until his death in 1926.

More than 60 years have passed since Eddie Plank last "fussed and fuddled" on a major league pitcher's mound. Sadly enough, it might just as well be 160. When Plank died in 1926, F. C. Lane wrote that "Matty stood for all that pitching could possibly mean, plus a character that appealed to the public. Plank was never, in the same sense, a popular idol. He was retiring, even eccentric, and a lefthander . . . and he never captured the hearts of the fans."

Today, Eddie Plank, the ninth winningest pitcher in major league history, is totally forgotten. Perhaps if Plank had won those seven World Series games, some fans might remember his name . . . but then again, how many fans today even know that there was once a team of Athletics in Philadelphia, a team composed of so many of baseball's greatest stars.

CARL MAYS

Nobody, it seems, ever remembers anything about me except one thing—that a pitch I threw caused a man to die. It was an accident. Nothing else . . .

I won 208 games and lost only 126 during my 15-year career. My lifetime earned run average was 2.92. I was a 20-game winner with the Red Sox, Yankees, and Reds. There were many other personal highlights . . .

But none of that matters. I might as well have had a one-game, or even one-pitch, career, because the only thing anyone remembers is what happened to me in August of 1920.

—The late Carl Mays

On August 16, 1920, the New York Yankees and Cleveland Indians met in an important ballgame at the Polo Grounds in New York City. The first-place Indians led the Yankees by three games in a pennant race that would go down to the wire before Cleveland edged out New York and Detroit.

On the mound for the Yankees was their submarine-throwing right-handed ace, Carl "Sub" Mays, who would go on to post a 26–11 record that year. The Indians countered with Hall-of-Famer Stan Coveleski, headed for a 24–14 mark.

Cleveland led, 3–0, when shortstop Ray Chapman stepped in to lead off the fifth inning. With the count even at one ball, one strike, Mays prepared to deliver a low fast ball, hoping to get ahead of the count. As Mays began his delivery, Chapman shifted his feet and bat to a "push-bunt stance," according to eyewitnesses. Mays responded the way any pitcher would—he switched to a high, inside fastball so as to make bunting a virtual impossibility.

The pitch struck Chapman on the left temple, fracturing his skull. He was assisted to the clubhouse, where he soon fell unconscious. For reasons which remain unknown, he was allowed to lie on the clubhouse trainer's table for about one hour before he was taken to the hospital. Chapman died at 5 A.M. the next morning.

"It's been near 60 years since that happened," teammate Bob Shawkey recalled. "And poor Carl went to his grave damned by a lot of people because of a freak accident. The man probably never saw the pitch because he never made an effort to get out of the way. In fact, I sort of thought he leaned into it.

"You have to know that Chapman was a very smart hitter with a unique stance," Shawkey continued. "He used to stand up straight, as close to the plate as was allowed. Then, when you started to pitch, he'd crouch over the plate so a pitch in the strike zone could even hit him."

Stan Coveleski never forgot that day, either.

"You'd expect a batter to fall away from a pitch like that," he said. "But Ray didn't. Maybe he never saw it . . . but the important thing is that Mays didn't mean to hit him. You know, Mays didn't even know he'd hit Ray because Mays fielded the ball and threw to first. Then, as their big first baseman (Wally Pipp) got ready to throw the ball around the infield, the whole ballpark was silent, and everyone stopped dead in their tracks. It was terrible when it happened, but no one had any idea that the man would die. When we found out, sure, we were angry at Mays, but we knew he didn't mean to hit him. Our ballclub went on record saying so, too, but it didn't do Mays any good."

No one bothered to call Mays when Chapman died. It was left to a forgotten member of the Yankee organization to inform Mays at about 10 A.M. that day.

The next day, the avalanche of letters and newspaper articles began, and those first few days were the most miserable of Mays's life. He later told reporters that the sheer cruelty and hatred expressed in those letters were inhumane and disgusting. Fortunately, after a few days, the tide turned completely, and the mail became overwhelmingly sympathetic.

And when Mays took the mound against the Detroit Tigers a week later, he received a standing ovation from the fans. His response was a shutout victory, the 100th win of his career.

But there was an ugly side of that victory, according to Bob McGarigle, author of *Baseball's Great Tragedy,* the only biography of Mays. Prior to the game, the clubhouse boy delivered a note from Ty Cobb which read: "If it was within my power, I would have inscribed on Chapman's tombstone these words: Here lies the victim of arrogance, viciousness and greed."

Mays read it twice, and swore that he wouldn't let the Tigers score a run if he had to pitch 27 innings to beat them. He needed only 9, and won, 10–0.

Lost somewhere in the sensationalism called history is the fact that Chapman himself exonerated and forgave Mays before he died.

"I'll be all right," the shortstop said while lying in the clubhouse. "Tell Mays I know it was an accident, and that he shouldn't worry." But the damage was done, and the name of Carl Mays is remembered solely as the answer to baseball's most morbid trivia question.

Who then, was Carl Mays, the pitching star of the Red Sox, Yankees, and Reds?

Born on November 12, 1891, in Liberty, Kentucky, Mays was one of eight children born to William and Louisa Mays. The family moved to Mansfield, Missouri, when Carl was two years old, and Mays's childhood memories began on their Mansfield farm.

Carl's father, a Methodist minister, died in 1904, putting an insufferable burden on the family, and forcing Carl to leave school in favor of work. It also forced the family to rely on hunting to supplement their farm produce, and Carl became a crack shot at killing squirrels and jackrabbits with hand-thrown rocks.

Carl's rock-throwing also produced an incredible example of foreshadowing. According to McGarigle, Mays bet a boyhood friend that he could hit the family calf on the rump from a long distance. The bet was made, the rock thrown, and both youths watched in horror as the calf turned toward them, lifted its head, and was struck in the left temple. The animal fell to the ground, stone dead, and Carl got a beating he never forgot—not so much for killing the calf, as for burying the meat-filled carcass.

Mays played his first baseball for a local semipro team, and was paid either $2.50 or $5 (depending upon the source) for each game they won. Losses were gratis! He soon embarked upon a long minor league career before being sold to the Detroit Tigers in 1915. Detroit subsequently sent him to Boston, and he went 5–5 with the Red Sox in 1915.

Carl improved to 19–13 (1916), 22–9 (1917), and 21–13 (1918). His future looked brilliant, and the Red Sox were world champions in 1916 and 1918, with Mays hurling the Series-clinching win in '18.

But, as was so often the case in his career, the happiness was short-lived. Mid-way through the 1919 season, Mays found himself struggling on a Boston team that would eventually finish sixth. As the bats grew ever more powerless, and the fielding more erratic, Mays grew increasingly frustrated. He also quarreled repeatedly with the new owner, Harry Frazee, and was not happy with the managerial decisions of Ed Barrow.

On July 12, 1919, after a 5–0 loss in Chicago dropped his record to 5–11, Mays shocked the baseball world by announcing that he would never pitch another game for the Red Sox.

"I have pitched the best ball of my life, but I am not winning," Mays told reporters. "Things have gone from bad to worse, and I don't know where I stand. The team just doesn't win when I'm pitching, so I'm going home to Pennsylvania."

And home he went, where he sat until a phone call from Yankee co-owner Cap Huston started the ball rolling to get Mays into a Yankee uniform. Huston asked Mays if he would consider pitching for the Yankees. Mays said yes, provided he received his full salary for the 1919 season. Huston quickly agreed, and a deal that sent shortstop Al Russell, pitcher Bob McGraw, and $40,000 to Boston landed the Yankees one of the best pitchers in baseball.

Of course, because it was Mays, and because he was such a talented pitcher, it would not be all that simple. After all, Mays's services had been sought by every team in the American League. One of those teams was the Cleveland Indians, the club that A.L. President Ban Johnson happened to have a substantial financial interest in. And, like any good businessman, Johnson was not about to let a rival business get the drop on him.

So, regardless of his "impartiality," Johnson suspended Mays indefinitely. The Yankees went to court, seeking an injunction against Johnson's suspension. Johnson tried to negate the trade, arguing that the best interests of baseball were not served when a player could determine when, and where, he would play. Perhaps persuasive on its face, but when the court heard about Johnson's ties to the Indians, it tossed Johnson, and his best interests of baseball, out on his ears.

The injunction was issued, and the Yankees went on to get injunctions in every major league city to guarantee no further interference with their new pitcher.

Mays went 9-3 in New York that year, 26-11 in that fateful 1920 season, and 27-9 in 1921. Once again Mays's future looked bright. The Yankees won their first pennant in '21, and were about to embark upon the dynasty that has made them a household word. Mays was 30 years old at the time, and at his peak. In the opening game of the World Series against the Giants, he tossed a five-hit, 3-0 shutout.

He returned to the mound for game four, and breezed through the first seven innings, before allowing three runs in the top of the eighth. The key hits were a triple by Irish Meusel, and a double by George Burns; and herein lies the real reason why Mays is not in the Baseball Hall of Fame. A great deal of controversy centers upon the pitch that Meusel hit. Huggins signaled for a fastball from the bench, but Mays threw a slow curve. After the game, the submariner explained that he had retired Meusel with that pitch in the first game, and had nailed him twice with the same pitch that afternoon.

The matter might have ended there, but for the testimony of an unnamed Broadway actor. The "informant" met with the late Fred Lieb, sportswriter emeritus, that night, and claimed that the game had been fixed.

"The actor's tale went something like this," Lieb recounted in his autobiography, *Baseball As I have Known It* (Coward, McCann & Geoghegan, 1977). "At the start of the eighth inning, Mrs. Mays allegedly flashed a signal to Carl by wiping her face with a white handkerchief. Some persons, he said, who regarded a Giants victory in the Series as absolutely necessary for their welfare, had offered Carl a rather substantial sum in cash if in close games, he would serve up enough hittable pitches to lose the game." The handkerchief signal was the pre-arranged sign that the money had been handed over.

Lieb went to Commissioner Landis, who listened to the actor's story, and started a full investigation.

Meanwhile, Mays pitched and lost the seventh game of the best-of-nine series, 2–1, this time on an equally controversial double by Frank Snyder. In 26 innings of World Series play, Mays had allowed 20 hits and six runs—but in two of those innings, he had allowed 4 runs on 7 hits. Rumors of a fix were never substantiated, and Lieb said Commissioner Landis' detectives uncovered no proof of wrongdoing.

In 1922, Mays slumped to 14–14, and again lost a strange World Series game. The Yankees led, 2–0, when the Giants exploded for four runs in the fifth inning. The key hit was a bad-hop single by Dave Bancroft, but once again, a privileged few were suspicious.

The matter might have ended there, but for a couple of conversations Lieb had with Yankee co-owner Cap Huston, and manager Miller Huggins. In 1928, Huston allegedly told Lieb that he knew that some of their pitchers had thrown games in both the 1921 and 1922 Series. Before Lieb could pursue the matter, Huston collapsed in a drunken stupor, and the reporter never brought it up again.

A year later, in Huggins's final season, the manager was discussing the misfortunes of several former ballplayers.

"Any ballplayer who played for me on either the Cardinals or the Yankees could come to me if he were in need and I would give him a helping hand," Huggins reportedly said. "I make only two exceptions, Carl Mays and Joe Bush. If they were in the gutter, I'd kick them."

Before Lieb could ask another question, the discussion had moved on, and the matter was never brought up again.

Whether the allegations were true or not, it is clear that Huggins carried on a personal vendetta against Mays for the rest of his life. During the spring of 1923, Huggins tried to send Mays down to the minor leagues, but was thwarted when five rival American League clubs claimed the hurler on waivers. So, Mays remained a Yankee, and saw very little action. His record dropped to 5–2 in 23 games (7 starts).

One game in particular stands out: July 17th, versus the Indians. Mays had not pitched an inning in weeks, when Huggins surprised him by using him in relief on the

16th. Imagine Mays's surprise when he learned he would be starting the next game! His arm was not ready for two straight days of pitching, and the Indians pummeled him for 13 runs on 20 hits. Worst of all, the manager left Mays in for the whole game, telling reporters afterwards that "Mays needed the work."

Huggins had accomplished his purpose. The other teams no longer had faith in Mays's arm, and the "former" star was waived to the Cincinnati Reds for $20,000. Mays went 20-9 for the fourth-place Reds in 1924. Mays had the last laugh, because the Yankees finished two games behind the Senators that year, and fans and sportswriters alike publicly wondered where the Yankees might have been had Mays still been around.

Mays had one more fine year, 1926, when he went 19-12 for the Reds. After that, age and arm troubles reduced him to a 14-9 mark over his remaining three seasons.

The question remains: How good was Carl Mays? His 208-126 mark was the fourth best percentage among the 200-game winners of his era, and ranks him 14th in baseball history. From 1916 to 1921, he went 128-60, with an earned run average of 2.19. He was a 20-game winner on five occasions, and in both leagues. Mays also pitched and won both ends of a doubleheader on August 30, 1918, beating the Athletics 12-0 and 4-1. He also used the Athletics to establish another baseball record: most consecutive wins by one pitcher against one team—23 straight. Mays also owns a World Series record: $31\frac{2}{3}$ consecutive innings without allowing a base on balls.

Clearly an outstanding pitcher, he was a star in his day. Unfortunately, as Mays lamented shortly before his death, he has been forgotten by all but trivia buffs, who recall him only as the man who threw the pitch that killed Ray Chapman.

CARL HUBBELL

I took baseball too seriously. I never got to enjoy it the way I should have. If I won a game today, I'd start thinking about the next game as soon as I got in the clubhouse. When I lost, I'd think the game over and over again, and I usually blamed myself for the loss.

—Carl Hubbell

I actually didn't think too much of it at the time, even though I did strike out the heart of the American League's batting order. After all, our league lost the game. But, the next day, so much was made of it in the papers that I started thinking about it. I guess it helped my career. Without it, I'd probably be forgotten. After all, a lot of people win 200 games. But, thanks to that All-Star Game, people think about me at least once a year.

—Carl Hubbell

On July 10, 1934, Carl Hubbell stunned the baseball world with the greatest All-Star Game pitching performance in major league history.

After surrendering a leadoff single to Charlie Gehringer, and walking Heinie Manush, Hubbell proceeded to strike out the heart of the American League lineup: Babe Ruth, Lou Gehrig, and Jimmie Foxx. In the second inning, he added Al Simmons and Joe Cronin to the list, before yielding a single to Bill Dickey. When Hubbell struck out his mound opponent, Lefty Gomez, to end the inning, he had recorded an unprecedented, and unequalled, All-Star Game record: six strikeouts in two innings.

The feat is all the more remarkable because every one of the strikeout victims is in the Hall of Fame, and, with the exception of Ruth, was at the height of his career. Gehrig would lead the league in batting (.363), homeruns (49), RBIs (165) and slugging percentage (.706). Foxx batted .334 (28 doubles and 44 homeruns) and drove in 130 runs. Simmons finished the season at .344 (36 doubles, 18 homeruns), 104 RBIs, and only struck out 58 times in 558 at-bats; while Cronin batted .284, drove in 101 runs, and *went down on strikes only 28 times in 504 at-bats.* As for Ruth, well, he was over the hill, but still managed to bat .288 (17 doubles, 22 homeruns). Similarly, Gomez was never much of a hitter (.147 lifetime).

Hubbell also retired the side in order in the third inning (two fly balls and a ground out), and departed to a thundering ovation from the Polo Grounds partisans.

To this day, fans are still asking how "King Carl" did it:

"Gabby Hartnett was my catcher that day," Hubbell recalled, some forty-three years later. "He had never caught me before, so we sat down before the game to go over the American League lineup. Well, we knew they could hit just about everything, but we also knew that no pitcher in their league threw the screwball. We hoped they'd have trouble with it, so we agreed that every strike would be a screwball, and every fastball would be wasted inside. Yeah, we knew they'd have a tough time with the screwball, but we never dreamed they would be handcuffed.

"I remember going out to watch them take batting practice to learn what they teed off on," he continued. "They weren't hitting anything into the seats—they were hitting everything over the roof! You can just imagine how that affected my confidence.

"I didn't start off well. I was terribly nervous, and once we got started, I was wild. I fell behind on Gehringer, three-one, and he singled. I walked Manush. I was on the verge of disaster. I stopped, called time out, and had a meeting with myself to regain my mental control. After that, I just bore down and followed our game plan. All things considered, I really wasn't under that much pressure, with Ruth up there and no outs. He, Gehrig, and Foxx had all hit homeruns off better pitchers than me, so I convinced myself that I had nothing to lose.

"We got Ruth on a screwball, called strike three. Gehrig fouled off a pitch, and then swung and missed. Foxx also went down swinging at the screwball. When I left the mound, knowing what I'd just done, I was satisfied, but I was already thinking about the next inning.

"When I got Simmons swinging at the screwball to lead off the second, and then nailed Cronin, I got caught up in the strikeout mania. I made a mistake and tried to strike out the next batter. I got two quick strikes on him. I figured I had Dickey, so I tried to waste a fastball outside, but he nailed it for a base hit. Looking back, I guess I blew it. I was never really a strikeout pitcher, I always preferred to throw one pitch and get a ground ball."

Carl Hubbell

* * *

When Carl Hubbell was a boy, he had no dreams of playing professional baseball. In fact, he did not even know it existed.

"I was born on June 22, 1903, on a farm in Red Oak, Missouri, and we moved into Oklahoma Territory when I was about three," he said. "It wasn't even a state in those days. We lived on a farm, and that meant one thing: work. Sure, I went to school, but we had no athletic programs. How could we—there were maybe a dozen of us in the one-room schoolhouse. There were no radios, let alone TVs, and with work on the farm, and a three-mile walk to and from school, who had time to read a newspaper. I guess we started to play something like baseball when I was around ten. I was lucky. There were five brothers to play with, or against."

By the time Hubbell was a junior in high school, the territory had become a state, and there were enough boys in his class to form a team.

"We asked the superintendent if we could form one, and he said okay, 'but who're you gonna play?'" Hubbell recalled. "Damned good question. The nearest school was 10 miles away. Still, we managed to play five or six games that year, and ten or twelve the next one. I hear that's about all they play in some parts of New York today, anyway, because of the weather in the spring."

When Hubbell graduated, there were no scouts knocking on his door.

"The thought of playing baseball for a living simply didn't even exist," he said. "I signed on with the Gypsy Oil Company in northern Oklahoma. We worked six days a week, and played in an oil field league on Sundays. One good thing was that we had batting practice every day, and that strengthened my arm."

Carl's only link with professional baseball came via the local newspapers, which devoted a few column-inches to the Tulsa club (Western League, Class A), "and it started something in my mind—the idea of *working* as a ballplayer.

"It got to the point where I felt I had to try it," he said, "so I took a leave of absence from the oil fields and went to see about a tryout with Cushing (Oklahoma State League, Class D). I took a room down there for 50 cents a night, and went to see the manager the next day. They were on a homestand, but the manager was reluctant to give me a look-see because it was the middle of the season and he had a full roster. I wasn't about to be put off, so I asked if I could pitch batting practice. He said yes, and after it was over, I asked if I could come back the next day. He said yes, and it went on that way all week.

"Finally, I was running out of money, and when I was about to go back to the oil fields, one of their pitchers got a teaching job and left. The manager signed me on the spot. My salary was $125 a month—$5 more than I was making in the oil fields."

As things would have it, the Oklahoma State League folded a year later, but Hubbell had impressed the manager so much that he sent the youth up to Oklahoma

City. He saw limited action, and went 1–1, but it was a valuable learning experience.

"They had two pitchers up there, Saw Mill Joe Brown and Lefty Thomas," Carl recalled. "Brown was very fast. He threw very hard, and I mean physically. He was also very wild. Lefty, on the other hand, threw a sidearm sinker that broke away from right-hand batters, and all he did was throw strikes. He was a finesse pitcher. Anyway, I looked at the two of them, and I said to myself, 'Why fire the ball like Brown when I can pitch like Thomas and let the other eight guys do the work in the field?'"

More importantly, Thomas showed Hubbell how to twist his wrist and make the ball break away from the righties, and Hubbell spent the winter working on the screwball. It paid handsome dividends. In 1925, Carl won eight straight games en route to a 17-win season, and the Tigers signed him.

"Ty Cobb was the manager, and he wouldn't let me throw the screwball," Hubbell recalled. "I was almost 22 years old. We played 28 exhibition games in spring training, and I never even threw an inning. Just threw batting practice. Didn't matter much, because without the screwball I was mediocre, so they released me to Beaumont of the Texas League. That was a reject team, and I was a reject pitcher. I was really at the bottom, and began wondering if I should go back to the oil fields. I had a conference with myself, and decided that the Tigers hadn't really given me a chance, and if I quit, then I'd blame myself for the rest of my life. So, I decided to stick it out for a while."

Hubbell's big break came in July of 1928, while his team was at Houston. The Democratic National Convention was in Houston that year, and it so happened that one of the Chicago delegates, Dick Consella, was a scout for the New York Giants. There was a lull in the proceedings, so Consella went out to the ballpark to watch Wild Bill Hallahan hurl for the home team. Hubbell was on the mound for Beaumont, and he beat Wild Bill, 2–1, in fifteen innings.

"It was my thirteenth win against nine losses," he recalled, "but I didn't think too much about it. Like I said, we were a reject team that was going no place."

Fortunately, Consella had other ideas. He rushed back to the convention hotel, and called manager John McGraw, *collect.*

"This had better be good," McGraw said, after accepting the call, "otherwise, you're fired."

"John, I just saw another Art Nehf," came the reply. "You've got to see him."

"If he's that good, sign him and bring him back with you," McGraw replied, and within a week, Hubbell was Giants property. The investment was good for 16 seasons.

"They gave me $750 a month," Hubbell said. "I was 24 years old, and that was more money than I'd ever dreamed of."

Carl joined the team in Chicago, and started against the Pirates a few days later.

"Pittsburgh got five runs off me in the third, and I figured I'd be back in Texas tomorrow," he said. "The next day, McGraw called me into his office, and my bags

Carl Hubbell

were already packed. Imagine my surprise when he told me not to worry, that he liked the way I challenged the hitters, and that if the team had played better in the field, we'd have won."

About five days later, Hubbell got another chance. New York's starter was kayoed in the third inning, and Carl came in with the bases loaded and Chick Hafey at the plate. (Hafey batted .337 that year, with 46 doubles, six triples, 27 homeruns, 111 RBIs, and just 53 strikeouts in 520 at-bats.) The count went to three balls, one strike, and Hubbell uncorked his first major league screwball—"more out of desperation than anything else." Hafey swung and missed, so Hubbell came back with the same pitch, and the .337 hitter swung and missed again for strike three.

"What the hell kind of pitch was that!" Hafey screamed out to the rookie. "You keep throwing that one, and ain't nobody gonna hit it!"

Hubbell went on to hold the Cardinals scoreless through the ninth, but the Giants lost, 4-3, in fifteen innings.

"I learned an important lesson that day," Carl recalled in 1980. "I learned that even the best hitters in the major leagues couldn't hit the screwball when it was breaking properly. Right then and there, I decided that it would be my bread-and-butter pitch, regardless of what it would do to my arm."

It was the beginning of an incredible career that spanned 16 seasons and included 253 wins against 154 losses (a .622 percentage), a lifetime 2.97 ERA, and election to the Hall of Fame in 1947. After a 10–6 rookie season, the 6-foot, 170-pound southpaw won 18 of 29 decisions in 1929, including a no-hitter against the Pirates on May 8. It was the only no-hit effort of his career, and was particularly tough because the Giants made three errors behind him. His only scare came in the ninth, when left fielder Chick Fullis dropped a line drive, and shortstop Travis Jackson bobbled a ground ball. The next two batters were Lloyd and Paul Waner, both Hall-of-Famers at the top of their careers. Hubbell got Lloyd on a called strike three; it was one of only 173 strikeouts in Lloyd's 18-year career. He ended the inning moments later by getting Paul to bounce back to the mound. Carl wheeled, threw to Jackson covering second for one, followed by the relay to first to complete the double play.

It was not until 1933 that Hubbell became an overpowering pitcher, and earned the nickname "The Meal Ticket" because of his ability to win crucial games and prevent losing streaks. He recorded a league-leading 23-12 mark, 1.66 ERA, 10 shutouts, and 308⅔ innings, while allowing only 47 walks and striking out 156. At one point, he ran off a streak of 46⅓ scoreless innings, including an 18-inning shutout in the first game of a doubleheader against the Cardinals in which he allowed six hits, struck out 12, and did not walk a man.

Hubbell capped the season off by pitching two complete game victories over the Senators in the World Series. "King Carl" opened the fall classic by hurling a five-hitter, striking out 10, and winning, 4–2, on a two-run homerun by Mel Ott. He came back three days later, scattered eight hits over 11 innings, and took a 2–1 decision when he induced pinch-hitter Cliff Bolton to bounce into a game-ending doubleplay with one out in the bottom of the eleventh. The lone Washington score was unearned.

"The Meal Ticket" received a hefty raise to $17,500 for 1934, and did not rest on his laurels. He repeated as the league's ERA champion (2.30), won 21 of 33 decisions, increased his innings-pitched to 313, and reduced his walks allowed to 37 (*barely one walk per nine innings pitched*)! Hubbell also recorded a league-leading eight saves!

Despite his outstanding statistics, and the aforementioned All-Star Game heroics, the Giants offered Hubbell the same $17,500 for 1935, and their "Meal Ticket" balked.

"I was furious," he recalled. "I'd done everything they asked, started and relieved, and I knew I deserved a raise. So, I called Bill Terry and asked him what a fellow has to do to get a raise, and he told me 'Win the pennant.'" Hubbell played the 1935 season at the same $17,500, and went 23–12, but the Giants finished third behind the Cubs, and again there was no raise in salary.

"It was ridiculous," he said. "I'd won 44 games in two seasons, and hadn't received a raise. But, what could I do? There were no free agents in those days, so I swore we'd win the pennant the following year, and we did."

Hubbell came through with his greatest season, winning 26 games while losing 6 (a league-leading .813 percentage), led the league with a 2.31 ERA, saved three games, and allowed 57 walks in 304 innings. He finished the season with 16 consecutive victories, and stifled the Yankees on a seven-hit, 6–1 win in game one of the World Series. He returned to the mound for game four, and was done in by Lou Gehrig's two-run homerun.

This time a raise was forthcoming, and the Meal Ticket came through with wins in his first eight games in 1937. That gave him 24 in a row, but Ford Frick ruled that no record had been set because the wins were split over two seasons.

"That's why we called him Mr. Milktoast," Hubbell said. "He tried to please everyone and gave the record to [Rube] Marquard. He did the same kind of thing to [Roger] Maris."

Hubbell finished with a league-leading 22 wins (8 defeats) and 159 strikeouts (the only time he led the league in that category) in what proved to be his last great season. His arm showed signs of weakness as the season wore on, no doubt caused by the tremendous strain of throwing the screwball, and his ERA went up to 3.20 in 261 2/3 innings. The Giants faced their cross-river rivals again in the World Series, and the Pinstripers thrashed "King Carl" in game one, 8–1. By the time he took the mound again, the Giants were down three games to one, so his 7–3 victory merely averted a sweep. It was his final World Series appearance.

After an off-year (13–10) in 1938, Hubbell underwent surgery for bone chips and calcium deposits in his pitching arm elbow. Although the operation was pronounced a success, the wing was never the same, and he never won more than 11 games in each of his remaining five seasons. After an 11–12 mark in 1940 (the only sub-.500 season of his career), Hubbell wanted to retire, but team owner Horace Stoneham convinced him to stick around for another year. That extra year lasted three seasons (11–9, 11–8, 4–4), and Stoneham rewarded the veteran for his loyalty by naming him Director of Minor League Operations upon his retirement. He remained with the Giants until 1977, when a stroke forced him into a part-time scouting job in Arizona.

On July 10, 1934, Carl Owen Hubbell did the impossible. He struck out five of the greatest hitters in baseball history before the home town fans at the Polo Grounds, and thereby vaulted into immortality. Those who were there will never forget the look of bewilderment in the eyes of the American League All-Stars who looked at, and swung at, a pitch they'd never seen before.

Ironically, the screwball that vaulted him into immortality, and made him a superstar, not only shortened his career, but left his left arm permanently disfigured, twisted out of shape.

"I have no regrets," he said. "They say baseball is a great life, and I'm living proof of it. They also say that left-handers are supposed to have bad control. Well, I guess that I am the living exception. For 16 years, I averaged less than two walks a game (724 allowed in 3,589⅓ innings). I made a living letting them hit the ball, and then spent the next 33 years trying to find other men who could do the same. But I learned one thing: Don't teach a youngster the screwball unless he has no other out pitch.

"I'll tell you something else. Today, wherever I go, whoever I meet, when they hear my name, they still remember that 1934 All-Star Game, and the fact that I threw the screwball and won a lot of games. Well, I'm 77 years old, and I'll tell you the truth: It's great to be remembered!"

DIZZY DEAN

By Judas Priest. By Judas Priest. If there were one more like him in all of baseball, just one more, as God is my judge, I'd get out of the game.

—Branch Rickey's reaction to a rookie named Dizzy Dean

One night, Dizzy Dean bumped into the president of the Texas League at 3 A.M.—well after curfew.

"Good morning, Pres," he said. "So, the ol' boy is a prowlin' around by himself tonight, eh? Well sir, I'm not the one to squawk. Us stars and presidents must have our fun."

"The trouble with them boys is they ain't got enough spart," Dizzy Dean told a radio audience. When pressed for an explanation of what he meant, Diz replied: "Spart is pretty much like fight or pep or gumption. Like the Spart of St. Louis, that plane Lindbergh flowed to Europe in."

Baseball has had its share of wild and crazy characters, but none of them has ever approached the sheer zaniness, and overwhelming popularity, of the legendary Dizzy Dean.

From 1932 to 1937, as one of the ringleaders of the equally legendary "Gashouse Gang" St. Louis Cardinals, Dean was more unpredictable than a spin of a roulette wheel, result of a horserace, and roll of the dice, *combined*! Nothing, and I mean nothing, was beyond the realm of the possible, when it came to Dean.

Who else but Dean would order his catcher to drop a pop foul with the bases loaded, and his team ahead by one run? That's exactly what happened one day against the Braves. Dean had bet a friend that he would strike out Vince DiMaggio every time the Boston outfielder batted. Sure enough, Diz nailed him the first three times, and stood to win 80 cents (ten cents doubled each at-bat) if he got Vince a fourth time. When rookie catcher Bruce Ogrodowski let the ball fall, manager Frank Frisch leaped out of his dugout seat and cracked his head against the dugout roof. By the time Frisch got back on his feet, Diz had already bored a fastball by DiMaggio for strike three!

Who else but the incredibly cocky right-hander would invade the clubhouse of a visiting team immediately before a game he was scheduled to pitch, and tell each batter exactly how he would pitch to him? "And then the big gorilla goes out and does exactly what he said he would, and shuts us out on three hits," recalled the late Casey Stengel, manager of the Brooklyn Dodgers at the time.

Then there was the time the Giants scored seven runs off him in one inning of an exhibition game. Diz was furious, told his infielders that "they're not gonna hit the master that way," and proceeded to hit the next seven consecutive batters with pitches! (Interestingly enough, the Giants went winless against him that year!)

And who else but the amazing Dean would amble over to the Tigers bullpen before game seven of the 1934 World Series, stop to watch his mound opponent, Eldon Auker, warm up, and then ask the veteran, "You don't expect to get anyone out with that stuff, do you?" Of course, Dean made two hits in one inning off the Detroit hurler to lead the Cardinals to an 11–0 victory!

Why, even so simple a task as telling reporters the details of his birth became a major production, when he gave three different dates and locations to three different newsmen in a matter of minutes! The first man heard "January 16, 1911, in Lucas, Arkansas." Number two was told "February 22, 1911, in Bond, Mississippi," while the third scribe learned that it was "August 22, 1911 in Holdenville, Oklahoma." When a fourth reporter confronted the wily hurler with the obvious conflict, Dean explained that he "wasn't lyin'. I was givin' 'em each scoops. That way they won't get in trouble for comin' in with the same story."

And who else but the 36-year-old Dean, who had not even picked up a baseball for six years, would ride the St. Louis Browns so unmercifully in his broadcasts, that club president Bill DeWitt would challenge him to don a uniform and see if the former All-Star could do better? Of course, Diz accepted the challenge, took the mound for the team's season finale against the White Sox, and yielded three hits, one walk, and no runs in four innings! (He even managed a base hit to left field, but it proved to be his undoing—Diz pulled a muscle stretching it into a double, and had to leave the game!)

He even remained the center of controversy and attention when he moved on to the CBS Television Game of the Week broadcasts, where he would mangle the English language to the point that grammar teachers throughout the land were deluging the network with complaints about runners who "slud" into third and returned to their "respectable" bases. Dean's response: "Criminy, now they's a tax on talkin'! Lots a people who ain't sayin' ain't, ain't eatin'."

Separating fact from exaggeration in the case of Dizzy Dean is no easy task. Historians have concluded that his real birthdate was January 16, the real location was Lucas, and the real name was Jay Hanna Dean (not the Jerome Herman he sometimes used!). Serious doubts remain about the year, largely because it was the only consistency, and because ballplayers of the day usually lied about their ages in hopes of extending their careers.

Jay was the third son born to the Albert Dean family. Mrs. Dean died when Jay was three and younger brother Paul was a mere infant. Albert was a dirt-poor sharecropper who traveled from town to town, following the harvests. School always took a back seat in the boys' lives, but Jay made it through second, third, or fourth grade—depending upon which version of his life he was telling.

Somewhere along the line, older brother Elmer was separated from the family.

"We used to travel in two cars," Diz recalled. "One day, we come up to a railway crossing and a big freight train wuz a-comin'. The car I wuz in made it across, but ol' Elmer had to wait for the train. We drove on, figuring Elmer would soon catch up, but the train stopped and blocked the road for at least 20 minutes. Then, Elmer must a took the wrong turn or somethin', cause he never did catch up with us. That was in 1925, and we never did see him again until 1930. We hunted for him, but none of us ever was much for writin', and besides, we didn't know where he was, so how could we write to, anywho.

"So, one day in 1930, Elmer gets hold of a Sunday paper with pictures, 'cause he never could read a lick, neither," or so the story goes. "And guess what he's seein'? A picture of Ol' Diz. So he goes and gits him a druggest who could write, and rattles off a letter to me and Paul tellin' us where he is and what's about, and we all goes and gits him. Never did lose nuthin' crossin' tracks again. No sir, never did make the same mistake."

By the time he was 10 years old, Jay was spending his days out in the cotton fields, earning 50 cents a day. On his 16th birthday, he "upped and ran away to enlist in the United States Army, where [he] took up baseball so [he] would have to do less soldiering." He soon developed into a tremendous pitcher, and earned the nickname "Dizzy" for driving his sergeant crazy. Toward the end of his three-year enlistment, the family scraped up $120 and bought Jay's freedom from the service (a common practice in that era).

After his release, Jay starred in semipro ball while working in San Antonio, until Cardinals scout Don Curtis signed him at the end of the 1929 season. The Cardinals sent him to St. Joseph, Missouri (Western Association), where he began establishing a reputation for cockiness, zaniness, and "winningness" on his first day. Before taking the mound in his first game, Diz visited the other team in their clubhouse, asked each player what pitches he liked to hit, and then threw them exactly what they had asked for. Of course, he won, 4–3! It was the first of 17 wins in 25 decisions, and earned him a promotion to Houston in August.

Diz had his first run-in with management in Texas, in the much-celebrated late-night meeting with League President Fred Ankerman at 3 A.M. (recounted at the beginning of the chapter), but managed to come away with just a $25 fine. He also pitched to an 8–2 mark in the final four or so weeks of the season, thereby earning a ticket to the big leagues, and a late-season start against the Pittsburgh Pirates.

"You're facing Pittsburgh, and they're mighty tough," owner Sam Breadon told the newcomer. "They've got Pie Traynor and the Waner brothers (Lloyd and Paul), all good hitters. You'd better be ready."

"They won't look so tough when they have to face ol' Diz," the 6'2", 182-pound cocksure hurler replied.

Sure enough, he beat the Pirates, 3–1, striking out five and scattering three hits, to fulfill the first of many "prophetic" performances.

During the off-season, Diz demanded that his salary be raised above the standard $3,000 paid to rookies. He even told General Manager Branch Rickey that he would "put more fans in the seats than Babe Ruth," during a four-hour session. Rickey somehow managed to listen to the brash rookie's drawl for endless hours, and finally emerged from his office with the quote: "If there were one more like him in all of baseball, just one more, as God is my judge, I'd get out of the game."

The only thing that prevented Diz from making the varsity in 1931 was Diz himself. He was constantly bragging about his own ability, and so infuriated the St. Louis veterans that they demanded that something be done about him. At first, Manager Street was inclined to let it go, but when Dean began sleeping through practice sessions, Street had had enough.

"Who the hell do you think you are, kid?" the enraged manager asked. "You come up outta' the bushes and act like the biggest busher of 'em all. Either you get to practice on time, or you're going back to Houston!"

That same afternoon, Street figured he would teach the kid a lesson, so he sent him in to pitch against the world champion Philadelphia A's. All Dean did was strike out the heart of their lineup: Al Simmons, Jimmy Foxx, and Mickey Cochrane. When he finished with Cochrane, Diz went up to Street and told him: "See, I don't need no practice. I can win games without workin' out. Let them other bums practice."

Diz dug his own grave even deeper by signing for just about anything he bought in spring training, expecting management to make good on it. Eventually, Rickey informed the merchants and restaurateurs that Diz was to pay cash, and he followed that up by putting the brash rookie on a one-dollar-a-day allowance. Each morning at 9 A.M., Dean reported to traveling secretary Clarence Lloyd, who handed the 20-year-old a $1 bill.

Even that embarrassment did little to tone Dean down, and eventually Rickey sent him down to Houston. Diz was shocked, and considered retiring, but friends reminded him that St. Louis was the defending champion, pointed out that the team did not need a 20-year-old wise guy, and convinced him to go back to the Texas club. (Rickey later admitted that he was convinced that the Cardinals would repeat without Dean. Besides, if they needed him, a quick telegram would have him in St. Louis in less than 24 hours.)

While the Cardinals were winning a world championship, Dean was having a great year in Houston: 26–10, 303 strikeouts, 1.57 ERA. He also met, wooed, and won Pat Nash as his wife, and she proved to be the Claire Ruth of his life. (Diz was something of a big spender until she began forcing him to save one-half of every paycheck... even though he had to borrow $2 from her for their marriage license!)

When Diz arrived at the Cardinals training camp in 1932, he came complete with a new moniker: "Ol' Diz." There was no point in sending him down again—he had not learned his lesson, and never would. Diz pitched in 46 games, 33 of them as a starter, and recorded an 18–15 mark with a league-leading 191 strikeouts, 4 shutouts, and 286 innings. He even batted .258. Perhaps his presence unsettled the rest of the veterans, because the team slumped to sixth place.

In 1933, Diz went 20-18, again leading the league in strikeouts (199), and adding the league title in appearances (48). He also became a national celebrity when the newspapers picked up his account of a spring training game: "I told the catcher [Jimmy Wilson] not to bother givin' me no signs no more because none of 'em could hit my .30-.30 fastball, anyway." He remained in the news by constantly getting in trouble for missing exhibition games, and the resulting fines that were imposed. Diz got off to a shaky start, but when Street was replaced by Frankie Frisch midway through the season (the team was 45–46), the team and its top pitcher responded.

On July 30, 1933, Dean set a record by striking out 17 Chicago Cubs. Among the victims were Kiki Cuyler and Babe Herman (three times). After the game, Diz told reporters, "If I'd'a knowed I was near to a record, I'd'a struck out 20 o' them bums, easy. Why, I just toyed with Billy Jurges a couple a times. He couldn't hit nuthin'!"

By the time the season ended, Dean was the talk of the National League. When spring training came around in 1934, he was earning $6,500, and had something new to talk about: His brother Paul had joined the team. When reporters asked Diz about the sibling half, the ever-quotable hurler said, "Me and Paul are gonna win the pennant for St. Louis. We'll win 45 games between us."

"How many will Paul win?" a reporter asked.

"As many as he can," Diz replied.

"And how many will you win?" he continued.

"Whatever number Paul don't," he replied.

Fans and writers alike began calling Paul "Daffy," but the nickname never stuck. He was a complete contrast to his cocksure, ever-verbal brother. Paul let his fastball do all of his talking, and went on to win 19 games (against 11 losses). Diz took 30 (against 7 losses, a 2.66 ERA, and league leading marks in strikeouts [195] and shutouts [7]). Of course, the Redbirds lived up to Diz's promise by winning the pennant, too.

Not that life was easy. The trouble began when Diz threatened a sit-down strike if Paul did not receive an immediate $2,000 raise above the standard rookie salary. On June 1st, he told Frisch that effective immediately, he would not pitch until Paul was earning $5,000. Frisch explained that a World Series share was a virtual certainty, provided Ol' Diz and Paul did not let the team down by striking, but Diz was not satisfied. Next, Frisch, with the help of the coaching staff, asked Paul whether he was unhappy about his salary, and when the rookie said no, they brought him to Diz. When Paul told the other half that he was satisfied, Diz withdrew the threat.

Eleven weeks later, controversy reigned again. This time, the problem involved the brothers' failure to accompany the team to an exhibition game in Detroit. Diz and Paul had pitched in the previous day's doubleheader (a rare double loss) with Chicago, and did not want to go. Diz claimed that he'd forgotten his baggage, and that his arm was so sore that he couldn't have pitched anyway. Paul said his ankle (injured in Philadelphia a week earlier) was so sore that he could barely walk. The club was not satisfied, so Diz was fined $100, Paul $50.

"I ain't payin' and I ain't playin'," Diz told the press the next day, not realizing that the fines would be deducted from his paycheck with or without his permission. "And, I ain't playin' until somebody up there apologizes."

This time, Frisch had no intention of catering to his pitching brothers. He ordered them on to the field for the next scheduled game (August 14th), and when both refused to play, Frisch suspended them indefinitely. Diz raged into the clubhouse and ripped up his uniform, swearing he would not play until Frisch also apologized. When reporters got wind of the histrionics, Diz restaged the uniform destruction with another set for the cameramen.

"They can't win without us," Diz announced. "Me an' Paul's won too many games." (He was 21–5, Paul 12–6.)

"Yes we can," Frisch replied, using the newspapers as his mouthpiece. "I'll use the old men (43-year-old Dazzy Vance and 41-year-old Jesse Haines) instead. We've got to have some discipline around here."

The next day, Diz learned that he had been fined an additional $36 for the two uniforms. He also learned that team owner Breadon was upholding Frisch's move (a 10-day suspension), and that their teammates were supporting the manager, too. Vance and Haines beat the Phillies that day, and then swept them in a doubleheader after a rain out.

Paul quickly realized that the team could do without him. He relented, paid the $50 fine, and issued a signed apology. The next day, he threw 7 solid relief innings, and won his 13th game.

Not so with Diz. He went to see Commissioner Kennesaw Landis, who agreed to hold a hearing in St. Louis on August 20th. Meanwhile, the Cardinals were winning game after game. Even Pepper Martin (third baseman) took a turn on the mound, pitching two scoreless innings in relief, as the Cardinals made it six wins out of seven games without Diz. A running verbal battle continued in the papers every day, and fans read in earnest the "blow by blow" descriptions coming out of St. Louis.

Finally, August 20th arrived, and after more than four hours of testimony, Judge Landis ruled that the fines and suspensions were valid. He rejected the Deans' explanations for missing the exhibition game, and left reinstatement up to Frisch and Breadon. The total cost to Diz would be $486 ($100 fine, $36 for the uniforms, and $350 for ten days' pay). The judge further ordered that Dean make a public apology to the team, and wire an apology to the Tigers.

As soon as the hearing was over, Diz was strangely satisfied. "Justice had been held," he told reporters, "and I'm a-goin' back on the field. I weren't meant to be no lawyer, anyway."

Four days later, Diz pitched a shutout, and the whole matter was forgotten. The Cardinals remained hot, battling Bill Terry's Giants down to the wire. At the end of the season, Diz was pitching with only two day's rest.

On September 21st, Diz threw a three-hit shutout against the Dodgers in the opening game of a doubleheader. He held the Brooklyns hitless for $8\frac{2}{3}$-innings, before letting up. Paul pitched a no-hitter in the nightcap, allowing just one baserunner (Len Koenecke's first-inning walk).

"If I'd a knowed Paul was goin' to pitch a no-hitter, I'd a throwed one, too," Diz told reporters afterwards.

The Cardinals wound up winning the pennant on the last day of the season, and moved on to Detroit to face the Tigers in the World Series. Diz had pitched the season finale, and speculation had it that Frisch would start Wild Bill Hallahan (8–12, but the hero of two previous Series) in game one.

"Opener, nuthin'," Dean announced. "I want to pitch the entire Series. Or maybe let Paul win one, too. I knows I can win four out of five."

Diz followed up on his remarks by ambling out to the field, where the Tigers were taking batting practice. He snatched a bat out of slugger Hank Greenberg's hands, stepped up to the plate, and drove the first offering into the seats.

"Hey Mo," he told Greenberg, "this is how it's done. And I'm the worst hitter on the club," he told the startled Tigers. "It's over already. The Cardinals are the champions."

His remarks and actions set the tone for a wild, hard-hitting, vicious-riding World Series. Diz seemed to take particular delight in taunting the young Greenberg, the lone Jew on either team. Diz started the opener, scattered eight hits, and went home an 8–3 winner. Greenberg touched Diz for a tremendous, albeit too-little, too-late homerun in the late innings, but Diz had an easy explanation.

"That Greenberg hit a curve that hung up there so long that a kid could have hit it," he said. "I could bring four National League teams over here and win the American League."

Later that day, he relayed his version of the game to Admiral Byrd, then exploring in Antarctica.

"Hello, big Byrd, down in Little America," Dean began. "I didn't have a thing out there today on my fastball or curveball. I finally staggered through and won a ballgame. I can pitch better than that. I would be tickled to death to pitch tomorrow's game. I think I would have my stuff tomorrow, and probably would shut the Detroit Tigers out."

Dean did not return to action until game four, when he was inserted as a pinch-runner for Spud Davis in the fourth inning. Diz led off first base, and Pepper Martin smashed a ground ball to Gehringer at second. A quick toss to Billy Rogell at the bag forced Diz, but the throw back to first nailed Diz in the head, knocking him out, cold.

The Cardinals ace was rushed to the hospital for X rays, which were negative. The next day, a newspaper headline earned eternal fame by informing its readers: "X-Rays of Dean's Head Show Nothing"! Diz spent the night in the hospital, but returned to the ballpark to pitch game five. He allowed three runs on six hits before yielding to Tex Carleton in the ninth inning of Detroit's 3–1 win.

Paul won the sixth game to even the Series, and thereby set up Diz's greatest moment: game seven. The cocksure hurler started the festivities by telling reporters that he would "twist the tail of the Detroit pussy cats," the day before the game! Before the game, he warmed up, then strolled over to the Detroit bullpen, where he told Eldon Auker that he shouldn't expect to get any of the Cardinals out with such lousy stuff. After finishing with Auker, he mosied on over to manager-catcher Cochrane and told him that Auker "jes' won't do, he jes' won't do."

Diz retired the Tigers in the first two innings, and led off the third with a routine hit to left field. When Goose Goslin was slow in fielding the ball, Diz lit out for second, and successfully stretched a single into a double. When Martin followed with a ground ball that Greenberg snared between first and second, the "stretch" became ultra-important. Had Diz been on first, Greenberg would have continued with his momentum and easily thrown the runner out at second. But with Diz already there, Greenberg's only play was a tough, cross-the-body throw to Auker covering first, and Martin beat the throw by a hair. Martin stole second, and Cochrane made the foolish mistake of walking Jack Rothrock intentionally to face Frisch. Frankie came through with a three-run double, and the Redbirds were off and running. The Cardinals scored 7 runs that inning, and Dean even got another hit (an infield single).

With a seven-run cushion, Dean began clowning. He took his time between pitches, taunting the Tigers batters. When the home team batted for the final time, he may have deliberately served up easy pitches to the men batting ahead of Greenberg so he could get one more shot at the slugger. Hank came up with two on and one out, and Diz struck him out again.

Frisch had proven himself to be a prophet, too. The World Series share was $5,389.57 for each St. Louis player.

Diz's next two seasons were also superb (1935: 28–12, 3.11 ERA, a league-leading 182 strikeouts; 1936: 24–13, 3.17, 195, and a league-leading 11 saves), but the Cardinals dropped to third and fourth. Meanwhile, the legend continued his antics on and off the field. One day, he and Pepper Martin interrupted a "high society" lecture-luncheon in Philadelphia by entering the ballroom dressed as house painters.

"We're here to re-upholster the joint," Dean told the stunned gathering. "Go right ahead with your program. You won't bother us."

Of course, the pair were recognized, and their high society fans invited them to sit down and stay for dessert!

Another day, two sick boys asked Diz to strike out New York's fine hitter, Bill Terry. Diz agreed to do it, knowing full well that the first baseman was a lifetime .341 hitter who rarely went down on strikes. The first two times Terry batted, Dean was unable to get the third strike past him. Terry's final at-bat came late in the game, with the bases loaded and two out. Dean fired a pair of fastballs past Terry, and then called time out.

"I'm gonna' have to strike you out, Bill," Diz told the astonished batter after walking in from the mound. "I promised some sick kids I would."

Sure enough, Ol' Diz returned to the rubber, threw another blazer, and "fogged" it past Terry before laughing his way into the dugout.

By the time the '37 season began, the 26-year-old Dean was on top of the baseball world. He had more than fulfilled his rookie year promise to Rickey—he had supplanted Ruth as the game's hottest drawing card. His cockiness was equaled only by his irrepressible wit. His wit was equaled only by his record: five seasons, 121–65, four straight years as the league's strikeout leader, and an ERA just over 3.00. His future looked brighter than ever. Experts figured he would win his 200th game sometime in late 1940 or early 1941, when Diz would be no more than 30 years old. He clearly had a shot at the all-time career marks set by Grover Alexander and Christy Mathewson (373 in the National League). His salary had climbed to $25,000, a remarkable figure for a Rickey employee. The world seemed to be in the palm of Diz's hands.

It was not to be. The downfall began before the 1937 All-Star break, when he bitterly criticized umpire George Barr for calling a balk on him in a close game. He later told a dinner group that Barr and National League President Ford Frick were "the two biggest crooks in baseball." When the remarks made the headlines around the country, Frick suspended Dean, pending an apology. Diz told the world, "I ain't signin' nuthin'," and he never did. The suspension was lifted a few days later (perhaps because Frick wanted to win the All-Star Game), and Diz returned to the mound.

The '37 season was also the year in which the managers selected the All-Stars, and Bill Terry tabbed Dean and his 12–7 record to start for the senior circuit. (Diz had hurled three scoreless innings in the '36 contest, and had allowed only one run on six hits in his seven total All-Star innings.) There was only one hitch—Dean did not want to play. He said he was tired, and probably still resented the suspension. Only last-minute lobbying by his wife prodded him into going to Washington, where he took the mound and retired the first eight men he faced, before allowing a single by Joe DiMaggio.

The next batter was Lou Gehrig, ever dangerous with men on base, and still in prime form (.351, 49 homeruns, 159 RBIs that year). Dean ran the count to three-and-two. Catcher Gabby Hartnett called for a breaking ball on the next pitch, but Diz refused. He wanted to "fog" one past the Iron Horse, but Gehrig was ready and creamed the pitch 450 feet to right field for a two-run homer.

The blow did more than put the Americans up, 2–0; it made Dean so angry that he lost his concentration and tried to "fog" one past Earl Averill, a notorious fastball hitter. The Cleveland outfielder jumped on the pitch and slashed a low line drive back to the mound. It struck Dean on the left foot and bounced away. Diz hobbled off the mound, grabbed the ball, and threw Averill out at first, but the damage was done. X rays revealed a fracture of the big toe, and Dean was warned not to return to the mound until the injury had completely healed.

Of course, Ol' Diz thought he knew more than the doctors, and he came back too soon. He faced the Braves, and struggled through six innings by using an unnatural motion that favored the injury. In the seventh, he felt something pop in his throwing arm, and the fastball was gone forever. He finished the season 13–10, with 120 strikeouts, the majority of which came before the All-Star break.

Rickey hated to see his top drawing card go by the boards, but he had no intention of holding on to a sore-armed fastball pitcher. St. Louis dealt Dean to the Cubs in the off-season, receiving $185,000 and three players (pitchers Curt Davis and Clyde Shoun, and outfielder Tuck Stainback). Diz showed up in spring training with a new motion. The old smooth, three-quarter-arm delivery was gone, replaced by a side-armed motion that featured curves and changeups. Pitching largely on guile and experience, Diz was able to keep the hitters off balance, and compiled a 7–1 record over 74⅔-innings with a 1.80 ERA. Chicago found themselves in a death-run with the Pirates, and when the two clubs met in Wrigley Field in late September, Manager Hartnett tabbed Dean as his starter in the second game of a three-game series.

As always, Diz came through with a tremendous outing. He held the Pirates at bay into the ninth inning, leading 2–0, before giving way to reliever Bill Lee. Lee allowed a run on a wild pitch, but held on for a 2–1 win.

When the Series against the Yankees began a week later, Hartnett announced that Dean would face the Bronx Bombers in game two. Again using that mixture of guile and off-speed curves, Diz took a 3–2 lead into the eighth inning. (It should have been 3–0, but for a weird play in the second inning. The Yankees had two men on, and one out, when a ground ball to the left side of the infield seemed a certain double play. However, Billy Jurges and Stan Hack cracked heads while trying to field it, the ball "split the defense," and Dean wound up chasing it into left field. Two runs scored.)

George Selkirk led off the Yankees' eighth with a single, but Dean retired the next two batters. Diz also thought he had retired Frank Crosetti on a called strike three, but the plate umpire disagreed. Diz lost his temper, and tried to "fog" one past the Yankees shortstop, but the "fog" was more a "bog," and Crosetti (who had not hit a homerun in 29 previous World Series games) slammed the pitch over the wall to put the Yankees ahead to stay.

For all intents and purposes, Dean's career was over. In 1939, he pitched 96⅓-innings and compiled a 6–4 mark. A year later, he went 3–3 in ten outings, and in 1941, he pitched one inning and then retired. His final mound appearance was reserved for the DeWitt challenge match mentioned at the beginning of the chapter.

After leaving the Cubs, Diz accepted an offer to announce the Browns games as a radio commentator. He was an incredible success, adding life to a team that was generally a disaster. His fractured English ("The runner slud into third" and "The players returned to their respectable bases") earned the ire of the English teachers of St. Louis, but the respect of thousands of listeners. In 1950, Diz told the world that he was "fed up with them sloggish Browns," and accepted a similar position with the Yankees' television network.

His first broadcast was hilarious. "Well, I'm through talkin' about things folks ain't seein,'" he told his audience. "And I'm just as calm and confidential in front of these cameras as anyplace else. Only difference between radio and television is they ain't so much to talk about in television. If a batter is taking his stanch [sic] at the plate, all you got to do is name him. They ain't no point in sayin' he's takin' his stanch [because] all you folks can see it. And, for an example, say that Roo-soo-toe [Phil Rizzuto] has got forked out while tryin' to steal second. If you got your eyes on your set, you seen him tagged out, or sees the empire [sic] signal. So they ain't no use for me to say much except to commertate [sic], maybe, why Roo-soo-toe takin' such a chance and tried to steal second."*

He was soon promoted to the CBS Game of the Week, where his gift of gab continued to fascinate audiences:

"That batter's shakin' his head—he don't know. I don't know what he don't know, but I know he don't know. Look at them empires, they don't know, neither. If I knowed what they don't know, folks, I'd sure tell ya. An' ol' Diz ain't awoofin'."**

Dean was so popular that Twentieth Century-Fox paid him $50,000 for the rights to his life story, and produced a so-so film entitled "Pride of St. Louis."

By the time Diz relinquished the broadcasting microphone, he was a well-to-do farmer-businessman with many solid investments. Even years after he retired from active life, he simply could not escape the public. More than 100 letters a day arrived at his home, seeking everything from an autograph to an interview, and he did his best to answer every one.

Pat's fine Southern cooking also helped Ol' Diz put on substantial extra pounds—he shot up to 300 of them! Of course, the extra weight prompted yet another famous story. Years back, when Diz and President Dwight Eisenhower were out on the links, the war hero asked, "Dizzy, for a man who plays golf so well, how can you permit yourself to get so overweight?"

"Mr. President," the answer began, "I was on a diet for the first 25 years of my life. Now that I'm makin' some real money, I'm makin' sure I eat good to make up for them lean years."

Dean's election to the Hall of Fame in 1953 was a foregone conclusion. He was so popular that nothing short of divine intervention could have kept him out.

When Jay Hanna Dean passed away on May 17, 1974, baseball lost one of its most popular, fun-loving, good-natured characters. They never will forget Ol' Diz.

---

*From "Disfergettable' Diz," by Pee Wee Reese, *The Sunday Bulletin,* April 6, 1975.
**From "Dizzy Dean—He's Not So Dumb," by Frank Tolbert, *The Saturday Evening Post,* July 14, 1951.

* * *

Jay Hanna Dean pitched in only 317 games in his career, and was washed up at the age of 27. His final "statics" (Dean's own word for statistics) show 150 wins, 83 losses, a 3.03 ERA, 26 shutouts, 1,155 strikeouts, and less than one hit allowed for each of the 1,966⅓-innings he pitched. Admittedly, these statistics are not overwhelmingly impressive, let alone good reason for admission to the Baseball Hall of Fame, in and of themselves.

Closer scrutiny is essential, and explains why Dean is not only enshrined in Cooperstown, but also walks among the true superstars of diamond history. Returning to the statistics, first—for 5½ seasons, Dean was the dominant pitcher of his day: 133-72, the league leader in strikeouts for four consecutive seasons, an ERA just over 3.00 (a much more difficult task in those days of complete games and dozens of .300 hitters). More significantly, Dizzy Dean dominated the sports pages like no man had since Babe Ruth. His every act was covered and printed for distribution from coast to coast. He became a living legend, performed like a superman in the 1934 World Series, and earned the respect and sympathy of the fans across the globe with his heartbreaking loss in the '38 Series. Then, when the arm was dead and his career had ended, he made the transition to the broadcasting booth, and thereby kept the Dean story alive. Did the years in the booth make a difference? Probably. But the fact remains that many other men have left the field for broadcasting careers—and they have been forgotten. The difference was that Diz had what it took, that charisma, that certain down-to-earth Americana quality, and that essential element of success that made him the superstar he clearly was. And, as Pee Wee Reese put it in eulogizing the late Dean, "I ain't awoofin'."

LEFTY GROVE

One day Hall of Fame shortstop Joe Cronin booted a ninth-inning ground ball. The error allowed the winning run to score, and Lefty Grove was tagged with the loss.

As soon as the game ended, Cronin raced for the clubhouse and locked himself in the manager's cubicle—a wire-mesh enclosed area.

Seconds later, Grove came charging in, only to find the errant shortstop out of reach . . . so Lefty climbed on a chair until his head was above the mesh, and blistered him until Cronin's hair curled.

"I couldn't even begin to repeat what he said," Cronin recalled, thirty years later. "He used every obscenity in the book, and a few I'd never even heard before. I could have killed him for it, but I knew all about his bad temper so I took it. When I think about it today, I still cringe. I had to be crazy."

And *Cronin,* not Grove, was the manager!

"He could throw a lamb chop past a wolf."
—Mickey Cochrane

When Philadelphia Athletics owner Connie Mack agreed to pay the Baltimore Orioles $100,000 for their ace southpaw, Robert Moses "Lefty" Grove, Orioles owner Jack Dunn saw an opportunity to garner a few extra headlines.

"Why not make the price $100,600?" he asked. "That way, we break the record 100-grand Boston paid me for Babe Ruth."

Mack had no objections. After all, Grove had compiled a 109-36 mark during his 4½ seasons with the Orioles, threw a fastball that rivaled Walter Johnson's, and was the hottest piece of minor league property in the country. Besides, Philadelphia had another major league team to contend with (Phillies) and the $600 would buy a lot of extra publicity that could help at the gate.

What did Connie get for his money? Everything he expected, and more. Grove went on to win 300 games (against 141 losses). He was a 20-game winner eight times, including marks of 28-5 and 31-4 in 1930-31. Lefty led the American League in earned run average *nine* times, and finished with a 3.06 ERA over 17 seasons.

"Robert," as Connie Mack always called him, was not only a winner, but was also a great strikeout pitcher. At 6-3, 190 pounds, Grove was an awesome-looking hurler who used his overpowering fastball to lead the league in strikeouts seven times (en route to 2,266 career "K's"). Walter Johnson probably threw harder, but Johnson lacked one thing Grove was renowned for. Walter was a pussycat. Grove was *mean*.

"Grove was what baseball people called 'pleasingly wild,'" said fellow Hall-of-Famer Joe Sewell. "What's more, he had a mean streak in him, and with his fastball, he inspired a fear in the batters that Johnson never did. You could dig in against Johnson. He wouldn't come inside and never threw at you. But Grove, well, he always looked angry, hateful, and we all knew about his temper. No one would dig in against him. We didn't wear batting helmets in those days, you know. A lot of good hitters were scared to death that he'd uncork one at them and end their careers, or their lives.

"However, I have to be frank with you," he continued. "I was very fortunate in my meetings with Grove. I batted over .400 against him lifetime, but even there, with that kind of success, I was scared. And, as the encyclopedias will tell you, not too many people did too much hitting off Grove."

Of course Lefty was often asked about his wildness, and his response never changed.

"I never threw at a hitter," he'd say. "If I ever hit a guy on the head with my fastball, he'd be through. I knew it, and the hitters knew it. However, I was naturally wild enough to give them something to think about."

"Old Mose," as he was known toward the end of his career, loved to throw his heat against the free swingers of his day, and was particularly proud of his success against Babe Ruth (9 homeruns allowed in 10 seasons). In fact, Grove had some of his greatest days against the Yankees, who were frequent victims of the "Lonaconing Express." The most memorable conquest of Ruth and company came in 1928, when Lefty struck out Ruth, Gehrig, and Meusel on 10 pitches while the winning run perched on third with no outs.

On another occasion, he struck out Earle Combs, Tony Lazzeri, Ruth, Gehrig, and Meusel on 16 pitches.

Not that the Yankees were his only victims. He consistently mastered the Red Sox,

Tigers, Indians, Browns, and White Sox during his days in an A's uniform. Only the Washington Senators gave him trouble—and plenty of it: They won their first 17 decisions against him!

If Grove had a weakness, it was his uncontrollable temper. His tantrums on, and off, the field were incredible. Perhaps the most famous occurred on August 23, 1931, in a game he lost to St. Louis, 1–0. Lefty started the day with a 16-game winning streak (equaling the league record set by Johnson and Joe Wood), and had high hopes of extending it against the hapless Browns. Prior to the game, outfielder Al Simmons had been given permission to go home to Milwaukee for personal reasons. Connie Mack started Jimmy Moore in his place. In the third inning, after a single by Goose Goslin, the luckless substitute misjudged a fly ball off the bat of Jack Burns, and Goslin came all the way around to score.

Grove went berserk in the clubhouse, destroying everything that wasn't nailed down, and then confronted the gentlemanly manager.

"Why the hell did you let him go home to Milwaukee?" Grove demanded, as he began a 15-minute tirade, the rest of which is best left unprinted.

But Mack was wise in the ways of baseball, and in matters pertaining to "Robert," so he let the enraged hurler talk himself out, and then silenced him by saying, "Now, now Robert. Calm down. It's only a ballgame." (Perhaps so, but Grove won his next six straight, and never forgave Simmons.)

Another Grovian eruption occurred after a 4–2 loss to the White Sox in 1936. By that time, Lefty had been traded to Boston, because the Depression had forced Mack to sell off his stars.

"Do you think Grove is going to throw his arm off for you hitless wonders?" he told his startled teammates.

"We're doing the best we can for you, like everybody else," replied slugger Jimmie Foxx. "Now you'd better shut up!"

And shut up he did, but he also avoided the team for a few days, refusing to ride with them to and from the park, opting for a 5-mile walk instead.

Only Jimmy Dykes seemed capable of soothing the savage beast on the field.

"I was his good friend off the field, so I was the only one allowed to go near him when he was on the mound," Dykes recalled. "If I saw his blood pressure going up, I'd get the ball and hold it for a while. After a few seconds, I'd go near him, but not too near. He'd snarl 'Give me the ball.'

"I'd step back and say, 'Wait a second, Lefty.'

"He'd growl, 'Gimme the ball!'

"I'd say, 'This is your buddy, Jimmy, talking. Now just relax.'

"But he'd keep snarling for the ball, and after a while I'd walk close enough for him to tear it out of my hand. It was quite a routine, and the fans loved it."

Lefty became the most respected tantrum thrower in baseball, and actually began tutoring teammates in the art of tantrum. One day Billy Werber came into the dugout, furious over a called strike three. He headed straight for the water bucket, and before Grove could warn him, lashed out at the bucket, toes first, and broke his big toe.

"When are you going to remember what I've told you about kicking buckets," Grove screamed. "You either make sure they are empty, or you use the bottom of your foot. How thick can you be?"

The media described Grove as surly, ill-mannered, and a grouch, but Lefty's lack of social grace was probably more a product of his background than intent. Born on March 6, 1900, in the western Maryland coaltown of Lonaconing (hence "The Lonaconing Express"), Grove had little experience with strangers and no training in etiquette. He was always uncomfortable around people who had more schooling than he, and spent most of his time sitting in hotel lobbies, watching the world go by.

"I know one thing," he said. "If I ever owned a ballclub, I'd want 25 guys as eager to win as I am and I don't care what their education is. All they have to know is baseball. Sometimes the smart guys with degrees are too smart!"

Until his 17th year, Grove never played organized ball, and when he finally joined the Midland minor league team, it was as a first baseman. That ended on a day when the starting pitcher never showed.

"I always thought it was ridiculous for the first baseman to throw harder than the pitcher," Grove said, in 1974. "You know, baseball looked pretty good to me. I'd had a taste of coal dust in those mines, and I'd worked as a railroad spikeman and in a glass mill. One day some guy asked me to play for Martinsburg, a Class D team. I told my dad that I didn't put the coal in there, and I didn't see why I should dig it out, and I went off to play ball for $125 a month.

"Unfortunately, Martinsburg didn't have a ballpark to play in, so we opened on the road while they built one," he continued. "A jerrybuilt grandstand was put up, but they ran out of money and couldn't put up a fence, so they sold me to the Orioles for $3,000. I was the only major leaguer ever traded for a fence."

He went 12–2 with the O's, led them to the Little World Series, and then went home to marry his childhood sweetheart, Ethel Gardner. Jack Dunn refused to sell him during the off-season, spurning many lucrative offers, and continued to hang on to his new wonder arm until Mack came around with the $100 grand.

"I was 25 years old when I joined the A's," Grove recalled. "My catcher was Mickey Cochrane, and we didn't even have signs. Sure, we went through the motions of giving and taking them, but it was just an act. All I ever threw that year was my fastball."

Lefty went 10–12 with a league-leading 116 strikeouts and 131 walks in his rookie year (1925) and improved to 13–13 with 194 strikeouts in 1926.

"His biggest problem those first two years was that he rushed every pitch," Mack recalled. "I tried to slow him down by having Mr. Cochrane waste time between pitches, but that only infuriated Robert. Finally, I told the youngster to count to 15 between pitches. That didn't work too well, either. The fans picked up on it, and began counting for him. That made him even angrier. Eventually, he learned to pace himself."

Robert exploded to a 20-12 mark in 1927, led the league in strikeouts for the third straight year, and reduced his walks to 79. The year 1929 was even better: 20-6, and two saves in the World Series against the Cubs.

In 1930 Grove had the first of two outstanding years: 28-5, 2.54 ERA, 209 strikeouts, 60 walks, and nine saves. He split two World Series starts, downing Burleigh Grimes, 5-2, in game one, but wasting a five-hitter in game four. Then, in one of his greatest moments, Lefty relieved George Earnshaw in game five, with the score 0-0. He held the Cardinals scoreless until Foxx's homerun in the ninth won the ballgame.

There were still a few non-believers, but Grove's 1931 performance put all doubts to rest: 31-4, 2.06 ERA, 175 strikeouts, 62 walks, and 5 saves. He also became the answer to a popular baseball trivia question: Who stopped the Yankees 308-consecutive-game scoring streak? Lefty. He defeated New York, 5-0 on August 3. Off the field, Lefty drew headlines by hurling his fastball through Libbey-Owens' new "shatterproof and breakproof" glass, leaving a hole the size of the ball.

Grove bested the Gashouse Gang two out of three again, but the A's lost the Series in seven games. Sadly enough, it was not only Connie Mack's final postseason appearance, but was also Grove's.

After two more fine years in Philadelphia (25-10, 24-8), he was sold to the Red Sox, along with Rube Walberg and Max Bishop, for $150,000 Depression dollars. Lefty's first year in Boston was a miserable experience. He developed arm trouble for the first time in his career, appeared in only 22 games, and finished 8-8.

"My fastball was never the same after I left the A's," he lamented. "Fortunately, by '34 I had developed a curve and a forkball. I began working on the curve when I was a rookie. The A's built me a special mound in spring training so I could throw on the sidelines. I started by just spinning the ball, not trying to put too much on it. My control improved, and by the time I lost some of the zip off my fastball, the curve was effective . . . but then I hurt my arm."

A winter of rest proved to be effective, and Grove rebounded to 20-12, and a league-leading 2.70 ERA. He remained effective for four more seasons, but the Sox never came close to catching the Yankees. In 1940, Lefty dropped to an arm injury-plagued 7-6, and when he did not improve in 1941, he retired.

Grove's final victory was the 300th of his career, and came after several losses and no decisions in search of the magic number. Afterwards, Lefty threw a gigantic party, attended by most, but not all, of his teammates. Noticeable by their absence were Joe Cronin and Ted Williams.

After his playing days were over, Grove owned and managed three bowling alleys for many years. He also maintained his connection with baseball, not as a professional, but as a Little League coach. His teams were always successful, and kept him in contact with the group of people he always got along with: children.

Sadly enough, Grove never received the credit for youth work he deserved, but this was because he was secretive about it. One of the few stories that ever leaked out involved a group of children who played in a sandlot near the A's ballpark. Lefty was headed for the park, when he observed the group, in rags, using an old ball that was covered with black tape. A few days later, every one of the youths had a sparkling new uniform, a bat, and two new baseballs. Only the A's trainer knew where they came from.

Grove was elected to the Baseball Hall of Fame in 1947. He died on May 23, 1975, in Norwalk, Ohio.

How great was Lefty Grove? Johnson, Koufax, Mathewson, and Alexander each won five ERA titles. Grove won *nine*. His .682 winning percentage ranks fourth among pitchers who won 200 or more games, and only two other southpaws have surpassed his 300 career victories: Warren Spahn (363-245) and Eddie Plank (327-192). His 2,266 career strikeouts place him 24th on the all-time list.

In 1969, he was not only selected the greatest living left-handed pitcher, but the greatest left-handed hurler in baseball history; but that vote was conducted among 100 veteran sportswriters, many of whom had seen Lefty pitch.

The fact is that Grove, for all his victories and strikeouts, never captured the hearts of his teammates, let alone the fans. There is no doubt that the tantrums he threw offended his teammates. There is no doubt that they also combined with his image as a mean, surly, uneducated man to alienate the fans, and his retiring nature did not help.

Then again, his best years came with the long since defunct Philadelphia Athletics, a team which went 40 years and two franchise shifts before winning another pennant, a team which has been forgotten. In another city, or another time, Grove might have become a superstar, but today he is yet another in the cast of forgotten stars.

There is one final note to the man that was Lefty Grove. Despite his truculence and uncontrollable temper, Grove was never thrown out of a game, never jumped a ballclub, never walked off the mound, and never had a fight.

SANDY KOUFAX

"What does a guy have to do to pitch around here?" a frustrated young Dodgers southpaw asked General Manager Buzzy Bavasi one day.

"Get somebody out," he snapped in reply.

"But how can you get 'em out when you never get to pitch?" the kid persisted.

"Get the ball over the plate when you do pitch," the general manager screamed. "Right now you've got only one pitch—high!"

"Taking batting practice against him (Koufax) is like playing Russian roulette with five bullets, and in batting practice he's only laying it over!"

—Jim Gilliam

For the first six years of his major league career, the youngest man ever elected to the Baseball Hall of Fame was a dismal failure. At 6'2", 210 pounds, the flame-throwing southpaw from Brooklyn could fire a baseball as hard as anyone in the history of the game, but he could not throw strikes with any consistency. One day, he'd strike out 14 Reds or 18 Giants. The next time out, he'd walk five and fail to last the first inning. Entering the 1961 season, the man who would dominate the National League for the next six years, pitch four no-hitters, and humble the mighty Yankees in the World Series, was a disappointing 36-40, with an ERA of 4.10. The worst of it came in 1960: 8-13, a 3.91 ERA, and a substantial salary cut.

The turning point came in spring training, 1961. The Dodgers were headed for an exhibition game, when catcher Norm Sherry (whose lone claim to fame was as the brother of relief ace Larry Sherry) was thinking about the erratic performance of the 25-year-old pitcher.

"You should have some fun out there," he told the startled hurler. "Don't throw so hard, and use more curves and changeups, especially when you're ahead of the hitters. Ease up. Remember: pitching is a science."

Incredibly enough, the words coincided with a dramatic improvement. Los Angeles faced the Minnesota Twins that day, and the "erratic" left-hander turned in 7 hitless innings. He went on to win 129 of his remaining 176 regular season outings, lead the National League in ERA for five consecutive years, and break the all-time single-season strikeout record by nailing 382 batters in 1965 (since broken by Nolan Ryan).

And then, when the 30-year-old superstar reached the height of his career, when sportswriters were predicting 300 career victories for the most dominant pitcher of his era, arthritis made it impossible for him to continue to pitch and he retired.

On December 30, 1935, Jack and Evelyn Braun gave birth to a son they named Sanford. Less than three years later, they were divorced, and Evelyn had married Irving Koufax. Sanford took the name of his stepfather, and soon became known as Sandy. The youth grew up in Brooklyn, New York, where he attended Lafayette High School. Sandy was a fair student, but devoted all of his spare time to sports, particularly basketball. That's right, basketball. And on those rare days when he played baseball, it was as a first baseman, not a pitcher . . . until a former semipro named Milt Laurie saw him throw.

"You've got a big league arm," he told Koufax. "Why don't you pitch for my club [the Parkviews]?"

Koufax agreed to give it a whirl, and found he liked being the center of the action. He also found success—he hurled a no-hitter in his second or third game.

When Sandy finished high school in 1953, several colleges offered him athletic scholarships—for basketball. He selected the University of Cincinnati, where he averaged 10 points a game as a freshman. When the season ended, he decided to try out for the baseball team, more because of its spring trip to New Orleans than for the love of the game. Koufax not only made the team, but won four of five decisions. He struck out 51 batters in 32 innings, including a school record 18 in one game.

Soon, scouts from the Giants, Pirates, Braves, and Dodgers were following his every move. He spent the summer working at a sleep-away camp, but Laurie arranged for him to have a ride to Brooklyn for every Parkviews game. The Giants arranged a tryout at the Polo Grounds, and it was a disaster. He was so wild that catcher Bobby Hofman eventually stormed off the field. When Sandy asked manager Leo Durocher if he could go into the clubhouse to get a soda, Durocher berated him and literally chased him out of the ballpark.

Sandy's next contact with a major league team was via Pirates scout Ed McCarrick. The Koufax family traveled to Pittsburgh to meet general manager Branch Rickey, formerly of the Brooklyn Dodgers. The meeting was cordial, but no offer was ever made—probably because the Pirates ownership did not have the money to be competitive in the bonus wars of the Fifties.

The Dodgers were next, in the person of superscout Al Campanis. The former second baseman had seen Sandy pitch many times, but still wasn't ready to make an offer. One day, columnist Jimmy Murphy came to Campanis and threatened to tell the Yankees how good Koufax really was, so Campanis made his move.

Less than a week before Koufax was scheduled to return to college, Brooklyn offered him a $14,000 bonus, plus the minimum major league salary of $6,000 a year, for two years. The Koufaxes agreed. There was one problem: Brooklyn had roster problems, and could not actually ink the contract until December, so Irving Koufax and Dodgers owner Walter O'Malley (both lawyers) cemented the deal with a handshake.

The handshake agreement was tested less than two weeks later, when the Braves offered a $30,000 package. Koufax reluctantly turned them down, and on December 14, 1954, the Dodgers sold Billy Cox and Preacher Roe to Baltimore, and added Koufax to their roster.

As things turned out, the bonus and salary were nice from a financial perspective, but they probably had a very negative effect on Koufax's career. A rule in effect at that time required that any player who signed for a bonus and/or salary in excess of $4,000 had to remain on the club's major league roster for at least two years. As a result, Sandy spent the 1955 and '56 seasons languishing in the Dodgers bullpen, getting an occasional start, but missing out on the minor league experience that might have accelerated his development.

Sandy made his first start in Pittsburgh. He threw 105 pitches, walked eight, and was kayoed in the fifth inning. In his next outing, he struck out 14 Reds, and allowed one hit. The rookie finished the season 2–2, struck out 30, and walked 28, in 41$\frac{2}{3}$ innings.

Over the next three seasons, Koufax showed flashes of brilliance, but remained terribly erratic. In 1959, he won three in a row for the first time in his career, and set a National League record by striking out 18 Giants in one game. A few days later, he set a night game record by nailing 16 Phillies. During the World Series against the White Sox, he tossed a five-hitter, but lost the game, 1–0.

The strong points overshadowed his mediocre 8–6 record and 4.05 ERA, and the Dodgers joined Koufax in expecting big things for 1960. As things turned out, 1960 was a disaster for Sandy and the Dodgers. Los Angeles slumped to fourth place, 15 games behind the pennant-winning Pirates, and Koufax did little to help: 8–13, 3.91 ERA, but with an intriguing 197 strikeouts in 175 innings. His personal disappointment was compounded by a 33-percent salary cut for 1961, and Sandy considered calling it quits before convincing himself to give it one more year. He went to spring training wondering if he would even make the team, took a fateful bus ride with Norm Sherry, and the rest is history.

"There's no doubt that Norm helped me," he later admitted. "But I still believe that the key was confidence. If there was any secret or magic formula to my sudden success, it was getting to throw every fourth day, knowing that I'd be out there again even if I had a bad outing."

Manager Walter Alston recalled hearing about the famous Sherry conversation, but gave the lion's share of the credit to pitching coach Joe Becker.

"Joe would have Koufax pitching with a windup and without a windup, trying to discover some method that would put some rhythm into his delivery," Alston said in his autobiography, *Alston and the Dodgers* (written with Si Burick). "And just like that, they found it one day—all at once—just a little rocking motion on the pitching mound was all it took."

Others gave a large part of the credit to club statistician Allan Roth, who was among the first in his field to break statistics down into dozens of specialized categories. Roth supplied Sandy with several vital tidbits, including the fact that lefties hit him for a substantially higher average than righties (exactly the opposite of what normally occurs). The reason was simple: Sandy's curve broke in slightly to lefties, almost like a screwball. The pitcher altered his grip on the ball, the curve began breaking away, and the improvement was dramatic. Roth also pointed out that the opposition was hitting his first pitch at a .350 clip. Again, the explanation was simple: Sandy was so worried about his control that he tended to just fire the ball over the plate on the first pitch to each hitter, rather than pitch to spots. Again, the pitcher came up with the cure—spotting that first pitch in a scientific manner, rather than trying to blow the hitters down. Again, the results were most satisfying.

In reality, it was as much a case of Koufax using his brain to overcome the control problems, as it was the help he received from his coaches and teammates.

In 1961, Koufax went 18–13 with a 3.52 ERA, and a league-leading 269 strikeouts in 255 2/3 innings (breaking the old N.L. mark of 267 by Christy Mathewson). He allowed only 96 walks. A year later, he was cruising along at 14–4, and the Dodgers appeared to be shoo-ins in the pennant race, when he was hit by a pitch thrown by Pittsburgh's Earl Francis. Koufax always feared being hit by a pitch, and, despite being a solid natural right-handed batter, insisted on batting lefty to protect his throwing arm. Ironically, the pitch struck on the bat, just above the left hand, breaking an artery in the fleshy part of the limb. It cut off the circulation to his index finger.

The finger remained numb for the next few days, and there was no sensation in it when Sandy took the mound to face the New York Mets on June 30th at Dodgers Stadium. He struck out the side on nine pitches to open the game, and went on to record 13 whiffs and 5 walks in his first no-hitter. The only tough out of the game came in the second inning, when shortstop Maury Wills had to go deep in the hole to field a ground ball by Frank Thomas, and just nipped him at first. The only other close call came with one out in the ninth, when Hot Rod Kanehl tried to bunt his way on. The crowd held its breath as the ball rolled along the baseline, but it hooked foul, and Kanehl bounced the next pitch to third. When Felix Mantilla popped out, the 29,797 fans on hand exploded to celebrate Sandy's 11th win of the season.

The finger remained numb, and a rare constriction of the blood vessels in the hand (Reynaud's Phenomenon) set in. Suddenly, Sandy could detect no pulse, and if he pressed the index finger, it turned white and stayed that way for hours. Pitching soon became out of the question, as doctors raced against gangrene to save the finger. Drugs and injections designed to dissolve blood clots eventually corrected the condition, but Koufax had missed more than 2 months, and the Dodgers had slumped badly. He returned to action on September 21st, against the Cardinals, and they drove him out in the first inning. Sandy lasted five innings in his next start, but was kayoed after one inning against the Giants in the best-of-three League Playoff.

Speculation was that Sandy was finished, and when a stiff shoulder caused him to miss three turns at the beginning of the 1963 season, the Dodgers feared the worst. Koufax returned to action after a two-week layoff, and while Alston and company held their breath, the southpaw came through with a marvelous 11–1 victory.

Koufax returned to the mound four days later, and pitched his most satisfying no-hitter, an 8–0 victory over the archrival Giants.

"I did not have overpowering stuff," he told reporters after the game. (He struck out only four and walked two.) "I felt it was coming in my last game, the win against St. Louis, because I only threw 87 pitches in that one. My control has come a long, long way."

There were several hard-hit balls, and one tough play. Lead-off batter Harvey Kuenn opened the game with a screamer right to centerfielder Willie Davis. In the fifth inning, Orlando Cepeda chopped a slow roller just past the pitcher's mound, but shortstop Dick Tracewski raced in to throw the big man out. Two innings later, Felipe Alou drove a fastball to the wall in left ("I thought it was out of the park," Koufax later said), but Tommy Davis caught it against the fence. Willie Mays drove the next pitch on the line—right to third baseman Jim Gilliam. The final out of the game was a one-hopper right back to the mound, and Koufax elected to take it himself, outlegging Kuenn to the bag.

Koufax went on to record a league-leading 25 wins against 5 defeats, a glistening

1.88 ERA (his second consecutive ERA championship—he had come in at 2.54 in his shortened 1962 season), and a league-leading 306 strikeouts (against 58 walks). He also hurled 11 shutouts, to lead the league in yet another category.

Yet, it was not until the World Series that Koufax's name vaulted from the ranks of the mere stars into those of the superstars. Los Angeles faced the awesome offense of the New York Yankees, and the world waited to see what the ace of the National League could do against the likes of Mantle, Maris, and Howard. In particular, writers and sportscasters alike relished the matchup of Koufax versus Ford on the mound, and Koufax versus Mantle (the greatest hitter of the era) at the plate.

Sandy faced the Yankees in game one, confident that he could handle their awesome lineup. The New Yorkers were eqully certain that Koufax wasn't really that fast, and that they could handle him. Their opinion changed after the first five batters (Richardson, Kubek, Tresh, Mantle, and Maris) had all struck out. By the time Tresh hit a two-run homerun in the eighth inning, the Yankees were behind, 5-0. Richardson, who struck out only 22 times in 630 regular-season at-bats, went down on strikes three times. When Harry Bright came up with two outs in the ninth inning, many of the Yankee Stadium fans were rooting for him to strike out, and thereby become the record 15th man to go down swinging in a World Series game. Bright cooperated magnificently, and Koufax had the record (broken by Bob Gibson a few years later).

Koufax returned to the mound for game four, and sealed the sweep with a 2-1 win. Whitey Ford pitched a two-hitter (Koufax allowed six safeties, including a homerun by Mantle), but it was not enough. The Bombers (?) were beaten.

"I can see how he won 25 games," Yogi Berra said after the Series was over, "but what I can't understand is how he lost five."

Koufax was now a superstar, and he demanded that the Dodgers pay him like one. The Dodgers gradually increased their offers to the $70,000 mark, but Sandy wanted $75,000. As spring training approached, a story appeared in several newspapers that Koufax was holding out for $90,000. According to Koufax, there was never any thought of $90,000, and he always believed that someone in the Dodgers front office had leaked that figure to pressure him into signing.

"I was maneuvered into a corner where I was forced to agree to their terms or else be regarded as a greedy, no-good bum," he said at the time. "But I never forgot it, either."

His contract hassles apparently resolved, Koufax appeared ready for another incredible season . . . but, once again, health problems interfered. His shoulder remained stiff through spring training, and the adhesions in it did not loosen until his third start of the regular season.

When the shoulder finally loosened, the southpaw continued to complain that he "Just didn't feel quite right" when he threw. Sandy carried a mediocre 5-4 record into June, which seemed to confirm that something was wrong. The team physician and trainers could find nothing physical, so Koufax began searching through the Dodgers' files to determine whether he had somehow changed his pitching motion. Sure enough, he discovered conclusive evidence that he was overstriding to his left. This defect caused him to throw across his body, and thereby rob himself of power and control.

When Sandy warmed up for his June 4th start at Philadelphia, he concentrated on correcting his stride, and by the time the game got under way, he was positive that everything would be all right. The game confirmed it. The Phillies' predominantly right-hand-hitting lineup managed only four outfield flies, and easily became his third no-hit victims. Had not Richie Allen worked out a walk on a 3–2 pitch in the fourth inning, Koufax would have achieved perfection.

"I'm still second-guessing myself about that 3–2 pitch," he recalled. "Catcher Doug Camilli had called for a curve, but I shook him off. Then, right in the middle of my windup, I realized that Allen would be expecting a fastball, and it broke my concentration. The pitch was low."

Sandy pitched most of the game under incredible pressure. The score remained 0–0 until the top of the seventh, when Jim Gilliam singled, Tommy Davis singled, and Frank Howard hit a towering homerun. The three-run bulge eased the burden a bit, and Sandy went on to strike out four of the final five batters. He finished the game with 12 strikeouts—the 54th time that he had set down 10 or more, tying him with Rube Waddell and Bob Feller for 10-strikeout performances. (He broke the record a few days later, and finished his career with 97 10-strikeout games.)

His motion problems solved, Sandy reeled off 11 wins in his next 12 decisions. Another 25-victory season seemed a certainty, but bad luck struck again. While diving back to second base on a pickoff play in early August, Sandy landed hard on his left elbow. The joint grew increasingly sore, but Sandy finished the game, and even pitched and won his next two starts.

"And then came that morning when I woke up and had to drag my arm out of bed," he recalled. "It was swollen from the shoulder to the wrist. My elbow was the size of my knee, and I couldn't straighten my arm out. Even worse, I could hear the liquid sloshing around inside it."

X rays disclosed traumatic arthritis, and the doctors ordered Sandy to take the rest of the year off. Without their ace, Los Angeles slumped, and by the time Sandy was pronounced ready to return, the Dodgers were out of the race. A brief consultation with the front office produced the agreement that Koufax should take the rest of the year off.

Again, the Dodgers and Koufax held their breath at the start of spring training, and again, the early going was discouraging. The arm began acting up, and it was feared that Sandy would become a once-a-week pitcher at best. Again, the heady southpaw did a little thinking of his own, and came up with his own solution: no throwing between starts.

It worked like a book. He won 26, lost 8, led the league in ERA (2.04), and set an all-time single-season strikeout record (382—which has since been broken by Nolan Ryan). The season also featured two heart-stopping moments, one of which resulted in a series of fines being handed out to members of the Dodgers and Giants, and the other of which produced Sandy's fourth no-hitter and only perfect game.

The Dodgers-Giants rivalry had followed the teams west from New York. In 1959, the Giants finished three games behind L.A. A year later, the teams finished fourth and fifth; in 1961, second and third. In '62, they tied, and the Giants won the pennant via a playoff. The roles more or less reversed for the next few years, with the Dodgers winning it all in 1963 and '65, and the Giants finishing within striking distance.

By the time their mid-August series rolled around in 1965, the rivalry was as intense as ever. The trouble began when Juan Marichal threw brushback pitches to Maury Wills and Ron Fairly. Despite the urgings of his teammates, Koufax refused to retaliate, so catcher John Roseboro took matters into his own hands. With Marichal batting, Roseboro returned an inside fastball to Koufax by coming perilously close to the Giants pitcher's ear. Marichal claimed the ball nicked him. Roseboro said it missed him by about three inches. Observers say that the pair exchanged words, and then Roseboro came up out of his crouch to take what appeared to be a swing at Marichal. Marichal beat him to the punch by cracking his bat on the left side of the catcher's head. Roseboro went after Marichal, and landed at least one solid blow. The fracas was eventually broken up, and National League President Warren Giles fined Marichal $1,750 and suspended him for eight games. Roseboro sued for $110,000, and eventually settled for $7,000.

And where was Koufax while all this was going on?

"Just staying out of it," he chuckled. "I was scared for Johnny, but I wasn't about to jump in there. With my luck, I'd have come face-to-face with Willie McCovey, and then what would I do? Besides, as I recall, Willie Mays got in there right away to break it up, and no one was going to take a swing at him, either."

The perfect game involved an equal amount of tension and emotion, but in a different way. Koufax's opponent, Cubs southpaw Bob Hendley, held the Dodgers hitless through the first $6\tfrac{2}{3}$-innings, before Lou Johnson was safe on a bloop double. It proved to be the only safety of the game. (Fortunately for Koufax, the Dodgers had nicked Hendley for a run in the fifth, but it came without the benefit of a base hit. Johnson led off with a walk, was sacrificed to second, stole third, and continued home when catcher Chris Krug threw the ball into left field.) Hendley did not allow another hit, and the Dodgers did not score any more runs.

Koufax carried the perfect game into the seventh inning. He retired the first two hitters, and then fell behind, 3–0, to Billy Williams. Koufax reared back and fired the fastball three times, and Williams was retired. In the eighth, Santo led off, and Sandy struck him out, along with Banks and Byron Browne. The streak continued into the ninth, with Krug and pinch-hitter Joe Amalfitano going down on strikes. The final batter was Harvey Kuenn, a lifetime .303 hitter, and particularly tough to strike out because he slapped at the ball. Koufax threw him three fastballs, and the star batter, who only struck out 16 times that year, was history.

The Dodgers went on to win the pennant, and opened the World Series against the Minnesota Twins on October 6th. Koufax was *not* on the mound (it was the Jewish High Holiday of Yom Kippur, the Day of Atonement, a day on which Sandy never pitched), and the Twins pounded Don Drysdale for an 8–2 win.

When Jim Kaat pitched the Twins past Koufax, 5–1, in game two, the Twin Cities began plans for a world championship celebration. Claude Osteen set them back in game three (4–0), Drysdale scattered five hits in game four (7–2), and then Sandy took the mound for game five. He struck out ten, scattered four hits, and whitewashed Minnesota, 7–0.

The teams returned to the Twin Cities for game six, and Minnesota rebounded behind the pitching and hitting of Jim "Mudcat" Grant (six-hitter and three-run homerun) to tie the Series.

It all came down to a seventh and deciding game. The rotation called for Drysdale to pitch that game, but Alston went with his ace, Sandy Koufax. The Brooklyn southpaw ended the World Series with a flourish, striking out ten, scattering three hits, and beating Killibrew and company, 2–0.

After the World Series, Koufax was determined to get his money's worth out of the Dodgers. He realized that the elbow would never really heal, and that his career could end any day, so he planned to ask for a three-year contract for $500,000. Willie Mays had just signed for $105,000, thereby becoming the highest-paid player in the National League, and Koufax felt he was worth a lot more. He was also disturbed by General Manager Buzzy Bavasi's tactic of comparing Drysdale (23–12 in 1965) and Koufax during the negotiation sessions as a means of forcing each pitcher to lower his demands. Koufax and Drysdale were friends, so they talked about it, and decided to present a united front.

The plan was simple: They would bargain together, and each demand $500,000. Neither would sign without the other. If the Dodgers would not come across with the money, both of them would retire.

Bavasi met with them about a month after the series ended, and laughed at their demands. His top offer was $100,000 for Koufax and $90,000 for Drysdale, and there would be no multiyear deals if he had his way. The duo countered by informing Bavasi that the rest of the negotiations would be handled by their agent, Bill Hayes, and the annoyed general manager responded by refusing to see him.

A few weeks later, a representative of Paramount Pictures asked the pair to appear in a movie. A meeting produced an agreement for a picture that would begin filming in the spring. It also contained an escape clause in the event the pitchers resolved their contract problems and signed to play baseball in 1966.

In November, the celebrated pitchers became celebrated hold-outs, when they lowered their demands to $450,000 apiece, and revealed their plan to retire in a press conference. A tremendous controversy ensued, with writers, broadcasters, and fans debating whether the pitchers were worth that kind of money. After all, many people reasoned, the President of the United States received only $100,000 a year.

The contract hassle dragged on through the winter, and into late March. The Dodgers broke training camp and headed west to open the season, and their aces began filming at Paramount. It looked as if Koufax and Drysdale would really sit out the season.

The deadlock broke suddenly. Bavasi called Hayes, and not only agreed to bargain with him, but increased the Dodgers offer to $110,000 for Koufax and $100,000 for Drysdale. When Drysdale heard about the offer, he stepped in and agreed to the principle of separate contracts, only if Sandy got $125,000 and he received $110,000. Bavasi surrendered on the salary issue, but won his demand for separate, one-year contracts. The great salary debate that had filled the newspapers for weeks was over.

What did the Dodgers get for their money? Koufax led the league with 27 wins, a 1.73 ERA, 27 complete games, 323 innings pitched, 317 strikeouts, and 5 shutouts. Drysdale slumped to 13–16 and was never the same pitcher he had been. The Dodgers found themselves locked in a wild three-way race with the Pirates and Giants for the pennant. For the month of September, every time Koufax pitched, he faced the ace of the other team's staff. He won five straight games, before Ken Holtzman beat him, 2–1, to cut the Dodgers' lead to 1½-games. Sandy came back with a September 29th win over St. Louis, and the Dodgers headed into the final weekend with a three-game lead. The Dodgers needed two wins to clinch. They lost the opener, 5–3, to Chris Short and the Phillies, while the Giants won in Pittsburgh. The lead was two games. It rained all day on Saturday, so the Dodgers stayed in their hotels and watched the Giants win again on TV. On Sunday, the Giants won again, and the Dodgers lost the opening game of the make-up doubleheader. Disaster loomed. If Los Angeles lost the second game, the Giants would play a rain-out make-up in Cincinnati the next day. A win in that make-up, and there would be yet another Giants-Dodger playoff.

Who would take the mound in that second game? Alston went to Koufax, asked him if he was ready, and the 30-year-old southpaw with the arthritic elbow said yes. The Dodgers scored six runs early, and Koufax coasted through the first four innings. With one out in the fifth, a sharp pain ripped through his back. He struggled through the inning, and ran to the clubhouse while the Dodgers batted. The Dodgers' trainers began working on him, and believed he had slipped a spinal disc. They tried massaging it back into place, but their efforts were unsuccessful. Time was running out on Koufax and the Dodgers, when former Dodgers pitcher Don Newcombe ambled into the clubhouse. Newk stood 6'4", and had added a few pounds to his playing weight of 220.

"What's the problem, and how can I help?" he asked.

"It's his back," Bill Buhler, one of the two Dodgers' trainers, replied. "Grab him under the arms and hold him tight. I'm going to pull down hard on his legs."

The two men went to work, and miraculously, the disc went back into place, and Koufax returned to the mound just in time to begin the inning. The lead, and his back, held up until the ninth, when an error and three hits cut the lead in half. Sandy reared back and struck out Bob Uecker, retired Bobby Wine on a ground out, and struck out Jackie Brandt to win the game and clinch the pennant.

The Dodgers opened the Series against Baltimore, and fell victims to a superb $6\frac{2}{3}$-inning relief performance by Moe Drabowsky. Moe struck out 11, and allowed one hit, leading the O's to a come-from-behind 5–2 victory.

Koufax was slated for game two. He matched scoreless innings with Jim Palmer until the top of the fifth. Boog Powell led off with a single. Dave Johnson sacrificed him to second. Paul Blair lofted a routine fly ball to centerfield. Willie Davis settled under it . . . and dropped the ball. The play was ruled an error (Koufax said it should have been a hit because Davis lost the ball in the sun), and the O's had runners on second and third. Andy Etchebarren, a .221 hitter, was next. Alston left it up to Sandy whether to walk the rookie catcher, or try to overpower him. Sandy pitched, and Etchebarren lifted a short fly to center. Willie came running in, settled under the ball, began waving his hands to try to block the sun, and, déjà vu, dropped the ball. Powell scored. Blair raced for third, and Davis's throw sailed over Jim Gilliam's head, enabling Blair to score, and Davis to a record three errors in one inning. Palmer struck out, but Louis Aparicio doubled to left, and the Dodgers trailed, 3–0. The lead increased to 4–0, and Alston pulled Koufax after the sixth inning, figuring he would need the extra rest to be ready for game five.

There was only one problem. There would be no fifth game. Baltimore won the next two, and the Dodgers were no longer the world champions.

The baseball world had an inkling of what was going on in Sandy's mind when he refused to accompany the Dodgers on a barnstorming tour of Japan. He told reporters that he would not go because his arm was too tired to do any throwing, and if he went along and did not pitch, everyone would be disappointed.

Sandy had warned Bavasi that this was his last season, and on November 18th, he held a private press conference that made it official.

"I've had too many shots and taken too many pills because of my arm trouble," he began. "I don't want to take a chance of disabling myself. I don't regret for one minute the 12 years I spent in baseball, but I could regret one season too many.

"I'm young," he continued, "and I want to live a lot of years after this. I don't want to become bitter because I pitched one year too many. I've got a lot of years to live after baseball, and I would like to live them with the complete use of my body. I am retiring, effective immediately."

His playing career over and done, Sandy was recruited by NBC to join their Game of the Week broadcasting crew. He was paid $100,000 a year, worked hard to become a polished broadcaster, found it really wasn't what he wanted to do, and gave it up after six years.

For the final five seasons of his 12-year-career, Sanford Koufax, a Jewish kid from Brooklyn who preferred basketball to baseball as a youth, was clearly the dominating pitcher in modern National League history. During that span, he won 111 games and lost 34—a sizzling .786 percentage—while leading the National League in ERA every year. He captured three unanimous Cy Young Awards, led the league in strikeouts three times, and was named the Most Valuable Player in 1963. When he was healthy, the Dodgers won the pennant every time (1963-65-66); when injuries shortened his season, they collapsed without him.

Admittedly, his overall won-lost statistics are not as impressive (165-87, 2.96 ERA). Similarly, his 4-3 mark in the World Series is slightly misleading, and requires a glance at his 0.95 ERA to be put in its proper perspective.

But in 1971, Sandy Koufax became only the sixth player in history to win election to the Baseball Hall of Fame in his first year of eligibility. It was not his overall record that got him in. It was his 2,396 strikeouts in 2,324$\frac{1}{3}$-innings, his four no-hitters, and his conquest of the mighty Yankees that made him an overwhelming choice.

In all of baseball's history, only one other man pitched more than 1,000 innings and struck out more batters than innings pitched: Nolan Ryan.

More than 14 seasons have come and gone since Sandy Koufax threw his final major league pitch, and the Dodgers still miss him. The year after he retired, Los Angeles sank to eighth place. In 1968, they finished seventh, and only recently have Dodgers fans again known postseason play. (Of course, their opponents were the

Yankees, but there was no Koufax to stifle Reggie Jackson and company in 1977–78.) And when the Dodgers regained the world championship, the nation clearly believed the Yankees had blown it, rather than the Dodgers "winning" it.

Perhaps it is in the area of attendance that the mark of the true superstar is best measured, and Koufax was no exception. The true superstar brings the fans out, and Koufax scored as well in that category as any. Los Angeles averaged more than 10,000 additional fans for every game that Sandy pitched in his glory years. Even Buzzy Bavasi publicly acknowledged his value as a drawing card—he allegedly offered Sandy $150,000 to come out of retirement and pitch one game a week in 1968! In 1966, more than 2,167,000 fans paid their way into Dodgers Stadium. A year later, without Koufax, the figure dropped below 1,664,000. In 1968, Los Angeles drew a record low: 1,581,093.

Without Sandy, the Dodgers were just another team. The rest of the league knew it, the standings reflected it, and the fans were not fooled, either. There was no superstar in Los Angeles in 1967, and the team would not reach the top again until 1981.

DON DRYSDALE

Everybody paid so much attention to Koufax that Drysdale was overshadowed, but no pitcher I've ever seen could handcuff right-handed hitters the way Drysdale could.
—Walter Alston, Manager
Los Angeles Dodgers, 1954–76

Sure I hit guys on purpose when I was pitching, but only after they had hit one of our guys on purpose. I had a rule: For every one of our players who went down, two of theirs did.
—Don Drysdale

On May 31, 1968, Los Angeles Dodgers pitcher Don Drysdale was involved in one of the most unusual calls in major league history. The 6′5″, 190-pound right-hander had pitched four consecutive shutouts, and was on the verge of a record-tying fifth, when the San Francisco Giants loaded the bases with no outs in the ninth inning. Los Angeles led, 3–0, but the record, and the game, were very much in doubt.

Dick Dietz, a .272 hitter, was the next batter. "Big D" ran the count to 2-and-2, before unleashing a sidearm fastball that hit Dietz. The Giants catcher started toward first base, the runner on third (Willie McCovey) headed home, and the shutout string was over.

Or was it?

"Wait, you're not getting first base on that one," plate umpire Harry Wendelstedt told the startled Dietz. "You didn't even try to get out of the way, so it's only ball three. You stay here."

215

Dietz could not believe his ears. Neither could San Francisco skipper Herman Franks, who protested loudly, said a few magic words, and was ejected from the game. When play resumed, Dietz flew out to shallow left field, and McCovey could not tag up. Ty Cline bounced a ground ball to first baseman Wes Parker, who threw home for a forceout. Jack Hiatt popped up.

The inning was over (so was the game), the Giants were shut out, and Drysdale had a share of the record.

"It was a gutsy call," recalled Drysdale's catcher, Jeff Torborg, now a coach with the New York Yankees. "I never saw it called that way before, although I later found out that Nellie Fox was once involved in the same situation."

(On June 3, 1956, Fox was denied first base in a similar situation. Two pitches later, he was clipped again, and this time umpire Hank Soar gave him first base.)

Giants Vice-President Charles "Chub" Feeney, now the president of the National League, has never agreed with Wendelstedt's call, but has mellowed over the years.

"It would have been 'gutsy' if he had made that call in our ballpark," Feeney said, repeating his reaction of 1968. "However, it doesn't matter anymore, and in a way I'm glad. Drysdale went on to set two records that our league is proud of."

(Don beat the Pirates, 5–0, in his next outing, for a record sixth consecutive shutout, and then broke Walter Johnson's 56-scoreless-innings streak by hurling $4\frac{2}{3}$-scoreless-innings against Philadelphia.)

Of course, Wendelstedt was right. Rule 6.08-b specifically denies the hit batsman first base if he "makes no attempt to avoid being touched by the ball." Of course, the definition of "attempt" is left entirely to the umpire's judgment, and allows for consideration of overwhelming speed, losing sight of the ball, etc. . . . and what else was Drysdale if he was not overwhelmingly fast!

Donald Scott Drysdale was born on July 23, 1936, in Van Nuys, California. As he remembers it, Don began playing ball with his father *and mother* when he was five years old. He developed into a fine infielder, and might very well have made the grade in that capacity, had fate not intervened.

One summer afternoon in 1953, Don's father, Scott, needed a pitcher for his American Legion team. The scheduled starter was late for the game, and after looking his roster over, Scott gave the starting job to his son. The 16-year-old future major leaguer normally played second base, and had never pitched before. In fact, Scott Drysdale had expressly forbidden Don to take the mound until that time, because he was afraid the boy would develop "Little League elbow" from throwing too hard at too young an age.

Don lasted five solid innings, and was replaced by the scheduled starter when the latecomer arrived. The following spring, the sidearming righty went 10–1 for Van

Nuys High School, and became one of the most sought-after seniors in the country. Scholarship offers from two major baseball schools, and dozens of lesser institutions, as well as bonus offers from major league clubs, poured in from all over. Eventually, Don opted for the Brooklyn Dodgers package: a $4,000 bonus and $600/month. He spent half a season at Bakersfield, played two more years in the minors, and stuck with the varsity in 1956.

"Big D" relieved in the ninth inning of Brooklyn's opening day contest, allowing no runs, no hits, one walk, and notching his first major league strikeout. A few days later, he made his first start, and defeated the Phillies, 6–1, on nine hits and nine strikeouts. He went on to make 25 appearances that year (12 in a starting role), and posted a 5–5 record, 2.64 ERA, and 55 strikeouts in 99 innings. He also saw action in game four of the World Series against the Yankees, in which he pitched two innings and allowed a two-run homerun by Hank Bauer in New York's 6–1 win.

Drysdale established himself as a starter in 1957 (17-9, 2.69 ERA, 148 strikeouts, and 61 walks in 221 innings), and was soon making life miserable for the league's right-hand batters. His sweeping sidearm motion by way of third base caught many a hitter leaning away from the plate. He further "endeared" himself to the opposition by nailing a hitter every now and then—he knocked down Hank Aaron twice in their first meeting, and the future homerun king subsequently labeled the 21-year-old flame-thrower "one of the meanest pitchers I ever saw."

The Dodgers and Drysdale both slumped in 1958, the club's first year in Los Angeles, but a year later, both bounced back. "Big D" led the charge, as the Dodgers battled Milwaukee to a regular season tie, posting a 17–13 win-loss mark, and leading the league with 242 strikeouts. He started game three of the World Series against the White Sox, and scattered 11 hits over seven innings. Relief hero Larry Sherry took over from there, and Big D was a 3–1 winner.

The 1960 season was a mixed bag: on one hand, Drysdale slumped to 15–14; but the win-loss figure was deceptive. Big D also pitched to a 2.84 ERA, and led the league in strikeouts with 246. A year later, he finished at 13–10, 3.69, and 182—a clear disappointment.

Again, Drysdale and the Dodgers rebounded to tie for the National League championship. This time, Big D was the key to Los Angeles' success: a league-leading 25 wins (against 9 losses) and 232 strikeouts to go with a 2.83 ERA. When Koufax was injured midway through the season, Drysdale became the ace of the staff, and virtually pitched the team into the playoff with San Francisco.

That playoff held the ultimate frustration for the 26-year-old star: Manager Walter Alston refused to use him in relief in game three "because he wanted me to be ready to open up the World Series," and the Dodgers blew a late-inning lead and were defeated. It was "an incredibly frustrating feeling to sit there and watch us lose, especially because the manager knew I was ready, but he was the manager," Drysdale later told reporters.

There was no stopping the Dodgers and Drysdale in 1963. Koufax was healthy all year, and although Big D's win-loss mark dropped to 19-17, he had a 2.63 ERA, and 251 strikeouts. In the World Series against New York, he started the third game, and beat Jim Bouton, 1-0, on a three-hit, 11-strikeout performance.

"That was the biggest win of my career," he recalled, some 15 years later. "There were a lot of people who never thought we had a chance against the Yankees. Then, when we came back from New York, up two-games-to-none, a lot of people said that the only way we'd win the thing was to take game three, and put them down, three-zip. I guess people figured Sandy would only pitch one more game or something, and that the rest of us couldn't beat the Yankees twice. Well, we won that one, and the next one, and we were the world champions again."

Of course, the team and Drysdale maintained their every-other-year pattern by slumping in 1964. Koufax was out for part of the season, again, and Big D, at 18-16, was the only other pitcher above .500 (18-16, 2.18 ERA, 237 strikeouts). Los Angeles finished sixth, two games under .500.

In 1965, the pattern continued. Drysdale went 23-12 in his last superlative season, Koufax played a full season, and the Dodgers edged out the Giants by two games to take the pennant. Drysdale added a 2.77 ERA, 210 strikeouts, and 7 shutouts to his career marks, and when Koufax was unavailable for the opening game of the World Series against Minnesota, Big D got the nod . . . and the knock. He lasted less than three innings, was tagged for six runs (three of them on a Zoilo Versailles homerun), and was tagged with the defeat for the first time in postseason play.

When the Twins clobbered Koufax the next day, and took a commanding two-games-to-none lead in the Series, the pressure was on the Dodgers to sweep the Twins in L.A. Claude Osteen spun a five-hitter in game three, and then Drysdale returned with a five-hitter of his own (including 11 strikeouts) to even the competition. Big D would have pitched the seventh game, had Alston stuck to the rotation, but the manager tabbed Koufax, and the lefty pitched a three-hit shutout, to win it all.

During the off-season, Drysdale and Koufax staged their famous holdout; it is covered in depth in the chapter on Sandy.

Drysdale was always well liked by his teammates, largely because he always took a real interest in everyone, and because he had a good sense of humor, according to catcher John Roseboro, author of *Glory Days with the Dodgers.*

"One day, we were getting ready to start the ballgame when 'Big D' notices that Elizabeth Taylor is sitting in the stands behind home plate in Dodgers Stadium," Roseboro recalled. "On the first pitch of the game, he uncorks a wild pitch that goes all the way back to the screen on a fly, and plops down at the base of the wall. I picked up the ball, got a good look at Taylor—she was wearing a revealing low-cut dress—and then went out to the mound."

"What the hell's the matter?" I asked him.

"Just taking care of my catcher," he replied, with a mischievous grin.

In '66, Drysdale slumped (13–16), but the Dodgers did not. For the second consecutive year, they edged out the Giants, and met yet another new team in the World Series: the Baltimore Orioles. Once again, Drysdale was tabbed to start game one, and again he was kayoed early. Frank and Brooks Robinson touched him for homeruns in the first inning, and he left the game trailing, 3–0. The Dodgers lost, 5–2.

Baltimore took games two (6–0, over Koufax) and three (1–0, over Osteen), leaving Drysdale to pitch the fourth game and try to avert a sweep. It was not to be. Frank Robinson took Big D downtown in the fourth inning for the only run of the game, as Drysdale and Dave McNally matched otherwise scoreless four-hitters. No one knew it at the time, but it was the end of the Dodgers mini-dynasty. Koufax was forced into premature retirement, and although Drysdale would go on to set the record for wins by a Dodger pitcher (since eclipsed by Don Sutton), and major league records for consecutive shutouts and scoreless innings, he was never again the dominant pitcher he had been.

In 1967, none of the Dodgers starters pitched better than .500 ball. Koufax was gone, Osteen dropped to 17–17, and Drysdale finished 13–16, as the team plummeted to eighth place among ten teams. A year later, Drysdale rebounded to 14–12 (2.15 ERA and 155 strikeouts), but the Dodgers moved up only one notch in the standings.

Of course, that '68 season was highlighted by Drysdale's consecutive-scoreless-innings streak. He began the assault on the record books with a 1–0 win over the Cubs on May 14th, allowing two hits, striking out seven, and walking three. Four days later, he goosed the Astros by the same score, this time allowing five hits, striking out six, and walking two. The Cardinals went down on the 22nd, 2–0, again on five hits (eight strikeouts and no walks), and the Astros became the only double-dip in the streak, losing a 5–0 decision on the 26th (six hits, seven strikeouts, two walks). The Giants (3–0, six hits, seven strikeouts, two walks) and Pirates (June 4th, 5–0, three hits, eight strikeouts, no walks) completed the shutouts string, but the scoreless innings continued into a game with Philadelphia on June 8th.

Gene Mauch, the Phillies scientific skipper, had as much a hand in ending the streak as anyone. Drysdale was always accused of greasing up the ball, and Mauch had determined to rattle the pitcher as much as possible. At the end of the third inning, he asked umpire Augie Donatelli to check Drysdale's left wrist, cap, and shirt for moisture, and the man in blue did.

"I was suspicious, so I told him that if he went to the back of his head again, it would mean automatic ejection," Donatelli recalled.

At the end of the fourth inning, Mauch complained again, and Donatelli frisked the pitcher for the second time. Apparently, this broke his concentration, because when Drysdale returned to the mound in the fifth, Tony Taylor and Clay Dalrymple both singled. After Roberto Pena struck out, Howie Bedell flew out to left, and Taylor tagged up from third base and scored. The Dodgers went on to win the game, 5–3, thanks to relief help from Hank Aguirre, but the streak was over.

The histrionics about Drysdale's "grease" led to a television commercial for a well-known "greaseless" hair tonic in which Drysdale is checked for grease, and goes into the dugout to produce his bottle of the "greaseless" tonic. The commercial proved exceedingly popular, and earned the tall righthander a hefty royalty.

Drysdale finished the season 14–12 (2.15 ERA), but was plagued by injuries. He got off to a slow start in 1969, was placed on the disabled list for a while, returned to win five of nine decisions, and was sidelined again with shoulder trouble. The diagnosis was a torn rotator cuff in the throwing shoulder, and the pain had become unbearable. He struggled from July 27 through August 11, and then announced his retirement, less than a month after his 33rd birthday.

In 1970, Drysdale signed a multirole contract with the Montreal Expos. He was designated broadcaster, minor league pitching coach, and public relations man, among other things. Two years later, he relinquished his Montreal duties in favor of handling the color commentary at the Texas Rangers games. A year later, he was back in California, handling the Angels broadcasts, a role he enjoyed for the next six years. In 1978, he was signed by ABC television, and he continues as a very interesting, ever-improving broadcaster to this date.

At the height of his career, Donald Scott Drysdale was probably the most feared right-hander in all of baseball. He not only compiled a fine 209–166 career won-loss record (2.95 ERA) and struck out 2,486 batters (against 855 walks) in 3,432⅓-innings, thereby setting Dodgers club records, but also set the National League record for most hit batsmen: 154. He had no qualms about that last record—"The only man I was afraid to throw at was Don Zimmer" (who has a metal plate in his head thanks to another beaning, at another man's hands). Aaron hated to face him; Mays preferred to face Koufax . . . The only man who had any confidence against Big D was Willie McCovey, who ate him for breakfast, lunch, and supper every time.

Yet, as feared as he was, and successful as he was statistically over his 14-year career, today, Don Drysdale is only a household name because of his broadcasting role. He has not been elected to the Baseball Hall of Fame, despite seven years of eligibility, and although he may some day win a plaque in that hallowed hall, the fact remains that Sandy Koufax, and not Don Drysdale, was *the* superstar of those great Dodgers teams of the early '60s.

Don Drysdale

In 30 years, they will still remember Koufax for his blistering speed, superb strikeout ratio, and premature arthritic retirement. They will also remember his two victories over the Yankees in the 1963 World Series.

But Drysdale will be forgotten. He was always overshadowed by Sandy (as Alston pointed out in the quote that opens this chapter), and deservedly so. The record speaks for itself. When Big D had his best year (1962), all the Dodgers managed was a heartbreaking loss to the Giants in the best-of-three playoff. Admittedly, the team was hurt by the absence of Koufax for part of the season, and admittedly, Manager Alston held Don out of the third game, thereby most likely blowing it . . . but the bottom line is that Drysdale could not carry the team alone. On the other hand, when Drysdale had an off-year (1966), but Koufax was on, Sandy could, and did, lead the Dodgers into the World Series . . . or at least that's the way the average fan remembers it. (Obviously, one man does not win a pennant—if he did, then where were the Senators during Walter Johnson's career!) What matters in the long run is the impressions the fans were under, and remain under to this day . . . and that impression has always been, and will always be, that Koufax was the man, and Drysdale was merely a supporting actor.

Furthermore, when Drysdale had the opportunity to vault into immortality, when he had the limelight to himself, he did not win the big game. In 1965, and again in '66, Koufax was unavailable for the first games of the World Series. Both times, Drysdale made the start, and in both games he not only lost, but was pounded out of the box in the early innings. Even Walter Alston had no difficulty distinguishing the superstar from the star—he pitched Koufax, on two days rest, in game seven, rather than take a chance on the well-rested Drysdale.

The sad fact is that, were Big D not in the ABC booth today, just 11 years after his retirement, the man who set two all-time pitching records, won 209 games in 14 seasons, and struck out nearly three times as many men as he walked (a two-to-one ratio is considered good), would already be fading into the obscurity that envelops the mere stars of baseball's past. In 30 years, he will be forgotten by all, save those who saw him pitch, and those who were hit by one of his blazers!

MEL STOTTLEMYRE

> He saved our necks in 1964, and all he ever got for it was a slew of last place and weak teams. I haven't seen the real old timers, like Waite Hoyt and Red Ruffing, but I'll tell you one thing: Mel Stottlemyre had to be as good as any of them. He won 20-or-more games three times. Whitey Ford only did that twice. Lefty Gomez and Red Ruffing and Bob Shawkey did it four times each—but look at the teams they played for. In my book, Mel was as good as any of them, and maybe better.
> —The late Elston Howard

On August 11, 1964, the New York Yankees were floundering. The defending American League champions had just dropped an important doubleheader to the front-running Chicago White Sox, and suddenly found themselves in third place, 3½-games off the pace. More bad news awaited manager Yogi Berra as he entered his private office after the twin bill—Whitey Ford's injured hip would sideline the ace of the pitching staff indefinitely. The outlook was grim.

Fortunately, help was on the way—or had actually already arrived. General manager Ralph Houk had summoned a 6'1", 178-pound right-hander from the Yankees' top farm club as a replacement for Ford. The 22-year-old newcomer would soon be named Minor League Player of the Year, based on a 13-3 record with Richmond. He would soon supplant Ford as the ace of the staff, using fine control and a natural sinking fastball to notch 164 wins and a 2.97 ERA over what amounted to less than ten full seasons.

It turned out to be the best move Houk made in his three-year stint as the club's general manager. The next day, the blond-haired, blue-eyed pitcher from Mabton, Washington, took the mound, and defeated the ChiSox, 8–3. Four days later, he defeated the first-place Baltimore Orioles, 4–1. By the time the Yankees clinched their twenty-ninth pennant on the next-to-last day of the season, the youngster had won 9 of 12 decisions, posted a 2.06 ERA, and virtually saved the final pennant the "dynasty" would ever win.

And on October 8th, the future twenty-game winner took the mound against future Hall-of-Famer Bob Gibson in game two of the World Series.

Born on November 13, 1941, in Hazelton, Missouri, Melvin Leon Stottlemyre is the son of a construction worker. The Stottlemyres moved to the farming town of Mabton while Mel was a youngster, where he eventually established himself as the best athlete at Mabton High School. Although he enjoyed the gridiron and basketball court competition, Mel's first love remained baseball, and his greatest success came on the pitcher's mound.

"I remember when I was a little kid, my brother and I would take turns throwing to each other," he recalled. "We tried to throw strikes, and we called each other's pitches. We must have been very young, but we threw a lot of strikes. The emphasis on throwing strikes is something that has sort of stuck with me all through my career."

Stott pitched Mabton High to three successive league titles, and lost only one game in his three-year career. Scouts were few and far between in that rural neck of the northwest woods, and despite Mel's outstanding schoolboy record, there were no professional or college scholarship offers. Mel wanted to continue to play baseball, and get a college degree, so he enrolled at nearby Yakima Valley Junior College.

In 1960, while pitching Yakima to the state championship, Stott caught the eye of Yankee scout Eddie Taylor.

"There was no great demand for him," Taylor recalled. "In fact, no one else was interested. But the kid had a beautiful free-throwing arm, a natural sinker, and fine form, and, every time I saw him pitch, he was getting the batters out. In fact, when I checked into it, I was very impressed by one thing above all else: he was always a winner."

A bonus was out of the question because there was no competition to sign Mel, but he did get $450 per month as his starting salary—pretty good money in those days. The Yankees sent Stott to their California State League club for two weeks, and then shipped him east to Harlan, Kentucky (Rookie League). Stott saw action in eight games, won five of six decisions, and was promoted to Auburn. In 1962, Mel moved up to Greensboro, North Carolina (AA), where he drew rave reviews while posting a 17–9, 190-strikeout, 2.50 ERA season. He advanced to Richmond in '63, where he split 14 decisions for a last-place club. The Yankees considered bringing him north at the start of the '64 campaign, but decided that another year of seasoning could not hurt. Stott got off to a slow start in Virginia, and was eventually demoted to long relief work, before a Memorial Day doubleheader opened up another starting assignment for him. He threw a two-hit shutout, won six of his next seven starts, and appeared ready for the leap into the majors.

"I kept telling them [the Yankees front office] he was ready," former Richmond Manager Preston Gomez said, "but they didn't decide to bring him up until Ford got hurt. They seemed to have decided that Mel would be a full-year rookie in '65, but it didn't work out that way."

He arrived in New York on August 11th, watched his teammates lose a doubleheader, and was told he would start the next day.

"The sportswriters were skeptical about Yogi's decision to thrust me into the fire right away," Stott recalled, "but I wasn't nervous. There was no sense to getting nervous. I'd been pitching the same way for years, so I figured I'd just go out there and see how effective I'd be in the major leagues."

Chicago's slugging first baseman, Pete Ward (.282, 28 doubles, 23 homeruns that year) was not surprised, either.

"We're not expecting a lamb," he told reporters before the game. "If this kid was 13–3 at Richmond, he must have something. I played in that league for a year, and it's damned good ball."

Ward made two hits off the rookie that afternoon, but had nothing but praise for the maiden winner afterwards.

"He keeps the ball down on you," Ward said. "He has a tremendous sinker and good control. He was good enough to win today, and I suspect he'll be good enough to win a few more before the season ends. He'll probably be their ace in a few years."

Ward proved to be a good prophet. Stott won four in a row, five of seven, and nine of twelve decisions, to lead the Yankees to the pennant. Perhaps his toughest victory came against the Minnesota Twins on September 8, when he beat their ace, Camillo Pascual, 2–1.

"As I remember it, they got some bad hop hits, and we made a couple of errors on ground balls," the sinkerballer recalled. "You know I relied on my infielders to get 15 or more outs every time I pitched, and on that day, we couldn't buy a break in the field."

Two ground ball singles put Mel in the hole in the first inning. Three ground balls later, the side was retired, but a run scored on a Harmon Killibrew forceout at second. In all, the Twins hit 13 grounders, two of which were converted into double plays, and 9 Minnesotans struck out. The Yankees tied the score in their half of the first, and scored the game-winning run in the seventh, when Roger Maris doubled and the late Elston Howard singled him home.

Minnesota's final threat came in the eighth. Jerry Kindall led off with a base hit. After Tony Oliva struck out, Harmon Killibrew ripped a perfect double-play ball to short—but the bouncer struck a rock and sailed over Tony Kubek's head, and the Twins had runners on first and second. Stott induced Jimmy Hall to slap a grounder to first. Again, it should have been a double-play ball; but this time, Joe Pepitone bobbled it and had to settle for an out at first while the runners moved up. The next batter was Bob Allison, and Mel induced him to hit the fourth ground ball of the inning. This one was hit to the sure-handed Clete Boyer at third, who fired over to Pepitone for the inning-ending out.

"There's no use getting rattled," Stott told the members of the media after the game. "Bad hops are part of the game. There's no use getting excited."

Stottlemyre never was one to get nervous or upset—not even the night before his first World Series outing. The 22-year-old hurler stayed up until 10 P.M., and then went to sleep. The next day, he faced Gibson and company, held them to seven hits, and won, 8–3. Actually, it was not as easy as the score indicates—the Yankees tallied four times in the ninth to blow the game open. Stott also tied a record at the plate—he struck out five times!

Mel and Bob hooked up again four days later in game five. Stott pitched well, allowing six hits in seven innings, but left the game trailing, 2–0. Tom Tresh's two-run homerun in the ninth inning got Mel off the hook, but the Yankees went on to lose the game, 5–2, when Tim McCarver hit a three-run blast of his own off reliever Pete Mikkelson in the tenth.

Stott and Gibson went at it again in game seven, each returning to the mound with just two days' rest. Again, Mel was respectable—three runs in four innings, largely thanks to some weak fielding—but the Cardinals went on to win, 7–5, making Mel a loser and ending the Yankees "dynasty."

In 20 World Series innings, the rookie had allowed 18 hits and seven earned runs, struck out 12 and walked six, and impressed an entire nation with his cool, calm attitude and ability to pitch out of trouble.

"We knew we had a good one in Mel," Houk told reporters after the Series was over. "He was the man we wanted, and when the chips were down, he came through fine."

After the Series, Mel went home to a hero's welcome in Mabton, where he scared the Yankees front office in December by spraining his ankle playing basketball. The injury proved minor, and had no effect on Mel's 1965 campaign: 20–9, a 2.63 ERA, a league-leading 18 complete games and 291 innings pitched, and 155 strikeouts versus 88 walks. Stott also hit an inside-the-park grand slam homerun against the Red Sox, and tossed four shutouts, but the Yankees slumped to sixth place.

A year later, Stott went from a 20-game winner to a 20-game loser, as the Yankees

Mel Stottlemyre

collapsed to 10th place—the worst finish in the club's history (although the last-place teams in 1908 and 1912 finished with worse percentages in the days of the eight-team league). Mel lost ten one-run ballgames that year, and the Yankees were shut out in six of the games he pitched.

Stott rebounded to 15-15 with the ninth place club of 1967, and came on strong at 21-12 for the fifth place '68 edition. A year later, he went 20-14 (2.82 ERA) and established himself as one of the finest pitchers in the American League.

"One of the things people tend to forget is the way Mel helps his own cause," former manager Ralph Houk said in 1969. "He is a great fielder, a superb bunter, and even surprises the opposition with an occasional homerun. That's part of the key to his success. He's a great all-around athlete."

The Yankees upped his salary to $70,000—the highest salary ever paid a Yankee pitcher up to that time. (Ford's top pay was $68,000.) A stiff shoulder limited his effectiveness in 1970, but he still finished at 15-13. That '70 season also featured the only game in which Stott was ejected during his entire career. The controversy concerned a play at the plate in which umpire Larry Napp ruled that Harmon Killibrew had beaten the throw. Mel argued vehemently, and eventually got the thumb, although he swore afterwards that the closest he came to profanity was telling Napp: "You stink!"

Over the next two seasons, Mel ran up 16-12 and 14-18 records (again leading the league in losses), but notched 7 shutouts in each campaign. Typically, he lost 15 one-run ballgames over the two years, and the Yankees were shut out nine times when he pitched.

Throughout his career, Master Melvin enjoyed tremendous success against two teams in particular: California and Washington/Texas. At one point, Mel ran off a string of 46 consecutive scoreless innings against the Angels, before they finally broke the schneid in a 4-3 loss on June 17, 1973. He finished with a 20-4 lifetime record against California. The Senators/Rangers were his second favorite on the mound (25-12), but his favorite at the plate—he had two 5-for-5 games against them. Actually, Stott did well against just about everyone. His career mark against Baltimore was 15-13—and the Orioles won four pennants and two eastern division championships during Mel's years. He finished 18-16 against Boston. Detroit gave Mel trouble (15-19), but in Denny McLain's 31-victory season, Stott beat him twice. Only Oakland proved a real challenge: Mel was 12-18 against them, but when Vida Blue was a rookie phenom, Mel decisioned him.

The 1973 season was Stott's final healthy year. He went 16-16 with a 3.07 ERA, but once again suffered as his teammates dropped out of the pennant race in August and finished a dismal fourth in their division. The front office recognized his solid performance with a raise that brought his salary up to $87,500.

In 1974, Mel got off to a slow start. He was struggling at 6–7 in June, when he injured his arm. At first, the diagnosis was a torn muscle, and after nearly six weeks on the disabled list, Mel pitched two innings of relief against the Red Sox on August 4th. The relief role ended his streak of 271 consecutive starts—an American League record. As it turned out, they were the last two innings of his major league career. The Yankees returned him to the disabled list on August 19 when X rays revealed that the injury was a torn rotator cuff. Doctors prescribed rest at first, but then decided that only an operation could restore the arm . . . and the odds that the surgery would be successful were less than 25 percent. Sadly enough, had Mel been healthy, the Yankees would have won their division. Instead, they finished two games behind Baltimore.

Mel rested all winter, and returned to Ft. Lauderdale hoping that the arm was sound. It bothered him from the start, and rumors surfaced that he would either retire or replace Whitey Ford as the Yankees pitching coach. He did very little game-conditions throwing in the spring, and was shocked when the Yankees placed him on waivers for the purpose of giving him his unconditional release on March 29, 1975.

"I'm not convinced whether or not I'm through," he told reporters, "but I am bitterly disappointed at the move because Gabe [Paul, Yankees general manager] told me to take my time getting ready. Then, all of a sudden, I'm released."

The move was greeted with severe criticism by the New York media, which labeled the Yankees ingrates for cutting Stott so quickly. When a glance at the major league collective bargaining agreement pointed out that any player who was on a team's roster at the end of spring training had to be paid two full months' salary, the reporters attacked what they called Yankee cheapness. After all, hadn't the club just signed Catfish Hunter for more than $3 million? Couldn't they afford to keep Mel around, especially because it looked like the club would win the A.L. East for the first time in 10 years?

After a week or so, the protests died down. By that time, former Yankee skipper Ralph Houk, then the Tigers manager, had offered Mel a conditional contract that allowed Stott to pitch his way into shape in Florida, and then join the Tigers in May or June. But the handwriting was on the wall, and Stott realized that without a risky operation, his arm would not improve. At the age of 33, when most pitchers are in their prime, Mel Stottlemyre decided against the operation, and retired.

Rating Mel Stottlemyre the top right-hander, and perhaps the greatest pitcher, in Yankee history, may shock some people, but when all relevant factors are considered, the conclusion is more than supportable. Statistically, Mel ranks among the leaders in virtually every pitching category: career shutouts (second—40, to Ford's 45); innings pitched (third—2,661 2/3); strikeouts (fourth—1,257); wins (fifth—164–139); ERA (seventh—2.97); and complete games (eighth—151). He was also an All-Star five times, led the team in wins in seven different seasons, and was the only quality player on the staff for several years.

But even the statistics do not tell the full story of Mel's greatness. From 1965 to 1973 (his nine healthy complete seasons), Master Melvin won 152 of the 716 games the Yankees won—nearly 22 percent! Furthermore, Stott's bread-and-butter pitch was the sinker, a pitch that produces numerous ground balls and relies on the infield to make the plays. The Yankee infield of that era was the worst in the team's history. It lacked speed, range, glovemen, and reliability. For example, in 1968, shortstop Tom Tresh led the league with 31 errors. Gene Michael gained the same dubious distinction two years later. The team finished ninth in overall fielding three times during Stott's career, including an astounding 93 infield errors in 1973 alone.

Perhaps the final point is best made this way: of the 167 games Mel won, 40 were shutouts. At times, if he did not shut the opposition out, he simply did not win. While Fritz Peterson was usually the beneficiary of high run production, the club rarely scored more than three runs in any game Mel pitched . . . partially because he always faced the ace of the opposition's staff.

Through all the years of frustration, Stott never complained, never stormed off the mound, and never demanded to be traded. (Not that the Yankees were not close to dealing him—the Red Sox once offered Carl Yastrzemski in return; the Senators, Frank Howard—but the team's general managers always believed that Mel was too good a pitcher to give up.)

What then, is the legacy of Melvin Leon Stottlemyre? He had all of the tools to win 200 games. He had the class that should only go with a champion. He was the heart and soul of his team for so many years. . . .

But, despite the Yankee tradition, despite the advantage of playing in New York, the bottom lines are winning and charisma. And while Stott did win 167 games, he simply did not win often enough to get by on wins alone. . . . And despite his two-to-one ratio of strikeouts to walks, he did not strike out enough batters to make the grade that way, either. . . . And, when a Yankees press release dated April 26, 1969, pointed out that Mel was "not the flamboyant type," they hit the nail right on the head—he simply was not an exciting pitcher to watch. No one went to the game to see Mel pitch—but they did go to see Vida Blue, Tom Seaver, and Bob Gibson.

Perhaps, if Mel had been born ten years earlier, or ten years later, things would have been different. He might have teamed with Vic Raschi, Ed Lopat, and Allie Reynolds to form the greatest starting rotation in Yankee history; or, he might have made headlines by battling Guidry down the wire for the most wins by a pitcher in 1978. But fate, in the form of his date of birth, played a cruel trick on Mel Stottlemyre—it ordained that he play for the worst teams the Yankees fielded in the last 60 years.

Sadly, the man who might have won more games than any other American Leaguer since Eddie Plank, Lefty Grove and Walter Johnson, never had the opportunity to attain superstar status. Instead, the quiet, unassuming, gentlemanly pitcher who lent the Yankees of the late '60s and early '70s a measure of respectability will fade from memory as the years go by, as much a victim of his own style as he was a victim of the teams he played for.

JUST PLAIN HEROES

GEORGE ROHE

George Rohe does not belong in the major leagues. He belongs in a factory somewhere, or in a mine digging coal or ore. He's about as valuable as a bat bag.
—Fielder Jones, Manager, 1906, Chicago White Sox

If Chicago White Sox owner Charles Comiskey and manager Fielder Jones had had their way, George Rohe's major league career would have ended long before the 1906 World Series. . . .

And the White Sox would never have been world champions.

History proves that Comiskey and Jones wanted to unload their 5'9" utility infielder before the season even began. Rohe had hit a dismal .212 in 34 games in 1905, and was just what the so-called "Hitless Wonders" didn't need—another limp stick.

A deal was arranged with New Orleans of the Southern League: Rohe, to go, for $5,000. All that remained was for the original "futility" infielder to clear waivers, and he would be out of Comiskey's life. (In those days, no major leaguer could be sent to the minor leagues unless he had been passed up on $1,000 waivers by every major league team.)

Enter John "Mugsy" McGraw, the unforgiving czar who reigned over the New York Giants. Mugsy had an outstanding grievance against New Orleans. The "mardi gras" club had refused to allow his Giants to use New Orleans for spring training, and McGraw had not forgotten.

"I never get angry, I just get even," Mugsy said, years later, when asked why he claimed Rohe. "There was no way I would allow a major league ballplayer of any caliber to go to that club."

Not that McGraw needed Rohe. Sammy Strang was the Giants' extra infielder, and he batted .319 that year, but McGraw didn't care. Besides, he was still annoyed at the American League for placing a team in New York, even if they were the hapless Highlanders.

So, Comiskey was faced with the choice of keeping his "bat bag," or selling it to the Giants for the bargain rate. Reluctantly, the Sox opted for Rohe. Hindsight proved it to be the right move.

George Rohe was born on September 15, 1875 in Cincinnati, Ohio. Virtually nothing is known about his childhood, adolescence, or anything else, until he appeared on the Baltimore Orioles roster in 1901. He batted .278 in 14 games, and was dispatched to the minor leagues. When Rohe resurfaced in the majors, the year was 1905, the team the White Sox, and the results even less impressive. In fact, his whole career consisted of 267 games over four years, and a lifetime .227 batting average. Worst of all, for a utility infielder, he was a positively horrendous fielder.

Rohe rode the pine for most of that 1906 season, batting .258, and fielding a dismal .935 on the team that led the A.L. in fielding. All summer long, Jones sizzled over the fact that Rohe was still on the team . . . until the day that shortstop George Davis broke his ankle. Suddenly, Jones needed Rohe, but the question was where to play him.

"I couldn't put him at second base because he would fall over the bag on double plays," Jones told reporters. "He was too slow for shortstop, and too small for first base. In the end, I moved [Jessie] Tannehill over to short, said a prayer, and played Rohe at third."

Up until that day, Rohe's major contribution to the Sox was as the organizer of the "Sandwich Club" in the bullpen. ("In those days, if you were way ahead or way behind, there was no way you'd get into the game, so we used to send out for sandwiches around the sixth inning," Rohe explained.)

Suddenly, Rohe was thrust into the heat of a pennant race, and would play third base in the World Series.

In game one of the fall classic, Rohe stunned the Windy City fans by hitting a run-scoring triple off Hall-of-Famer Mordecai Brown. The blow tied the score, and the Sox went on to win, 2–1. Ed Ruelbach silenced Rohe and his teammates with a one-hitter in game two (a seventh-inning single by Jiggs Donahue was the only safety), but Rohe roared again in game three by blasting a bases-loaded triple in the Sox 3–0 win.

By now, Rohe had developed quite a following, and the fans greeted his every at-bat with a new sound: applause. Brown shut out the Sox in game four, allowing two hits, and knotting the Series at two each, but Rohe and company went to work on a trio of

Cubbies in game four, and the Sox stumbled to an 8–6 win. Rohe had three hits—and three of his team's six errors! When the Sox went on to take game six, and the Series, he had a world championship ring and a Series-leading .333 batting average. He was a hero.

It would be nice to report that Rohe went on to a long and illustrious career with the White Sox. It would also be nice to hit 100 homeruns in one season. Both require miracles, and neither has occurred.

With the start of the 1907 season, Rohe reverted to form. He survived the year, somehow, and hit .213. In November, he was finally sold to New Orleans, and this time Mugsy could do nothing to prevent it. The rules had been changed, and major leaguers were chattels to be dealt with as the club pleased.

Rohe bounced around the minors for seven years, and ended his professional career with Richmond. He returned to the steel mills from which he came, and spent 20 years as a laborer. When age and illness forced him to retire, he became a reporter for a Columbus, Ohio, newspaper, and did some freelance photography. He died on June 10, 1957, in Cincinnati.

Today, George Rohe is still remembered. Not by every fan, but by those who delve into baseball history, back to the early years, to the "Hitless Wonders," who pulled off the greatest upset in World Series history. He was a "zero" for most of his four-year career, but took advantage of luck, fate, an injury, and whatever ability he had, to create a niche for himself as the first World Series hero.

JOHN "HOME RUN" BAKER

When I played the game, everything was legal. I'd like to see what today's hitters would do against the dead ball. Then, I'd like to see 'em swing at the spitters, shiners and emory balls I used to look at. Course, the worst of all was the "dark" ball, which was coated with mud and tobacco juice. When that came whizzin' in from Walter Johnson, it was about as easy to see as a Negro boy in a watermelon patch in the dark.

—John Franklin "Home Run" Baker

Was not the Great Mathewson present at the same clubhouse meeting at which Mr. McGraw discussed Baker's weakness? Could it be that Matty, too, let go a careless pitch when it meant the ballgame. . . ? Or maybe "Home Run" Baker doesn't have a weakness.

—As Rube Marquard wrote after Game Three of the 1911 World Series in his column.

John Franklin Baker was not a great homerun hitter by today's standards. He led the American League in homeruns for four consecutive seasons (1911–14), but his totals were 9, 10, 12, and 8. His 93 career blows were spread over 13 seasons (Ruth usually bettered the figure in two seasons), and average out to a mere 7 per campaign (less than what dozens of players have hit in a month).

But Baker's name remains as closely linked to the four-bagger as the names of Ruth, Aaron, and Maris because, in 1911, the Hall of Fame third baseman slammed a pair of crucial round-trippers that carried the Philadelphia Athletics to the world championship, and forever earned him the sobriquet "Home Run."

Not that Baker was the first major leaguer to hit two homeruns in one World Series. There had been seven World Series and 41 games prior to game two of the 1911 classic, and seven homeruns had been hit. Boston's Patsy Dougherty drove out a pair in game two of the 1903 Series against Pittsburgh, and Fred Clarke had reached the seats in two games of the 1909 Series, but neither of those occasions proved as important to the outcome of the Series as Baker's. Nor were they hit off a pair of Hall of Fame pitchers like Rube Marquard and Christy Mathewson.

Born on March 18, 1886 on a farm in Trappe, Maryland, Baker grew up working in one field, and playing baseball on the other. Future major leaguer Buck Herzog saw enough of the 20-year-old infielder to invite him to join Herzog's semipro team in Ridgely in 1906. John Franklin was an immediate success, and attracted the attention of talent expert Jack Dunn, who brought him up to the Baltimore Orioles for a tryout. Baker played in five games, went 2-for-15, and committed two errors before being released for being "too awkward," according to Dunn. It proved to be a rare error in judgment by the man who discovered Babe Ruth, Lefty Grove, and dozens of other big leaguers.

The 6-foot, 175-pound youth was farmed out to Reading, where the A's Connie Mack spotted him. Mack kept an eye on the kid for a year and a half, and purchased his contract toward the end of the 1908 season.

"He wasn't afraid of making an error," Mack recalled in 1930. "He'd go way into the hole to get the ball, and, despite his awkward walk, threw well and had good speed on the bases. He was so cool and calm in practice, and personable with the other players, that I immediately inserted him at third base. It certainly worked out—didn't it?"

Baker faced Hall-of-Famer Ed Walsh in his "season opener," and hit two doubles off the White Sox spitballer. From that day on, for the next six seasons, Baker was the hot corner of what soon became known as the A's fabled "$100,000 infield" (Stuffy McInnis at first, Eddie Collins at second, Jack Barry at short, and Baker at third).

The 23-year-old third sacker started his sophomore season with a bang. Philadelphia opened at Boston, and when Baker came up in the first inning, the bases were loaded with two outs. Righty Frank Arellanes delivered, and the left-handed slugger drove the ball over the fence in right field for the first homerun of his career, and the only grand slam he would ever hit. The A's won the game, 4–1, and Baker was a homerun hero for the first time. He finished the season at .305 (27 doubles, a league-leading 19 triples, 4 homeruns, 89 RBIs and 4 stolen bases).

In 1910, Baker started off with a bang of a very different type. In an early-season game, the Tigers elected to test Baker's courage, and Ty Cobb slid into third spikes up,

John "Home Run" Baker

knocking him down, and cutting him. Although reputedly a mild-mannered fellow, Baker leaped up and attacked Cobb, precipitating a near-riot.

"Home Run" saved his best performances for the World Series. In 1910, after a disappointing .283 regular season, he exploded at a .409 clip to lead the A's past the Cubs in five games. His single, two doubles, and two RBIs were decisive in Philadelphia's opening game 4-1 victory. Baker added another key double and five singles before the Series ended.

But 1911 was his year. After an outstanding regular season (.334, 40 doubles, 14 triples, a league-leading 9 homeruns, 115 RBIs and 38 st0len bases), Baker vaulted into immortality with a pair of clutch homeruns against the Giants in the Series.

Christy Mathewson won the first game, 2-1, and the New Yorkers sent 24-game winner Marquard to the mound in game two. The teams battled to a 1-1 tie through five innings, when Eddie Collins doubled with two outs. Baker came up next, and he drove a Marquard offering into the seats for the game-winning homerun.

The fun began the next day, when Matty's ghostwriter, Christy Walsh, blistered Marquard for pitching carelessly to the third baseman. At a clubhouse meeting prior to the game, the article proclaimed, Manager John McGraw had gone over each of the A's hitters and explained what should and should not be pitched to them. Obviously, Rube had disregarded the manager's instructions.

When the Series resumed a day later, Matty was back on the mound. He had not lost to Philadelphia in four World Series appearances dating back to 1905 (when he shut them out three times), and both teams believed that the winner of game three would take the crown. For eight innings, Matty was superb. New York led 1-0, thanks to hits by Chief Meyers and Matty, and a ground out by Josh Devore, as the teams entered the ninth inning. The A's sent the heart of their lineup to the plate. Collins led off and grounded out to third base. The best hitter on either team was out. Matty, who had allowed just 1 run in 44.3 World Series innings, appeared to be in full control. For him to allow a run, let alone a homerun, was unthinkable.

Baker stepped in, swinging his 52-ounce club in readiness as the crowd cheered their hometown pitcher on. The first pitch was a curve at the knees. Baker swung and missed. Matty came back with the same pitch, and Baker took it for strike two. Ahead 0-2 in the count, Matty had the slugger right where he wanted him. Everyone expected Matty to uncork one of his famous "fadeaway" pitches (actually a screwball) to get the third strike. He took a slow, deliberate windup, as if seeking pinpoint accuracy on the next pitch. Matty unleashed the ball, and Baker sent his bat in motion. Ball and bat made serious contact, and the Polo Grounds drew dreadfully silent as the ball changed direction and arched high in the air, deep to right, and into the seats for a stunning game-tying homerun. The A's went on to win, 3-2, in 11 innings.

That second homerun not only solidified Baker's hold on the "Homerun" nickname, but made his name a household word. Newspapers across the country were filled with banner headlines about the "Magnificent Masher of Mathewson and Marquard."

The blow also gave Marquard's ghost a chance to get even.

"Will the great Mathewson tell us exactly what pitch he made to Baker?" the column screamed. "I seem to remember that he was present at the same clubhouse meeting at which Mr. McGraw discussed Baker's weakness. Could it be that Matty, too, let go a careless pitch when it meant the ballgame for our side? Or maybe Home Run Baker just doesn't have a weakness?"

Rain interrupted the Series for seven days, and the nation held its breath, waiting to see if Baker could do the impossible and hit yet another homerun in the Series. Twice, the new hero slammed the ball deep to right field, and on both occasions, it hit off the wall for run scoring doubles in the A's 4–2 win. Baker was strangely silent in the final two games, producing no extra-base hits, but finishing the series with 9-for-24 (.375), 2 doubles, 2 homeruns, 7 runs scored, and 5 RBIs.

A raise to $8,500 encouraged Baker to improve for 1912, and he did: .347, 200 hits, 40 doubles, 21 triples, a league-leading 10 homeruns, and 133 RBIs, 116 runs, and 40 stolen bases. Unfortunately, the rest of the club slumped, and the A's finished 15 games behind the Red Sox.

Baker had another solid season in 1913, and led the league in homeruns (12) for an unprecedented third straight year, and in RBIs. More importantly, his teammates rebounded to win the pennant, and the Giants found themselves facing their old nemesis in the World Series. Baker took up right where he had left off, hitting a decisive two-run homerun off Marquard to lead the A's to a 6–4 win in the opener. He did not reach the fences again, but continued to rip McGraw's hurlers at a .450 clip with 7 RBIs.

"I don't know what to do about him," McGraw lamented, after the Giants lost the final game, 3–1. "We just can't seem to get him out when we have to. It's uncanny. You know I'm a superstitious man, and, well, he's a jinx."

It was Baker and the A's who were jinxed in 1914's fall classic. The "Miracle Boston Braves," who came from miles behind to capture their first N.L. flag, capped their season by sweeping the heavily favored Mackmen. Baker had turned in yet another fine season (.319, 23 doubles, 10 triples, his final league-leading homerun total of 8, and 97 RBIs), but was held to two singles and two doubles in the Series.

The dismal World Series was only the beginning of the troubles that beset Baker and the A's. Mr. Mack was disgusted with his team's lackluster performance, and wanted his stars to take cuts in their salaries. He could not cut Baker, who had signed a three-year, $10,000 year deal after the 1913 season. Then along came the Federal League, which offered "Home Run" a multiyear deal at $15,000/season. Baker mulled

John "Home Run" Baker

it over and then confronted Mack with a demand for a raise. Mack would not hear of it, arguing the sanctity of contract and the financial problems confronting the ballclub. When other Federal League teams made similar offers to some of Mack's stars, he began selling them to other teams, rather than lose them for no compensation.

Meanwhile, Baker sat home and remained undecided. His wife was not well, and all the travel had exhausted him. He thought more and more in terms of just sitting out the 1915 season, and in the end, that's exactly what he did.

"I understood Mr. Mack's financial problems," he said, years later. "I also had a responsibility to my family."

When Mack's attempts at luring the hero out of retirement seemed deadlocked, he resigned himself to doing without yet another one of his starters ... but when Baker balked at returning for 1916, Mack had had enough, and sold the third baseman to the New York Yankees for $37,500.

At first, Baker refused to report, but Manager Miller Huggins pursuaded him to return to the major leagues. He played in 100 games as a Yankee in 1916, batted .269, and drove in 52 runs. His statistics steadily improved over the next three seasons, but then disaster struck again: His wife died. Faced with the problem of caring for young children, "Home Run" decided to sit out the 1920 season to mourn his wife, care for his family, and run the farm.

When Baker returned in 1921, he shared the hot corner with Mike McNally, and batted .294 in 94 games. The Yankees won their first American League pennant, and suddenly Baker found himself facing his old friends, John McGraw's Giants. As things turned out, Art Nehf and company were able to do what Matty and Rube could not: they held Baker to a pair of meaningless singles in 8 at-bats. Furthermore, Baker also suffered the ignominy of hitting into the Series-ending double play, although it was not his fault. The Giants led the last of McGraw's preferred best-of-nine World Series, four-games-to-three, as the teams began the eighth game. Mugsy's boys took a 1–0 lead into the bottom of the ninth inning, and Art Nehf appeared to be on the verge of giving the Giants the championship. With one out, Aaron Ward drew a walk, and Baker stepped up. Déjà vu? Close, but no cigar. Baker ripped a sizzling ground ball to the right side for what seemed to be a sure base hit, but second baseman Johnny Rawlings dove to his left and stopped the ball. From the sitting position, he threw to first, and just did nip Baker. Ward, who had been running with the pitch, believed the ball went through for a hit, and continued nonstop toward third. First baseman George Kelly had anticipated such a move, and had no sooner stepped on the base to retire Baker, than he was firing over to third. Frank Frisch took the throw, and as Ward slid into the bag, Frisch slapped the tag on him to complete the unique 4-3-5 series-ending double play.

Baker played one more season, batted .278 in 69 games, and was replaced as a regular by Joe Dugan. "Home Run" hit his final round-tripper on May 22nd. The victim was former teammate Urban Shocker. It was the 96th of his career, but the total was later reduced to 93 because of scoring changes. He went 0-for-1 in the World Series, which was won by the Giants in four games (there was a tie in game two).

After his retirement, Baker returned to his farm in Trappe, Maryland. He discovered that he missed the game, and gladly accepted an offer to manage the nearby Easton team in the Eastern Shore League. That team featured a powerfully built, 17-year-old catcher named James Emory Foxx, who began driving the ball with awesome power and consistency. At first, Baker offered the youth to the Yankees, but they were satisfied with Wally Schang, and may have already had their eyes on Bill Dickey. When New York turned him down, Baker went straight to Mr. Mack.

"I think you'd better sign him," Baker told the Grand Old Man. "You won't find his likes anywhere else."

Mack agreed, paid the $2,000 Baker wanted for the phenom, and later admitted that it was a steal.

"Homerun" continued to serve the Easton Club, and was eventually named president, a post he retained until 1942. Thirteen years later, he was elected to the Baseball Hall of Fame. A stroke disabled him in 1962, and a second one took his life on June 22, 1963.

How great a "homerun" hitter was Home Run Baker?

"If he had played with the livelier ball, he would have rivaled Mr. Ruth," Connie Mack said, nearly 30 years after Baker's retirement. "He hit the fence dozens of times, and those shots would have carried over the wall today."

Baker felt much the same way, but was never bitter about the jackrabbit ball.

"Dozens of balls I hit every season came within inches of clearing walls," he said in 1955. "The year I hit 12 homeruns to lead the league, I hit the right field fence 38 times. All of those would have been gone with the lively ball."

When John Franklin Baker hit two homeruns in the 1911 World Series, he became a national celebrity and earned a very unique nickname. Many players have duplicated the feat, and as recently as 1977, Reggie Jackson hit three in one game! More than a dozen players have hit four times as many homeruns in a season than Baker did in his best year. Names like Ruth, Foxx, Greenberg, and Mantle all come to mind, and all of them drove at least 238 more baseballs over fences in their careers than Baker did in his.

Yet, for all the four-baggers and round-trippers so many other ballplayers have hit, for all the consistency and awesome power they may have demonstrated, only one man in the history of baseball ever earned the nickname "Home Run": John Franklin Baker.

Just ask any kid who John Baker was, and you'll get a blank stare . . . but call him "Home Run" Baker, and the eyes will light up in recognition of one of baseball's first World Series heroes.

There is one other way to look at it. Baker was clearly not the most gifted member of the fabled "$100,000 infield." Second baseman Eddie Collins was far and away superior. He played 25 years, batted .333, and was inducted into the Baseball Hall of Fame in 1939. Similarly, John "Stuffy" McInnis was probably also Baker's superior: He played 19 seasons and batted .308. Baker, by comparison, saw action in only 13 big league campaigns (although he sat out two years by his own choice) and finished at .307.

Yet, today, Collins has faded into obscurity, and McInnis is not even enshrined in Cooperstown . . . but such is the fate of a pair of mere stars when matched against the man who rose to the occasion in the 1911 World Series and became an immortal hero.

GEORGE WHITEMAN

> I was the classic example of the right guy in the right place at the right time. I was also lucky, damned lucky—but, then again, that was always my nickname, "Lucky."
> —George Whiteman, Boston Red Sox, 1918

Most of America's heroes in 1918 wrote their names into history through acts of valor in France and Belgium.

And most of America's baseball players were "over there," or at least off the field and working in wartime support industries.

But one man who became a hero that year performed his miracles on fields that bore no resemblance to Flanders and Ypres. He wore a cap instead of a helmet, and spikes instead of steel-tipped boots, and his weapons were made of leather and wood. Best of all, none of his victims died, but he actually held an entire nation captive for almost two weeks.

The hero's name was George Whiteman, a 36-year-old journeyman outfielder whose major league career totaled 85 games, but who rose to the occasion in the 1918 World Series to lead the Red Sox to their last world championship.

Whiteman was one of those ballplayers who dominated minor league pitching, but never could hit the sharp-breaking curve that distinguishes the big leagues from the bushes. His first visit to the majors lasted exactly three games. The Boston Red Sox, for whom he later performed minor miracles, gave him a three-game tryout in 1907. Six years later, the New York Highlanders (Yankees) purchased his contract, and George batted .344 in 11 games, but was totally inept afield. The New Yorkers elected not to retain his rights for 1914, and he returned to Toronto, convinced that he would never play another major league game.

But storm clouds were brewing over Europe, and it would be only a matter of time before the United States entered World War I. General Enoch Crowder, Provost Marshall for the United States, declared baseball a non-essential industry, and off to war marched dozens of big leaguers. The Red Sox lost outfielders Duffy Lewis and Chick Shorten, first baseman Dick Hoblitzell, shortstop Jack Barry, and pitcher Dutch Leonard. Stuffy McInnis was acquired to fill the first base hole, Everett Scott replaced Barry at short, and the club knew that its big four of Babe Ruth, Sam Jones, Joe Bush, and Carl Mays would provide more than adequate pitching, but there was still a gaping hole where Lewis and Shorten had played.

Someone, history does not recall who, suggested that Whiteman be brought back. The minor league star had had another superlative season (.372 with 7 homeruns), and despite his advanced years, was summoned back to Fenway.

George was quietly mediocre at the plate during the regular season. The 5'7", 160-pound, Peoria, Illinois, native batted .266 with 14 doubles and 1 homerun in 71 games, primarily facing left-handers and trying to defend left field. Unfortunately, George's best years in the field were well behind him, and he finished with a dismal .935 fielding percentage on a team that led the American League in defense! Strangely enough, it would be his fielding that overshadowed his hitting during the World Series against the Cubs.

Game one featured Ruth against Hippo Vaughn in a classic pitchers' duel. The teams were deadlocked at zero, when Whiteman sandwiched a single between hits by McInnis and Dave Shean, to produce the game's only run. The real surprise was Whiteman's catch of a pair of late-inning line drives in the left-centerfield alley, both of which stymied Cubs' rallies, and both of which were labeled "flukes" by Chicago first baseman Fred Merkle.

Game two went to the Cubs, 3-1, as Lefty Tyler bested Bush, but not before Whiteman gave the Chicagoans a big scare in the ninth inning. Amos Strunk singled to open the inning, and Whiteman's two out triple brought him home, but Tyler retired the dangerous Hooper to end the game.

By now, the Cubs fans had had enough of the veteran outfielder, and they began calling for his return to the old age home, but George was not quite ready to retire. In game three, after the Sox scored twice in the top of the fourth inning, Chicago's Les Mann hit a one-out double down the right field line in the home half of the frame. Up to the plate stepped Dode Paskert, who drove a tremendous fly ball to the deepest part of left field. The fans rose in unison, anticipating a game-tying homerun, only to watch in horror as the ancient Whiteman plodded back to the fence and made an incredible catch. Mann had wisely tagged up at second base, but any thoughts of trying to take two bases on the sacrifice fly were ended when Whiteman wheeled and made a perfect throw to the relay man.

(The game ended on a rare note when Charlie Pick, who stole only seven bases all year, was out trying to steal home in the ninth inning.)

Whiteman's glove was silent in game four, but his bat produced a rally-starting base hit that led the Sox to a thrilling 3–2 win. The victory was "marred" by the end of Babe Ruth's 29⅔-innings of scoreless World Series pitching, but the Babe was "just happy to win the game."

Chicago breathed a loud sigh of relief when Whiteman's name was not in the lineup for game five, but the sigh seemed a bit premature when the players from both teams balked at taking the field as a protest over the minuscule World Series shares they would receive ($890 to the winners, $535 to the losers). The owners were not to blame—the minimal shares were caused by the splitting of gate receipts with second, third and fourth place teams in each league, and a donation to the National War Charities. Hooper and Mann acted as representatives of each team, and demanded a meeting with the three-man National Commission that supervised the Series. American League President Ban Johnson convinced the players to take the field, and promised that there would be no reprisals, but after the Series, the participants were informed that they had forfeited their World Series emblems (a diamond collar stud). The game was played, Chicago won, 3–0, and the fans were embittered by the near strike while thousands of men were dying in Europe.

Whiteman returned to left field for game six, and resumed right where he had left off. Once again, the Sox jumped ahead, 2–0, and once again the Cubs rallied. This time, the score was 2–1 in the eighth inning when Turner Barber stepped up to the plate and slashed a wicked line drive to left. Out of nowhere came Whiteman, who made a spectacular somersaulting catch to end the threat.

The catch also ended Whiteman's Series—he separated his shoulder—and it proved to be the last play he ever made in the major leagues. However, it was his 15th putout of the Series, a record for an outfielder, and his .250 batting average led the victors, who batted .186 as a team!

Whiteman returned to Toronto in 1919—the war had ended, and he was no longer needed. The hero batted .302 with 39 doubles and four homeruns, and came in at .271, 27 and 6 in his final year as a player (1920). Whiteman spent his next ten years as a minor league manager, and later worked as a scout until his death on February 10, 1947.

The year 1918 has remained very special in the hearts of Red Sox fans. The team has not won another world championship, and the fans still long for the days when a 36-year-old outfielder named George Whiteman became a hero.

HOWARD EHMKE

When Hall-of-Famer Al Simmons learned that Howard Ehmke, a "36-year-old bag of bones," was going to open the World Series on the mound for the Philadelphia Athletics, he nearly choked.

"My God, Mr. Mack," Simmons exploded, "are you really going to pitch him?"

"Yes, Mr. Simmons, I really am," Connie Mack replied. "Is it all right with you?"

"Yes, Mr. Mack," the stunned outfielder replied. "If it's all right with you, it's all right with me—I guess."

About a month before the 1929 season ended, Philadelphia Athletics manager Connie Mack faced the unpleasant task of telling 16-year-veteran pitcher Howard Ehmke that the time had come for them to part.

"I called Old Howard off to one side, and told him that he had to go back to the minors," Mack recalled, "and Old Howard came back with just the answer I wanted to hear."

"Mr. Mack," he said, "I've been 16 years in this game and have always wanted to take part in a World Series. Now, we both know that the Athletics have got the pennant won this year, and I know I still have one great game left in this old arm before I quit."

"So, I left Old Howard in Philadelphia," Mack continued, "and told him to scout our opponents, the Cubs, when they played the Phillies at the end of the season, because he'd be our starting pitcher in game one of the World Series.

"The season ended a couple of weeks later, and the pennant was ours," Mack said.

"We came home amid a great deal of fanfare, and even more speculation as to whether Lefty Grove, George Earnshaw, or Rube Walberg would open the Series for us. Every newspaper claimed they had the inside scoop, and picked their favorite, but I didn't announce my starter until 15 minutes before game time. The fans were astonished when Old Howard went out to the box, as were most of my players."

And so were the Chicago Cubs—13 of them struck out, as Ehmke scattered eight hits, set the strikeout record (which has since been surpassed), and won, 3–1.

"I won only 7 games that year, and I could pitch only once every three weeks," Ehmke recalled, nearly 30 years later. "But when Mr. Mack told me on September 14, 1929, that I'd be the starting pitcher on October 8, I knew I would win it for him.

"He even said he would take all the responsibility if we lost," Ehmke continued. "I was ready when the eighth came around, and I never had better stuff or better control."

Not that Old Howard had an easy time of it. The A's did not score until Jimmy Foxx's solo homerun in the seventh inning broke a 0–0 deadlock. Prior to that, the Cubs had posed the only serious threat, when they posted runners on second and third with one out in the third inning. Up to the plate stepped the dangerous Hack Wilson, and Ehmke struck him out on sidearm curves. The next hitter was Rogers Hornsby, the greatest right-handed batter in the history of the game, and Ehmke snuck a slow curve past him for another "K."

Old Howard tied Ed Walsh's record (12 strikeouts, set in game three in 1906) in the seventh, when he struck out Gabby Hartnett for the second time (he also nailed Wilson and Hornsby twice), but did not get another until the ninth . . . when Ehmke himself was nearly kayoed.

After the A's added a pair of runs in the top of the ninth, Wilson led off the bottom of the inning by ripping a line drive back at Ehmke. The 36-year-old took the shot in the groin, fell down, picked up the ball, and threw Wilson out at first base before collapsing in agony.

After considerable delay, Ehmke rose to his feet and refused to leave the game. Kiki Cuyler stepped up, and slammed a ground ball to short, where Jimmy Dykes threw it over Eddie Collins' head at first, putting Cuyler on second. Riggs Stephenson singled to left, scoring Cuyler, and cutting the lead to 3–1. Charlie Grimm drove a base hit into right field, and Mack ordered Lefty Grove to start warming up. But Ehmke settled down and induced Footsie Blair to bounce into a forceout, and then caught pinch-hitter Charlie Tolson looking at a called strike three to set a new record.

In retrospect, Mack's "gamble" was not as risky as it may have seemed. Ehmke had gone 7–2 during the season, hurling 54 2/3-innings over 11 games, so he had been effective when he pitched. More importantly, Mack was acutely aware of the Cubs' reputation as fastball hitters who murdered lefthand pitchers, and by using Ehmke, he was putting a righthanded "junkballer" on the mound. Furthermore, the first game was in Wrigley Field, with its spacious bleachers, which would be filled with white-shirted fans—a tough background for hitters to see the pitch, and even tougher when the pitcher threw sidearm the way Ehmke did.

Until his heroic performance in game one of the '29 Series, Ehmke's major claim to fame centered on the no-hitter he threw against the A's on September 7, 1923, and the near-no-hitter he pitched against the Yankees in his next start. In that second contest, New York's lead-off batter, Whitey Witt, hit a hard shot to third, where Boston third baseman Howard Shanks booted it, and the official scorer ruled it a hit. Ehmke retired the next 27 consecutive batters, and the fans spent the afternoon, and the next few days, clamoring for a change in the scoring, but to no avail.

Old Howard was also credited with inventing the "hesitation" pitch, a sidearm changeup in which Ehmke delayed bringing his arm forward to deliver the ball until after his body had finished its forward motion. Interestingly enough, it continued to baffle the hitters for years, and was particularly effective against the Cubs in the World Series.

Statistically, Ehmke finished his career at 167-166, with a 3.75 ERA. He won 20 games once (20-17 for the Sox in 1923), and followed that with a 19-17 mark in 1924. When he dropped to 9-20 a year later, and got off to a 3-10 start in 1926, Boston decided that his arm was dead, and dealt him to Philadelphia. Ehmke won 12 of 16 decisions for Mack that year, came in at 12-10 in 1927, and 9-8 in '28. His ERA was consistently between the 3.60-3.90 marks—rather unspectacular by today's standards, but pretty good in the days when teams often averaged .280 or better at the plate.

Ehmke came from a family of baseball players. His older brothers, Frank (pitcher) and Charley (outfielder), both starred for Brown University. Charley subsequently wrote to John McGraw and Mack about their younger brother, Howard, while the future World Series hero was the ace of the Glendale High School staff in Los Angeles. McGraw never replied, but Mack sent along a nice letter, promising to keep Howard in mind. Thirteen years later, Connie kept his promise, when he acquired the 32-year-old from the Red Sox.

Howard began his professional career on April 24, 1914, his 20th birthday, when he joined the Los Angeles entry in the Pacific Coast League. He was sold to the Washington Senators after the season, but jumped to the Buffalo Bisons of the Federal League, where he went 0-2 in 1915. Ehmke wanted to return to L.A. for 1916, but manager Frank Chance would have no part of any Federal League refugees, so Ehmke stayed in New York and latched on with Syracuse. It proved a tremendous windfall for the upstate club. Ehmke went 31-7 with 195 strikeouts, and was sold to the Tigers for a substantial sum at the end of the season. Howard went 3-1 for Detroit that year, and with the exception of a short stint in the Navy in 1918, remained in the majors for the next 14 years.

Ehmke's success in game one of the '29 Series convinced Mack to start him in game five, but this time the veteran was less of a mystery to the Cubs, who knocked him out of the box with two runs in the fourth inning. Rube Walberg relieved him, and Philadelphia came from behind to win the game, and the Series, with a three-run ninth inning (a two-run homerun by Mule Haas, followed by consecutive doubles by Simmons and Bing Miller). (That was also the year the A's scored 10 runs in the seventh inning of game four to overcome an 8–0 Chicago lead.)

The Series outing also convinced Mack to sign Ehmke for 1930, but Old Howard's arm had gone dead, and he retired with an 0–1 mark in three games, and an embarrassing 11.70 ERA.

After leaving baseball, Ehmke and his wife operated a canvas-fabricating business until he contracted spinal meningitis and died on March 17, 1959, in Philadelphia, Pennsylvania. He had lived long enough to hear Connie Mack tell the world that Ehmke's win was the greatest thrill in Mack's 50 years in baseball. He had also lived to see his record eclipsed by Carl Erskine, the Dodgers' right-hander who struck out 14 Yankees in game three of the 1953 Series.

Fifty years ago, an "old bag of bones" was saved from the scrap heap for that one final moment of glory. Many of the fans who saw Ehmke go out to the mound that fateful day must have thought the fix was on, and that Mack had sold out to gamblers. What man in his right mind could overlook George Earnshaw (24–8), Rube Walberg (18–11), Ed Rommel (12–2), and the immortal Lefty Grove (20–6) in favor of Old Howard? Evidently, Mr. Mack knew something the experts in the bleachers didn't.

Fifty years have passed, and today's baseball fan will easily overlook Earnshaw, Walberg, and Rommel, mere stars in the galaxy of baseball greats. They may remember Grove as *the* star hurler of that team, but one thing is certain: Anyone who knows anything about World Series history will never forget the hero of the '29 classic, a 36-year-old junkballer named Howard Ehmke.

AL GIONFRIDDO

Joe DiMaggio up, holding that club down at the end. The big fella sets, [Joe] Hatten pitches—a curveball, high outside for ball one.

So, the Dodgers are ahead, 8 to 5, and the crowd well knows that with one swing of the bat this fellow is capable of making it a brand new game again.

Joe leans in. He is one-for-three today, six hits so far in the Series. Outfield deep, around towards left. The infield overshifted.

Here's the pitch—Swung on. Belted! It's a long one, deep into left center. Back goes Gionfriddo, back, back, back, back, back—He makes a one-handed catch in front of the bullpen! Ooooh doctor!
—Red Barber (the play-by-play of Al Gionfriddo's great catch in game six of the 1947 World Series)

When the Brooklyn Dodgers obtained outfielder Al Gionfriddo from the Pittsburgh Pirates, sportswriter Bill Roeder wrote that "they weren't even sure he could spell his name."

Other sources claimed the 5'6" outfielder was included as a courier to carry the estimated $250,000 the Dodgers received in exchange for pitchers Kirby Higbe, Hank Behrman and Cal McLish, catcher Homer Howell, and outfielder Gene Mauch.

Everyone agreed that the lifetime .276 hitter would never be a regular in Brooklyn, and most expected him to come to rest on the Dodgers farm club up in Montreal.

Yet, less than six months later, the unheralded 5′6″ "courier" rose up and cast a giant shadow over the greatest player of that era, Joe DiMaggio.

The setting was game six of the '47 World Series. New York led the Series, three games to two, with games six and seven slated for The House That Ruth Built. The Dodgers had their backs to the wall as pitchers Allie Reynolds and Vic Lombardi squared off in what most fans expected to be the final game of another Yankee championship.

Gionfriddo began the game where he had spent most of his four-year career—on the bench. Brooklyn went with Gene Hermanski in left field, followed by Eddie Miksis in the fifth. When the Dodgers opened their second three-run lead of the ballgame (8–5), Gionfriddo went in to left field as a defensive replacement.

In the bottom of the sixth, the Yankees rallied against reliever Joe Hatten. George Stirnweiss led off with a walk. After two outs, Yogi Berra delivered a base hit, and up to the plate stepped the tying run, in the form of Joe DiMaggio. The record crowd of 74,065 surged forward, anticipating another stroke of the Yankees' patented "five o'clock lightning." (DiMaggio's fifth-inning homerun, and pair of outstanding catches, had proven decisive the day before.)

Out in the vast expanse of left field at the old Yankee Stadium (301′ down the line, but 402′ to straightaway left field, and 457′ to left-center), the tiny Gionfriddo looked like a lonely island of blue and white in a sea of green. Strangely enough, he had a hunch that "Joltin' Joe" would drive the ball his way.

"When DiMaggio came to bat, I thought to myself: 'Two men on. If he hits one out of here, it ties the game. He's been hot and he can hit anyone, and he likes to hit up the alley.' So, I'm ready to go back towards the fence, and that's why I got such a good jump on the ball."

DiMaggio wasted no time. He jumped on Hatten's second pitch, driving it deep to left center, toward the 415 marker on the bullpen.

"I took off as soon as it was hit," Gionfriddo recalled. "I turned my head once to get a bead on it, put my head down, and just kept going. When I got to the fence, I leaped and sort of twisted around, snaring the ball in my webbing, and simultaneously slamming into the bullpen fence. Man, it seemed like I was running forever.

"When I realized I made the catch, I started trotting towards the dugout," he continued. "Carl Furillo picked up my cap and said 'nice catch.' It wasn't until I got to the dugout, and all of the Dodgers were standing up on the top step, slapping me and hollering, that I realized the significance of it."

The fans could not believe it. DiMaggio was stunned, and in a rare display of frustration, kicked second base as he reached the bag. To this day, Red Barber says it was "not the greatest catch in baseball history, but simply an impossible catch."

Gionfriddo's heroics killed the rally and preserved the Brooklyn lead. When the

Al Gionfriddo

Yankees rallied again in the ninth, Hugh Casey came on to retire the side and send the Series to a seventh game.

"It would have meant a lot more to me if we had gone on to win the seventh game, or if the Dodgers had kept me around for another 10 years," Gionfriddo said, "but neither event occurred. The Yankees won the deciding game 5–2, and Eddie Miksis played left field."

In fact, Gionfriddo never played another major league game! The following spring, Al was beaned by teammate John Van Cuyks during an exhibition game, and was out for two weeks. No sooner did he recover from that blow, than general manager Rickey dealt him another.

"He wanted to send me down to Montreal, but didn't have the courtesy to tell me," Gionfriddo recalled. "I found out that I'd been sent down when I heard it on the eleven o'clock news. The next day, I went up to see him, and the receptionist said she'd tell Mr. Rickey I was there. She went into his office, came back, and told me Mr. Rickey would see me in a little while.

"So, half an hour goes by, an hour, two hours, and finally I'm getting disgusted," he continued. "Then, out comes Branch Jr., his kid, who says to me 'who you waitin' on Al?' I told him I wanted to see his dad, and the kid replied 'He's not here. He's out of town.' Right about then, the receptionist sort of disappeared.

"Eventually, I did get to see the old man, and he promised me that if I'd go down to Montreal, and have a good year, he'd bring me right back. Well, I hit .310 with 25 homeruns, so the next spring comes around, and I'm expecting to be back in Brooklyn, and what do you think happens? He tells me he wants me to go to Hollywood in the Pacific Coast League for 1949. Said something about how they'd never seen me play out there, and how I would draw large crowds and make the Dodgers a lot of money. So I told him that if he wanted me to go, and make the Dodgers a lot of money, he'd have to pay me $10,000 and I'd do it. Naturally, he wouldn't pay me, so they sent Chuck Connors instead, and I stayed in Montreal."

The following year, Rickey wanted Gionfriddo to go to St. Paul, to work his way back from an injury the outfielder had suffered while sliding into third base. Gionfriddo refused to go, and accepted an appointment as a player-coach with Fort Worth in the Texas League. After that, he managed the Drummondville minor league team in Canada, and when that club folded, he hooked on with Ventura in California. Gionfriddo hit over .300 during his three years there, and retired in 1956.

In retrospect, getting to Brooklyn in the first place was quite an achievement for Gionfriddo, one of 13 children born to an Italian-American family in Dysart, Pennsylvania. There was no baseball team at his high school, so he lettered in football and track, running the 100-yard dash in 10 seconds. He played American Legion baseball, and impressed his manager enough to have letters sent out to all of the major league teams. The Cubs asked him to appear at Forbes Field for a tryout during a road trip in 1943, but rain canceled the game and the tryout. Later that year, a Pirates affiliate in Harrisburg asked him to try out, and a year later, they sent him a contract. Gionfriddo's minor league career was a big success. In 1944, he stole 52 bases for Albany in the Eastern League, and the Pirates called him up in September.

He stayed with Pittsburgh for the next two years, seeing relatively little action, and finding himself chained to the bases.

"I hit .284 in 122 games in 1945," he recalled, "but I only stole a handful of bases. The Pirates simply did not care to run. Our manager was Frankie Frisch, and he never let you run on your own. He was from the old school and controlled the whole game from the bench.

Gionfriddo went to spring training in 1947 determined to win the regular job in left, but broke his ankle just before the season started. He returned to the Pirates in the beginning of May, and played in one game, before he was dealt to Brooklyn.

"We were in Brooklyn for a game," Gionfriddo recalled. "It was rained out, but the manager told us to stay close to our hotel rooms because there was a trade in the works, and at least one outfielder was going to go. So, I was sitting around, when a messenger comes in and tells me I'm wanted in the manager's room, and I knew I was gone.

"I was upset at the trade," he continued. "My competition in left was Jim Russell [10 years, .267], and I believed I could have beaten him out. But, baseball was baseball. You didn't have an agent in those days, and you couldn't reject a trade. It was even more upsetting to read all those articles about me being a courier or message boy to carry the money."

In 38 games with Brooklyn that year, Gionfriddo batted .175, with two stolen bases. However, he seemed to lead a charmed life in the World Series. Most fans have forgotten the role he played in spoiling Yankee pitcher Bill Bevens' no-hitter in game four that same year. The Dodgers entered the ninth inning hitless, and trailing 2–1. With one out, Carl Furillo walked. After a foul out, Gionfriddo ran for Furillo, and while pinch-hitter Pete Reiser was at-bat, Gionfriddo broke for second. Contemporary reports claim that a decent throw would have nailed the speedster, but Berra's shot down to second was high and wide of the base. Gionfriddo was safe, and the tying run was in scoring position. Manager Bucky Harris countered with a controversial walk to Reiser, thereby putting the tying run on first base. The Dodgers sent Cookie Lavagetto up to pinch-hit for Eddie Stanky, and Lavagetto doubled off the right field wall to end the no-hit bid and win the game. Had Gionfriddo not stolen second, Reiser would never have been put on, and Bevens might have gone home a no-hit winner.

After his retirement from baseball, Gionfriddo stayed on the West Coast, selling insurance. He subsequently opened a restaurant, Al's Dugout, in Santa Barbara, but gave it up after several successful years. Today, he is the trainer and equipment manager at San Marcos High School in Goleta, where he receives several letters a day, most of them from children who never saw him play, asking for his autograph.

On October 5, 1947, an obscure utility outfielder with a lifetime .266 batting average made an incredible—no, impossible—catch. Thirty-five years have come and gone since that day. Eddie Miksis, Hugh Casey, and Joe Hatten, all of whom were better ballplayers than the "courier from Pittsburgh," have long since been forgotten. The Dodgers did not even win the World Series, and the man who made the catch never played another major league game, but baseball fans around the world will never forget the name of Al Gionfriddo, a true hero.

DUSTY RHODES

He was the worst fielder who ever played in a big league game. Any time you see a fielder get under a ball and pound his glove—even in the Little League—you know he's going to catch it. I have seen Dusty Rhodes pound his glove and have the ball fall twenty feet behind him. I have seen more balls fall into his glove and fall right out again. Didn't bother Dusty one bit. He'd come running in at the end of the inning with a big grin on his face.

"Better get me out of theah, Skip. Ah'm going to get kilt. You know I can't ketch the ball."
—Leo Durocher, Manager, New York Giants (From *Nice Guys Finish Last,* published by Simon & Schuster)

When the New York Giants clinched the 1954 National League pennant, the experts all agreed that that was as far as the Giants would go.

Their World Series opponents, the Cleveland Indians, had won an American League record 111 games, and featured one of the greatest pitching staffs ever assembled. Hall-of-Famers Early Wynn (23–11, 2.73), Bob Lemon (23–7, 2.72) and veteran Bob Feller (13–3, 3.09) spearheaded a starting rotation that included the League's ERA champion (Mike Garcia, 19–8, 2.64) and Art Houtteman (15–7, 3.35). The bullpen was equally effective: Don Mossi (6–1, 7 saves), Ray Narleski (3–3, 13 saves), and veteran Hal Newhouser (7–2, 7 saves).

Offensively, second baseman Bobby Avila led the league at .341, with 15 homeruns and 67 RBIs; Larry Doby led all hitters with 32 homeruns and 126 RBIs, and third baseman Al Rosen batted an even .300 with 24 homeruns and 102 runs batted in.

Most of the sportswriters picked the Indians, and many went on record by predicting a sweep.

Not that New York was such a bad team. Johnny Antonelli (21–7, league-leading 2.50) led a pitching staff that had won 97 games. Ruben Gomez (17–9, 2.88), Sal Maglie (14–6, 3.26), Don Liddle (9–4, 3.06) and Jim Hearn (8–8, 4.15) filled starting roles, while Marv Grissom (10–7, 19 saves) and Hoyt Wilhelm (12–4, 7 saves) put out many a rally.

Offensively, Willie Mays had returned from the service with a great year: a league-leading .345 average, 41 homeruns, 33 doubles, 13 triples, and 110 RBIs. Don Mueller was the runner-up at .342. Hank Thompson (.263, 26 homeruns, 86 RBIs), Alvin Dark (.293, 20 homeruns, 70 RBIs) and Monte Irvin (.262, 19 homeruns, 64 RBIs) filled key supporting roles, but no one in their right mind was picking the Giants.

"New York will need another miracle," said sportscaster Mel Allen, in reference to Bobby Thomson's homerun. "On paper, Cleveland's got this thing won."

Allen and the rest were right, up to a point. There would indeed be a sweep, and the Giants would indeed need a miracle. The miracle's name was James Lamar Rhodes.

Born on May 11, 1927, the six-foot, 178-pound Rhodes was as unlikely to lead the Giants to the world championship as Don Larsen was to pitch a perfect game. Dusty had never even played baseball as a child. His first amateur club, the St. Andrew's Gaels, drafted him because of his extraordinary power as a softball hitter. Rhodes' first game in a Gael uniform came on a day when the regular centerfielder failed to show, and it established a career-long pattern: two homeruns, a triple, and two errors.

Nashville Sounds scout Bruce Hayes spotted Dusty in 1946, signed him for $125, and sent him to Hopkinsville (Class D). His progress up the minor league ladder was steady—and so was his drinking. Eventually, manager Charlie Root sat his hell-raiser down, and warned Rhodes that he'd better cut down on his drinking, or he would never make it to the big leagues.

"So I took his advice, and cut down by fifty percent," Rhodes told reporter Barney Kremenko. "I stopped drinking chasers."

By 1952, Rhodes had advanced to the Sounds, and was stroking the ball at a .347 clip before the Giants summoned him to New York. Dusty batted .250 in 67 games with New York, and quickly convinced manager Leo Durocher that he could never be a regular outfielder.

"He is the worst fielder I have ever seen," Durocher told the world. "Granted, he can hit, and with power, but his glove is useless."

When Rhodes dropped to .233 the following year, Leo demanded that club owner

Horace Stoneham unload the outfielder, but Stoneham would have no part of it. Durocher wondered why—and found out the following year, when he found the pair doing some pregame drinking in the owner's office.

As things turned out, it was the best trade the Giants *never* made. Dusty exploded at a .341 rate for the '54 season, including 15 homeruns and 50 RBIs in just 164 at-bats. He was 15-for-45 as a pinch-hitter, and came through with at least a dozen game-winning hits.

When the World Series rolled around, Durocher made it clear that he would not take a chance on Rhodes' glove (or lack thereof), so Dusty figured he would be lucky to pinch-hit once or twice.

The Series opened in New York, and featured two memorable events. The first came in the eighth inning, when, with the score tied 2–2, and two men on base, Cleveland's Vic Wertz belted a drive to deep centerfield. Willie Mays turned his back on the ball, raced out toward the clubhouse in dead centerfield, and caught the ball on the dead run. Without breaking stride, Mays wheeled and fired the ball back into the infield to hold the runners and save the game.

And then came Rhodes. Mays led off the tenth inning with a walk. After Mays stole second, starter Bob Lemon intentionally walked Hank Thompson (a lefty) to get at Monte Irvin (a righty). Durocher countered with a move of his own: Dusty Rhodes.

Lemon threw him a slow curve, and the pinch-hitter deluxe lofted a high fly ball some 260 feet down the right field line. In any other ballpark, the "drive" was an out... but in the Polo Grounds, the sign at the foul pole read 258. The ball landed in the first row of seats for a stunning three-run homerun.

"That had to be the biggest shock of my playing career," Lemon recalled, some 25 years later. "And, I don't think the ballclub ever recovered. You know, you make a perfect pitch, a tough hitter hits a routine fly ball, you breath a sigh of relief, and it lands in the seats. In our park, the right fielder would have been moving in to catch it!"

Rhodes struck again in game two. New York trailed 1–0 when Mays led off the fifth with another walk. Thompson singled with one out, and Durocher summoned Rhodes again. This time, Rhodes dumped an Early Wynn offering into centerfield to score Mays, and Durocher rewarded the utility player by keeping him in the ballgame, figuring Rhodes' hot bat might be useful later on. (Durocher later admitted he also hoped that nothing would be hit Dusty's way.) Sure enough, in the bottom of the seventh, Rhodes took Wynn downtown, driving the ball off the facade in right field to give the Giants an insurance run. Antonelli scattered eight Indians hits, and the Giants won, 3–1.

By now, the newspapers had dubbed the hero of the first two games the "Colossus of Rhodes," and everyone expected him to be in the starting lineup for game three.

Durocher had other ideas, and went with Irvin ... until the Giants loaded the bases in the third inning. New York trailed 1–0, so Leo called on Rhodes again in place of Irvin, and the Colossus lined a single to right to put the Giants ahead to stay.

Rhodes was rewarded with another visit to the outfield, but went hitless in his next two at-bats. He did not play in game four, largely because the Giants took an early 7–0 lead, and held on for a 7–4 win. Rhodes had taken an early lead on the Babe Ruth Award, and he held on to win, too.

"I still have the bat I used," Rhodes recalled. "You can recognize it by the spike marks that Willie Mays put there when he kicked it. You see, Mays broke one of my bats near the end of the season, and I had to have three bats flown in air mail special delivery for the World Series. Well, he came to me and asked if he could borrow another bat. I said no, and he got so angry he kicked the bat and caught his spikes in it."

Rhodes also refused to give the bat to the Baseball Hall of Fame, but offered his glove instead! He also claims he laid off the whiskey once he got to the majors, or at least before games.

"Could a man hit a baseball that was thrown at 90 miles per hour if he were drunk?" Rhodes said, unaware, or ignoring, the fact that a wide range of his peers (Mickey Mantle, according to Jim Bouton's *Ball Four,* for example) were quite successful at it. "Leo Durocher started those stories. They were good after-dinner jokes, and I didn't mind because he treated me very good."

Dusty's heroics (and his friendship with Stoneham) earned him a $4,000 raise (to $12,000) for 1955, and he turned in another fine year (.305, including 11-for-44 as a pinch-hitter). When Durocher left the Giants after the '55 season his replacement, Bill Rigney, named Rhodes the starting left fielder in spring training. Perhaps it was the shock of getting a chance to play regularly, or perhaps it was the alcohol he never drank before games, but Dusty's bat went strangely silent, and he was benched after four games. He finished the year at .217, and when he came in at .205 in 1957, he was sent down to Phoenix.

Perhaps the warm climate dried him out, but Rhodes's bat came alive in 1959, and the Giants recalled him while he was batting .320. Unfortunately, he simply was no longer the power hitter he had been, and after going 9-for-48, he was released.

In 1960, Rhodes drew headlines again, not for baseball, but for a divorce. Fourteen years later, Rhodes' face was again splashed all over the New York papers, but this time it was because his son Jeff had been shot and nearly killed in New York City. Today, Dusty works on a tugboat in New York Harbor, transferring trap rock barges from New York to New Jersey.

The year 1954 was more than a year for heroes. It proved to be the last hurrah for

Dusty Rhodes

the New York Giants. The team slumped to third place in 1955, and plummeted to consecutive sixth-place finishes in '56 and '57. By the time the 1958 season began, the Giants were in San Francisco.

Rhodes and baseball parted ways 20 years ago. The Polo Grounds were torn down five years later. Names like Lockman, Irvin, Mueller, Antonelli, Maglie, and Grissom have all faded into the obscurity reserved for trivia buffs. All of them were better ballplayers than Rhodes. All of them had longer careers. All of them were more distinguished.

Yet, for all of their statistics, longevity, and success, those men are forgotten. Not many people remember that there were once Giants in New York . . . but they do remember one man—James Lamar "Dusty" Rhodes: Three days in a life that has lasted more than 19,200. Six at-bats in a career that included 1,178. Four hits. Two homeruns. Seven RBIs. Doesn't sound like much, does it, but in 1954, it was a good way to create a hero.

For Dusty Rhodes, it was the perfect formula for immortality.

SANDY AMOROS

> Everybody talk about catch I make. They still wonder how I make it. It really too good to describe.
> —Sandy Amoros (recalling the catch that saved the 1955 World Series for the Brooklyn Dodgers, *Sports Scene Magazine,* November 1971)

On October 4, 1955, Edmundo Isasi "Sandy" Amoros had a date with destiny.

The part-time outfielder, whose mediocre major league statistics never approached the outstanding numbers he recorded in the minor leagues, was about to play the hero's role in the only World Series the Brooklyn Dodgers ever won.

The site was the "Old" Yankee Stadium, a hallowed baseball ground, whose dimensions served as a concrete-and-steel reminder of the left-handed power hitter for whom it was built, Babe Ruth. The right field foul pole stood a mere 296 feet from home plate. Straightaway right field was a very reachable 344, and even the 367 marker in right-center was frequently passed over by homeruns into the Stadium's vast outfield bleachers. For a left-handed pull hitter like Yogi Berra, the "Big Ballpark in the Bronx" was paradise.

As kind as the dimensions were to lefties, they were equally cruel to righties. The left field foul pole was only 301 feet away, but that number was more of a tease than a chip shot. Only the deadest of pull hitters were able to take advantage of it. The four-foot-high outfield fence curved sharply away from home plate as it made its way to the 461-foot marker in dead center field. Straightaway left was 402 feet, and left-center was a titanic 457.

Most of the seats in the huge triple-decked grandstands that extended from the home team's bullpen in right field, around behind home plate, and out to the visitors' bullpen in left, were filled. The remainder of the 62,465 fans on hand were crowded into the vast bleachers that spanned the outfield, creating a noisy sea of humanity that provided a colorful commentary for every pitch. Few of those present could have imagined that the outcome of the World Series would center upon a catch by Amoros on a ball hit by Berra—down the *left* field line!

The events leading up to the seventh game of the 1955 World Series had been very predictable. Each team had won all of its home games. The opening contest (6–5) and game two (4–2) went to the New Yorkers, behind southpaws Whitey Ford and Tommy Byrne. The latter's performance capped a 16–5 regular season, and was the first complete game victory by a left-hander over the Dodgers that whole year.

A shift to Ebbets Field for the middle set produced a trio of Brooklyn triumphs. Johnny Podres took game three, 8–3, scattering seven Yankee safeties. Homeruns by Roy Campanella, Gil Hodges, and Duke Snider powered the Dodgers to an 8–5 win in game four. A day later, rookie hurler Roger Craig and relief ace Clem Labine combined for a 5–3 victory, sending the Bombers reeling back to the Bronx with their backs to the wall.

Ford was magnificent in game six. The Hall-of-Famer allowed one run on four hits, and rode Bill Skowron's three-run homerun to an easy victory. There would be a seventh game after all.

The Yankees and Dodgers were no strangers to postseason play, though their fates had been very different. In 20 postseason appearances up to 1955, the New Yorkers had won 16 championships, including their last seven in a row. The National League prayed in unison for the years in which other franchises won the American League pennant!

The Dodgers, on the other hand, were 0-for-7 in the World Series, 0-for-2 in National League Playoff Series, and had even managed to lose the pennant on the last day of the 1950 season. Five of their World Series defeats had come at the hands of the Yankees, some of them in the strangest of circumstances. In 1941, catcher Mickey Owen's infamous passed ball cost the Dodgers a Series-tying victory in game four, and enabled the Yankees to take a three-games-to-one lead. A day earlier, a line drive hit by Yankee pitcher Marius Russo broke Dodgers' hurler Fred Fitzsimmons' knee cap, forcing the Brooklyn ace to leave the game with a 1–0 lead. Reliever Hugh Casey allowed a pair of eighth inning runs, and the Yankees won that game, too. A four-hitter by Tiny Bonham ended the Series the next day.

The teams clashed again in 1947. Cookie Lavagetto became the first of several Dodgers World Series heroes when he pinch-hit a two-out, game-winning double in the bottom of the ninth inning in game four. The blow was all the more significant because Yankee starter, Bill Bevens (7–13 in regular season play), had stumbled through 8⅔-innings without allowing a hit. The near-historic performance ended in a loss for Bevens, in what proved to be his final major league appearance, and knotted the Series at two games apiece.

A Yankee victory in game five set the stage for another Brooklyn hero, Al Gionfriddo. With the Dodgers leading, 8–5, in the sixth inning, the Yankees placed runners on first and second with two outs. Up to the plate stepped Joe DiMaggio, who drove a Joe Hatten fastball deep to left field, straight for the bullpen. Back went Gionfriddo, back, back, back, back, back to make a one-handed catch in front of the bullpen. The Dodgers hung on for an 8–6 win, setting up a seventh game . . . won by the Yankees, 5–2.

Two years later, a highly touted Brooklyn club was dispatched in a mere five games. Duke Snider (.143), Jackie Robinson (.188), Carl Furillo (.125), and Gil Hodges (.235) found the offerings of Allie Reynolds, Eddie Lopat, and Joe Page virtually unhittable. The Dodgers, a .274 squad in the regular season, batted a woeful .210 against the Bombers.

Of all the losses to the Yankees, the one in 1952 was the toughest to swallow. The Dodgers had run away with the National League pennant, finishing with a 105–49 record, 13 games ahead of the second-place Braves. They led the league in virtually every offensive category, and dominated the Yankees in regular season statistics. Worst of all, the Dodgers took a three-games-to-two lead home to Ebbets Field, and proceeded to lose the final pair. Vic Raschi and Reynolds combined for a 3–2 win in game six, aided by a balk and error by Brooklyn starter Billy Loes. Game seven was lost when New York second baseman Billy Martin grabbed an infield fly at his shoe tops with the bases loaded in the seventh, and the score 4–2, New York.

A year later, Martin set a record with 12 hits in a six-game series, and Mickey Mantle added a pair of game-winning homeruns, as Casey Stengel's troops won their fifth consecutive world championship.

Add on: a five-game series loss to the Red Sox in 1916; an unassisted triple play by Bill Wambganss and the first World Series grand slam (Elmer Smith), both coming in the pivotal fifth game of the 1920 Series against the Indians, won by Cleveland in seven games; Bobby Thomson's sudden death homerun in 1951; a loss to the Cardinals in the 1946 League Playoff; and a loss on the final day of the 1950 season to cost a tie for the pennant. Is it any wonder that Brooklyn fans seriously doubted that their team would ever win a World Series?

In the world of heroes, fate often plays a strange role in creating the setting for the great deed that vaults the mortal ballplayer into the ranks of the gods. In Sandy Amoros' case, this was no exception.

If things had gone according to plan, Sandy never would have left the Dodgers' bench during game seven, and Brooklyn might never have won a World Series. The Yankees started Byrne, meaning that right-hand-hitting Jim Gilliam would replace Amoros in left field.

It was a situation that Amoros had come to expect, and perhaps accept. Sandy came to the Dodgers amidst great expectations when he signed for $1,000 in 1952. He tore up the International League with St. Paul, where manager Bert Haas coined the nickname "Sandy" because the 5'7", 170-pound Cuban was built like prizefighter Sandy Saddler. Rave reviews came in from all corners.

"He reminds me of Pete Reiser," said Billy Herman, manager of Amoros' Cuban League team.

"He can throw as well as Musial," Dodgers manager Charlie Dressen announced. "They say he's as fast as [Sam] Jethroe, and about as good a hitter as Rhodes, but in a better league."

Amoros batted .340 with St. Paul, and earned a late-season look-see from the varsity. In 20 games, he batted .250, with three doubles, one triple, and three RBIs. A year later, he finished the season at Montreal with an International League-leading .353, and was touted as Brooklyn's answer to Willie Mays and Mickey Mantle.

But it never worked out that way. He began the '54 season at Montreal, where he was batting .361 when the Dodgers summoned him on July 12th. He was impressive in 79 games, batting .274 with 18 doubles, 6 triples, 9 homeruns, and 34 RBIs. When spring training 1955 rolled around, Brooklyn's new manager, Walter Alston, penciled him in as his starting left fielder.

Unfortunately, it did not take long for Amoros to play himself out of the full-time job. He simply could not hit the major league left-hander, and also found the off-speed delivery impossible to deal with. In 119 games, he batted a disappointing .247, but produced 10 homeruns and 51 RBIs in 388 at-bats.

The World Series had been no different. Sandy sat the bench against Ford and Byrne in the opening games. When the scene shifted to Ebbets Field, and the Yankees rolled out their righthanders, Sandy contributed a run-scoring single in game three, and a game-winning two-run homerun in game five. (After the game-winner, would-be interviewers were shocked to discover that Amoros spoke only two words of English: "yes" and "coive," Brooklynese for "curve.")

The seventh game of the '55 Series opened with Byrne retiring the first nine Dodgers he faced, before Roy Campanella doubled in the fourth inning. One out later, Gil Hodges singled him home, and Brooklyn led, 1–0. In the sixth inning, the visitors scratched out another run. Pee Wee Reese led off with a base hit. Duke Snider laid down a sacrifice bunt which Byrne fielded and tossed to Skowron at first base. The easy out by stepping on the bag was the obvious move, but Skowron elected to tag Snider, and had the ball knocked out of his glove. Campanella followed with a sacrifice. Byrne intentionally walked Carl Furillo, and was replaced by Bob Grim. Hodges greeted the righthanded reliever with a sacrifice fly to centerfield, and Brooklyn led, 2–0.

Grim compounded matters by uncorking a wild pitch, and then walking Don Hoak, to re-load the bases. The next batter was scheduled to be second baseman Don Zimmer, a weak stick from the right side of the plate, so Alston summoned George Shuba as a pinch hitter. "Shotgun" rocketed a ground ball right to Skowron, who stepped on the base to retire the side.

With Zimmer out of the game, Alston had to make a defensive change. Gilliam was pulled out of left field, and shifted to second base. Shuba, never much with the glove, and slow afoot, was too risky to send to left, so Amoros, a left-hand fielder, trotted out to the sun field at Yankee Stadium.

And what of the vaunted Yankees' bats, while all this was going on? Well, Dodgers' starter Johnny Podres had struggled through the first five innings, pitching in and out of jam after jam. Skowron doubled with two outs in the second, but was left stranded. Only a fluke play prevented the Yankees from scoring in the third. Phil Rizzuto drew a two-out walk. Billy Martin singled. Gil McDougald chopped a slow grounder towards third. Had Hoak charged in and fielded it, he would have had no play, so he elected to lay back, and watched in amazement as the batted ball struck Rizzuto sliding into third. Phil was called out, and the inning was over.

Berra opened the fourth inning with a pop fly double that fell between "Alfonse" Gilliam and "Gaston" Snider. The young Dodgers southpaw dug in on the mound and retired Hank Bauer on a fly to right, Skowron on a bouncer to second, and Bob Cerv on an infield pop up.

Billy Martin opened the Yankees half of the sixth with a walk on four straight pitches. McDougald followed with a surprise bunt single, Martin stopping at second. The next batter was the New Yorkers best clutch hitter, their pull hitter emeritus, Yogi Berra.

Out in left field, Amoros was battling the sun, and his nerves. He knew Berra was a dead pull hitter, but for some unexplainable reason, Sandy positioned himself close to the foul line, as if Berra were a righty.

With two Yankees on base, and no outs, the crowd began chanting for a hit. Berra responded by driving a high, outside fastball deep down the left field line. The crowd rose, and strained to see whether it would be a double, homerun, or foul. That the ball could be caught was simply inconceivable. That it would be caught seemed impossible.

"I was looking for a changeup," Berra recalled in 1980. "The fastball caught me a little late with the bat, but when I hit it, I figured double, triple, homerun or foul."

As 62,465 pairs of eyes watched, the tiny round sphere headed straight for the 301 marker in the left field corner, and as it did, a frantically running Amoros could be seen headed for exactly the same spot.

"I ran as hard as I could," Amoros said (in Spanish, of course). "I was worried about the ball, the sun, the wall, and falling. Just as I reached the wall, I reached up and back with my glove, and caught it. Then, I hit the wall. I came off the wall, turned, and threw to Pee Wee. He threw to first base, and we got a double play."

Only a left-handed fielder with great speed, positioned in the wrong place, could have made the catch ... and as fate would have it, Amoros fit the bill. The catch killed the rally (Bauer followed with an infield out), but the Yankees were not dead yet.

In the eighth inning, Rizzuto singled. After Mantle lined out, McDougald was safe on a smash off Hoak's shoulder, and Berra was up again. This time, there would be no heroics by either team. Yogi lofted an easy fly to Furillo in right. Bauer struck out. The Yankees went down in order in the ninth. The Dodgers were the world champions. Amoros had achieved immortality.

After the game, Berra stopped in to congratulate the winners. He put his arm around Amoros and smiled for the cameras—but only after pretending he was angry, and making some threatening, but purely comical, gestures toward the new hero. As for Amoros, he smoked a huge Havana cigar, waved a can of beer, and chatted gleefully in Spanish, with anyone who would listen.

It would be nice to report that Sandy went on to a great career with the Dodgers or some other team, but that was not the case. In 1956, he batted .260 (including 11 doubles, 8 triples, 16 homeruns, and 58 RBIs) and played a very strange role in the Dodgers' chase for the pennant. He started the final week of the season with a disastrous game against the Phillies, dropping a fly ball that led to 3 unearned runs, and a 7-3 loss. The newspapers blasted the hero of the '55 classic, and lamented the Dodgers' drop to a full game behind the Milwaukee Braves.

Alston refused to heed the warnings that Sandy was inadequate, and Amoros rewarded his loyalty a few days later by hitting a pair of homers in the Dodgers' 8-6 pennant-clincher over Pittsburgh.

Brooklyn and New York clashed again, but a new hero emerged: Don Larsen. Strangely enough, Amoros almost encored in the hero's role. In the top of the fifth inning, moments after Mickey Mantle's backhand catch of Gil Hodges' drive up the left-centerfield alley, Sandy drove a Larsen fastball deep down the right field line. The crowd rose in unison, waiting for the umpire's signal—homerun or foul. At the last second, the ball hooked to the right of the foul pole, and the perfect game was preserved.

Amoros finished the Series 1-for-19, and the Dodgers lost in seven games. The 1957 season was more disappointing. Although Sandy's batting average improved to .277, his overall production tailed off to 7 doubles, 7 homeruns, and 26 RBIs. In the off-season, he was demoted to Montreal, where he pounded the baseball again. The Dodgers brought him back for 5 games in 1959, but traded him (with outfielder Rip Repulski) to the Tigers for Gail Harris after the ninth game of the 1960 season. It proved to be his final year in a major league uniform.

Sandy disappeared from public view for two years, but re-surfaced when he was detained in Cuba by dictator Fidel Castro. Sandy had returned to Cuba to see his wife and daughter, and Castro refused to allow him to report to the Mexico City team. Instead, he insisted that Amoros manage the Cuban National Team. When the former major leaguer refused, he was denied an exit visa for five years, and was prevented from obtaining employment. Fortunately, Sandy had saved quite a bit of money from his baseball days, and invested part of it in a $30,000 ranch with plenty of cattle.

Eventually, the money ran out, and Sandy wrote to a friend in New York, begging for help. A refugee delivered the letter, and the ensuing public outcry opened the door for Amoros to leave the Caribbean Island—but not before the state confiscated his ranch, cattle, car, and all remaining personal property.

Sandy returned to New York, and lived in squalor. When his destitute situation was brought to the attention of former Dodgers general manager Buzzy Bavasi, along with a note that Sandy needed only 7 days on a major league roster to qualify for a $250/month pension, Bavasi signed the hero to a one-month contract ($1,200).

After the brief return to baseball, Amoros returned to New York, and an apartment in the South Bronx. He obtained employment as the manager of an appliance store, until the business closed in 1971. At that point, he was forced onto the welfare roles, unable to find gainful employment, according to *Sports Scene Magazine* (November, 1971). Today, he still lives in the Bronx and is a regular at Old Timers' Days.

With one incredible catch, Edmundo Isasi Amoros saved the only world championship the Brooklyn Dodgers ever won. That one play overshadowed the outstanding hitting of Snider (.320, 1 double, 4 homeruns, 7 RBIs) and pitching of Podres (2-0, 1.00 ERA). Ironically, on a team best known for its heavy hitters, for a franchise that won only one world championship, the thing the fans remember is a catch by a man who could speak neither English, nor Brooklynese.

Today, Amoros resides in New York . . . which is more than one can say for the Dodgers.

DON LARSEN

The only thing Larsen fears is sleep.
—Jimmy Dykes, Manager, 1954 Baltimore Orioles

I'm not what you'd really call a praying man, but once I was out there in the ninth inning I said to myself, "Help me out, somebody."

—Don Larsen

The odds of a major league pitcher hurling a perfect game in 1956 were about 11,500 to 1.*

The odds that one would be thrown in the pressure-packed fifth game of the World Series were incredible.

And the odds that the pitcher would be Donald James Larsen, a journeyman righthander best known for leading the American League in losses (3–21 with Baltimore in 1954), and wrapping his car around a telephone pole at 5:30 A.M., were simply incalculable.

Not that Larsen was such a bad pitcher that year. He had gone 11–5, and at times showed signs of the great potential that originally attracted general manager George Weiss' attention. In fact, when he adopted a no-wind-up delivery in September, Larsen won his last four games of the season impressively (a three-hitter and three four-hitters), and appeared to be on the verge of the outstanding career everyone had predicted.

*More than 68,000 games had been played since 1900, and only six perfect performances had been turned in.

At least one thing held him back: his love for the night life. Larsen's day usually began at noon, or later, and did not end until the wee hours of the morning. In spring training that year, he had "seriously wounded a telephone pole and demolished a mailbox" when he drove his car off the road at 5:30 A.M. Curfew was midnight, according to manager Casey Stengel, "and where he was going and what he was doing remains a mystery, but he couldn't have done it in a museum." Larsen was not fined, perhaps because of his 0.69 spring ERA, or because Stengel knew Larsen would not change his ways, but he was tagged with the nickname "Night Rider."

"Truth of the matter is that the one time I did go to bed early, I had the worst game of my career," Larsen recalled. "That was against the Dodgers in game two of the '56 Series. We were ahead 6–0, but I couldn't get anybody out. When Casey Stengel came out to get me, I was furious, and I told him 'that's the last time I'll ever go to bed early.'"

Actually, the fact that Larsen was still a pitcher was almost a miracle. Had he hit better as an outfielder with Globe-Miami (Arizona-Texas League) in 1949, he would never have pitched again. Had Marty Marion remained the manager of the Browns when they shifted to Baltimore after the '53 season, Larsen would have been converted into an outfielder because "he was the fastest man on the team, a good hitter (.242 lifetime), and a questionable pitcher," according to Marion.

And to top off all the "ifs" and "odds," if the Dodgers had not kayoed him in the second inning of game two, Larsen never could have been ready for game five.

But there he was, standing on the pitcher's mound in the top of the ninth inning, with the eyes of 64,519 fans focused on his every move, rooting for him to retire the Dodgers without allowing a man to reach base.

There had been a few close calls. Larsen had gone 3 balls on Pee Wee Reese in the first inning, but the shortstop struck out. Jackie Robinson had come within a half-step of breaking up the no-hitter in the second, when his hard grounder to the left side of the infield deflected off third baseman Andy Carey's glove ... only to bounce directly to shortstop Gil McDougald, who threw Jackie out by an eyelash.

In the fifth, Gil Hodges drove a slider toward the 457 marker in left center, but Mickey Mantle raced up the alley and made a brilliant backhand grab. Sandy Amoros followed with a line drive down the right field line that landed in the seats about six inches outside the foul pole. In the eighth, Carey came through again, this time making a one-hand stab of Hodges' line drive.

As the tension mounted, Larsen began "sweating up a storm."

"Some time during the sixth or seventh inning, I realized I had not allowed a man to reach first base," Larsen recalled. "By then, the guys on the bench wouldn't even look at me when we were batting. Everyone was nervous, afraid of breaking the no-hitter or jinxing it. Me, I was scared to death. Forget the no-hitter, which was enough to worry about; the score was only 2–0 and we had to win the game.

"When I came to bat in the eighth, the crowd gave me a tremendous ovation, or so they tell me," he continued. "I was so nervous that I don't really remember it. Anyway, I struck out on three pitches, went back to the dugout, took a deep breath, hitched up my pants, and headed out to the mound."

The hour of decision had arrived.

Carl Furillo, a lifetime .299 hitter, led off the top of the ninth. He fouled off the first two pitches, took a ball, fouled off two more, and then flied out to Hank Bauer in right.

Roy Campanella was next. The Dodger catcher was still a powerful stick, and a dangerous clutch hitter. He jumped on Larsen's first offering and sent a towering drive into the upper deck in left field, foul by 20 or 30 feet. The next pitch was the only curveball the "Night Rider" threw that inning, and Campy bounced to second for out number two.

The third man scheduled to bat was pitcher Sal Maglie, who had matched Larsen's perfection with a five-hitter that would be wasted. Manager Walter Alston summoned veteran Dale Mitchell, a lifetime .312 hitter, to bat for Maglie. It was to be the last at-bat of his career. It would also be the most memorable.

"He really scared me up there," Larsen recalled. "But as I look back, he had to be just as nervous as I was."

The first pitch was wide of the plate. Umpire Babe Pinelli, working the final game of his illustrious career, called the next pitch a strike. When he swung and missed on the third pitch, the crowd rose to its feet.

Larsen set, and delivered his 97th offering of the day—a chest-high fastball over the outside corner—"Strike three!"

"And then," as Larsen likes to remember, "all hell broke loose." Catcher Yogi Berra came racing out to the mound and jumped on the man of the hour.

"People never give Yogi enough credit for that perfect game," Larsen said. "Twice, I shook him off, and both times Yogi insisted on the pitch he wanted, so I gave in. He had them off balance all day."

After the game, Larsen was named the winner of the *Sport Magazine* Corvette for the most outstanding player in the Series. There was no sense in waiting for games six and seven.

In the noisy clubhouse after the game, a reporter reminded Yankee co-owner Del Webb that Dodger owner Walter O'Malley had rewarded his pitchers with $500 bonuses when they tossed a no-hitter.

"Are you going to give Larsen $500?" he was asked.

"Who's got O'Malley's money," replied the Yankee owner, himself a multi-millionaire.

Born on August 7, 1929, in Michigan City, Indiana, the 6'4", 228-pound Larsen attended Jefferson Elementary School and was a good student. He grew into an outstanding high school outfielder-pitcher, and was signed by the Browns in 1948. During a 4-year minor league career, Larsen showed great potential, and a 17-11 mark in 1952 earned him a shot at the varsity in '53. "Night Rider" went 7-12 and batted .284 for St. Louis, but when the franchise shifted to Baltimore, he plummeted to 3-21. But 1954 was not only a bad year for Larsen; it was a year in which the Yankees failed to win the pennant for the first time since 1949. Not that they did all that badly, winning 103 games. The problem was that Cleveland won 111, and George Weiss decided that the *real* problem was an aging pitching staff. When Allie Reynolds retired, Weiss needed at least one new arm. The solution: a 17-player deal with Baltimore that brought Larsen and "Bullet Bob" Turley to New York.

The postseason shift would prove to be a blessing, but Larsen got off on the wrong foot. His pitching was so erratic that he had to be sent down in early 1955, but a 9-1 mark at Denver led to his midseason recall. "Night Rider" went 9-2 with the Yankees, but lost game four of the '55 Series against the Dodgers (8-5, lasting less than five innings).

Don signed for $8,000 for 1956, and the Yankees expected headline performances from their 26-year-old hurler. The celebrated telephone pole accident was the first of several headlines Larsen garnered during spring training, much to his chagrin and Weiss' displeasure.

"The next day, he complained of a bad back," Stengel recalled. "The day after that, his shoulder hurt. Finally, I told him that since he couldn't bend and he couldn't throw, he should start taking laps around the ballpark. Funny thing about laps. They seem to cure a lot of things that modern medicine don't."

By the time the season began, Larsen had become Casey's favorite reclamation project, and his 0.69 spring training ERA made the project look like a success. When the bell rang, Larsen got off to a slow start, but eventually earned his salary with an 11-5, 3.26 mark.

"He'd pitch a beautiful ball game one day, and get pounded his next time out," Stengel said. "Then we found out what was happening. The base coaches on the other teams were picking up his pitches by the way he held the ball in his windup because Mr. Larsen didn't conceal the ball too good. So he switched to this here no windup throwing and the results are plain to see."

Larsen shut out the Red Sox, and pitched superbly in his three other September starts, which came after the club had clinched the pennant.

"I never would have experimented with that no windup motion if we hadn't already clinched it," he told reporters.

Stengel tabbed Larsen to start game two, and as has already been recounted, "Night Rider" was kayoed. When he named Larsen to start game five, Stengel was second-guessed by thousands of fans. Not only was it a pivotal game (the teams were tied with 2 wins each), but the final two games would be in Ebbets Field, where the Yankees had lost five straight, and seven of their last eight.

One man who shared Casey's faith in "Gooney Bird" was third baseman Andy Carey's father.

"My dad and Don went out the night before the game," Carey recalled. "At some point in time, they separated, but Dad went up to Times Square to that place that prints up any headline you want. He had two made up: 'Larsen Wins Game Five' and 'Gooney Bird Pitches No-Hitter.' He stuck them on Larsen's hotel room door, but went back later and ripped the no-hitter sign down. Dad was afraid he'd jinx him.

"Dad not only proved a prophet, but I played a key role in keeping the no-hitter going," he continued. "I was also involved in scoring our second run. We were ahead, 1-0 on Mantle's homerun off Maglie when I came up to lead off the sixth. I got a hit, went to second on Larsen's bunt, and scored on a hit by Bauer.

"You really can't imagine the tension on the bench by the time the seventh inning rolled around," he said. "I remember watching guys making sure they'd get the same spots when they sat down. I can remember worrying about the ball being hit to me, even after I made that catch on Hodges's line drive. On top of that, we had a ballgame to win, and two runs against Brooklyn didn't mean much."

After the Series, Larsen earned nearly $35,000 in postseason appearances at a rate of $1,500 a show (compared to the $100 he received before the perfect game). Unfortunately, his celebrity status lasted only about six months. "Night Rider" posted a 10-4 mark in 1957, but remained erratic (87 walks, 81 strikeouts, and a 3.74 ERA). He split two World Series decisions against Milwaukee, winning in relief of Turley in game three (12-3) but dropping the finale to Lew Burdette (5-0).

The year 1958 was more of the same, but Don dropped to 9-6 and appeared in only 19 games, all in a starting role. He won his only decision against the Braves in the World Series, a six-hit shutout in game three, and started game seven, but went to no-decision in a game the Yankees came from behind to win, 6-2.

A slump to 6-7 (4.33) in 1959 encouraged Weiss to deal Larsen to Kansas City in the off-season. Even in parting, Larsen made a solid contribution: the key to the deal was a young outfielder named Roger Maris.

Larsen's next six years were spent shuffling between six clubs. His best effort was as a part-time starter, part-reliever for the White Sox in 1961 (7-2), but they sent him to San Francisco in the off-season. "Night Rider's" last stop was with the Cubs in 1967, for whom he pitched three innings, allowed three earned runs, and was tagged with his 91st career loss. It was his final appearance on the mound.

Today, Larsen is an employee of Blake, Moffit & Towne Paper Products. Everywhere he goes, at every introduction, he is always asked: Are you the same guy who . . . ?

On October 8, 1956, Casey Stengel handed a baseball to Donald James Larsen and asked only one thing: Give me the best game you've got left in that arm.

Larsen did more than try. He did more than win. He wrote a page in the baseball history book by turning in the greatest pitching performance in World Series history. He rose to the occasion, and not only won a pivotal game, but attained perfection.

On that afternoon, as Joe Trimble put it, "The imperfect man pitched the perfect game" and became a hero forever.

BILL MAZEROSKI

> When I walked up there, all I thought about was "get on base." But deep in my mind, I just thought we were going to lose. You couldn't feel too bad to take the Yankees to the seventh game and lose in extra innings.
>
> —Bill Mazeroski (thoughts as he stepped up to bat in the ninth inning)

On October 13, 1960, William Stanley Mazeroski had a date with destiny.

He was about to play the hero's role in a drama that proved that the best team does not always win.

The site was ancient Forbes Field, home of the National League Champion Pittsburgh Pirates, where 36,683 fans were on hand for game seven of the 57th Annual World Series. The oddsmakers had installed the New York Yankees as heavy favorites to crush the upstart Pirates and capture their 18th world championship, and despite the unexpected extension to seven games, the world "knew" the Yankees would win.

After all, hadn't the New Yorkers won games two (16–3), three (10–0), and five (12–0) by lopsided scores? Weren't they leading the Pirates in every offensive category, including a 46–17 margin in runs scored and eight homeruns to Pittsburgh's one? And if offense wasn't enough, how about the Yankee edge in team earned run average (less than three runs as against more than six)?

There were a handful of Pirates fans who were not convinced. Hadn't Pittsburgh combined clutch hitting, gutsy pitching, and superior defense to edge the New Yorkers in games one (6–4), four (3–2), and five (5–2)? Wasn't the only statistic that really mattered the one under the "W" column?

As things turned out, the experts were wrong. The Pirates were about to win the kind of game they had no business winning: a high-scoring slugging match. They were about to prove that, just as statistics do not create a superstar, they do not win a World Series.

Ralph Terry also had a date with destiny that afternoon. The 24-year-old right-hander was the fifth pitcher summoned by manager Casey Stengel, and the summons had been issued one pitch too late. Jim Coates had come on with no one out, runners on first and second, and the Yankees leading 7–5 in what had been a wild ballgame.*
Coates yielded a successful sacrifice bunt to Bob Skinner, induced Rocky Nelson to pop out, but then gave up a run-scoring infield hit to Roberto Clemente, and a three-run homerun to Hal Smith.

Terry retired the side without further ado, and nervously watched as the Yankees came up in the top of the ninth. Bobby Richardson led off with a single. Pinch hitter Dale Long singled. Mickey Mantle singled home Richardson. Yogi Berra followed with a ground ball to first base. Nelson fielded it, stepped on the bag, and watched in amazement as Mantle slid back into first base, thereby preventing a double play! Long scored on the strange play, and Terry had a chance to avenge his 3–2 heartbreaking loss in game four.

For Bill Mazeroski, the 1960 World Series had been an outstanding success. In game one, he drove a Coates fastball into the seats for the gamewinning two-run-homerun, and turned the defensive gem of the game when he stabbed a Hector Lopez ground ball and started a ninth inning double play. Maz's bat remained hot and he finished the Series at .320. Time after time, Maz went deep in the hole between first and second to rob the Yankee batters of what left their bats as sure base hits.

As he stepped up to the plate to lead off the bottom of the ninth, all he hoped to do was hit the ball hard. Bill's job was to get on base, to get something going... but deep down, he expected to lose.

---

*Pittsburgh jumped ahead 2–0 in the first on a two-run homerun by Rocky Nelson off starter Bob Turley. The Pirates added a pair in the second on a two-run single by Bill Virdon, kayoing Turley and bringing in Bill Stafford. Bobby Shantz took the mound for New York in the third, and held the Pirates scoreless into the eighth inning.

The Yankees came back with a run in the fifth on Bill Skowron's homerun off starter Vernon Law, and took the lead in the sixth on a run-scoring hit by Mickey Mantle and a three-run-homerun by Yogi Berra. New York added two insurance runs in the top of the eighth and, with Shantz cruising along, the 18th world championship seemed a sure thing.

Gino Cimoli opened the Pirates half of the eighth with a single. Virdon followed with a wicked ground ball to shortstop Tony Kubek. It struck a pebble and nailed Kubek in the throat, converting a double play into an infield hit, and eventually forcing the premature ending of Kubek's career. Dick Groat singled home Cimoli.

Stengel responded with a controversial pitching change, summoning the slow-footed Jim Coates, despite the obvious bunt situation, and the fact that the next batter, Bob Skinner, was a lefty (as was Shantz). Shantz also had a reputation as the best fielding pitcher in the league, so the move was all the more absurd.

Terry knew the book on Mazeroski. A tough out and good contact hitter. Not much power, though, so blow the fastball by him . . . or so the Yankee scouts said.

Terry was no longer nervous. He believed his teammates would win it for him in the top of the tenth. All he had to do was retire the side. It seemed too easy.

The 6'3" right-hander followed the book. His first pitch was a high, hard slider, taken for ball one. The next offering was a fastball, just above the waist, and at 3:37 P.M. on the ancient centerfield clock, Mazeroski launched Pittsburgh's version of "the shot heard round the world."

The ball landed in the seats in left center, where 14-year-old Andy Jerpe retrieved it, brought it to the clubhouse and presented it to the new hero.

"You keep it son," Maz told the youth, while he autographed the baseball. "The memory is good enough for me."

A *Sporting News* poll voted the blow the Number One Sports Thrill of the Year, despite the incredible Olympic Hockey victory over the Soviets, and Floyd Patterson's knockout of Johansson. Maz also won the Hickock Belt as the Professional Athlete of the Year, and the Babe Ruth Award for the outstanding World Series performer. The postseason banquet circuit netted him another $20,000 to go along with the handsome raise he received from the Pirates for 1961.

Athletic honors were nothing new to Mazeroski. Born on September 5, 1936, in Wheeling, West Virginia, Bill inherited much of his dad's athletic ability and developed into a standout performer at Warren Consolidated High School in Tiltonsville, Ohio. (The elder Mazeroski had been signed by the Indians in 1935, and moved steadily upward through their organization until an off-season mining accident resulted in the amputation of part of his left foot, and an end to a budding career.) On the basketball court, Bill averaged 27.8 points per game, and ranked among the top five scorers in Ohio. However, his first love remained baseball, and under the guidance of coach Al Burazio, the future major leaguer developed into a standout shortstop-pitcher. He once hurled both ends of a state championship doubleheader, winning a five-hitter in the opener, but dropping a three-hitter in the nightcap.

Maz was pursued by colleges and pro teams in both sports, and opted for an immediate baseball career by signing with the Pirates for a $4,000 bonus in 1954.

"My father did a good job of convincing me that the thing to do was to play minor league ball," Mazeroski later told reporters. "There was a lot to be learned, and the way he felt I should learn it was by playing on a minor league team, not by sitting on a major league bench." (In those days a bonus baby had to remain on the major league roster for his first two seasons.)

After two years in the farm system, Maz joined the Pirates in mid-1956 and batted .243 over 81 games. A year later, he was installed at second base full time, and came through with a .283 mark (the best in his 17-year career). In 1958, "the ballplayers' second baseman," as he quickly became known, batted .275 with 19 homeruns, and earned a trip to the All Star Game. During the pregame warm-ups, the greatest stars of the day interrupted their pre-game activities to watch the youth field ground balls, much the same as they would stop to watch Ted Williams, Willie Mays, and Mickey Mantle take batting practice.

A look at Mazeroski's glove, and one wonders about his success. The premier second baseman used an old pancake-style glove which appeared to have been left out in the rain for a week or two. It barely covered his hand, but also enabled him to get the ball out quickly. As the years went by, his stack of Gold Gloves grew and grew (he would take home eight), and he set virtually every defensive modern record for second baseman.*

Strangely enough, as quick as he was around the infield, Dazzlin' Maz was equally slow on the bases. Only catcher Jim Pagliaroni finished behind the hero, leading Pag to quip that "Maz can fall faster than he can run." And when a Hollywood film company needed a batter to hit into a triple play for use in the film version of Neil Simon's "The Odd Couple," what better man than Maz? (Roberto Clemente was originally cast as the batter, but the slow-footed Mazeroski was a far more convincing character.)

Mazeroski remained the Pirates' regular second baseman until 1969, when injuries reduced him to a .229 average in 67 games. He played more often in 1970, but the average did not improve, and a kid named Dave Cash came along and batted .314. Maz wanted to retire, but the Pirates convinced him to hang on for another shot at the World Series. In 1971, he batted .254 in 70 games, and the Pirates rewarded him by reaching the fall classic again. The hero of the '60 triumph made his only appearance as a pinch-hitter in game one and did not reach base. His teammates did not let him down, and went on to win the Series in seven games.

After the Series, the front office pressured him to stay on, and he decided to give it one more shot. By this time, his mobility afield was drastically reduced, and his batting average plummeted to .188, forcing a reluctant retirement.

Mazeroski has remained active in baseball, and currently serves as a coach with the Seattle Mariners. He also owns and operates a nine-hole golf course in Rayland, Ohio.

For 12 of the 17 years he spent in the major leagues, William Stanley Mazeroski was

---

*Established major league records for the most double plays by a second baseman in one season (161) in 1966; most games at second in a season (163) in 1967; most years leading the league in assists as a second baseman (9); most doubleplays by a second baseman, lifetime (1,706); most consecutive years leading the league in doubleplays by a second baseman (8); most years leading the league in doubleplays by a second baseman (8).

Established National League records for most chances in a career (11,659), most games as a second baseman lifetime (2,094), most putouts lifetime second baseman (4,974); most assists by a second baseman, lifetime (6,685); and most years leading the league in chances accepted by a second baseman (8).)

the premier second baseman in the National League. He took home eight Gold Glove awards, and was selected to numerous all-star teams. His countless fielding records have already been recounted.

During that career, Maz came to bat 7,755 times, and averaged .260—not bad by today's standards for infielders.

Yet, 20 years later, 7,754 of those at-bats might just as well have never taken place. Few fans can tell you whether he batted lefty or righty, and most of the younger generation answers in silence when questioned on his position.

But there is one at-bat they do remember, and it came on October 13, 1960, at 3:37 P.M., when a slick-fielding .260 hitter unleashed a World Series–clinching homerun, and became an instant hero.

AL WEIS

> There goes my chance of ever playing in a World Series.
> —Al Weis's reaction to learning that he had been traded to the New York Mets.

Anyone who predicted that the New York Mets would win the 1969 World Series in spring training would have been laughed out of the bar.

And anyone who picked Albert John Weis as the hero of that fantasy would have been measured for a straight jacket and slapped in a padded cell!

Why, ever since their inception in 1962, the Mets had been an embarrassment to the City of New York, and the National League. At first, they were so bad it was funny. The originals clowned their way to four straight last place finishes. In 1966, they edged their way up to ninth place, but collapsed back into tenth a year later. The '68 squad nosed out Houston for ninth (by one game), and there had been very few changes in personnel as the team opened the '69 campaign. The addition of aged slugger Donn Clendenon, and a young reliever named Tug McGraw, gave the fans little reason to expect a dramatic improvement in the team's fortunes.

As for Weis, a utility infielder acquired from the White Sox* in May, 1968, well, the 6-foot, 160-pound stringbean was a brilliant fielder who could not hit a lick. In seven previous major league seasons, the quiet, modest gloveman averaged .223, with a career total 29 doubles, 8 triples, 4 homeruns, and 80 runs batted in—a mediocre year for many of his contemporaries! His lone claim to fame was a well-photographed collision with Baltimore's perennial all-star, Frank Robinson, in June 1965, which

---

*With centerfielder Tommy Agee, for left fielder Tommy Davis and pitchers Jack Fisher and Billy Wynne.

sent Weis to the hospital for knee surgery, and left Robinson with a concussion, and double vision.

During the off-season, Weis spent hours working out, and, by the time the bell rang for spring training 1969, the "Mighty Mite" had put on 15 pounds of newly acquired muscle. Manager Gil Hodges believed the extra poundage would add some punch to his utilityman's bat, and as things turned out Weis raised his batting average 43 points: from .172 to .215. That his batting average would improve was predictable. That he would hit consecutive game-winning homeruns in a crucial mid-season series with the Chicago Cubs, and be the offensive star of the World Series, was inconceivable.

Needless to say, that is exactly what happened.

Born on April 2, 1938, in Franklin Square, Queens, New York, Weis's family moved to Springfield Gardens (about 10 minutes from the site where Shea Stadium was subsequently erected) when he was a toddler. In 1940 the family moved east to Bethpage, Long Island, New York, where Al went to Farmingdale High.

"I did not play any baseball for the school until my junior year," he recalled. "I just never thought I was that good, and never dreamed of a career in the pros. I played the infield, and even did some catching in a summer league, but I said to heck with the catching.

"There weren't any pro scouts rushing to sign me when I graduated," he said, "so I went into the Army, where I played a lot of service ball. The Dodgers liked me, and offered a free trip to Florida for a tryout, but I wanted a real contract. When the White Sox came along and offered one, I signed for a minimal amount. I never regretted it, well, except for the day when I learned that I'd been traded to the Mets.

"You see, after four years in the minor leagues, I'd played six straight seasons in Chicago, and was working for the club as a winter ticket salesman. I walked in the door for lunch one day, and the phone rang. My wife answered it, and said it was John Murphy, the general manager of the Mets. At first, I thought it was a joke, but when she said it was person to person, I took it.

"Well, he told me I'd been traded to their club, and how glad they were to get me. I was dazed, and very unhappy. We'd just bought a new home, and now we'd have to move. Worst of all, I was going from a pennant contender to a last-place club. I thought to myself: There goes my chance of ever getting into a World Series."

As often seems to be the case with a just plain hero, Weis never would have been in the starting lineup against the Cubs on July 15, 1969, had it not been for events beyond the control of his team's manager. New York's regular shortstop, Bud Harrelson, was serving a two-week tour with the Army Reserve, and Weis was the designated replacement.

At least Hodges had known about the reserve duty prior to the season. What he had no way of knowing was that at that late date, the Mets would trail the first-place Cubs by a mere 4½ games, as the teams opened a three-game series at Wrigley Field on the 14th.

Chicago took the opener, 1–0, as Bill Hands bested Tom Seaver. Weis went 1-for-3 (a leadoff single in the third inning), and was pinch-hit for by Clendenon, with a runner on first and two outs in the ninth. Clendenon lined out to Glenn Beckert, and the game was over.

The next day, the Mets sent right-hander Gary Gentry to the mound to face former New Yorker Dick Selma. Weis again led off the third inning with a single, went to second on a sacrifice, and scored on Agee's triple off the ivy-covered centerfield wall. Chicago countered with a run in the bottom of the frame. Jim Qualls led off with a single, was sacrificed to second, stole third, and came around on a sacrifice fly by Don Kessinger.

Art Shamsky led off the Mets half of the fourth with a base hit, and moved up a base on a hit by Ed Kranepool. Hopes of a big rally dimmed when Selma struck out Wayne Garrett, and faded when J. C. Martin did likewise. The next batter was Weis.

"He threw me two curveballs, and had me 0-and-2," the righthand hitting infielder recalled. "I was in my protective stance, choking up on the bat, just trying to make contact. The next pitch was a letter-high fastball, over the heart of the plate, and I guess I got all of it."

"No doubt about it," Selma said. "I made a mistake. Everyone knew he couldn't hit a curve. My catcher called for a curve on the 0–2 pitch, but I insisted on trying to blow the fastball by him."

The ball arched high and deep to left field, sailing over the screen, and putting the Mets ahead, 4–1. Ken Boswell added a solo shot in the next inning, and New York appeared headed for an easy win. However, the Durochermen struck back for a run in the sixth on a single by Ernie Banks and a two-base error by Agee, and then closed to within one on solo homeruns by Billy Williams and Ron Santo in the seventh. Hodges summoned reliever Ron Taylor, and the right-hander nailed down the victory.

Wrigley Field's seating capacity was officially listed at 36,667, but the third game of the series attracted more than 38,000 screaming Cub-ophiles. The silence was "deafening" when the Mets opened a 4–0 lead in the first inning, and added one more in the second, but the home team rallied in the bottom of the frame. A run in the third tied matters at five, and that's the way the score read as the Mets batted in the fifth inning.

Weis faced lefty reliever Rich Nye in the fifth, and drove another shot deep to left field.

"Oh, no. Not again," cried Cubs play-by-playman Jack Brickhouse. "It's in the bleachers."

New York eventually forged a 9–5 victory, and the Cubs lead was down to 3½ games.

"Let's face it. I'm no homerun hitter," Weis told the press after the game. "I'm not even any kind of hitter. My place on this team is as a utility infielder, and I am not complaining."

When Harrelson returned from the reserves, Boswell left, so Weis shifted to second base, and remained in the lineup.

"One of the reasons the Mets got me was because I had finished all of my military obligations," Weis recalled. "As it turned out, I hit well enough over that span to win a part-time starting job. When Boswell returned, he only played when we faced a righthander."

The Mets slumped in late July and early August, and eventually fell 9½ games behind Chicago, before catching fire. They won 38 of their final 49 games, including a two-game sweep of the Chicagoans at Shea Stadium in early September. On September 10th, they took over first place. Two weeks later, they clinched the pennant. A sweep of the Atlanta Braves in the National League championship series sent them hurtling into the World Series.

By the time the fall classic versus the Baltimore Orioles began, Weis's homeruns against the Cubs had been merged into the unfolding miracle that was the whole season. The fact that Weis would see action whenever southpaws Mike Cuellar and Dave McNally pitched was not considered when the oddsmakers installed the Orioles as 9–5 favorites to win the Series.

Cuellar faced Seaver in the opener. Weis was 0-for-1 when he came to the plate in the seventh inning. The bases were loaded. Cuellar, a master curveball and changeup artist, snuck strike one past him. Three consecutive balls followed, succeeded by a second strike. On the payoff pitch, Weis lofted a fly ball to medium left field. Clendenon tagged at third, and scored the club's only run in the 3–1 loss.

McNally started game two. Mets hurler Jerry Koosman pitched no-hit ball until the seventh inning, when Paul Blair singled, stole second, and scored on a two-out hit by Brooks Robinson. The run matched Clendenon's fourth-inning homerun, and the score remained tied as the teams entered the top of the ninth inning.

The first two Mets went down easily. Ed Charles kept the inning alive with a base hit. On a two-two pitch to Jerry Grote, the 36-year-old Charles took off for second base, and Grote completed his half of the run-and-hit play by singling to left field. Given the head start, Charles continued on to third, and Weis came to the plate with the go-ahead run 90 feet away.

McNally delivered, and Weis smacked the offering into left field, putting the Mets ahead by a run.

"I didn't order McNally to walk Weis because the next batter was Koosman," Orioles skipper Earl Weaver subsequently explained. "If we had walked Weis, they'd have pinch-hit for Koosman, and I wanted him in there when we batted in the bottom of the ninth. You see, Koosman had pitched a hard eight innings, and I'd rather have my hitters face a tired arm than a fresh reliever."

Koosman got the first two Orioles in the bottom of the inning, before facing Frank Robinson. Hodges called time, and ordered Weis out of the infield, and into the left field corner—a unique four-outfielder defense designed to deny the extra-base hit (short of a homerun) to the Baltimore slugger. As things turned out, the strategy was irrelevant. Robinson walked on a three-two pitch.

Boog Powell batted behind Robinson, and the huge left-handed first baseman also drew a walk on a 3–2 pitch.

Hodges had seen enough, and the call went out to the bullpen for Taylor. Again, the count went to 3–2. On the payoff pitch to Brooks Robinson, the All-Star third baseman smashed a hot ground ball to third. Charles grabbed it, threw low and in the dirt to first, but Clendenon scooped it up for the final out. The Mets had achieved a split in Baltimore, and would return home to Shea for the middle three games.

Baltimore sent right-hander Jim Palmer to the mound for game three, relegating Weis to the bench until the late innings. By then, the Mets led, 5–0, the score by which they won.

Cuellar returned for game four, and Weis took up right where he had left off. The utility infielder touched him for two singles in his first three at-bats, but did not figure in the Mets 1–0 lead as the teams entered the top of the ninth inning. (Clendenon's homerun accounted for the run.) With one out in the ninth, Frank Robinson singled. Powell singled. Brooks Robinson ripped a line drive into right centerfield—a sure triple—until Ron Swoboda came from nowhere to make a sensational diving catch. Frank Robinson tagged up and scored the tying run, but the score remained 1–1 as the teams entered the bottom of the tenth.

Grote led off the Mets half of that extra frame, and was safe at second when Don Buford misplayed his fly ball to left field. (It was scored a double.) This time, Weaver walked Weis intentionally, and Hodges sent J. C. Martin up in place of Seaver. The backup catcher laid a bunt down the third base line. Reliever Pete Richert grabbed it, and fired the ball past Powell at first, allowing the winning run to score.

With their backs to the wall, the Orioles assigned McNally the task of keeping their hopes alive, and he got off to a great start. The southpaw pitched shutout ball for five innings, and added a two-run homerun to help build a 3–0 lead. It was not enough.

Cleon Jones led off the sixth and was sent to first base on a controversial hit-by-pitch call. Clendenon followed with his third homerun of the Series. The Orioles did not score in the top of the seventh.

When Weis stepped up in the seventh inning, he did not know that 220 homeruns had been hit in Shea Stadium that year. One thing he did know was that he had not hit one in his home ballpark. In fact, he had never hit one in Shea since joining the Mets.

However, Weis had tagged McNally for a homerun back in his American League days, and with the way the "Mighty Mite" was wrecking the Orioles' staff, perhaps the southpaw should have been more cautious when Al came up in the seventh. At any rate, McNally pitched, and Weis delivered: a long drive to deep left centerfield, over the 371 marker, to tie the ballgame up, and send the fans into delirium.

"Was I shocked when I hit it?" Weis responded to a reporter's question. "Hell yes! All I'd tried to do was meet the ball, hit it hard, get a single.

"When I saw Don Buford start in toward the infield, I figured it was a fly out," he continued. "Then, he started back, and I figured I had a hit, but I never thought it would carry out of the park. I haven't hit many homeruns, so I don't know a homerun off the bat. I didn't realize it was gone until I reached second base.

"I couldn't wait to get into the dugout. I didn't want to break a smile, but I couldn't keep a sober face. They mobbed me when I got there. I didn't even know where the ball landed."

In the eighth inning, the Mets forged ahead on doubles by Jones and Swoboda. The final score was 5–3, and the miracle was complete.

According to newspaper reports, the hero of the '69 season received a $7,000 raise (to $25,000) for 1970. He continued to fill the utility role, seeing action in 75 games, and batting .207 (7 doubles, 1 triple, 1 homerun). The Mets slumped to third place, six games behind the Pirates.

In 1971, Weis was limited to 11 games before being placed on waivers on July 26th.

"Releasing Weis was the hardest thing I ever had to do," Hodges said afterwards. "He gave me everything he had on the field. He never complained, and he spent hours teaching our young infielders how to play."

After his release, Weis returned to the home he had purchased in Chicago in 1968, and a job as the manager of a furniture warehouse. He resides in the same home today, with his wife and two teenage children.

In 1969, Albert John Weis was part of a baseball miracle. There were other heroes on that Mets team, but Weis's name stands out, a cut above the rest, because, from his bat, a clutch hit was least expected, and most shocking.

"I'm living in Chicago now, and those homeruns and hits in '69 come up just about every day," he said in 1981. "Most of my friends are, and were, Cubs fans, and they never let me forget it. Then again, why should I want to forget it: those were the greatest moments of my career."

CHRIS CHAMBLISS

> Now I think I know how Bobby Thomson felt. I hit it and watched it go out. I didn't realize what I'd done until the fans started pouring on to the field. I didn't think I'd make it around the bases. People were ripping at my cap and clothes . . .
> —Chris Chambliss, October 14, 1976

When Chris Chambliss stepped into the batter's box to lead off the bottom of the ninth inning of game five of the 1976 American League championship series, the mood of most of the record 56,821 fans jammed into Yankee Stadium bordered on despair.

Their hometown heroes had squandered a 6–3 lead in the eighth inning (thanks to a three-run homerun by George Brett), and had barely escaped a bases-loaded, two-out situation in the ninth. Only a bang-bang force at second had retired the Royals and kept the score tied.

The issue was very much in doubt as Mark Littel, a strong left-hander, warmed up before the Yankees came to bat.

It had been a very satisfying season for the Yankees first baseman. Chris had joined the club amidst a great furor in 1974. Fans and players alike openly criticized the deal that sent four popular pitchers (Fritz Peterson, Fred Beene, Tom Buskey, and Steve Kline) to Cleveland, in return for Chambliss and two pitchers (Dick Tidrow and Cecil Upshaw).

That first season had not been easy. Chris's new teammates made no secret of their resentment of the trade, which had broken up the country club atmosphere that pervaded the Yankees' clubhouse. The situation was made worse by Chambliss, and the rest of the club, getting off to a slow start. However, things began to change after the All-Star break. The Yankees and Chambliss got hot together, and soon found themselves locked in a four-way race for the division championship. Although Baltimore ultimately took the title by two games, a new generation of Yankee fans had high hopes for the future.

Then came the year of disappointment: 1975. The team added Bobby Bonds to its roster, got off to a great start, and then collapsed. Injuries played a major role in the team's demise, and although Chambliss finished at .304, the fans were not happy with his 72 RBIs.

But 1976 had been great. The team had returned to the remodeled Yankee Stadium and gotten off to a great start. Chambliss had come through with several big homeruns, including a blow that beat the Red Sox in a big series. The fans had warmed up to his .293 average and 96 RBIs.

The 1976 season had also been a sweet success for the 23-year-old Littel. He had burst upon the scene with an 8–4 win-loss total, and 16 saves. Only one batter had hit a homerun off him in 60 innings, and his ERA was a sparkling 2.08. The hard-throwing southpaw expected big things in the future, and honestly believed the Royals could go all the way.

For Chambliss, the championship series had been more of the same, only better. His two-run homerun and three RBIs had been decisive in the Yankees 5–3 win in game three. Game five had already been good to Chris: a sacrifice fly in the first inning to tie the score (2–2), a run-scoring ground ball that broke a 3–3 tie in the third, a double in the fifth, and a single, stolen base, and run scored in the Yankees two-run seventh. Now, he was set to lead off the ninth against Littel, knowing he would see fastballs, and just hoping to hit the ball hard.

The series had also been good to Littel. He had relieved starter Larry Gura with two outs in the ninth inning of game one and retired the only batter he faced. He came into game three with two on and one out in the sixth, and set the Yankees down in order. Of course, the Royals had lost both games, but it was not his fault.

As Littel began warming up, the fans (?) began littering the field with rolls of toilet paper and debris. By the time he was ready, the umpires were not—the field had to be cleared of debris, and Chambliss' at-bat was delayed for about five minutes.

"I was all warmed up and ready when that last barrage came down from the stands," he recalled. "I got angry about the delay and lost my concentration, but when

Chambliss stepped in, I was ready. I figured, throw the fastball, get ahead in the count. I knew I could get him out."

At 10:54 P.M., Chambliss stepped in, Littel took the sign from catcher Buck Martinez, and the first pitch of the inning was on its way. Chambliss had guessed right. It was a fastball. The 35-ounce bat swept across home plate, meeting the ball just in front of the base, sending it rising on a line toward the wall in right centerfield.

"I stopped to watch it in flight," Chris recalled. "It felt good when I made contact. I thought it had a chance to go out . . ."

Out on the mound, Littel knew he was in trouble.

"As soon as he hit it, I knew it would go a long way, up the alley, but I was hoping that someone would run it down," Littel recalled. "I watched them leap at the wall, and then it was over. My heart dropped to my shoes, and all I could think about was getting the hell out of there, and how close we'd come, and why did I have to be the one to give up that one."

When "chance" became reality, Chambliss jerked his arms into the air and did a little victory dance before starting his trek around the bases. By the time he reached first base, the infield was a sea of humanity. When he reached second, he had to use his hand to touch it—a youth had already pried it out of the ground and was carrying it away as a souvenir.

"I never did touch third," he admits. "It was gone by the time I got there, and I didn't touch home plate until much later on, when my teammates sort of dragged me out of the dugout and made me touch it to make the pennant official."

Carroll Christopher Chambliss, the hero of the 1976 A.L. series, was born on December 26, 1948, in Dayton, Ohio. His father is a Navy chaplain, and the commitment to the armed forces necessitated several relocations during Chris's childhood.

The future major leaguer first attracted attention as the All-Avocado League shortstop in his junior year at Oceanside High School (Oceanside, California) in 1966. A year later, he shifted to first base, where he won All-League honors again. Upon his graduation from high school, the 6'1", 185-pound slugger enrolled at Mira Costa Junior College, where he had an outstanding baseball career. Each June, the Cincinnati Reds drafted Chambliss, and each June, he spurned their offers (which went as high as a $12,000 signing bonus alone).

In 1969, Chambliss graduated from Mira Costa and enrolled at UCLA, where he batted .340 (15 homeruns and 45 RBIs). The Cleveland Indians made him the number one draft choice for all of major league baseball in 1970, and he inked an Indians contract that included a $35,000 bonus.

Cleveland originally planned to send him down to their Reno (Class C, California League) farm club, but he was so impressive in spring training that Wichita (AAA) manager Ken Aspromonte convinced the Tribe's front office to send him there. All he did was lead the league with a .342 batting average, making him the first rookie ever to win an AAA League batting crown. When Ken Harrelson retired to pursue a short-lived professional golf career, Cleveland summoned Chambliss as his replacement.

Chris batted safely in his first six games, including a game-winning two-run single in his first major league contest, and went on to win Rookie-of-the-Year honors, with a .275 batting average. He improved to .292 a year later, dropped back to .273 in 1973, and was off to a great start when the Indians dealt him to New York on April 24, 1974.

"It was a shock," the mild-mannered, quiet first baseman recalled. "I guess I had the idea that I would be in Cleveland for some time. I didn't want to go to New York. We had just gotten married, and had moved into our first apartment . . . and then boom, the trade."

The reception awaiting him in New York was even more shocking. The trade had upset most of the veterans on the Yankees' ballclub, and when Chambliss got off to a slow start, there were grumblings about him being the second coming of Matty Alou. (Alou batted .305 as a Yankee in 1973, but rarely drove in any runs.)

"They made no secret about their displeasure over the deal," he said. "It was nothing personal against me. It was just a wave of negative feelings that sort of focused on me."

As the season wore on, Chambliss and the Yankees got hot, and were not eliminated from the division title race until the next-to-last-day of the season. Chris finished with an 18-game hitting streak, and was suddenly very much appreciated (despite final statistics of .255 with 50 RBIs).

"I guess you have to give the front office credit after all," said veteran pitcher Mel Stottlemyre, one of the more vociferous opponents of the deal. "Chris and Dick Tidrow have done a great job for us."

(As things turned out, the players sent to Cleveland never did much for the Indians. Peterson went 24-25 over three seasons, the last of which was split with Texas. Beene went 5-4 with 4 saves in two years. Kline recorded a 3-8 mark over his two remaining major league campaigns, and Buskey continues to enjoy moderate success as a short relief man after saving 16 games for the Indians in 1974.)

What was Chambliss' reward for the strong finish? The Yankees opened spring training by working left fielder Roy White at first base. What was Chris' reaction? He lent White his glove.

When Roy injured his wrist, Chambliss reclaimed the position and had an outstanding year. He followed the .304 1974 season with the heroics of '76. While most of his teammates were silenced by the Reds in the World Series, Chambliss hit .313.

This time, he was rewarded handsomely—at least by the salary standards that were in effect at that time. The Yankees inked him to a five-year $1,200,000 deal that gave Chris everything he wanted—except a no-trade clause. He responded with another superior season in 1977 (.287, 32 doubles, 6 triples, 17 homeruns, and 90 RBIs), slumped badly in the ALCS (1-for-17 against the Royals this time), but rebounded with a solid World Series performance (.292). Most fans have forgotten that it was Chambliss' two-run homerun that opened the Yankees' scoring in the sixth and final game, but that is because the less spectacular Chambliss was overshadowed by Reggie Jackson's three homeruns that day.

Chambliss was bothered by nagging injuries in 1978, but still came in with solid statistics: .274, 26 doubles, 3 triples, 12 homeruns and 90 RBIs. He missed three World Series games against the Dodgers due to an injured wrist, after batting .400 against the Royals in the playoffs.

The off-season was rough psychologically. Chris' hand was not healing properly, and to add to his worries, the newspapers were filled with reports that the Yankees planned to deal him to the Twins in exchange for Rod Carew.

By the time spring training began, Carew had signed with the Angels, but Chambliss would not get any peace of mind. Jim Spencer, a power-hitting left-handed first baseman, complete with a Gold Glove, was his competition at first base, and with the abundance of lefty power, Chris feared he was expendable. The wrist eventually healed, and Chris eventually got on track, but Spencer had a tremendous year in a part-time role, and the Yankees decided to deal Chambliss in the off-season.

"In retrospect, I knew I was gone when they signed Spencer to a four-year deal," Chambliss said at a press conference three days after he learned he had been traded to the Toronto Blue Jays as part of a six-player trade that brought Rick Cerone and Tom Underwood to New York. "I am very disappointed that George Steinbrenner did not call me and let me know what his plans were. I still haven't heard from him, nor have I heard from any of my teammates.

"I'm not bitter about the trade," he continued, "and I am not retiring, despite speculation to the contrary. The fans in New York have been very kind to me and my family, and I appreciate their support.

"I am well aware that players of equal or less ability made more money than I did because of their relationship with George Steinbrenner. Being quiet and non-controversial cost me a lot of money. I have no regrets because I knew what I was doing. I reacted to every situation the way my personality dictates."

Less than five weeks later, the still-shaken first baseman was jolted again. Toronto had dealt him to the Atlanta Braves.

"I was beginning to get used to the idea of going to Toronto because I like the city," he said. "But, it sounds like Atlanta really wants me. It's going to be all right. I know they were last in the N.L. West last year, but I've been in the cellar before. Cleveland once lost 106 games while I was there. Besides, I'm a low ball hitter, and this is supposed to be a low ball league."

The switch to the cozy Atlanta ballpark did not hurt Chris' production, either. He batted .282 (37 doubles, 18 homeruns, 72 RBIs, and 13 game-winning hits). The Braves even made a run at the divisional title, but collapsed in the final two weeks of the season.

"We've got a very young ballclub, and the future looks bright," he said in the 1980-81 off-season. "I'm looking forward to some very exciting baseball in this city next year."

On October 14, 1976, Carroll Christopher Chambliss used one swing of the bat to gain a place in the hearts of Yankee fans that will never be forgotten. Odds are that if the quiet, uncontroversial, intelligent, gentlemanly Chambliss had not hit that one homerun, he would already be buried among the solid ballplayers still active in the major leagues. He would have remained overshadowed by the more spectacular performers, like Rod Carew, and the more controversial actors, like Reggie Jackson.

Ironically, Carew, the man who Chambliss was very nearly traded for, will be forgotten in thirty years. Ironically, Spencer, the man who made Chambliss expendable, will fade out of the fans' minds even sooner. But Chambliss, the man they traded, the man who stayed quietly in the shadows, will be remembered because when the chips were down, and the pennant was on the line, he took Mark Littel downtown, and became an eternal hero.

BUCKY DENT

All I was thinking about was hitting the ball hard. I knew how Torrez pitched—he'd been with us the year before. I was hoping for something waist high and a little inside—up in Fenway Park, that wall is always on your mind. When I hit it, well, seeing that ball go up on that screen was the greatest thing in the world. It was a fairy tale come true.

—Russell Earl "Bucky" Dent

On October 2, 1978, the New York Yankees and Boston Red Sox had a date with destiny. The eternal archrivals had finished the regular season tied for first place in the American League Eastern Division. A one-game playoff would begin at 2 P.M. that afternoon, at the site of the only previous tie-breaker in American League history, ancient Fenway Park.*

The significance of the Boston ballpark extended well beyond the vocal, capacity hometown fans. Fenway's dimensions (315 feet down the left field line, a gradual slope back to the 388 mark just to the left of center) overwhelmingly favored right-hand hitters, a commodity with which the Sox were well stocked (Rick Burleson, Carlton Fisk, Jim Rice, George Scott, Butch Hobson, and Dwight Evans).

The Yankee lineup, on the other hand, was loaded with lefthand power designed to pepper the short porch in the Stadium's right field corner, and was far less effective in Boston. In fact, historically, the Yankees rarely won more than four or five games a year in Fenway, a four-game sweep that September notwithstanding.

---

*A coin toss held three weeks earlier had been won by Boston.

As things turned out, the short fence in left field did play a crucial role in the ballgame. A right-hand hitter lofted a fly ball onto the screen, about ten feet fair of the 315 marker. There were two runners on base, and the blow extinguished a 2–0 deficit.

Ironically enough, the heroic blow was not launched by a noted power hitter. In fact, the batter was not even an occasional power hitter—he had hit 22 homeruns in 4½ years.

There was one final irony. The hero did not wear the red and white flannel with a large "B" on the cap. The Red Sox were beaten by their own ballpark, beaten by a .243 hitter, beaten by Bucky Dent.

That the Yankees and Red Sox would square off in an October playoff game seemed impossible in July, and wishful thinking in September. On July 19th, the injury-plagued New Yorkers trailed Boston by 14 games. During the ensuing 52 days, the Yankees healed and won, while the Sox suffered similar injuries and lost. By the time the squads opened a mid-September series at Fenway, the gap had been reduced to four games.

Beginning on September 7th, and continuing through all four games, the Yankees launched an offensive display that left the Sox reeling. The Bombers abused the Boston pitching staff for 42 runs, and swept a four-game series in Boston for the first time since 1949.

Two days later, a Yankee win over Detroit, coupled with a Boston loss to Toronto, pushed the New Yorkers a half game ahead. As the week wore on, the lead grew to 3½ games, and the teams entered the final 14 days of the season with the momentum favoring the Yankees.

Somehow, the Bostons rallied, gaining 2½ games before the teams entered the final week of play. For six straight days, they matched wins. On the final Sunday of the season, Cleveland smashed the New Yorkers, 9–2, and Boston beat Toronto, 5–0, to force the playoff.

It had been a rough year for Russell Earl "Bucky" Dent. He batted a disappointing .243 in 123 games, the first time in his five-year career that he had played less than 153 games. Rumors of family problems, coupled with a pulled right hamstring muscle, and the final year of his contract, served as potent distractions for the handsome 5'11", 182-pound shortstop.

Most of all, Bucky was frustrated by manager Bob Lemon's policy of pinch-hitting for him whenever there were men on base in the late innings of a close ballgame. Lemon reasoned that with power hitters like Jim Spencer and Cliff Johnson, and better average hitters like Roy White and Lou Piniella, the odds favored pinchhitting, and using reliable Fred Stanley in Dent's stead. Dent longed for the opportunity to prove himself. One would be forthcoming.

Michael Augustine Torrez also had a date with destiny that afternoon. The 32-year-old right-hander, 16–12 (3.96) during the regular season, had drawn the starting assignment from Sox skipper Don Zimmer. His opponent would be the easy Cy Young Award winner, Rapid Ron Guidry, 24–3 (1.74), a 28-year-old southpaw in his second season with New York.

Their careers could not have been less similar. Torrez was a crafty 11-year veteran with a career 130–96 mark. His win-loss statistics were deceptive—his 3.60 lifetime earned run average more accurately reflected the fact that Torrez was a winner because his teams scored a lot of runs for him. He was not a strikeout pitcher, and occasionally had control problems. He also tended to give up at least one hit per inning pitched.

Guidry, on the other hand, spent most of six seasons in the minors, showing flashes of brilliance, but failing in spring training and brief visits to the varsity. Ironically, the 5'9" southpaw was nearly traded for Bucky Dent in 1977—only the protestations of former manager Billy Martin saved him.

When Guidry finally broke into the starting rotation in 1977, he went on to post a 17–9 mark, with a 2.82 ERA, 176 strikeouts, and a reputation as one of the best young hurlers in the game. In 1978, he had that unforgettable season: 25–3, 1.74, 248 strikeouts, 13 straight wins at the start of the season.

As between Torrez and Guidry, there was no doubt that Gid was the better man on the mound, when well rested. But the playoff game forced the left-hander to pitch on just three days' rest, breaking his season-long four-days-between-starts routine. He was also a left-hander, pitching in a ballpark that Whitey Ford rarely pitched in because it was a graveyard for southpaws.

Yet, the ultimate irony had to be that less than a year before, almost to the day, Mike Torrez was pitching the New York Yankees to a world championship. His heroic relief role in game five of the American League Championship Series with Kansas City, coupled with two wins over the Dodgers in the World Series, made him a much sought after free agent after the '77 campaign. Torrez asked Yankee owner George Steinbrenner for a five-year deal, and the shipbuilder balked. The Red Sox needed pitching, and what better place to get it than from their arch rival's stable.

When word of Torrez' signing with Boston hit the papers, Yankee fans openly wondered whether a major error had been made. President Al Rosen told the public that all they had lost was a .500 pitcher, words he probably regretted for about an hour and a half on October 2, 1978.

As things turned out, Torrez would make another significant contribution to a Yankee world championship. This time, the aid was limited to one game, in fact, to one pitch, one moment in which he served up a three-run homerun to our hero, Bucky Dent.

And what of Russell Dent, or rather Russell O'Dey, or Russell Stanford? Bucky Dent was born on November 25, 1951, in Savannah, Georgia. His parents were divorced when Bucky was an infant, and his mother sent him to live with her relatives, Sarah and James Dent. Bucky grew up in Hialeah, Florida, and did not learn about the real facts of his birth until he was 10 years old. One day, his "Aunt" Dennis came to visit, and told him that she was his mother. The child was stunned.

"That's all she said, and then she dropped it," he told reporters. "I didn't know what to think at first. I had no feeling for her, and couldn't accept her as my mother, so I continued to call my Aunt and Uncle 'Mom and 'Dad' because they deserved it.

"Whenever I saw my real mother, I'd ask about my real father, and she'd never tell me anything."

Thus began a 15-year search for his real father, a search which ended when his mom finally revealed that the man was Russell Stanford, and he was living near Savannah. Eventually, Bucky located his dad, and the pair have more than made up for the 25-year separation.

In the interim, Bucky starred as an All-State tailback for Hialeah, and an All-County third baseman. He spent a year at Miami Dade North Junior College, and earned All-America Honorable Mention at third and short. In 1970, he signed with the White Sox, and joined the parent club in 1973. A year later, he was the starting shortstop, batted .274, and finished runner-up in the rookie-of-the-year balloting.

In 1975, Dent had his best season in Chicago, batting .264 with 29 doubles, 4 triples, 3 homers, and 58 RBIs. He led all American League shortstops with 840 total chances, 283 putouts, 541 assists, and a .981 fielding average, while making just 16 errors.

In 1976, he slumped to .246, and was dangled as trade bait during the off-season. The Yankees were not satisfied with their shortstop, Fred Stanley, and were quick to pursue the highly touted Dent. Originally, the Sox wanted Ron Guidry as part of the deal, but they eventually settled for lefty slugger Oscar Gamble, and pitchers Bob Polinsky and Dewey Hoyt.

Bucky was moderately successful in his first season in pinstripes: .247, 18 doubles, 4 triples, 8 homeruns, and 49 RBIs. He also batted .263 against the Dodgers in the World Series. His 1978 statistics showed a mixed change: .243, 11 doubles, 1 triple, 5 homeruns, 40 RBIs, but limited to 123 games.

Bucky Dent

That Dent would be a hero in the playoff game seemed unlikely.

By the time Bucky Dent came to bat in the top of the seventh inning of the first-ever American League Eastern Division Championship Game, Yankee fans were wondering out loud about Steinbrenner's refusal to sign Torrez. For six innings, the turncoat righthander had been nearly untouchable. Only Mickey Rivers' third inning double, and Lou Piniella's fourth inning infield hit, marred an otherwise superb outing. Torrez had struck out Thurman Munson, the Yankees' best clutch hitter, three times, twice with Rivers on second. He also had the luxury of a 2-0 lead, thanks to a second inning solo shot by Carl Yastrzemski, and a sixth inning, run-scoring single by Jim Rice.

Graig Nettles opened the seventh with a fly ball to right field. Chris Chambliss followed with a hard single to left. When Roy White slashed a liner into center, Zimmer headed for the mound, and a conference with Torrez. They talked about pinch-hitter Jim Spencer, reviewed the way to pitch to him, and induced the lefty stick to fly out to left field. The next batter was Bucky.

"Quite frankly, I never expected to bat in that situation," Dent recalled, "but we were without Willie Randolph because of a hamstring injury, so Lem [manager Bob Lemon] had no choice but to let me hit. We were out of infielders because Spencer pinch-hit for Brian Doyle."

Dent took a pitch for ball one, then fouled one off his left ankle. He hobbled around in pain, and mysteriously switched bats.

"I told him to use the one the batboy brought out," Rivers later explained. "It was the bat he was supposed to use all along. You see, he'd been using my bats, and I had two. One was chipped, and he'd gone out there with the chipped one, which is bad luck. So I told the kid to do anything—hit him, strangle him, scream at him, but get that damned chipped bat out of there."

Dent returned to the plate. Torrez uncorked a fastball that was supposed to be low and away. It stayed belt high, and inside.

"He'd thrown that to me before, and handcuffed me," Dent said. "I was hoping I'd see it again, and when I did, I jumped on it."

The ball sailed high and deep down the left field line, and landed atop the screen, about 10 feet fair.

The Yankees went berserk. Steinbrenner and Rosen began cheering wildly. The Boston ballpark was strangely silent. The Yankees were ahead, 3-2.

Torrez lasted one more batter—a walk to Rivers—and was replaced by Bob Stanley. Munson doubled Rivers home, and in the top of the eighth, Reggie Jackson drilled the ball 420 feet for what appeared to be an "insurance" homerun, making it 5-2. As things turned out, it was the best insurance money could buy.

Jerry Remy led off the eighth with a double off Yankee reliever Rich Gossage. After Rice flew out, Yaz singled Remy home. Fisk singled Yaz to second, and Fred Lynn's base hit to left closed the gap to 5–4. With more than 32,000 fans screaming for a game-tying hit, Gossage settled down and retired Hobson on a fly to right, and Scott on three strikes.

The ninth inning was heartstopping. Gossage retired pinch-hitter Dwight Evans, but walked Burleson. Remy followed with a line drive to right that Piniella lost in the sun. The veteran outfielder raised his arms, faking a bead on the ball, and watched, hoping to pick it up before it bounced past him. The ball landed five feet in front of him, and bounced to Lou's left. If it went past, a triple and a tie, with Rice coming up—but Lou snared it and fired to third, holding Burleson at second. The play became all the more significant when Rice flew out to deep right, Burleson advancing to third (instead of scoring). The next batter was Yaz. The heart of the Bostons for 20 years stood on the threshhold of superstardom, took ball one, and then popped up to Nettles at third, ending the ballgame.

"It was the greatest ballgame I ever saw," Dent said. "When I was a kid, I used to dream about things like this. It's a fairy tale that came true. I can't help but think of Bobby Thomson's homerun. I didn't see it, but every fan has heard the announcer [Russ Hodges] screaming 'The Giants win the pennant, the Giants win the pennant.' Well, this homerun is similar, and hopefully the fans will remember it, and me, for a long time."

Dent returned to mediocrity for the four-game ALCS versus the Royals, managing three hits in 15 at-bats, and driving in four runs, but in the World Series, he rose to the occasion again. He had a hit in each of the first four games against the Dodgers, and contributed three hits in the Yankees' 12–2 victory in game five. His two-run single in the second inning of game six (the first of three hits that day, too) drove in what proved to be the Series' winning run, as the Yankees rebounded from a 0–2 deficit to take Los Angeles in six games. Bucky finished 10-for-24 (.417) with 7 RBIs, and received the Babe Ruth Award as the outstanding World Series performer.

Bucky's success in the World Series made him a national hero. He made dozens of off-season appearances and endorsements as the world sought to take advantage of his good looks and big hits. He paid for his success in several ways. He did not stay in shape in the off-season, and reported slightly overweight for 1979. He also ran into serious marital problems, and temporarily separated from his wife. To top it off, he was in the option year of his contract, and the Yankees made no secret of the fact that they did not plan to sign him, especially after he collapsed to .230 at the plate.

"When I packed my bags at the end of the season, I really didn't expect to be back," he recalled. "I didn't even know if I wanted to be back. We had talked informally with California, and I was leaning toward a move. Then, my agent, Nick Buoniconti, called, and told me the Yankees had made an offer. I talked it over with my wife, and we decided that we'd rather stay in New York. The kids were happy, and so was I when George came through with a five-year deal that includes a two-year no-trade clause."

Bucky responded with his best year ever, batting .262 with 26 doubles and 52 RBIs, and remains the darling of the fairer sex in New York baseball.

On October 2, 1978, a lifetime .250 hitter took one swing of the bat and vaulted into immortality. He had many other things going for him: good looks, fine ability, a thriving baseball career in New York, a World Series ring on his finger, and a promising future in New York. No one would argue that Dent was as good a hitter as Spencer, Nettles, Randolph, Piniella, Rivers, White . . . but long after they are forgotten, the name of Russell Earl "Bucky" Dent will survive, because he rose to the occasion and became a hero by hitting an unexpected homerun that completed a miracle.

CONCLUSION

The creation of a superstar begins with a tremendously talented athlete who is either outstanding in every aspect of the game (e.g., Willie Mays), or whose weakness is so overshadowed by strengths as to be overlooked (e.g., that Ted Williams was a mediocre fielder).

Next, there is the element of success. The player must be successful, his team must win pennants, and somehow, that player must become identified as "the straw that stirs the drink good." Thus, men who had tremendous ability, but were cursed with weak teams (i.e., George Sisler) never attained superstar status. Similarly, great ballplayers who were overshadowed by even better teammates (i.e., Sandy Koufax masking Don Drysdale) never make the vault into immortality.

Even the great player who does "stir the drink," who is successful, and whose team does win pennants, will be overlooked without that certain special appeal called charisma. The player must have that sixth sense for dealing with the fans, and use it to build a love affair of sorts with the tens of thousands he performs before every day. There must be some aspect of his character that the public can focus in on, and attach itself to. He must be godlike on the field, yet demonstrate human frailties off it. The fans focused on Babe Ruth's feats on the diamond, and his warm, boyish personality off it. In many ways, he was leading the life that every male in America dreamed of: the greatest athlete by day, the wildest playboy by night.

The importance of good relations with the media cannot be overemphasized. If a great athlete's name and feats do not get into print, and on the airwaves, he has no chance of attaining superstar status. If he is portrayed in a consistently unfavorable light, the public will adopt that negative attitude as its own. Regardless of the player's on-the-field performance, judgment will be passed by the knights of the keyboard and denizens of the catbird seat, and irreparable harm may occur.

Franchise location is also a consideration. The larger the city, the greater are the opportunities for endorsements, speaking appearances, and the like, and the larger the base from which fans may be drawn. More fans mean more income, and tend to stabilize the franchise. Such stabilization leads to continuity, and such continuity is important. (Perhaps if there were still A's in Philadelphia, Lefty Grove, Jimmy Foxx, Al Simmons, and George Earnshaw might be remembered.)

Another factor is the popularity of the sport in the location. Seattle has never been a sports-minded town. One franchise has already failed there, and the Mariners are in trouble. Similarly, while some cities are capable of supporting two teams, or even three, others simply cannot. The Braves were never a financial success in Boston. Likewise, the A's in Philadelphia and the Browns in St. Louis.

In the end, the element of luck plays a part, too. A bad hop on a ground ball gives Bill Mazeroski a chance to become a hero, a tragic illness enables Lou Gehrig to overcome the shadow cast by Babe Ruth and become a superstar, defensive changes necessitated by pinch-hitters force a manager to put Sandy Amoros in left field and open the door to the hall of heroes... all a combination of luck and fate... all crucial factors in the search for immortality and superstardom.

GENERAL INDEX

Note: Names and page numbers in italic indicate that a chapter is devoted to that person. See also the Index of Teams.

Aaron, Henry (Hank), xiv, 18, 103, 112, 117, 217, 220, 237
Abrams, Cal, 120
Adams, Ace, 116
Adams, Charles (Babe), 21, 143
Addis, Bob, 109
Agee, Tommie, 285, 287
Aguirre, Hank, 220
Alexander, Dale, 98
Alexander, Grover Cleveland, xv, 53, *132-33, 147-52,* 154, 156, 190, 200
Allen, Richie (Dick), 207
Allison, Bob, 226
Alou, Felipe, 205
Alou, Matteo (Matty), 294
Alston, Walter (mgr.), 204-5, 209-11, 215, 217-18, 221, 268, 270, 275
Amalfitano, Joe, 209
Amoros, Edmundo (Sandy), xviii, 125, *265-71,* 274, 306
Anson, Adrian (Cap), xv, *5-11,* 131
Antonelli, Johnny, 260, 261, 263
Aparicio, Louis, 211
Archdeacon, Maurice, 158
Arellanes, Frank, 238
Ashburn, Richie, 120, 123
Aspromonte, Ken (mgr.), 294
Atwell, Toby, 109
Auker, Eldon, 182, 188-89
Averill, Earl, 190
Avila, Bobby, 259

Baker Bowl, 50, 114, 148
Baker, Del, 72
Baker, Gene, 120
Baker, John (Home Run), 4, 98-99, 142-43, 163, *237-44*
Bancroft, Dave, 171
Bankhead, Dan, 108
Banks, Ernie, xvii, 209, 287
Barber, Turner, 247
Barnes, Don, 31
Barnes, Roscoe, 3
Barnhart, Clyde, 43
Barnie, Bill (mgr.), 10
Barr, George, 190
Barrow, Ed (mgr., g.m.), 85, 169
Barry, Jack, 238, 246
Bauer, Henry (Hank), 217, 269-70, 275, 277
Bavasi, Buzzy (g.m.), 121-22, 123, 201, 209, 213, 271
Beck, Erwin T., 3
Beckendorf, Henry (Heinie), 156
Becker, Joe (coach), 204
Beckert, Glenn, 287
Bedell, Howard (Howie), 220
Beene, Fred, 291, 294
Behrman, Hank, 253
Bench, Johnny, 73
Bender, Charles (Chief), 164
Benswanger, Bill (owner), 58-59
Bentley, Jack, 157
Bevens, Bill, 256, 267
Bishop, Max, 199
Blackenship, Cliff, 154
Blair, Clarence (Footsie), 250
Blair, Paul, 211, 288
Bolton, Cliff, 178
Bonds, Bobby, 292
Bonham, Ernest (Tiny), 91, 266

307

Borchert, Otto (owner), 58-9
Boswell, Ken, 287-88
Boudreau, Lou, 93
Bouton, Jim, 218, 262
Boyer, Clete, 45, 226
Branca, Ralph, xvii
Brandt, Jackie, 211
Braves Field, 66, 138
Breadon, Sam, 151, 184, 187
Bresnahan, Roger, 58, 131
Brett, George, 291
Brickhouse, Jack (broadcaster), 287
Bridges, Tommy, 70-71
Bridwell, Al, 134
Briggs Stadium, 86, 91
Briggs, Walter (owner), 66, 72, 73, 92
Bright, Harry, 206
Brock, Lou, 18
Broeg, Bob (writer), 59, 157
Brown, Joe (Saw Mill), 176
Brown, Mace, 44
Brown, Mordecai (Three-Fingered), 133, 234
Browne, Byron, 209
Browning, Pete, xv
Brush, John (owner), 136
Buford, Don, 290
Burdette, Lew, 277
Burich, Si (writer), 204
Burkett, Jesse, xv
Burleson, Rick, 297, 302
Burns, George, 54, 170
Burns, Jack, 197
Bush, Joe, 246
Buskey, Tom, 291, 294
Byrne, Tommy, 266, 268-69

Camilli, Doug, 207
Campanella, Roy, 123, 124, 126, 266, 268, 275
Campanis, Al (scout), 203
Cantillon, Joe (mgr.), 153-54
Carew, Rod, 295-96
Carey, Andy, 274, 277
Carleton, James (Tex), 188
Carlson, Hal, 113
Carrigan, Bill (mgr.), 53
Casey, Hugh, 255, 257, 266
Cash, Dave, 282
Cavaretta, Phil, 71
Cepeda, Orlando, 205
Cerone, Rick, 295

Cerv, Bob, 269
Chambliss, Chris, xvii, *291-96,* 301
Chance, Frank, 251
Chapman, Ben, 75-81, 102-03
Chapman, Ray, 47, 54, 72, 157, 167-69, 172
Charles, Ed, 288-89
Chase, Hal, 94, 137
Chiozza, Lou, 115
Cimolli, Gino, 280
Clarke, Fred, 23, 238
Clarkson, John, xv, 5
Clemente, Roberto, 280, 282
Clendenon, Donn, 285, 287-89
Cleveland Municipal Stadium, 83
Cline, Ty, 216
Coakley, Andy, 163
Coates, Jim, 280
Cobb, Tyrus Raymond (Ty), xv, 5, *13-19,* 21, 24-25, 34, 36, 50-51, 55-56, 60, 62, 81, 93, 103, 164, 168, 176, 238-39
Cochrane, Gordon (Mickey), 60, *65-73,* 86, 98, 100, 184-85, 198-99
Cohen, Andy, 113
Collins, Eddie, xv, 36, 48, 161-62, 238-39, 243, 250
Combs, Earle, 14, 196
Comiskey Park, 97
Comiskey, Charles (owner), 156, 233
Connery, Bob (scout), 31-32
Connolly, Tom, 164
Connor, Roger, 3
Connors, Chuck, 255
Consella, Dick, 176
Coombs, Jack, 148, 163
Coveleski, Stan, 157, 167-68
Cox, Billy, 45, 203
Craig, Roger, 266
Cramer, Roger (Doc), 92
Crawford, Sam, 18, 164
Cronin, Joe, 58, 173-74, 195, 200
Crosby, Bing (owner), 92
Crosetti, Frank, 191
Curtis, Don (scout), 184
Cuyks, Jon Van, 255
Cuyler, Hazen (Kiki), 185, 250

Daley, Arthur (writer), 144
Dalrymple, Clay, 220
Daniel, Dan (writer), 144
Dark, Alvin, xvii, 124, 260

General Index

Davis, Curt, 191
Davis, George, 137, 234
Davis, Harry, 86, 164
Davis, Spud (Virgil), 188
Davis, Tommy, 205, 207, 285
Davis, Willie, 205, 211
Dean, Jay Hanna (Dizzy), 70, 87-88, 94, 181-93
Dean, Paul (Daffy), 87-88, 94, 186-88
Delahanty, Ed, xv, 153
DeLancey, Bill, 88
Dent, Russell (Bucky), xvii, 297-303
Derringer, Paul, 91
DeSautels, Gene, 102
DeVore, Josh, 239
DeWitt, Bill (owner), 182, 191
Dickey, William (Bill), 58, 65, 72-73, 79, 97, 173, 242
Dietz, Dick, 215-16
DiMaggio, Joe, xii, 35, 47, 80, 106, 117, 190, 253-54, 267
DiMaggio, Vince, 182
Doby, Larry, 56, 259
Dodgers Stadium, 205, 213
Dolan, Tom, 50
Donahue, Jiggs (John), 67, 234
Donatelli, Augie (umpire), 219-20
Donovan, Bill, 164
Dougherty, Pat (Patsy), 238
Downing, Al, xiv
Doyle, Brian, 301
Doyle, Jack, 23, 24
Doyle, Larry, 163
Drabowsky, Myron (Moe), 211
Dressen, Charlie (mgr.), xvii, 121, 268
Dreyfuss, Barney (owner), 24, 26
Drysdale, Don, 209-10, 215-21, 305
Dubuc, Jean (scout), 85
Dugan, Joe, 242
Dunn, Jack (mgr., owner), 195, 198, 238
Durocher, Leo (mgr.), 111, 116-17, 202, 259, 260-62
Dygert, Jimmy, 164
Dykes, Jimmy, 18, 60-61, 197, 250, 273

Earnshaw, George, 69-70, 199, 250, 252, 305
Ebbets, Charlie (owner), 144, 145
Ebbets Field, 108, 111, 127, 128, 266, 268, 277
Ehmke, Howard, 249-52
Eisenhower, President Dwight D., 13, 121, 192

Engel, Clyde, 53, 134
Engel, Joe (scout), 85
Erskine, Carl, 252
Etchebarren, Andy, 211
Evans, Bill (umpire), 157
Evans, Dwight, 297, 302
Evers, Johnny, 134

Fairly, Ron, 208
Feeney, Charles (Chub) (g.m., N.L. President), 216
Feller, Bob, 84, 159, 207, 259
Fenway Park, 102, 297
Fields, W. C., 35
Finn, Mickey, 52
Fisher, Jack, 285
Fisk, Carlton, 297
Fitzsimmons, Fred, 266
Fogel, Horace (mgr.), 136
Fohl, Lee, 54
Forbes Field, 21, 26, 106, 108, 110, 251, 279
Ford, Henry, 94
Ford, Whitey (Edward), 126, 206, 223, 227, 228, 266, 268, 299
Foreman, Frank, 162
Fox, Nellie, 216
Fox, Pete, 88
Foxx, James Emory (Jimmie), xiv, xvi, xvii, 60, 62-63, 69, 76, 97-104, 173-74, 184, 242, 250, 305
Francis, Earl, 204
Franks, Herman (mgr.), 216
Frazee, Harry (owner), 169
Freeman, Andrew (owner), 10
French, Larry, 71
Frick, Ford (Comm. of Baseball, writer), 93, 151, 178, 190
Frisch, Frank, 30, 87, 94, 157, 182, 185, 186-87, 188, 241, 256
Fuchs, Emil (owner), 30
Fullerton, Hugh (writer), 10, 16
Fullis, Chick, 177
Furillo, Carl, 123-24, 126, 254, 256, 267, 269-70, 275

Gafney, John (umpire), 10
Galan, Augie, 71
Galbreath, John (owner), 92
Galehouse, Denny, 83
Galvin, James (Pud), xv, 5

Gamble, Oscar, 300
Garcia, Mike, 259
Gardner, Larry, 53
Garigiola, Joe, 109
Garrett, Wayne, 287
Gassaway, Milt, 91
Gavin, Mike, 121, 124
Gehrig, Henry Louis (Lou), xii, xv, 14, 34, 35, 39, 44, 76, 78-80, 86, 89, 94, 101, 103-4, 111, 117, 125, 173-74, 178, 190, 196, 242, 306
Gehringer, Charlie, 70-71, 86, 88, 173-74, 188
Gentry, Gary, 287
Gessler, Dan, 52
Gibson, Robert (Bob), 148, 206, 224, 226, 229
Gibson, George, 43
Giles, Warren (N.L. pres.), 208
Gilliam, James (Jim, Junior), 201, 205, 207, 211, 268-69
Gionfriddo, Albert (Al), 56, *253-57,* 267
Gomez, Vernon (Lefty), 21, 32, 79, 97, 173-74, 223
Gomez, Pedro (Preston), 225
Gomez, Ruben, 260
Goslin, Leon (Goose), 70-71, 86, 98, 197
Gossage, Richard (Goose), 302
Gowdy, Henry (Hank), 157
Grahame, Frank (writer), 45, 66, 111
Greenberg, Henry (Hank), xvii, 70-71, 76, *83-95,* 102, 104, 107, 108, 188-89, 242
Griffith, Clark, 9, 55, 61, 156
Grimes, Burleigh, 54, 60, 100, 199
Grim, Bob, 269
Grimm, Charlie, 250
Grissom, Marv, 260, 263
Groat, Dick, 280
Groom, Bob, 36
Grote, Jerry, 288-89
Grove, Robert Moses (Lefty), xvi, 63, 70, 78, 104, 159, 161, *195-200,* 229, 238, 250, 252, 305
Gruber, John (writer), 25
Guest, Edgar (poet), 83, 87
Guidry, Ron, 229, 299
Gura, Larry, 292

Haas, Bert (mgr.), 268
Haas, George (Mule), 60-61, 252
Hack, Stan, 71, 191
Hadley, Irving (Bump), 65, 71, 73, 98

Hafey, Charles (Chick), 177
Haines, Jesse, 149, 187
Halahan, William (Wild Bill), 101, 176, 188
Hall, Jimmy, 226
Hamilton, Billy, xv
Hands, Bill, 287
Harper, George, 113
Harrelson, Derrel (Bud), 286, 288
Harrelson, Ken (Hawk), 294
Harris, Stanley (Bucky), 70, 86, 157, 256
Harris, Gail, 271
Hart, James A. (owner), 10
Hartnett, Charles (Gabby), 44, 73, 79, 89, 174, 190-91, 250
Hatten, Joe, 253-54, 257, 267
Haugstad, Phil, 108
Hayes, Bill, 210
Hearn, Jim, 260
Heilman, Harry, xv, 51, 59
Heinemann, Ernie (owner), 112
Hendley, Bob, 208
Henrich, Tommy, 106
Herman, Floyd (Babe), 185
Herman, William (Billy), 268
Hermanski, Gene, 109, 254
Herzog, Charles (Buck), 238
Hiatt, Jack, 216
Hildebrand, George (umpire), 36
Higbe, Kirby, 253
Hilltop Park, 15
Hines, Pinky, 8
Hoak, Don, 269-70
Hoblitzell, Dick, 246
Hobson, Clell (Butch), 297, 302
Hodges, Gil, 123, 124, 126, 266-69, 270, 274, 277, 286-87, 289
Hodges, Russ (broadcaster), 302
Hofman, Bobby, 202
Holtzman, Ken, 210
Hooper, Harry, 52-53, 134, 246-47
Hoover, J. Edgar, 80
Hornsby, Rogers, xv, xix, 3, 18, *29-34,* 36, 39, 57, 149-50, 152, 250
Houk, Ralph (mgr.), 223, 225, 227-28
Houtteman, Art, 259
Howard, Frank, 207, 229
Howard, Elston, 206, 223, 225
Howell, Harry (scout), 16
Howell, Homer, 253
Hoyte, Dewey, 300

General Index

Hoyt, Waite, 44, 223
Hubbell, Carl, 112, 114, 117, *173-79*
Huggins, Miller (mgr.), 31-32, 56, 161, 171-72, 241
Hulbert, William A., 9
Humphries, Johnny, 84
Hunter, Jim (Catfish), 228
Hurst, Don, 151
Huston, Cap (owner), 170-71

Irvin, Monte, xvii, 260-63

Jackson, Joseph (Shoeless Joe), xv, 5, 16-17, 48
Jackson, Reggie, xii, 36, 62, 213, 242, 295-96, 301
Jackson, Travis, 115, 158, 177
James, Bill, 163
Janowicz, Vic, 109
Jansen, Larry, 116
Jennings, Hughie, 17, 23-24
Jethroe, Sam, 268
Johnson, Ban (A.L. pres.), 15, 55, 170, 247
Johnson, Cliff, 298
Johnson, Dave, 211
Johnson, Lou, 208
Johnson, Walter, xv, 37, 43, 133, 150, *153-60,* 196, 197, 200, 216, 221, 229, 237
Jones, Charlie, 3
Jones, Cleon, 289-90
Jones, Davey, 17
Jones, Fielder, 233-34
Jones, Sam, 54, 246
Judd, Oscar, 116
Judge, Joe, 158
Jurges, Billy, 71, 185, 191

Kaat, Jim, 209
Kaline, Albert (Al), 93
Kanehl, Roderick (Hot Rod), 205
Keefe, Timothy, xv, 5, 143
Keeler, William (Wee Willie), xv
Keller, Charlie, 106
Kelly, George, 157, 158, 241
Kessinger, Don, 287
Killibrew, Harmon, xvii, 209, 225-26, 227
Killifer, Bill, 148, 151
Kindall, Jerry, 226
Kiner, Ralph, 92-93, *105-110,* 128
Klein, Charles (Chuck), 50, 114

Klem, Bill (umpire), 33, 163
Kline, Steve, 291, 294
Klippstein, Johnny, 124
Koenecke, Len, 187
Koosman, Jerry, 288
Koufax, Sanford (Sandy), 156, 159, 160, 200, *201-13,* 215, 217, 218-21, 305
Kowalik, Fabian, 89
Kranepool, Ed, 287
Krichell, Paul (scout), 85
Krug, Chris, 208
Kubek, Tony, 206, 226, 280
Kuenn, Harvey, 205
Kuzava, Bob, 124

Labine, Clem, 266
Lajoie, Napoleon (Nap), xv, 16
Lakefront Park, 3
Landis, Judge Kennesaw Mountain (commissioner), 29-30, 36-37, 39, 55, 61, 69, 171, 187
Lane, F.C. (writer), 165
Lannin, Joe (owner), 53-54
Larsen, Don, 260, 270, *273-78*
Lavagetto, Harry (Cookie), 256, 266
Law, Vernon, 280
Lazzeri, Anthony (Tony), 149-50, 152, 196
League Park (Cleveland), 54, 83-84
Lee, Bill, 191
Lemon, Bob, 259, 261, 298, 301
Leonard, Hubert (Dutch), 55, 246
Leuker, Claude (fan), 15
Levy, Sam (writer), 59
Lewis, George (Duffy), 52-53, 246
Liddle, Don, 260
Lieb, Fred (writer), 170
Lindstrom, Freddie, 114, 157
Liska, Ad, 60
Littel, Mark, 291-93, 296
Lockman, Carroll (Whitey), 263
Loes, Billy, 267
Lombardi, Vic, 254
Long, Dale, 280
Lopat, Ed, 229, 267
Lopez, Al (mgr.), 93
Lopez, Hector, 280
Lynn, Fred, 302

McAleer, Jim, 52
McCarrick, Ed (scout), 203

McCarthy, Joe, 31, 78–79, 89, 100, 147–49
McCarver, Tim, 226
McCovey, Willie, 208, 215–16, 220
McCreery, Tom, 10
McDougald, Gil, 269–70, 274
McGarrigle, Bob (writer), 168–69
McGinnty, Joe, 134, 163
McGraw, John (mgr.), 3, 6, 11, 22, 23–25, 30, 52, 56, 58, 85, 111–14, 117, 133, 137, 141–42, 144, 159, 176, 233–34, 237, 239–40, 241, 251
McGraw, Frank (Tug), 285
McInnis, John (Stuffy), 238, 243, 246
McKechnie, Bill (mgr.), 43
Mack, Cornelius (Connie) (mgr.), 56, 59–61, 68, 69–70, 72, 98–99, 100, 101–2, 104, 133, 162, 195–96, 197–99, 238, 240–41, 242, 249–52
McKinney, Frank (owner), 92
McLain, Dennis, 227
McLish, Cal, 253
McNally, Dave, 288, 289–90
McNally, Mike, 241
McNeely, Earl, 158
McQuinn, George, 92
McRoy, Bob, 54
Maglie, Sal, xvii, 116, 260, 263, 275, 277
Mails, John (Duster), 48, 54
Mann, Les, 246–47
Mantilla, Felix, 205
Mantle, Mickey, xii, xiv, xx, 108, 125–26, 128, 206, 242, 262, 267–68, 270, 274, 277, 280, 282
Manush, Henry (Heinie), 173–74
Maranville, Walter (Rabbit), 43, 149
Marcum, John, 102
Marichal, Juan, 127, 208
Marion, Marty, 274
Marquard, Richard (Rube), 53, *139–45,* 163, 178, 237–38, 239–40
Maris, Roger, 31, 103, 178, 206, 225, 237, 277
Martin, Alfred (Billy), 14, 125, 267, 269, 299
Martin, Joseph (J.C.), 287, 289
Martin, Pepper (Johnny), 69–70, 187–89
Martinez, John (Buck), 293
Mathews, Ewin (Eddie), xiv, xvii, 117
Mathewson, Christopher (Christy), xv, 22, 53, *131–38,* 142–43, 145, 150, 156, 163, 164, 190, 200, 204, 237–38, 239–40
Matthews, Wid (coach), 119
Mauch, Gene (mgr.), 219–20, 253

Mayo, Jack, 92
Mays, Carl, 47, 72, 157, *167–72,* 246
Mays, Willie, xv, xvi, xviii, 47, 56, 117, 125–26, 128, 205, 209, 220, 260–61, 268, 282, 305
Mazeroski, William (Bill), xvii, *279–83,* 306
Medwick, Joe, 87–8
Menke, Frank, 142, 145
Merkle, Fred (Bonehead), 53, 134–35, 246
Metkovich, George, 109
Meusel, Bob, 44, 49, 56, 69, 150, 196
Meusel, Emil (Irish), 157, 170
Meyer, Billy (mgr.), 108
Meyers, John (Chief), 53, 239
Michael, Gene, 39, 229
Miksis, Eddie, 254–55, 257
Milan, Clyde, 154
Miller, Edmund (Bing), 62, 252
Mills, Howard, 83
Minor, Ben (owner), 156
Mitchell, Dale, 275
Mize, Johnny, 107
Moore, Jimmy, 197
Moore, Wilcy, 44
Moran, Pat (mgr.), 137
Morgan, Joe, 81
Moriarty, George, 84
Mossi, Don, 259
Mueller, Don, xvii, 260, 263
Munson, Thurman, 301
Murphy, Jimmy (writer), 203
Murphy, Johnny, 286
Musial, Stan, 92, 103, 109, 112, 117, 268

Nahin, Lou (owner), 58–59, 67–68
Napp, Larry (umpire), 227
Narleski, Ray, 259
National Association, 8
National Baseball Hall of Fame, xi, 11, 76, 80–81, 93, 103, 113, 128, 144, 151, 161, 174, 177, 192–93, 200–201, 212, 242, 243, 262
Navin, Frank (owner), 15, 70
Nehf, Art, 157, 176, 241
Nelson, Glenn (Rocky), 280
Nettles, Graig, 45, 301–2, 303
Newcombe, Don, xvii, 211
Newhouser, Hal, 259
Newsom, Norman (Bobo), 83
Niles, Harry, 52
Nichols, Charles (Kid), xv, 22

General Index

Nye, Rich, 287

O'Brien, Eddie and Johnnie, 109
O'Connor, Jack (mgr.), 16
O'Doul, Francis (Lefty), 32
Ogrowdoski, Bruce, 182
Oliva, Tony, 226
O'Malley, Walter (owner), 121, 203, 275–76
O'Neill, James (Tip), 8
Orsatti, Ernie, 88
Osteen, Claude, 218, 219
Ott, Melvin (Mel), xiv, 111–18
Owen, Marv, 70
Owen, Mickey, 266

Pafko, Andy, xvii
Page, Joe, 267
Pagliaroni, Jim, 282
Palika, Erv, 108
Palmer, Jim, 211, 289
Parker, Wes, 216
Pascual, Camillo, 225
Pasek, John, 10
Paskert, George (Dode), 246
Pasquel, Jorge (Mex. League pres.), 33–34
Paul, Gabe (g.m.), 228
Peckinpaugh, Roger, 44, 158
Pena, Roberto, 220
Pepitone, Joe, 226
Pennock, Herb, 44
Perkins, Cy, 68, 100
Perry, Gaylord, 154
Peterson, Fred (Fritz), 229, 291, 294
Pick, Charlie, 247
Pinelli, Babe (umpire), 275
Piniella, Lou, 298, 301–3
Pipgras, George, 44
Pipp, Wally, 38, 168
Plank, Edward (Eddie), xv, 161–65, 200, 229
Podres, Johnny, 125, 266, 269
Polinsky, Bob, 300
Pollet, Howard, 106
Polo Grounds, 58, 111, 112–15, 117, 132, 134, 141, 157, 167, 174, 179, 202, 239, 261, 263
Potter, Nelson, 92
Povich, Shirley (writer), 159
Powell, Jake, 89
Powell, John (Boog), 211, 289

Qualls, Jim, 287
Quinn, Jack, 68–69

Radbourn, Charles (Old Hoss), xv, 5
Randolph, Willie, 301, 303
Ransom, Dude, 52
Raschi, Vic, 229, 267
Rawlings, Johnny, 241
Reagan, Ronald, 150
Reese, Harold (Pee Wee), 120, 126, 193, 268–69, 274
Reiser, Pete, 256, 268
Remy, Jerry, 302
Rennie, Rud (writer), 79
Repulski, Eldon (Rip), 271
Reynolds, Allie, 124
Rhodes, Gordon, 102
Rhodes, James (Dusty), 259–63, 268
Rice, Jim, 297, 301–2
Richardson, Bobby, 206, 280
Richert, Pete, 289
Rickey, Wesley (Branch) (g.m.), 36–37, 41, 73, 78, 80, 105, 108, 122, 181, 184, 185, 190–91, 203, 255
Rickey, Wesley Branch, Jr., 255
Rigney, Bill (mgr.), 262
Ring, Jimmy, 90
Rivers, John Milton (Mickey), 301, 303
Rizzuto, Phil, 192, 269–70
Roberts, Doak, 51–52
Robinson, Bojangles, 76
Robinson, Brooks, 45, 219, 288–89
Robinson, Frank, xvii, 219, 285–86, 289
Robinson, Jackie, 75–77, 81, 122–23, 124, 126, 267, 274
Robinson, Wilbert (mgr.), xix, 142, 144
Roe, Elwin (Preacher), 203
Roeder, Bill (writer), 253
Rogel, Billy, 188
Rohe, George, 233–35
Rommel, Ed, 158, 252
Root, Charlie, xvi, 89, 260
Roseboro, John, 208, 218
Rosen, Albert (Al), 39, 259, 299, 301
Rossman, Claude, 164
Roth, Allan (statistician), 204
Rothrock, Jack, 189
Rowe, Lynwood (Schoolboy), 70
Rucker, George (Nap), 22
Ruel, Herold (Muddy), 157
Ruelbach, Ed, 234
Ruffing, Charles (Red), 223
Rusie, Amos, 22, 136, 159
Russell, Allan (Al), 170

Russell, Jack, 114
Russell, James (Jim), 256
Russo, Marius, 266
Ruth, George Herman (Babe), xii, xiii, xv, xvi,
    4–5, 10–11, 18, 25, 34, 36, 39, 44, 56, 62,
    70, 76, 78, 80, 83, 90, 95, 98, 100–101,
    102–4, 105, 108, 110, 111, 117, 120, 125,
    145, 150, 152, 159, 173–74, 184, 190, 193,
    195–96, 237–38, 242, 246–47, 265, 305, 306
Ryan, Nolan, 159–60, 202, 208, 212

Salsinger, H.G. (writer), 70
Santo, Ron, 209, 287
Savino, George, 102
Schaeffer, Herman (Germany), 17
Schang, Wally, 98–99, 242
Schulte, Bob, 109
Schulte, Fred, 114
Scott, Everett, 157, 246
Scott, George, 297, 302
Seaver, Tom, 229, 287, 288
Selkirk, George, 191
Selma, Dick, 287
Sewell, Joe, xv, 47, 48–49, 157, 160, 196
Sewell, Luke, 92
Seymour, Cy, 134
Shamsky, Art, 287
Shantz, Bobby, 280
Shawkey, Bob, 168, 223
Shea Stadium, 286, 288–89
Shean, Dave, 246
Shelton, Ben, 52
Sherdel, Bill, 149
Sherry, Larry, 202, 217
Sherry, Norm, 202, 204
Shibe Family, 68
Shibe Park, 58, 98
Shocker, Urban, 44, 242
Shore, Ernie, 53
Short, Chris, 210
Shorten, Charles (Chick), 246
Shotten, Burt (mgr.), 119–20
Shoun, Clyde, 191
Shuba, George, 269
Simmons, Aloysius Harry (Al), xv, *57–63,* 69,
    99, 173–74, 184, 197, 249, 252, 305
Simmons, Curt, 121
Sisler, Dave, 39
Sisler, Dick, 39, 120
Sisler, George, xiv, xv, xvi, *35–39,* 51, 114, 305

Sisler, George, Jr., 39
Smith, Elmer, 267
Smith, Hal, 280
Smith, John, 135
Snider, Edwin (Duke), 119–28, 266, 267–69,
    271
Snodgrass, Fred, 53, 134–35, 143
Snyder, Frank, 171
Soar, Hank (umpire), 216
Spahn, Warren, xv, 161, 200
Spaulding, Al, 8
Speaker, Tristam (Spoke), xiv, xvi, xviii, *47–56,*
    114, 134
Spencer, Jim, 295, 298, 301–2
Spohrer, Al, 33
Stafford, Bill, 280
Stainback, George (Tuck), 191
Stallings, George (mgr.), 42
Stanky, Eddie, 256
Stanley, Bob, 301
Stanley, Fred, 299–300
Stengel, Charles (Casey), 112, 124, 182, 267,
    274, 276–77, 278, 280
Steinbrenner, George (owner), 295, 299, 301,
    303
Stephenson, Riggs, xv, 250
Stirnweiss, George, 254
Stoneham, Horace (owner), xvii, 30, 115, 179,
    261, 262
Stottlemyre, Melvin (Mel), 223–30, 294
Stovey, George, 7
Strand, Paul, 59, 68
Strang, Sammy, 234
Street, Charles (Gabby), 155–56, 184–85
Strunk, Amos, 164, 246
Swoboda, Ron, 289–90

Tannehill, Jesse, 234
Taylor, Eddie (scout), 224
Taylor, Jack, 22
Taylor, Ron, 287
Taylor, Tony, 220
Terry Ralph, 280–81
Terry, William (Bill), xv, 32, 36, 94, 114–15,
    178, 187, 189–90
Tesreau, Jeff, 143
Texas League, 122, 255
Thomas, Frank, 205
Thomas, Fred, 54
Thomas, Clarence (Lefty), 176

General Index

Thompson, Hank, 260-61
Thomson, Robert (Bobby), xviii, 116, 124, 260, 267, 291, 302
Thurston, Hollis (scout), 106
Tidrow, Dick, 291, 294
Tinker, Joe, 134
Torborg, Jeff, 216
Torrez, Mike, 297, 299-302
Tracewski, Dick, 205
Traynor, Harold (Pie), 26, 41-45, 184
Tresh, Tom, 226, 229
Trimble, Joe (writer), 278
Truman, Harry, 101
Tucker, Ernest (coach), 77
Turley, Bob, 276-77, 280
Turner, Tom (owner), 67
Tyler, George (Lefty), 246

Uecker, Bob, 211
Underwood, Tom, 295
Upshaw, Cecil, 291

Vance, Clarence (Dazzy), 187
Vaughn, James (Hippo), 246
Veeck, Bill (owner), 31, 56, 93
Versailles, Zoilo, 218
Vidmer, Dick (writer), 79
Virdon, Bill, 280

Waddell, George (Rube), 104, 141, 162, 163-64, 207
Wagner, Al, 23
Wagner, Honus, 21-27, 81, 152
Wakefield, Howard, 140
Walberg, George (Rube), 68, 199, 250, 252
Walker, Fred (Dixie), 123
Walker, Harvey (Hub), 92
Walker, Moses & William, 7
Walsh, Christy (writer), 239
Walsh, Ed, 238, 250
Walters, William (Bucky), 91
Wambsganss, William (Bill), 50, 267
Waner, Lloyd, 177, 184
Waner, Paul, xv, 44, 177, 184
Ward, Aaron, 241
Ward, John Montgomery, 7
Ward, Pete, 225

Ward, Preston, 109
Warneke, Lonnie (Lon), 89
Weaver, George (Buck), 48
Webb, Del (owner), 275
Webb, Earl, 86, 288
Webb, James (Skeeter), 92
Weis, Albert (Al), 285-90
Weiss, George (g.m.), 273, 276, 277
Welch, Mickey, xv
Welsh, Jimmy, 113
Wendelstadt, Harry (umpire), 215-16
Werber, Billy, 198
Wertz, Vic, 261
West Side Park, 3
White, Roy, 294, 298, 301, 303
Whiteman, George, 245-48
Whitted, George (Possum), 43
Wilhelm, Hoyt, 260
Williams, Billy, 209, 287
Williams, Harry (owner), 112-13
Williams, Theodore (Ted), xv, xix, 103, 200, 282, 305
Williamson, Edward (Ned), 3
Wills, Maury, 205, 208
Wilson, Art, 143
Wilson, Lewis (Hack), 151, 157, 250
Wiltse, George (Hooks), 22
Wine, Bobby, 211
Witt, Lawton (Whitey), 251
Wood, Joe, 55, 159, 197
Worthington, Al, 34
Wrigley Field, 120, 251, 287
Wynn, Early, xvi, 259, 261
Wynne, Billy, 285

Yastrzemski, Carl, xvi, 94, 229, 301-2
Yerkes, Steve, 53, 134
Yankee Stadium, 42, 44, 71, 76, 78, 81, 92, 94, 106, 149, 206, 254, 265, 269, 291, 292, 297
York, Rudy, 90-92
Young, Cy, xv, 22, 50, 150
Youngs, Ross, 157

Zamlock, Carl (scout), 67-68
Zeller, Jack (g.m.), 90
Zimmer, Don, 220, 269, 299, 301

INDEX OF TEAMS

Note: Major league teams are listed by nickname; i.e., Yankees, New York; minor league teams are listed by nickname when available.

Aberdeen, 58
Akron (Ohio-Penn League), 37
Albany, 106, 256
Alburquerque, 127
Alexandria, 127
Angels, California (A.L.), 220, 227, 295
Astros, Houston (N.L.), 219
Athletics (A's), Philadelphia (A.L.), xiv, 8, 14, 15, 47, 56, 60–61, 68–69, 70, 72, 91, 98–101, 104, 109, 135–36, 141–43, 161–65, 184, 195, 198, 200, 238–40, 249–52, 306
Athletics, Kansas City (A's) (A.L.), 277
A's, Oakland (A.L.), 227
Atlanta (Southern League), 144
Auburn, 224

Bakersfield, 217
Bears, Newark (International League), 56, 158
Beaumont, 176
Birmingham, 43
Bisons, Buffalo (Federal League), 251
Blue Jays, Toronto (A.L.), 295, 298
Blues, Kansas City, 56
Blues, Veracruz (Mexican League), 33–34
Braves, Boston (N.L.), 30, 33, 36, 39, 42, 61, 109, 124, 137, 139, 143, 164, 182, 191, 240, 267, 306
Braves, Milwaukee (N.L.), xiv, 202–3, 217, 270, 277
Braves, Atlanta (N.L.), xiv, 288, 295–96
Brewers, Milwaukee (A.L.), xiv
Brewers, Milwaukee (American Association), 58–59
Browns, St. Louis (A.L.), xv, 16, 31, 35–38, 48, 52, 78, 83, 91–92, 98, 109, 137, 156, 164, 182, 192, 197, 274, 276, 306

Canton, 141
Cardinals, St. Louis (N.L.), 10, 22, 29, 31, 38, 60–61, 69–70, 76, 87–88, 100–01, 107, 147, 151, 171, 177, 181, 184–86, 199, 205, 210, 219, 226, 267
Chicago (Federal League), 156
Cleburne (North Texas League), 51
Clippers, Columbus (International League), 37, 39, 141
Cubs, Chicago (N.L.), 3, 22, 30, 33, 43, 60, 69, 70, 79, 83, 89, 102, 105, 109, 113, 133–34, 143, 146, 151, 178, 185, 186, 191, 199, 208, 219, 234, 239, 246, 249–52, 256, 277, 286–88, 290
Cushing (Oklahoma State League), 175

Denison, 31–32
Denver, 276
Dodgers, Brooklyn (N.L.), xvii, xix, 23, 29, 39, 54, 111, 116, 119–25, 136, 139–40, 144, 182, 187, 202–3, 217, 253–57, 165–71, 274, 276–77
Dodgers, Los Angeles (N.L.), 127–28, 201–2, 203–4, 206, 208–12, 215, 217–20, 271, 286, 295, 299, 300, 302
Dover (Eastern Shore League), 67
Drummondville, 255

Easton (Eastern Shore League), 99, 242
Expos, Montreal (N.L.), 127, 220

Feds, St. Louis (Federal League), 164
Forrest Cities, Rockford, 8
Fort Worth (Texas League), 255

Giants, New York (N.L.), xvi, xvii, xviii, 10, 22,

317

30, 52–53, 58, 111, 114–17, 123–26, 131–37, 141–45, 157–59, 163, 170–71, 176–79, 182, 187, 202–3, 233, 239–42, 259–63
Giants, San Francisco (N.L.), 127, 201, 208, 215–16, 217, 219, 263, 277
Globe-Miami (Arizona-Texas League), 274

Harlan, 224
Harrisburg, 256
Hartford, 86
Highlanders, New York (A.L.), 24, 155, 234, 245
Hollywood (Pacific Coast League), 255
Honesdale, 135
Hopkinsville (D League), 260
Hornets, Greensboro, 224
Houston (minor league), 184–85

Indianapolis, 140–42
Indians, Cleveland (A.L.), 16, 37, 47–48, 54–55, 61, 83–84, 93, 98, 101, 109, 141, 144, 157–58, 167, 170–71, 197, 259–62, 276, 281, 293–94, 296, 298

Jacksonville (Florida State League), 144

Kenwick, 127
Keokuk, 140

Los Angeles Angels (Pacific Coast League), 251

Mariners, Seattle (A.L.), 282, 305
Martinsburg, 198
Mets, New York (N.L.), 31, 34, 105, 109–10, 127, 205, 285–90
Midland, 198
Montreal (International League, Dodgers), 122, 253, 255, 268, 271
Mudhens, Toledo, 7, 58

Naps, Cleveland (A.L.), 140
Nationals, Cleveland (N.L.), 109
Norfolk, 135

Oklahoma City, 175–76
Orioles, Baltimore (A.L.), 203, 211, 219, 224, 227–28, 273–74, 276, 285, 288–90, 292
Orioles, Baltimore (International League), 144, 195–96, 198, 238, 270
Orioles, Baltimore (N.L.), 6, 23

Patterson (Louisiana), 112–13
Padres, San Diego (N.L.), 127
Pelicans, New Orleans, 112, 233, 235
Phillies, Philadelphia (N.L.), 39, 50, 53, 75–76, 79–80, 102, 109, 114, 116, 120, 124, 135, 143, 148, 150–51, 187, 196, 203, 207, 210, 216, 217, 219, 249, 270
Phoenix, 262
Pilgrims, Boston (A.L.), 24, 238
Pirates, Pittsburgh (N.L.), 21–26, 37, 39, 41, 83, 92–3, 105–9, 133, 143, 158, 163, 176, 184, 191, 202–4, 210, 216, 219, 238, 253, 256, 270, 279–82, 290
Portland, 67–68
Portsmouth, 43, 102
Providence, 144

Raleigh (Piedmont League), 86
Rangers, Texas (A.L.), 220, 227
Red Legs, Cincinnati, 3
Red Sox, Boston (A.L.), xiii, xvi, 39, 42, 47, 50–54, 61, 80, 92, 98, 102, 104, 109, 134, 145, 157, 167, 169, 170, 196–97, 199, 226, 227, 228–29, 238, 240, 245–47, 251, 267, 276, 292, 297–99, 301–2
Red Sox, Milwaukee, 58, 86
Reds, Cincinnati (N.L.), 26, 31, 34, 39, 49, 50, 61, 73, 80, 90–91, 120, 132, 136, 137, 144, 146, 167, 169, 172, 201, 203, 210, 293–94
Reno (California League), 294
Richmond, 80, 223, 224, 245
Royals, Kansas City (A.L.), 291, 292, 295, 299, 302

St. Paul, 123, 255, 268
Senators, Washington (A.L.), 36, 39, 43, 55, 60–61, 79–80, 85, 89, 91, 109, 114, 140, 153, 156, 158, 164, 177–78, 197, 221, 227, 251
Shreveport, 58–59
Sounds, Nashville, 260
Spokane, 127
Steubenville, 22
Syracuse Chiefs (International League), 251

Tacoma (Pacific Coast League), 154
Tampa (Florida State League), 76, 80
Taunton, 135
Tigers, Detroit (A.L.), 14–15, 21, 24, 39, 55, 61, 66–67, 69–71, 73, 83, 86–93, 102, 107, 155,

Index of Teams

163, 167, 168, 182, 186–89, 197, 227–28, 238, 251, 271, 298
Toronto (International League), 106, 245, 246, 247
Tulsa (Western League), 175
Twins, Minnesota (A.L.), 202, 209, 218, 225–26, 295

Ventura, 255

Waterloo, 140
White Stockings (N.L.), Chicago, 3, 6, 9

White Sox, Chicago, 3, 34, 47–48, 55, 61, 93, 106, 110, 127, 137, 156, 158, 169, 182, 197, 203, 217, 223–24, 233–35, 238, 277, 285–86, 299–300
Wichita, 144, 294

Yankees, New York (A.L.), xii, 36, 43, 44, 47–49, 55, 61, 69, 70, 73, 75–77, 80, 83, 85, 90–91, 98–99, 102, 109, 115, 123, 124–25, 126, 149, 157–58, 161, 164, 167, 169, 170, 178, 192, 199, 201, 203, 206, 212–13, 216–18, 221, 223–30, 241–42, 251, 254–55, 266–70, 273–77, 279–81, 291–92, 294–96